Short-Term Group Therapies for Complicated Grief

Short-Term Group Therapies for Complicated Grief

Two Research-Based Models

William E. Piper, John S. Ogrodniczuk, Anthony S. Joyce, and Rene Weideman

American Psychological Association • Washington, DC

Published by
American Psychological Association
750 First Street, NE
Washington, DC 20002
www.apa.org

To order
APA Order Department
P.O. Box 92984
Washington, DC 20090-2984
Tel: (800) 374-2721; Direct: (202) 336-5510
Fax: (202) 336-5502; TDD/TTY: (202) 336-6123
Online: www.apa.org/books/
E-mail: order@apa.org

In the U.K., Europe, Africa, and the Middle East, copies may be ordered from
American Psychological Association
3 Henrietta Street
Covent Garden, London
WC2E 8LU England

Typeset in Goudy by Circle Graphics, Inc., Columbia, MD

Printer: Maple-Vail Book Manufacturing, York, PA
Cover Designer: Mercury Publishing Services, Rockville, MD

The opinions and statements published are the responsibility of the authors, and such opinions and statements do not necessarily represent the policies of the American Psychological Association.

Library of Congress Cataloging-in-Publication Data

Short-term group therapies for complicated grief : two research-based models /
William E. Piper . . . [et al.]. — 1st ed.
       p. cm.
  Includes bibliographical references and index.
  ISBN-13: 978-1-4338-0843-2
  ISBN-10: 1-4338-0843-9
  ISBN-13: 978-1-4338-0844-9 (e-book)
  ISBN-10: 1-4338-0844-7 (e-book)
1. Grief therapy. 2. Group psychotherapy. 3. Loss (Psychology) I. Piper, William E.

  RC455.4.L67S377 2011
  616.89'14—dc22
                                        2009054456

British Library Cataloguing-in-Publication Data

A CIP record is available from the British Library.

Printed in the United States of America
First Edition

To my colleagues and family, who provide me with the inspiration
and energy to write books such as this one.
—*William E. Piper*

To Jennifer, Mikayla, and Ethan—your unconditional love continues
to remind me of what is most important in life.
—*John S. Ogrodniczuk*

To my long-time colleagues WEP and JSO (and MM): It's been a
privilege to share my work life with you, and I will always be grateful.
—*Anthony S. Joyce*

To the memory of my father, Johan.
—*Rene Weideman*

CONTENTS

ACKNOWLEDGMENTS

As we have experienced, the implementation of large-scale clinical trials requires the collaboration of a large number of people. Just collecting the data can take several years. If we consider carrying out three such projects over a 20-year period, which is essentially what we did, the number of key collaborators is considerable. The therapists in the project (in addition to R. Weideman) were J. Fyfe Bahrey, Andrea Duncan, Scott C. Duncan, and Judith Fiedler. Those who conducted interview assessments of complicated grief, quality of object relations and other variables were Gary Alward, Douglas Ginter, David Hutnyk, John G. O'Kelly, Mary McCallum, Gregory Passey, Heather Paul, John Rosie, David Shih, Paul I. Steinberg, and Alan Wong.

There were several research project coordinators who worked closely with a large number of research assistants: Maarit H. Cristall, Clara Hungr, Chirstine Lamarche, Cheryl Melder, and Hillary Morin. The research assistants were Suzanne Bachelor, Sherryl Basarab-Ostrander, Treena Blake, Elizabeth Colangelo, Carys Cragg, Martin Debbane, Linda Deng, Karen Evans, Suzanne Gill, Janice Grant, Sharmaine Gray, Shellene Greer, Shannon Hancock, Anacaona Hernandez, Tamara Hilscher, Nancy Hurst, Susan Hurst, Sandra Inamasu, Agnes Kwong, Claire Leighton-Morris, Corey MacKenzie, Myriam

Marrache, Doris Martens, Kathleen McCallister-Munn, Jennifer Michel, Ward Nicholson, Ellen Perrault, Jaime Pinzon III, Colleen Poon, Diane Priebe, Brandy Reed, Tamara Schuld, Carlos Sierra H., Tara Simpson, Bonnie Stephanson, Stan Tubinshlak, Vuokko Van Der Veen, and Jill Zimmerman.

In addition, we are especially grateful for the administrative support provided by heads of the Departments of Psychiatry, Roger C. Bland and Glen B. Baker in Edmonton, Alberta, Canada, and Athanasios Zis in Vancouver, British Columbia, Canada. We are also appreciative of the grant support provided by the National Health Research and Development Program of Health and Welfare Canada, the Canadian Psychiatric Research Foundation, the Alberta Mental Health Research Fund, the Medical Research Council of Canada, the American Group Psychotherapy Foundation, and the Canadian Institute of Health Research.

Short-Term Group Therapies for Complicated Grief

INTRODUCTION

Losing a significant person through death is a painful human experience that unfortunately increases in frequency as people grow older. Typical grief reactions include shock, denial, sadness, irritability, insomnia, preoccupation with the loss, yearning for the lost person, searching for the lost person, and experiencing intrusive images and memories about the lost person. Whether such reactions are regarded as normal or abnormal depends on their intensity and their duration. If they are experienced at mild to moderate intensities for short periods of time (e.g., 1 or 2 months), they tend to be regarded as normal and appropriate. However, if they become intense and enduring, the grief reactions are regarded as unresolved and perhaps in need of treatment. This is particularly the case when there are comorbid complications such as depression; anxiety; health-compromising behaviors such as excessive drinking or smoking; and social, occupational, and familial dysfunction. Currently, there is no standard definition or official diagnostic category for *complicated grief* (CG) in the *Diagnostic and Statistical Manual of Mental Disorders* (American Psychiatric Association, 2000). Nevertheless, there is reasonable consensus among experts in the field as to what constitutes CG. The combination of unresolved grief symptoms and continuing dysfunctional complications is generally regarded as CG (M. S. Stroebe et al., 2000).

CG is usually treated through individual therapy, but in today's cost-conscience environment, administrators and practitioners alike view group therapy as an increasingly attractive treatment modality. Given the benefits of group therapy, we developed and extensively tested two evidence-based group therapy treatment models for CG: interpretive and supportive group therapies. The purpose of this book is twofold: to summarize the research that supports these models and to present these models so that clinicians can administer them. In the remainder of this chapter, we (a) discuss the benefits of group therapy, (b) explain how our models differ from common grief support groups, (c) note the limitations of short-term group therapy, and (d) explain how the rest of the book is organized.

BENEFITS OF GROUP THERAPY

Long known to be cost-effective and time efficient, group therapy has a wide range of applications and established efficacy, as demonstrated by mounting research evidence (Burlingame, MacKenzie, & Strauss, 2004; Johnson, 2008). Based on a comprehensive review of the literature concerning prevalence of use, the surgeon general's report on mental health indicates that group therapy is used by mental health professionals in a variety of inpatient and outpatient settings with clients of all ages and stages of development (U.S. Department of Health and Human Services, 1999). Successive reviews of the outcome literature have found considerable evidence for the efficacy of group therapy (often on par with that of individual therapy) in the treatment of situational difficulties, behavioral problems, psychological disorders, and physical conditions (Fuhriman & Burlingame, 2001; McDermut, Miller, & Brown, 2001; McRoberts, Burlingame, & Hoag, 1998; Smith, Glass, & Miller, 1980).

We have argued that group therapy may be the treatment of choice for CG (Piper, McCallum, & Azin, 1992). Many problems that patients present with have their origins in complex human attachment, interpersonal relationships, and social milieus (I. D. Yalom & Leszcz, 2005). Thus, the social learning opportunities that group therapies provide are particularly well suited for addressing a variety of problems (Phares, 1992) such as CG.

Hughes (1995) provided an exhaustive list of beneficial features of groups for people who have suffered a death loss. Group treatments are capable of mobilizing strong forces for change. The group, which is sometimes referred to as a *cohesive social microcosm*, can exert considerable pressure on patients to participate. It is capable of eliciting the typical maladaptive behaviors of each patient. The other patients can observe, provide feedback, and offer suggestions for change. The patient can subsequently practice adaptive behavior. This process is commonly referred to as *interpersonal learning*. Other patients may learn through observation and imitation. Simply recognizing that other patients share one's difficulties (universality) and helping other patients with their problems (altruism) can be therapeutic. These various processes (cohesion, interpersonal learning, imitation, universality, and altruism) are regarded as powerful and unique therapeutic factors of group therapy (I. D. Yalom & Leszcz, 2005).

There are other facilitative features of group therapy as well. Intense negative transference toward the therapist is less likely to occur in group therapy than in individual therapy because the situation is less intimate, and strong affects such as rage are diluted because there are multiple targets for expression. Similarly, feedback from the therapist in the individual therapy situation may be dismissed as biased, but this is much less likely to occur in response to feedback from several peers in a therapy group. In addition, because of the variety of affects expressed by different patients, integration of positive and negative affects is facilitated. In the case of short-term group therapy, time limitations may also provide unique opportunities for therapeutic understanding and change. In the case of CG, limited time is an especially relevant issue because it creates an impending loss for the patients and brings to the forefront all of their emotions and behaviors associated with loss.

In addition, common events in groups, such as patients' lateness to sessions, absenteeism, and dropping out, often trigger feelings and conflicts similar to the reactions that patients had experienced toward people whom they were losing and people whom they eventually lost. Although such events are usually regarded as disruptive and problematic in most therapy groups, they can be examined and used productively in loss groups. Termination of the group, as well, provides an opportunity for patients to examine their reactions to an immediate loss, compare them with previous reactions, and attempt adaptive reactions. Similar to the other naturally occurring events, termination can be used productively.

INTERPRETIVE AND SUPPORTIVE THERAPY GROUPS VERSUS COMMON SUPPORT GROUPS

Our two treatment models—interpretive group therapy and supportive group therapy—have all the benefits of group therapy but differ from common support groups in several critical ways: They are customized to address issues specific to CG; they have formal evidence of effectiveness; and they are always led by professional mental health specialists. The following sections describe each type of treatment in detail.

Common Support Groups

There are many different types of grief groups, characterized by such features as purpose (e.g., adjustment to a recent loss or alleviation of a chronic maladaptive grief reaction), duration (e.g., time limited or open-ended), status of the group leader (e.g., peer, professional), theoretical orientation of the group (e.g., psychodynamic, cognitive–behavioral), and the group's target population (e.g., a group for older widows or for parentally bereaved children). According to a recent review by Currier, Neimeyer, and Berman (2008), the most extensive of its kind to date, most group interventions have addressed immediate grief reactions among those with recent losses and those who are devoid of any clinically significant symptoms or behaviors associated with their loss. These kinds of group interventions are often referred to as *support groups*. Very few group interventions have focused on people suffering from CG. In fact, Currier et al. did not include a single study of a group intervention for people with CG. This reflects a considerable inconsistency between the abundant clinical literature on the etiology, signs, symptoms, and prognosis of CG and the scarce literature concerning its treatment, especially with regard to using group interventions.

In support groups, people who have experienced the recent loss of a significant other come together and, with the help of a leader, discuss feelings and reactions to their losses, learn new skills, meet new people, and adapt to life without the person who has died. People who attend support groups do not necessarily suffer from any significant impairment associated with their loss. Rather, they recognize the value of a helping hand and seek the support of others who are in a similar situation. Support groups can be led by a trained professional who has had a great deal of experience working with death and loss or by a layperson (i.e., peer) who has experienced the loss of a significant person and successfully adapted to the loss and wants to help others through a similar situation. Support groups typically have an educational or self-help orientation, yet they can also offer a forum for members to discuss their feelings associated with their loss.

Support groups are often geared toward helping people with specific types of losses. For example, there are support groups for widowed persons, suicide survivors, survivors of homicide victims, parents who have experienced the death of a child, survivors of persons killed by drunken drivers, and children who have lost a parent. Such specialized groups have an advantage in that the group members experience relief of finally being around others who, because of the similarity of their loss, seem to really understand (Hughes, 1995). It is more comfortable to be with people who are close enough to the problem that they do not need long explanations to achieve understanding. However, specialized support groups are not always available in every community. It is not always possible to offer separate groups for each type of loss because smaller communities do not have the population to maintain segregated support groups or cannot find appropriate and willing leaders. Nevertheless, mixed support groups benefit participants because they learn that all loss engenders grief and that grief is a common human experience.

Table 1 provides examples of various grief support groups, including those of the mixed variety and those oriented toward people with particular types of losses. Support groups are located in a variety of settings, including local hospices, senior centers, churches, Red Cross centers, local hospitals, and religious-affiliated social service organizations. The Internet is also a very useful tool for locating support groups. For example, the website of the BC Bereavement Helpline (http://www.bcbereavementhelpline.com/index.php?mode=links) posts a list of 40 local, provincial, national, and international agencies that offer support services to the bereaved.

Although many participants of support groups attest to the usefulness of these groups for helping them adjust to life without the person who died, formal evidence of the effectiveness of such groups is often lacking. For example, in their review of bereavement interventions, Currier et al. (2008) found that interventions directed toward people with recent losses but with no indication of a CG reaction fail to benefit them. Although such findings may reflect the reality of the limited efficacy of support groups, they may also reflect the possibility that studies of such interventions have failed to assess aspects of the lives of support group participants that are affected by such interventions (e.g., improvement in instrumental and emotional support). Nevertheless, in the event of a death loss and absence of significant impairment by the survivor, support groups may serve a useful purpose for those who would like assistance in adjusting to their loss.

TABLE 1
Examples of Grief Support Groups

Organization	Focus of support group
THEOS (They Help Each Other Out Spiritually)	Young and middle aged widows
Parents of Murdered Children and Other Survivors of Homicide Victims	Survivors of murder victims
MADD (Mothers Against Drunk Driving)	Friends and family of people killed by drunk drivers
Compassionate Friends	Anyone who has experienced the death of a child
Rainbows	Children in grief
GriefShare	Anyone who has suffered a significant death loss

Overview of Interpretive Group Therapy and Supportive Group Therapy

In contrast to common support groups, our two models of therapy for CG—interpretive group therapy and supportive group therapy—are professionally led groups for adults with CG. The work of our clinical and research group likely reflects one of very few, if not the only, programs dedicated to developing and testing group therapy models for people suffering from CG. Our models each contain 12-session groups that are led by a single therapist.

For ease of communication, many people refer to interpretive therapy and supportive therapy as if they were distinct entities. Others argue that it is preferable to think in terms of a continuum with interpretive therapy at one end and supportive therapy at the other. Although the concept of a continuum is more complex than a dichotomy, it too is an oversimplification. This is evident if one tries to specify the nature of the dimension that defines the single continuum. It quickly becomes clear that the therapies on the continuum differ on many features. Thus, there are actually many continua, one for each feature. This multidimensional perspective is conceptually more cumbersome than a dichotomous perspective or a unidimensional perspective, but it is much more accurate in representing the complexity of the therapies. Consistent with the multidimensional perspective, we have defined features as including overall therapy objectives, session objectives, and therapist techniques or behaviors (Piper, Joyce, McCallum, Azim, & Ogrodniczuk, 2002). In an attempt to reduce conceptual difficulties, we suggest the following definitions and formulations. *Overall objectives* refer to the general or ultimate aims of therapy. Although helping patients solve their presenting problems is an overall objective of both interpretive and supportive forms of psychotherapy, the pathways differ. In supportive psychotherapy, presenting problems are addressed directly. In interpretive psychotherapy, they are addressed indirectly. Sometimes the terms *primary objectives* versus *secondary objectives* are used to make this distinction.

From our viewpoint, the primary (or direct) objective of supportive psychotherapy is to improve the patient's immediate adaptation to his or her life situation. To restore the patient's equilibrium, symptoms must be reduced, self-esteem boosted, and stressors reduced. There is a focus on the immediate needs of the patients. In many cases, there is a crisis-intervention orientation, even if the "crisis" is relatively minor and repetitive. Thus, there is an attempt to initiate restorative procedures as soon as possible and strengthen them as therapy proceeds. The secondary (or indirect) objective of supportive psychotherapy is to teach the patient problem-solving skills that can be used in the future. This includes such skills as learning how to define problems, consider alternative solutions, consider the advantages and disadvantages of solutions, try out solutions, and evaluate the outcomes of attempted solutions. In psychodynamic parlance, this is referred to as building ego strength.

From our viewpoint, the primary objective of interpretive psychotherapy is to enhance the patient's insight about repetitive conflicts (intrapsychic and interpersonal) and trauma that underlie and sustain the patient's presenting problems. This is part of a process of achieving self-understanding and control that continues beyond the termination of psychotherapy, which in psychodynamic theory is achieved through the process of working through. Typical conflicts include wanting yet fearing a close relationship with someone, wanting to be self-sufficient yet fearing isolation, and experiencing ambivalent feelings toward the lost person. It is assumed that insight into such common conflicts will allow patients to resume a normal mourning process, which has been impeded. A related objective was to help the patients develop tolerance for ambivalence toward the people whom they have lost. The secondary objective of interpretive psychotherapy is to help the patient successfully adapt to and, when possible, alleviate the presenting problems that brought the patient to the therapist.

To some extent, what is primary for interpretive psychotherapy tends to be secondary for supportive psychotherapy and vice versa. During each therapy, there is an oscillation between working on primary and secondary objectives, which tests the skills of the therapist.

Session objectives are general goals that indicate what the therapist is trying to achieve during individual sessions. They do not represent the specific techniques (behaviors) the therapist uses to achieve such objectives. For example, the session objective in interpretive psychotherapy is to create a state of tolerable deprivation and provoke anxiety during the session. Faced with the same material in supportive therapy, the objective would be to create a state of gratification and decrease anxiety. How the therapist actually brings about the desired results depends in part on the specific techniques the therapist uses. In interpretive psychotherapy, the technique of interpreting transference can lead to a state of deprivation and anxiety. In supportive psychotherapy, the technique of offering praise can lead to a state of gratification. Exhibit 1 lists features (i.e., session objectives and techniques) that have been used in the literature to differentiate interpretive therapy from supportive therapy. Although each is identified with one or the other form of therapy, each may be viewed as representing a continuum. For each continuum, the more the therapist emphasizes the feature, the more he or she is working interpretively or working supportively.

If there is considerable emphasis on interpretive features or supportive features, a therapy session is regarded as interpretive or supportive, respectively. For example, a therapist who mainly focuses on unconscious transference manifestations in the context of parental relationships, through the use

EXHIBIT 1
Features of Interpretive Group Therapy and Supportive Group Therapy

Interpretive features	Supportive features
Create a state of tolerable deprivation and anxiety in the session	Create a state of gratification in the session
Create pressure on the patient to talk by being nondirective	Relieve pressure on the patient to talk by being directive and conversational
Provide interpretations	Provide noninterpretive interventions, for example, reflections, questions, clarifications
Focus on the patient–therapist relationship	
Explore and interpret positive and negative transference	Focus on patient relationships that are external to therapy
Focus on early relationships	Facilitate positive transference and redirect negative transference
Explore the patient's subjective impressions of others	Focus on current relationships
Focus on unconscious processes	Focus on realistic impressions of others
Explore the meaning of uncomfortable emotions.	Focus on conscious processes
Explore and interpret mature and immature defenses	Allow the expression of uncomfortable emotions
Internalize responsibility for difficulties	Facilitate mature defenses and discourage immature defenses.
Make links among therapist, parental, and significant other relationships	Externalize responsibility for difficulties
	Engage in structured problem solving
	Provide guidance and advice
	Offer praise
	Provide self-disclosures about personal information, opinions, and values

of interpretations that arouse tension in the patient, is conducting an interpretive session. In contrast, a therapist who mainly focuses on alternative ways to relate to a current partner, through the use of questions, guidance, and praise of the patient's past efforts, which is gratifying, is conducting a supportive session.

The following vignettes help illustrate the differences in therapists' technical approach in interpretive group therapy and supportive group therapy.

Supportive Group Therapy Vignette

The following vignette illustrates supportive group therapy. It is from the third session of a 12-session treatment. The vignette takes place early in the session in which one of the male group members, Mike, is talking about the suicide death of a close friend and the anger he is feeling.

> Mike: It broke my brother's heart absolutely, but it also broke mine. I don't know, my brother doesn't like to talk about it,

but I know how I feel. I feel really extremely angry with him and ah . . .

Therapist: Well, you know, when someone does commit suicide the truth is that they're, they're depriving themselves of a life and other people of relationships, right? So I think that it's an understandable human reaction that we can't kinda sweep under the rug. It's a reality; it is a feeling that many people report. Although as you say, there is a sort of delicacy about it. You don't want to say that you feel angry.

Mike: No.

Therapist: Because it seems like it's inappropriate.

Mike: No, Ron, he's, he's 32 now, and he's a, he's a very strong intelligent person and uh, he, I know he has problems dealing with it, but when we sit down and talk I let him open up and we'd just talk about it, but he um, he doesn't seem to be as angry as I am. I just, uh, I can't, I have a hard time accepting it. I've lost people in the past, through, you know, from car accidents and such, and uh, but this one just, it just blew me away, it just, and that's 4 years ago, almost 4 years ago.

Therapist: Well, how do people get to accept things they feel angry about? Even if it takes a while, how do people do it?

Ed: You say, "My anger doesn't change a thing. I can be, can be as angry as I like, but he, you know, he made his mind up."

Mike: I would like to know, 'cause the word comes up like, if, if he lived, you know, if he had phoned me, if he had done this. Well obviously he didn't do that, now I don't know if anybody else has been in that case where, uh, and that's what, I guess, using that word "if" . . . "If, if," you know it's like, it's a small word, big meaning, but that's never going to happen, and I guess that's part of my, my problem with dealing with it, you know.

Ed: That's OK man, I mean it's natural for you to think, "If . . . if only . . . " That's your imagination, but then you can think of alternatives, like other ways of how it could have been, right?

Mike: Mmm-hmm.

Therapist: You put yourself in another story. Is there anything useful about that, imagining an alternative, or does it only hurt?

Sue: It seems like people do that naturally, they consider oh, if only, or if this had happened and then that had happened.

> If you think that different histories might have occurred, is that a way for your mind to try and adjust to what really did happen?

Sandra: Isn't that sort of like sweeping it under the carpet?

Sue: Well, I'm not sure.

Sandra: I know that's not what you're suggesting but . . .

Therapist: Yeah. You think, this happened. It wasn't this; it wasn't that. It was this, right?

Sandra: Mmm-hmm.

Therapist: So maybe it's a way of getting the past into focus even though it's hard to get into focus by contrasting it with what didn't happen or the other thing.

Interpretive Group Therapy Vignette

The following vignette, from the final session of the 12-session treatment, illustrates interpretive group therapy. The focus of the vignette is on Ed as he struggles to accept and express ambivalent feelings about his losses and the loss of the group. His only daughter died of cancer 10 years ago after a prolonged illness. She was 4 years old. And recently his dad died.

Alice: If we don't get our daily—our weekly—here—where are we going to get it—our—for me a crying jag—for anyone else— [pause] the interaction with people that understand.

Therapist: Yeah, the fear is there that, uh, the thing that people have a hard time embracing are the feelings around the disappointing group or the bad group—the ending group. You don't really want to deal with these except by trying to make me answer questions or force me to do this or that [pause] and you're still holding on to something for everyone. Ed, you're the most—you've been pushing for this for 4 weeks in a row now. I think you owe it to yourself to give up your stubbornness and try to get into what it is you're trying to get from me. What is it about the me that's been frustrating you—the me that hasn't been enough for you—that might be related to how stuck you got after losing your girl and your dad?

Ed: I don't know.

Therapist: You gotta go farther than that . . .

Ed: I just don't know.

Therapist:	What is it? It's about emotions—what you're feeling. Try to put them into words. [*silence*]
Ed:	[*looking stricken*] It's not going to come. [*pause*] It's not going to come.
Therapist:	This is everybody's dilemma, not just Ed's. Brenda, you're the second most pushy in terms of asking questions—trying to get something—so my guess is you're also in touch with the same thing this guy's in touch with. If only somebody could start putting it into words. What's behind all this pressure on me.
Brenda:	Well, my feeling is that our conditions are hopeless. This didn't help.
Therapist:	That's definitely the feeling.
Brenda:	We had high expectations. I did.
Gloria:	Maybe Ed felt hopeless when he lost his daughter and he lost his dad. She was his daughter. He couldn't save her. Being a parent you think that you're supposed to be able to protect your children from all the bad in the world. That's gotta be a helpless feeling to not be able to help them. [*pause*] You have no control over your circumstance. When I look at Ed I get so anxious for some reason. Fiona and Ed both have so much pain. They can't let go. I worry about Fiona because she said if this didn't work she didn't know what she'd do.
Therapist:	It's going on inside of you as well—the very same thing.
Gloria:	Maybe.
Therapist:	You're on the verge of tears too. It's all about you. All of you are in the same boat.
Helen:	You feel like they do so you can relate to the same pain.
Gloria:	I guess I feel for them.
Therapist:	And for yourself.
Gloria:	Getting up in the morning and seeing hope for the future, not just getting through another day. [*silence*]
Alice:	But isn't that why we're asking where do we go from here? Because we know we're not whole yet? [*silence*]
Therapist:	Can you speak for yourself? Do you know you're not whole?
Alice:	Yeah!

Therapist:	And what does that feel like?
Alice:	Well—frustrating for one thing. After putting in this period of time I know I'm better, but I'm still not whole.
Therapist:	Maybe people just cannot admit at this point that you're feeling a lot of anger that this thing's coming to an end.
Brenda:	I think the way we feel is that we could almost start all over again. [*a few people laugh*]
Therapist:	Well, it's a nice fantasy you could use to try to cope with what you're feeling now. [*pause*] But you're angry.
Ed:	Well, I'm not happy.
Therapist:	You're angry.
Ed:	Mmm-hmm.
Therapist:	You're angry with me.
Ed:	Not really. [*silence*]
Irene:	Nothing personal but . . .
Alice:	I have a hard time dealing with anger.
Therapist:	You can join the club today.
Alice:	When I get upset and angry with somebody, I end up in tears even when I'm giving them a piece of my mind. I will cry through the whole thing. I can't handle my anger or anger from anyone else. More often than not I end up crying [*pause*] unless I completely block it out. [*silence*]
Therapist:	Ed, when you ask, "Is this normal?" I think you're trying to avoid how angry you are. [*silence*]
Ed:	I don't know what's wrong. [*silence*]
Gloria:	Try to get it out. [*silence*]
Therapist:	[*to the group*] Does he look happy with me to you?
Irene:	No. I can feel his anger from here. [*silence*]
Ed:	I respect you.
Therapist:	Is that easier to say than . . .
Ed:	I don't know you that well.
Therapist:	Do you like me? You know, whatever *liking* means in this context?

Ed:	Yeah. [*silence*]
Therapist:	So you don't know what to do with liking me and hating me at the same time because you're losing me—hating me because you don't feel I've been enough for you. [*silence*] What do you feel? You're feeling something very powerful— so is everybody. [*pause*] You loved your father.
Ed:	A lot.
Therapist:	You couldn't possibly be angry at him for leaving you, could you? [*silence*] You loved your daughter.
Ed:	Mmm-hmm. [*pause*] You're trying to get me to go to a place I don't want to go.
Therapist:	I'm not trying to. You're already there. [*pause*] You couldn't possibly feel angry with her for leaving you. [*pause*] You couldn't possibly be angry at me for how you see me as responsible for ending this group, not answering questions and all that stuff. [*pause*] You're all in the same boat, by the way, with your attempts not to deal with that part of the group. [*silence*]
Ed:	I don't want to go there. [*pause*]
Therapist:	No. You can't go there with me. You can't go there with your dad. You can't go there with your daughter. [*silence*]
Ed:	No. [*silence*]
Gloria:	What if you know it would make you feel better to let go?
Ed:	It doesn't. It hurts too much.
Therapist:	You're not angry at those people?
Gloria:	I don't know if I'm angry. I don't think I am. [*pause*] Let's talk about Ed, ha ha.
Therapist:	You see what I'm getting at? [*pause*] I think in your own ways—in the ways things come about in groups like this— you've come to love this group and love each other and I guess love me. You just don't seem to be able to handle being furious with group—with me—for its frustrating parts.
Alice:	I don't know how you can be angry at someone for leaving you—for dying when they didn't have a choice. If they had had a choice, they wouldn't have. [*pause*] So how could you possibly be angry?
Therapist:	Nice try.

Alice:	Well rationalized, eh?
Therapist:	For all the good it does you . . .
Alice:	Yeah. [*pause*]
Therapist:	Just check out your feelings; you'll know you can be. [*silence*]

Determining the Optimal Treatment Approach

Given the different emphases of supportive and interpretive therapy, how should clinicians determine which treatment is right for which patient? Several factors should be considered, such as patient needs and expectations. However, our research shows that one factor may be particularly important in this regard. *Quality of object relations* (QOR)—that is, a person's capacity for interpersonal relatedness—has been shown to strongly influence the indicated treatment. Patients with high QOR (i.e., those who tend to form mature relationships characterized by reciprocity and stability) seem more likely to benefit from interpretive therapy than supportive therapy, and those with low QOR (i.e., those who tend to form primitive relationships characterized by destructiveness and instability) are more likely to benefit from supportive therapy than interpretive therapy. However, both high-QOR and low-QOR patients benefit most when the group contains at least a certain proportion of high-QOR members. Therefore, our models rely on careful assessment of QOR, among other factors, to determine optimal treatment approach and group composition.

LIMITATIONS OF SHORT-TERM GROUP THERAPY

Clinicians often raise the legitimate question, What can be accomplished for my patient in a group that lasts only a short time? In a long-term therapy group, patients can work over an extended period of time toward changing interpersonal patterns that took a long time to develop. Eventually, all patients become the focus of the therapist's attention. In the case of short-term group therapy, the nature of the therapist's attention to individuals is less certain. It is clear that the benefits of short-term group therapy for CG should not be oversold. To do so would diminish its credibility. It should not be promoted as a cure-all or as a means of bringing about lasting personality change. In short-term group therapy for CG, considerable improvements were found for loss-specific symptoms and general psychiatric symptoms. In contrast, improvements involving interpersonal distress, social (role) dysfunction, and interpersonal dependency were relatively small. This suggests that interpersonal traits are less likely to change after 12 sessions of group therapy. Similarly, it would be unrealistic to expect short-term group therapy to bring about significant characterological changes in patients with CG who also have personality disorders.

ORGANIZATION OF THIS BOOK

This book contains two parts. In Part I, we discuss the research that informs and supports our model treatments. In Chapter 1, we first review the effectiveness of various therapies in alleviating CG, including individual therapy, group therapy, peer counseling, psychodynamic therapy, cognitive–behavioral therapy, exposure therapy, psychoanalytic therapy, primary interventions, secondary interventions, tertiary interventions, interventions that target CG specifically, and interventions that target bereavement broadly. We then describe three extensive trial programs that support our models. Essentially, the efficacy of predominant therapies (which are mostly individual therapy treatments and have small effect sizes) is contrasted with the efficacy of our own treatment models (which are group therapy treatments and have large effect sizes).

In the remaining chapters in Part I, we explore the prevalence of CG (Chapter 2); risk factors for CG (Chapter 3); and the effects of patient characteristics (Chapter 4), process variables (Chapter 5), and group composition (Chapter 6) on therapeutic outcome.

In Part II, we present our model treatments and provide practical guidance for administering them. In Chapter 7, we explain how to administer the preliminary stages of short-term group therapy for CG, including assessing patients, developing treatment plans, forming groups, and preparing group members for treatment. In Chapter 8, we describe the common components of the two models, including the focus on themes and roles, the use of group-as-a-whole interventions, and the significance of termination. In Chapter 9, we describe the techniques of our interpretive group therapy model and in Chapter 10, the techniques of our supportive group therapy model. Finally, in the Afterword, we describe future directions for research and practice.

Although Part I will appeal primarily to researchers and Part II primarily to practitioners, both parts are vital for understanding the etiology and outcome variables of CG.

I

RESEARCH THAT INFORMS THE SHORT-TERM GROUP THERAPY MODELS FOR COMPLICATED GRIEF

1

EFFECTIVENESS OF INDIVIDUAL AND GROUP THERAPIES

Creating a therapy group that has the potential to be effective treatment for patients, a rewarding experience for therapists, and an accessible intervention for referral sources is a complex endeavor. It actually involves the creation of two groups. The first group consists of the patients who have come for treatment. The second, less obvious group consists of colleagues whose referral decisions greatly affect the viability and success of the therapy group. Each of the two groups requires preparation and education by the therapist. The better informed that patients are about the objectives and processes of the group, the smoother will be their entry into the group, and the more likely that they will attend and remain. The more informed the colleagues are regarding the objectives and processes of the group, the more likely the referrals will be appropriate and the more likely the group will operate smoothly without internal or external interference or disruption.

Before discussing such topics as prevalence, risk factors, preparation, and education, which are covered in subsequent chapters, we provide an overview of treatment effectiveness for complicated grief (CG). How effective are other treatments compared with our own treatment models? In this chapter, we review the effectiveness of several common treatments—such as peer counseling, psychodynamic, cognitive–behavioral, exposure, and psycho-analytic therapies—and our own group treatment models.

In the field of psychotherapy, effectiveness is often expressed in terms of effect size. It is a statistic that expresses the amount of change in a single sample (e.g., from pretreatment to posttreatment) or the difference in the amount of change between two samples (e.g., treated and control group). Because it is expressed in terms of standard deviation units, comparisons can be made across outcomes and treatments. In this book, effect size is generally defined as the mean of the pretreatment outcome score minus the mean of the posttreatment outcome score divided by the standard deviation of the pretreatment score. It is commonly symbolized as d.

We begin the chapter by discussing literature reviews of effectiveness that have been conducted by other researchers. Next, we describe specific studies conducted by other researchers. Both of these sections reveal relatively small effect sizes of common treatments, though it is not known whether this is due to methodological flaws of the studies. We then describe three extensive trial studies testing our own model treatments, short-term interpretive group therapy and short-term supportive group therapy. The trial studies demonstrate methodological rigor and yield greater effect sizes than other tested treatments.

LITERATURE REVIEWS

During the past decade, a small number of literature reviews of the efficacy of bereavement interventions have been conducted. Although it would have been desirable for the reviews to have provided the basis of a consensus concerning the efficacy of bereavement interventions, this has not been the case. To the contrary, reviewers have criticized various aspects of each other's review methodology as well as the conclusions drawn from the reviews. At times the criticism has been quite sharp and accusatory. For example, Larson and Hoyt (2007) have suggested that Fortner (1999) and Neimeyer (2000) misrepresented empirical findings and damaged the reputation of grief counseling.

In a review of 35 bereavement interventions, that is, interventions that were not specifically focused on CG, Allumbaugh and Hoyt (1999) found that individual therapy produced an average effect size of 0.65, whereas group treatment produced an average effect size of 0.40. This difference was marginally significant ($p < .10$). Allumbaugh and Hoyt pointed out that this difference, which favors individual therapy, runs counter to the general finding of no significant differences in the outcome literature comparing group and individual therapies (Bednar & Kaul, 1994). Allumbaugh and Hoyt noted that their result was likely due to the confounding of treatment modality and practitioner training in the studies that they reviewed. More highly trained clinicians produced better results than nonprofessional therapists or therapists in training, and there was a tendency for the highly trained clinicians to be used in the studies of individual therapy.

Allumbaugh and Hoyt presented an "omnibus effect size" in their review ($d = 0.43$), which is somewhat smaller than effect sizes commonly reported in psychotherapy outcome studies. They recommended that future researchers try to include self-selected participants rather than recruited participants. Of note, in the six studies that "used participants who were likely similar to real-world patients because they voluntarily sought treatment" (Allumbaugh & Hoyt, 1999, p. 376), their effect sizes ranged from 1.17 to 3.05. In short, their evidence suggested that treatment with self-selected patients is likely to be as effective or even far more effective than what is typical of psychotherapy outcome research in general.

They also recommended attention to time duration since loss. Control groups in this review showed a relatively small spontaneous recovery rate, which might be expected given that the mean length of time since the loss was more than 2 years. Much of the initial spontaneous recovery may have already occurred in the first 3 to 6 months. Likewise, in the treatment groups, the effects of therapy after a long interval of untreated reactions to the loss may have been attenuated relative to the possible effects of earlier treatment. Allumbaugh and Hoyt estimated that the omnibus effect size would have been 0.70 if treatment had begun within 3 or 4 months of the loss.

Kato and Mann (1999) provided an overview of four major theories of bereavement together with qualitative and quantitative analyses of the studies they selected. They summarized four main approaches to the treatment of bereavement: psychoanalytic, stage, stress, and social support theories. In their qualitative overview, they summarized findings from four studies of individual therapy. Three of these reported small and inconsistent improvements in the physical health of treated subjects. The fourth reported some improvements in stress reactions but not in physical health. Methodological flaws in all of the studies made results hard to interpret. Kato and Mann stated that more research is required before conclusions about the effects of individual therapy can be drawn. In their quantitative overview, they restricted consideration to just 11 studies meeting certain basic methodological criteria, including random assignment to treatment or control groups and use of the same recruitment methods for both control and treatment subjects. Interventions were not clearly aligned to theories of bereavement, and outcome measures reflecting depression and coping were not included.

When individual therapy was combined with group and family therapy, the average effect size for bereavement interventions, including measures of depression and grief, physical symptoms, and other psychological symptoms, was only 0.11, a very low number. Were the interventions ineffective or not powerful enough, or did limitations such as small sample sizes prevent potential effects from being shown? Kato and Mann (1999) left these questions open. Given Allumbaugh and Hoyt's (1999) findings on a larger sample of studies and given the findings of other reviews to be summarized in the paragraphs that follow, it appears likely that Kato and Mann surveyed studies that were particularly methodologically limited.

Larson and Hoyt (2007) subsequently criticized Kato and Mann's (1999) procedures. They pointed out that Kato and Mann had limited the keywords in their electronic search to *bereaved* and *bereavement*. If *grief, grieving*, or *griever* had been used, more studies would have been included. Also, Larson and Hoyt objected to the procedure of calculating a separate effect size for each measure because multiple measures within a single study would surely not be statistically independent of each other. Accordingly, Larson and Hoyt were skeptical about the reported low aggregate effect size.

Neimeyer (2000) provided a meta-analytic review that included 23 studies in which there was random assignment to treatment and control groups. The overall effect size was low (0.15). The modality of treatment (individual vs. group therapy) was not associated with effect size, whereas higher risk levels (sudden violent death or evidence of chronic grief) were related to increased effect sizes. Alongside each other, these findings suggest that the individual experiencing grief may be more relevant to treatment outcome than the modality of treatment that he or she receives. Neimeyer's review subsequently generated controversy (Bonanno & Lilienfeld, 2008; Fortner, 2008; Hoyt & Larson, 2008; Larson & Hoyt, 2007) because it relied heavily on an unpublished dissertation completed by Fortner in 1999, who used a statistic called treatment-induced deterioration effect, which had not been subjected to peer review prior to its citation by Neimeyer (2000). On one side of this debate, Larson and Hoyt (2007) and Hoyt and Larson (2008) alleged that misunderstandings and unwarranted pessimism in the professional community and popular press have followed the misconceived application of the treatment-induced deterioration effect statistic by Neimeyer. Perhaps the most upsetting conclusion of Neimeyer was the suggestion that the treatment appeared to be harmful to 38% of the sample. Even on the other side of the debate, however, which is characterized by a more skeptical view of therapeutic claims for the treatment of bereavement, Bonanno and Lilienfeld have continued to recognize that there is a population of 10% to 15% of bereaved people who have enduring or extreme CG features requiring treatment. Although the treatment of CG is a somewhat independent and specialized topic, treatment providers for this condition are likely to remain interested in the controversies over treatment of what is called *normal grief* and the question of possible iatrogenic treatment effects.

Schut, Stroebe, van den Bout, and Terheggen (2001) provided a review of bereavement intervention research in which they distinguished between primary, secondary, and tertiary interventions after loss. Primary interventions were described as those for the bereaved population in general. Secondary interventions were for people who were defined as being at high risk for bereavement-related problems, including bereaved parents, people who experienced sudden traumatic deaths, and people who had high preintervention symptomatic distress. Schut et al. (2001) concluded that most of the 16 primary intervention studies that they reviewed had methodological problems and that there was hardly any empirical support for the effectiveness of the described interventions. Results were more mixed for seven secondary intervention studies. When effects were found, they were described as follows: "generally rather modest and there are some indications that improvement is only temporary" (Schut et al., 2001, p. 725). Tertiary interventions provided to people who had already developed a complicated mourning response were described in seven studies. Effects were described as positive and lasting, although often modest. There was a tendency in these seven studies for participants to self-refer, whereas in the primary and secondary interventions participants tended to be recruited by researchers. Self-referral of participants tended to be associated with more favorable results than were found when participants were recruited by researchers. People who ask for help are probably more motivated than those who are recruited. Although tertiary intervention studies were not free of methodological problems, they did at least incorporate preintervention–postintervention comparisons, unlike some of the primary intervention studies and nearly all of the secondary intervention studies. Schut et al. (2001) concluded that "the general pattern emerging from this review is that the more complicated the grief process appears to be, the better the chances of interventions leading to positive results" (p. 731).

Another conclusion from the Schut et al. (2001) review was that interventions provided later in the bereavement process tended to be more successful than those provided earlier. This is relevant in the light of diagnostic criteria for CG that require symptom disturbance of at least 6 months, such as the criteria proposed by Zhang, El-Jawahri, and Prigerson (2006). Jordan and Neimeyer (2003) pointed out that the evidence regarding optimal timing of bereavement interventions is mixed and that the optimal timing may be curvilinear—not too soon and not too late. They concluded tentatively that full interventions 6 to 18 months following a loss may be optimal, although they qualified this by recommending "early contact with newly bereaved clients to establish a relationship and provide psychoeducation" (Jordan & Neimeyer, 2003, p. 782).

Currier, Neimeyer, and Berman (2008) provided the most comprehensive review of the field to date. They included 61 controlled studies of psychotherapeutic interventions for bereaved persons. Only 25% of the interventions they reviewed were of individual therapy. For group therapy, the figure was 63%; for family therapy, it was 12%. There were no significant overall differences favoring group, individual, or family modalities at posttreatment. In a classification that is conceptually similar to the primary, secondary, and tertiary classification proposed by Schut et al. (2001), Currier et al. distinguished between universal, selective, and indicated interventions. Universal interventions were aimed at anyone who experiences bereavement, regardless of risk factors or functioning levels. Selective interventions were aimed not at highly distressed grievers per se but at particular bereaved people who were considered to have an increased risk of experiencing distress, for example, a parent whose child died a violent death. Indicated interventions were aimed at people who already showed problems adapting to loss: They may have experienced a disorder such as depression, clinically significant problems such as intrusive thoughts related to the loss, anxiety, or guilt feelings. The overall conclusion from the qualitative and quantitative literature was that interventions for indicated grievers have some empirical support, but universal and selective interventions have little. Effect sizes for indicated interventions (0.53 for posttreatment effects, on the basis of 5 studies; 0.58 for follow-up effects, on the basis of 2 studies) were described as comparable to effect sizes that have been reported for psychotherapy in general. For universal and selective interventions, there were positive changes, but the evidence suggests that positive changes also occur with time for the majority of bereaved people. In their review of bereavement research, M. S. Stroebe, Hansson, Schut, and Stroebe (2008) came to a similar conclusion, that is, that the greater the pathology in bereavement, the more likely the treatment is to be efficacious.

Currier et al. (2008) concluded that interventions had small effects at posttherapy and negligible effects at follow-up. Clearly, CG fits under the category of indicated interventions. Currier et al. (2008) wrote that "the present results are largely mute concerning complicated or prolonged grief" (p. 658). However, they balanced that conclusion with the view that "such an empirically derived diagnosis as a criterion for treatment deserves further consideration, especially in view of the growing evidence for the relative efficacy of specific treatments for this disorder" (p. 658). In this connection, they cited Boelen, de Keijser, van den Hout, and van den Bout (2007) and Shear, Frank, Houck, and Reynolds (2005) whose studies are summarized in the section that follows. They also noted that only five studies of indicated interventions assessed outcomes at posttreatment, only one of which screened for CG as it is currently understood (Wagner, Knaevelsrud, & Maercker, 2006, which is discussed in the section that follows),

In contrast to previous reviews, Currier et al. (2008) concluded that the evidence did not show support for timing of interventions as an important moderator of outcome. This lack of evidence can be said to raise a question concerning the assumption that therapy for bereaved people is better delivered earlier than later. Even with universal and selective samples in which clinicians might hypothesize that intervention could protect against later deterioration, differential effectiveness based on time since the loss was not shown. One shortcoming of their study was that 16 of the 61 studies included in their review were dissertations.

SPECIFIC STUDIES

Next, we outline the findings in specific research studies that include individual treatment. These studies provide representation of diverse theoretical approaches and methods of intervening with a focus on complicated or traumatic grief.

Peer Counseling

Although it has not been extensively investigated by CG researchers, peer counseling is more widely provided for bereaved individuals than formalized treatment by professional clinicians. A study of widow-to-widow counseling was conducted by Vachon, Lyall, Rogers, Freedman-Letofsky, and Freeman (1980). Of 185 widows who were approached in the Toronto area, 162 agreed to participate in the study. The median age of the widows was 52 years. Their husbands had died at 67 years and younger. The researchers wished to reduce the risk of confounding problems related to aging with those related to bereavement. Participants were interviewed at 1, 6, and 24 months after the husband's death. They had been randomly assigned to an experimental widow-to-widow program or to a control group who received only the interviews. Interventions were provided by 1 of 6 widows who had taken part in a training seminar that covered bereavement problems, supportive counseling, and information about appropriate community resources. One-on-one support was provided at first, either by phone calls or face-to-face meetings. Communication could be initiated by either the widow contact or the widow. At a later stage, small group meetings were available. The article does not provide information on the proportion of all the meetings that took place within a small group format. On the basis of General Health Questionnaire scores, a high-distress group of 67 women was identified; those in this group who received the intervention were significantly more likely to regard their health as above average and significantly less likely to anticipate difficulty in adjusting to widowhood. A "pathway of adaptation" was described: Although both intervention and control subjects appeared equally distressed at 1 month postbereavement, by 6 months, when, the authors suggested, the immediate postloss support had ebbed away and the reality of the loss was more fully experienced, the control subjects showed more depressive symptoms and pre-occupation with the past. At 12 months, the control subjects had recovered in what the authors called intrapersonal adaptation, catching up with the intervention subjects in this respect. However, the intervention group was ahead of them in the resocialization process, and they maintained that lead over the next year, that is, up to 24 months postloss.

There are several implications of this interesting study. Peer counseling may well be effective, and even brief training of certain peers may be helpful to this effectiveness. Highly distressed widows may be particularly likely to benefit from peer interventions. Finally, interventions may have differential effects at different stages of bereavement, including attenuation or preven-tion of depressive features in the first 6 months and acceleration of adaptive resocialization after the intrapersonal adaptation has occurred.

Notwithstanding considerable interest in the study by Vachon et al. (1980), it received criticism from Schut et al. (2001) along with their endorse-ments of the randomized design and of the low initial refusal rate. Specifically, Schut et al. noted that other measures were used in the study, but data from these other measures were not included in the article. Readers were thus left uncertain whether the other measures yielded consistent conclusions. Also, 39% of the participants had dropped out by the time of the 2-year follow-up. The dropouts "had lost younger husbands, were of lower socioeconomic class and seemed to have more psychological problems and less support available" (Schut et al., 2001, p. 717). The concept of the pathway of adaptation is not necessarily invalidated by the problems arising from selective dropouts, but Schut et al. raised a legitimate question about the true extent of its applicabil-ity to different groups. Schut et al. also emphasized that the intervention worked most clearly for the widows who were categorized as highly distressed. This was notable in their view because they reported that the study by Vachon et al. has often been cited as having shown that primary preventive interven-tions are efficacious—a conclusion with which Schut et al. disagreed.

Brief Dynamic Therapy

Even by the often limited standards of methodological quality in the research literature on individual therapy for CG, psychodynamic interventions have in general not been well represented by strong methodological studies.

Horowitz, Marmar, Weiss, DeWitt, and Rosenbaum (1984) used brief dynamic therapy to treat 52 bereaved patients, including 28 diagnosed with adjustment disorder and 14 diagnosed with posttraumatic stress disorder (PTSD). The latter group, which may have resembled a group of patients who would now be described as having CG, had experienced bereavements following deaths that were "entirely or predominantly unanticipated and followed by high intrusive or denial symptoms" (Horowitz et al., 1984, p. 440). The study did not make clear how much time had elapsed since the deaths experienced by the different diagnostic groups. The average time between deaths and the first evaluation for the study was 35 weeks, but the range was extensive, between 2 and 159 weeks, with an SD of 29. The study did not explicitly compare outcomes between diagnostic groups. Also, it did not include a no-treatment control group or a group that received another form of treatment. There was a finding that participants with higher initial symptoms had significantly more decline in their distress. Most of the variables that were analyzed in the study concerned therapy processes. More exploratory therapists' actions were found to be more suitable for patients who were highly motivated for therapy and/or at a higher developmental level of object relations and less suitable for patients who were less motivated and/or at lower, less organized developmental levels of object relations. On the other hand, more supportive therapists' actions were found to be more useful for patients at lower levels of object relations and less useful for patients at higher levels. These findings were very similar to the findings of the individual therapy matching study by Piper, Joyce, et al., 2002, and the group therapy comparative trial by Piper, McCallum, Joyce, Rosie, and Ogrodniczuk, 2001.

Marmar, Horowitz, Weiss, Wilner, and Kaltreider (1988) followed with a study comparing brief dynamic individual therapy provided by experienced clinicians with mutual-help group therapy under the leadership of trained nonclinicians. The participants were 61 widows who had unresolved grief reactions 4 to 6 months after the deaths of their husbands, randomly assigned to one or other of the treatments. There were improvements in both conditions, particularly in stress-specific and general symptoms and to a lesser extent in social and work functioning. There was significantly greater attrition in the group treatment condition. Treatments were equally effective when two subgroups that had completed at least 8 of 12 sessions were compared. Patients in both conditions tended to rate their improvement more highly than clinicians did. The authors reported their impression that "group treatment placed greater emphasis on support, role modeling, and exchange of practical information," whereas the individual dynamic therapy "emphasized the identification and resolution of recurrent maladaptive relationship patterns and idiosyncratic obstacles to the mourning process" (Marmar et al, p. 208). The greater attrition in the group treatment condition appeared to be the clearest difference between the treatments in this study, but, given the difference in training between the individual therapists and the nonclinician group leaders it was not possible to conclude that attrition is a predictable group therapy liability for this population.

Behavioral and Cognitive–Behavioral Studies

There is more research-based literature on behavioral and cognitive–behavioral approaches to individual bereavement interventions than there is on other approaches.

In an early controlled clinical trial of behavior therapy, Mawson, Marks, Ramm, and Stern (1981) provided "guided mourning," an exposure intervention, to 6 of 12 randomly assigned bereaved adults who had experienced chronic grief for at least 1 year. The other 6 received "antiexposure," which included instructions to avoid contact with distressing bereavement-related situations. In both conditions, participants received just six sessions lasting between 60 and 90 minutes delivered over 2 weeks. One month after treatment, the exposure group had better scores on the Texas Inventory of Grief and showed less avoidance of bereavement cues. However, the difference on the Texas Inventory of Grief did not persist at 2 months, and other measures did not show differential effects of the two interventions. Six sessions is very little treatment, and six subjects per condition is a very small number. It is possible that these limitations did not allow the real differences between the approaches to emerge.

In a follow-up behavioral study, Sireling, Cohen, and Marks (1988) randomly assigned 26 adults with *morbid grief* to exposure (*n* = 14; three then dropped out) or antiexposure conditions (*n* = 12; three then dropped out). Participants received 10 sessions over 14 weeks. Morbid grief was identified by avoidance features and duration, that is, distress lasting longer than 1 year following the loss. Both the guided mourning and the antiexposure groups improved on the Texas Revised Inventory of Grief and on measures of global symptom severity and work and leisure experience. Such differences were maintained up to 54 weeks later. Overall, however, antiexposure led to fewer significant changes on a variety of measures. The authors suggested that both the treatment and control groups were helped by contact with a therapist and encouragement to try new activities.

Frank, Prigerson, Shear, and Reynolds (1997) provided an exploratory report on exposure-based treatment of chronic bereavement-related distress in elderly individuals. They viewed bereavement-related distress as *traumatic grief*, which they conceptualized as treatable by the approach that Foa, Hembree, and Rothbaum (2007) had developed for the treatment of PTSD. They regarded CG as a term that implied different clinical features, including possibly psychotic features, which have not been considered in more recent presentations of CG in the literature. Generally, CG has been favored as a term that avoids confusion with PTSD (Ott, 2003). Frank et al.'s therapeutic interest was in avoidance (e.g., avoidance of the circumstances of the loss). They emphasized tasks such as reliving the moment of the death and saying goodbye to the deceased. They did not yet have objective data on treatment outcome. As Raphael, Minkov, and Dobson (2001) pointed out, this approach is similar to the guided mourning techniques described by Sireling and colleagues (1988).

Shear et al. (2001) reported on a pilot study of traumatic grief treatment in which traumatic grief was operationalized as a score greater than 25 on the Inventory of Complicated Grief (ICG; Prigerson, Maciejewski, et al., 1995). Of the 21 subjects who began treatment, 13 completed a full 4-month course (16 sessions). The treatment was manualized. It included imaginal exposure, that is, reexperiencing the scene of death and in vivo exposure to situations that were being avoided. Interpersonal therapy (IPT) methods were used to promote reengagement of relationships with others. The completer group ($n = 13$) and the intent-to-treat group ($n = 21$) both showed significant pretreatment–posttreatment differences on the ICG and on measures of anxiety and depression. Traumatic grief treatment provided substantially better results (the effect size for symptom changes was 1.82) than IPT alone with similar subjects. The authors noted that a randomized controlled trial was needed to confirm the traumatic grief treatment approach. That was done and reported by Shear et al. (2005), who conducted a randomized controlled individual therapy study that compared IPT with a targeted complicated grief treatment (CGT). Participants had scores of at least 30 on the ICG; at least 6 months had elapsed since the death of a loved one; and an independent evaluator judged CG to be the most important clinical problem. As Shear et al. (2005) pointed out, IPT is a well-studied, efficacious treatment for depression. In this study, IPT had a grief focus; there was sometimes a secondary focus on role transitions or interpersonal conflicts. CGT was unlike IPT in its attention to traumalike symptoms. CGT was delivered on the basis of the dual-process model of bereavement coping (M. S. Stroebe & Schut, 1999): The therapists in this condition attended to the processes of loss adjustment, on one hand, including an exercise that involved *revisiting* the loss through telling the story of the death, and on the other hand, restoration of a satisfying life. The loss focus included cognitive–behavioral therapy techniques, whereas the restoration focus included IPT strategies. Thus, CGT was conceptualized as going beyond IPT. Shear et al. (2005) made the claim that CGT was the first treatment "to target complicated grief symptoms directly" (p. 2607). The mean number of sessions for treatment completers in both conditions was 16. Data were analyzed for 49 patients in the CGT condition and 46 patients in the IPT condition. Treatment completion rates did not differ between groups, but there was a 26% dropout rate from both treatments. Also, notably, an additional 10% of participants refused to participate in the imaginal exposure exercise in CGT, which they found too difficult. The overall response rate was greater for CGT (51%) than for IPT (28%)—this difference was statistically significant. The time to response was significantly faster for CGT. The authors called for more research to confirm findings, test potential moderator variables such as medication, and improve treatment acceptance.

Cognitive–Behavioral Therapy via E-mail

Wagner, Knaevelsrud, and Maercker (2005) described an entirely e-mail-based cognitive–behavioral treatment program that was developed to address PTSD and CG. In a pilot study involving a mother whose 15-year-old son had committed suicide, 10 writing sessions were conducted over 5 weeks. The tasks for the patient were structured in the following sequence: self-confrontation, cognitive reappraisal, and sharing and farewell ritual. The therapist provided feedback after every second essay and tailored the tasks to the patient's needs. There were clear reductions on measures of intrusion, avoidance, anxiety, and depression, although some of the gains were not as strong at 3-month follow-up.

Wagner et al. (2006) followed their pilot study report with an article on a cognitive–behavioral Internet-based treatment program for CG viewed in terms of Horowitz's (1986) stress-response model. It conceptualized CG as sharing with PTSD the central features of intrusion, avoidance, and failure to adapt. A group of 55 bereaved individuals who sought help through the Internet were randomly assigned to treatment or to a waiting-list control condition. Treatment, which lasted 5 weeks and involved extensive e-mail communication with trained psychologists, consisted of 3 modules: exposure to bereavement cues, cognitive reappraisal, and integration and restoration. Therapists promoted tasks such as the development of rituals and other means of integrating the deceased person into one's life and reactivation of social connections. There were two weekly 45-minute writing assignments; therapists provided feedback and psychoeducation. The study recruited people who had experienced a traumatic or complicated bereavement, including a high proportion of parents who had lost a child (61%). The average age of participants was 37 years. Notably, 51 of the 55 patients were female. The treatment group showed better outcomes than the waiting-list group, with effect sizes for the former of 1.50 for pretreatment to posttreatment changes and 1.60 from pretreatment to 3-month follow-up. Change was clinically significant: Of the treatment group, 19% reported symptoms of intrusion and avoidance at posttreatment compared with 67% of the control group over the equivalent period. The authors suggested that the cognitive–behavioral treatment protocol, together with its associated stress-response theoretical model, was one possible explanation for the effectiveness of the treatment. They likened the treatment procedures in this study to the face-to-face procedures described by Shear et al. (2005).

The Internet-based therapeutic relationship was evidently experienced as strong and positive. The dropout rate was low (8%). The anonymity of the

Internet was seen as possibly conducive to personal disclosure. Also, the Internet is not geographically restricted and is not inconvenient for socially isolated patients. On the other hand, the authors cautioned that there could be misunderstandings during Internet-based treatment interactions and that crisis interventions would be difficult for Internet-based therapists to provide.

Models of Therapy Compared

Research comparisons of models of therapy within single studies tend to be consistent with the well-known dodo bird verdict that different types of therapy produce similar outcomes. However, apart from general replication of that familiar pattern, there were specific findings of particular interest, including another result that supported the value of exposure and a study that showed differential responses by men and women to different kinds of counseling.

Kleber and Brom (1987) compared three individually provided therapies, trauma desensitization, hypnosis, and brief dynamic psychotherapy, with each other and with a control group. Each therapy was provided over approximately 15 to 20 sessions. Participants were 83 Dutch adults (60 women and 23 men) who had experienced *pathologic grief* from death losses within the previous 5 years. The average time since the loss was 23 months. Participants were referred by a general practitioner or sought treatment in response to newspaper advertisements. The authors, who were interested in the posttraumatic stress response features of intrusion and denial, described all participants as experiencing psychological disorders. Between pretreatment and posttreatment, each of the therapies showed significant declines for intrusion and denial and for somatic symptoms, psychoneurotic symptoms, and state anxiety. In the control group, the equivalent variables did not show significant changes. However, when residual gain scores were calculated, that is, when the test of efficacy became more rigorous, the three therapies were superior to controls for intrusion and denial pretreatment–posttreatment comparisons but not uniformly so for other variables such as somatic symptoms and psychoneurotic symptoms. Intrusion and denial thus received empirical confirmation as variables of interest in pathologic grief. Overall, none of the therapies emerged as clearly superior, although psychodynamic therapy alone showed significant gains for psychoneurotic symptoms and state anxiety, even in the residual gain score comparisons with the control group. Nontreated patients also recovered, although to a lesser extent. In regression analyses, it was found that hypnotherapy and trauma desensitization were more successful with younger than with older patients, whereas psychodynamic therapy was almost equally successful with older and with younger patients. Higher income patients did better with psychodynamic therapy, whereas lower income patients did better with trauma desensitization.

Kleber and Brom (1992) treated prolonged or abnormal grief in a program that compared 12- to 15-session psychodynamic therapy with hypnotherapy and behavioral therapy and with waiting-list controls. All treatments were effective. Although avoidant behaviors were more resistant to intervention, the psychotherapeutic interventions were the most helpful approach to avoidance.

Schut, Stroebe, de Keijser, and van den Bout (1997) conducted a study on gender differences in contrasted bereavement interventions. A group of 23 widows and 23 widowers, who were all regarded as experiencing mildly complicated bereavement on the basis of General Health Questionnaire scores, were randomly assigned to either problem-focused or emotion-focused coping counseling. There was also a nonintervention control condition. These 46 participants each completed seven counseling sessions, starting between 14 and 17 months after bereavement. Data were collected at posttreatment and at follow-up (25 months after bereavement). In general, problem-focused counseling produced slightly better effects than emotion-focused counseling, and both led to somewhat better effects than no intervention. Gender differences emerged: Men, who were seen as predisposed to be more problem-focused, benefited more from emotion-focused counseling; whereas women, who were seen as predisposed to be more emotion-focused, benefited more from problem-focused counseling. The authors accounted for the gender differences by proposing that each gender could benefit by extending beyond the characteristic coping repertoire, for example, men needed to extend beyond their usual problem-focused coping style. In an overlapping characterization, the authors suggested that each gender could obtain help within less familiar spheres. The interaction of treatment approach with the client characteristic of gender is clinically interesting. Would atypical emotion-focused men benefit more from problem-focused counseling, and would atypical problem-focused women benefit more from emotion-focused counseling?

Boelen et al. (2007) compared cognitive–behavioral individual therapy with supportive individual counseling for people with scores more than 25 on the ICG. There were two cognitive–behavioral conditions: 16 participants completed cognitive restructuring (CR) + exposure therapy (ET) in which 6 sessions of CR were followed by 6 sessions of ET, and 20 participants completed ET + CR, in which the order of the pair of 6 sessions was reversed. In the supportive counseling condition, there were 12 sessions, completed by 7 participants in which therapists were unconditionally supportive of attempts to solve various emotional, social, and practical difficulties without giving exposure instructions or addressing cognitions. For all measures, effect sizes in both cognitive–behavioral conditions were higher than those for supportive counseling. Also, ET + CR was more effective than CR + ET, yielding larger clinical improvement and higher pretreatment to posttreatment effect sizes.

Notably, the effect size on the ICG for ET + CR completers was 1.80, which is an impressively high result. Dropout rates were higher during CR sessions than during ET sessions. Midtreatment comparisons showed more improvement after 6 sessions of ET than after 6 sessions of CR. Boelen et al. (2007) concluded that the "findings do suggest that encouraging patients to confront and work through the loss is important in treating CG and more helpful than targeting thinking patterns" (p. 283). One way to summarize this study is to say that exposure received strong empirical backing; cognitive restructuring received moderate backing; and supportive therapy received some backing.

The authors provided caveats to their conclusions, including the possible lack of power to detect differences that followed from relatively small sample sizes and the possibly compromised outcomes that may have resulted from comorbid conditions that were not measured at intake.

TRIAL STUDIES FOR INTERPRETIVE GROUP THERAPY AND SUPPORTIVE GROUP THERAPY

The development of interpretive group therapy and supportive group therapy for CG involved a repeated cycle of clinical work, observation, research, consideration of clinical implications, and modification of clinical work. The research included a prevalence study for CG (Piper, Ogrodniczuk, Azim, & Weideman, 2001; see Chapter 2, this volume) and three randomized group therapy clinical trials. These included a controlled trial that focused on the efficacy of interpretive group therapy for CG (Piper, McCallum, & Azim, 1992), a comparative trial that focused on the relative efficacy of the two forms of group therapy for CG as well as on quality of object relations (QOR) as a potential patient matching variable (Piper et al., 2001), and a composition trial that focused on the impact of group composition defined as the proportion of patients in the group with high-QOR scores (Piper, Ogrodniczuk, Joyce, Weideman, & Rosie, 2007). In the following sections, we discuss the administration and results of the trial studies. Table 1.1 summarizes the effect sizes of the three trials.

Controlled Trial

In 1986, several members of our team of researchers and clinicians (W. Piper, M. McCallum, and H. Azim) worked for the outpatient walk-in clinic of the Department of Psychiatry, at the University of Alberta Hospital in Edmonton, Alberta, Canada. We conducted an informal in-house review of the objectives and achievements of several therapy groups provided in the clinic, particularly time-limited short-term therapy groups. Our review revealed

TABLE 1.1
Effect Sizes for the Controlled, Comparative, and Composition Trials

Outcome variable	Controlled trial	Comparative trial	Composition trial
General symptomatic distress	1.00	.47	.40
Depression	.76	.61	.56
Intrusion	.56	1.09	.56
Avoidance	.70	1.05	.85
Target severity (patient)	1.50	1.47	1.38
Target severity (assessor)	2.00	1.37	1.63
Mean	1.09	1.01	.90

Note. Data from Piper, McCallum, and Azim (1992); Piper, McCallum, Joyce, Rosie, and Ogrodniczuk (2001); and Piper, Ogrodniczuk, Joyce, Weideman, and Rosie (2007).

that the short-term therapy groups appeared to be experiencing *task overload*. That is, the groups seemed to be trying to achieve too much: crisis intervention; support for day-to-day problem solving; assessment of suitability for long-term group therapy; training for new therapists who were inexperienced with group therapy; and treatment for symptom reduction, insight, and development of interpersonal skills and personality change. Thus, in our feedback to the clinic, we concluded that the short-term therapy groups would likely benefit from having a narrower focus with a more limited but more realistic set of objectives. Because the topic of loss was very prevalent among the patients who were participating in the short-term therapy groups, we decided to conduct a pilot therapy group to determine how well a short-term therapy group that focused on loss and that had more limited objectives would work. As it turned out, the group worked very well. After discussions with the therapists and clinic administrators, we began providing loss groups for patients who met criteria for CG.

Success in bringing the loss groups from the drawing board to the clinic can be attributed to at least one additional factor that proved to be very important. Because the loss groups were a new form of treatment, there was a need to carefully monitor their process and outcome. Although we could have achieved this by administering some relatively simple quality assurance measures of outcome before and after therapy and some brief process ratings after each session, we were interested in doing considerably more than that. We wished to evaluate the loss groups in terms of their specific potential to be an effective treatment for patients with CG and as an object of study of events regarded as important in the field of group therapy. Thus, at about the same time that we were testing the pilot group in the clinic, we were designing a randomized clinical trial to test the efficacy of the treatment. We submitted applications for external funds to support a formal investigation of treatment efficacy. We were successful in obtaining funds from two federal granting agencies (Health and Welfare Canada, Canadian Psychiatric Research Foundation). From a technical perspective, the funds allowed us to conduct a more thorough and more time-consuming battery of assessments with the help of research assistants. From a collaborative perspective, the funds seemed to serve as an endorsement of the legitimacy and importance of the project.

The methodology of the project called for the collaboration of almost everyone in the clinic. Psychiatrists managed medications for the patients and conducted interview assessments. Receptionists fielded questions from potential patients and referral sources. Clinic therapists served as assessors, referral sources, and eventually loss group therapists. As therapists in the project, they had to treat patients who had been assigned randomly to treatment condition and therapist; they had to audiorecord their sessions; they had to follow a treatment manual; and periodically they had to complete sets of forms about their patients and groups. We believe that the granting agency endorsements helped sustain the willingness of the clinic staff to complete the research tasks, which inevitably required them to devote extra work time to the project. On the positive side, there was the possibility of discovering interesting findings. Also on the positive side, the research project helped standardize many of the clinic's procedures for assessing patients, making treatment recommendations, and maintaining patient files. The 1992 book *Adaptation to Loss through Short-Term Group Psychotherapy* (Piper et al., 1992) presented the findings from our randomly controlled trial. The project also provided data for a dissertation topic for one member of the team (M. McCallum) and contributed to introducing large-scale clinical research projects to the staff of the clinic.

On reflection, we realized that in designing a research project to examine the usefulness of loss groups, we had constructed a treatment model for CG that was based on a considerable number of assumptions about loss, about people experiencing loss, and about the role of psychotherapy in coping with loss:

- We assumed that the loss of a significant other through death is a nearly ubiquitous event in people's lives. Perhaps the sole exception is a child who loses his or her own life before having experienced the loss of others.
- Although experts differ in defining normal and abnormal reactions to loss, we assumed that extreme and prolonged symptomatic manifestations or the complete absence of symptoms are abnormal.
- We assumed that losses have permanent effects, some of which remain outside of conscious experience.
- We assumed that reactions to recent losses that seem out of proportion to the event can be indicative of failure to resolve important previous losses.

- We assumed that it is doubtful whether anyone fully resolves the loss of significant relationships or is ever totally free of the effects of such losses.
- We assumed that people's responses to loss are influenced by stable factors such as one's defensive style and personality. Also relevant is how well a person has dealt with long-standing conflicts over such issues as trust, dependence, intimacy, and aggression.
- Although people's needs following loss are also diverse, we assumed that the need for catharsis and support are universal.
- We assumed that most people experiencing loss do not request or need psychotherapy.
- We assumed that group treatment approaches reduce social isolation and diminish the belief that one's difficulties are unique.

The group therapy in the trial was interpretive, or what some investigators refer to as *expressive*, in nature. It was based on the notion that recurrent internal conflicts whose components are largely unconscious serve to perpetuate maladaptation. Conflicts concerning the issues of independence versus dependence and intimacy versus privacy in the context of loss were commonly examined. The objective of therapy was to help patients solve their presenting problems by achieving insight into the ways their difficulties were related to unresolved intrapsychic conflicts, hence, initiating a process of working through that would continue beyond the treatment sessions. The technical orientation emphasized an active therapist role in which interpretation and clarification were emphasized over support and direction. Relevant here-and-now events in the group, including transference, were highlighted and explored. Patients were encouraged to contribute to the therapeutic process of other patients. A total of 154 patients completed their initial assessments and were randomly assigned to one of 16 therapy groups in either the immediate treatment condition or the waiting-list control condition. The lengths of the therapy group and the waiting-list period were the same (12 weeks). After 12 weeks, the control patients were offered group treatment. A comprehensive battery of 16 outcome measures was administered on three occasions: just before the onset of therapy, just after therapy ended, and at follow-up 6 months after therapy ended. A number of different areas were represented. These included interpersonal functioning, psychiatric symptomatology, self-esteem, life satisfaction, and personalized target objectives. The sources of evaluation included the patient, the therapist, and an independent assessor. Of the 16 outcome variables, significantly greater improvement for treated patients over control patients was found for 10 variables. Examination of the effect sizes for each variable and clinical significance for several variables that had sufficient normative data provided further evidence of strong treatment effects. Finally, the overall pattern of change from posttherapy to 6-month follow-up indicated either maintenance of improvement or additional improvement for nearly all 16 variables. Taken together, the analyses provided strong evidence of the efficacy of the treatment. Nevertheless, not all of the patients completed treatment once they began and not all patients benefited. A total of 109 patients began therapy and 33 dropped out prematurely for a dropout rate of 30.3%. Although undesirable, this percentage is well within the range of what therapists often experience with group forms of treatment.

A number of characteristics distinguished our approach to treatment from that of others. First, it was a psychosocial form of treatment, in contrast to a biological form such as medication. Second, it was a form of psychotherapy, which means that it focused more on internal psychological events than on overt behavior. Third, it was psychodynamic in orientation with a conceptual emphasis on conflictual components such as wishes, anxiety, and defenses, and a technical emphasis on clarification, confrontation, and interpretation. Fourth, it was a group form of treatment, thereby involving an entire set of patients in interaction with a therapist and one another as opposed to a more private one-to-one relationship between patient and therapist. Fifth, it was a time-limited form of treatment with a predefined beginning and ending as opposed to a form of therapy with an open-ended contract. Sixth, patients were expected to decide what to talk about at the beginning of each session and throughout treatment, rather than being directed by the therapist as in the case of cognitive–behavioral approaches. Given these characteristics, we named the treatment time-limited short-term dynamically oriented group therapy.

In the 1980s, several books (Rockland, 1989; Werman, 1984) and reviews (Winston, Pinsker, & McCullough, 1986) focused on dynamically oriented individual therapy of a supportive nature for patients with a large range of outpatient problems. The objective was to improve immediate adaptation to the patient's current life situation rather than to enhance insight about internal conflicts. In general, supportive therapy focuses on conscious processes, reality, and current relationships with people outside the session rather than unconscious processes, fantasy, early relationships, and the patient–therapist relationship. In response to the patient's efforts, the therapist offers praise, not scrutiny, and attempts to minimize rather than accentuate anxiety and regression in therapy sessions. Rockland and others argued that contrary to popular belief supportive therapy is characterized by specific technical features that should be a part of every psychotherapist's repertoire. In his 1989 book, Rockland concluded:

> Supportive therapy is probably more effective for less healthy, poorly motivated patients, exploratory therapy for healthier, better motivated patients. Supportive therapy deserves more study, particularly of its outcomes, when applied to patients across the diagnostic spectrum who have

varying motivations, degrees of psychological mindedness, and so on. (pp. 242–243)

For more than 30 years, our research team has studied the impact of two particular personality variables on such variables as working, dropping out, and benefiting from various forms of psychotherapy. They are psychological mindedness (PM) and QOR. We have defined PM as the ability to identify dynamic (intrapsychic) components and refer them to a person's difficulties. The person being assessed viewed a videotape of a patient speaking to his or her therapist. The person being assessed was then asked to comment about what he or she thought was troubling the patient on the videotape. An external rater used a scoring manual to assign a score ranging from 1 (low) to 9 (high). We have defined QOR as a person's internal enduring tendency to establish certain kinds of relationships that range along an overall dimension from 1 (primitive) to 9 (mature). An assessor conducts a 1-hour interview that focuses on the nature of the patient's relationships during three stages of life (childhood, adolescence, and adulthood). The assessor uses a scoring manual to determine the overall score. In some of our earlier studies, only one or the other of the two personality variables was assessed. In more recent studies, both were assessed. In the currently discussed controlled trial, however, only PM was assessed. In the trial, PM was directly related to patient work in therapy. Although work was directly related to therapy outcome, PM was not related to therapy outcome. This is sometimes referred to as the three-variable problem in statistical analysis. It usually suggests that a powerful undetected additional variable is affecting the relationships among the three variables. In addition, PM was inversely related to dropping out of therapy.

Comparative Trial

At the same time that we were conducting the controlled trial for our loss groups, we were conducting a comparative (matching) trial in the clinic that involved two forms of time-limited short-term individual therapy (interpretive, supportive) for a general outpatient sample. The patient personality variable was QOR. We hypothesized that high-QOR patients would benefit more from interpretive individual therapy and that low-QOR patients would benefit more from supportive individual therapy. The findings were consistent with these hypotheses. Consequently, we wondered whether similar hypotheses would receive support in the cases of interpretive group therapy and supportive group therapy for loss patients and QOR. Thus, we embarked on a similar comparative (matching) trial with 16 new loss groups and QOR as the primary personality variable. We were funded for this comparative trial from the Medical Research Council of Canada. The findings were as predicted. High-QOR patients benefited more from interpretive group therapy, and low-QOR patients benefited more from supportive group therapy.

In the comparative trial, the composition of each therapy group was mixed (heterogeneous) in terms of the patients' QOR scores. We wondered whether the significant matching findings would be even more pronounced in groups composed of all high-QOR patients who received interpretive therapy and groups composed of all low-QOR patients who received supportive therapy. This led to a decision to conduct a new clinical trial. It involved 18 groups and was called the composition trial.

Composition Trial

The composition trial was funded by the Canadian Institutes of Health Research. Given that several members of our team had moved to Vancouver to work at the University of British Columbia and two of its affiliated hospitals, the project was conducted as a two-site study (Edmonton and Vancouver).

Four conditions were created in the study: (a) homogeneous high-QOR interpretive groups, (b) homogeneous low-QOR supportive groups, (c) heterogeneous mixed-QOR interpretive groups, and (d) heterogeneous mixed-QOR supportive groups. Our primary hypothesis was that patients in the two homogeneous conditions would experience greater benefit than would patients in the two heterogeneous conditions.

Therapy groups were created in the following manner. When approximately 16–20 patients were available, they were allocated to a group in one of two ways. If two heterogeneous mixed-QOR groups were being formed, when possible patients were matched as closely as possible in pairs on the basis of their QOR scores, use of medication, and age and sex. One patient of each pair was assigned randomly to an interpretive therapy group and the other to a supportive therapy group. Then the pair of groups was assigned to a therapist, who led both groups during a 12-week period. If a homogeneous high-QOR group and a homogeneous low-QOR group were being formed, the patients were ranked from high to low on the basis of their QOR scores, with the upper half of the patients assigned to an interpretive group and the lower half of the patients assigned to a supportive group. The high-QOR group was then assigned to a therapist who provided interpretive therapy, and the low-QOR group was assigned to the same therapist, who provided supportive therapy.

A few exceptions occurred for two reasons. First, there was no control over the patients' QOR scores for each set of 16–20 patients that accumulated. Thus, it was not always possible to form two homogeneous groups or two heterogeneous groups. Second, there was no control over who dropped out of therapy and how that affected the composition. We required that a patient be a completer (attended 8 or more of the 12 sessions) and that the composition of the group be defined by completers. Thus, each completer in a group was exposed to a very similar interpersonal environment over a substantial number of sessions.

A total of 135 patients started therapy in a group. Following the procedure described in the previous paragraph, 62 patients were randomly allocated to interpretive therapy ($n = 32$) or supportive therapy ($n = 30$). In addition, 73 patients were assigned to create a high-QOR or low-QOR group composition for interpretive ($n = 35$) or supportive ($n = 38$) therapy, respectively. From the total, 25 patients (15 from interpretive therapy, 10 from supportive therapy) dropped out (attended seven or fewer sessions). The difference between the dropout percentages—22% for interpretive therapy and 15% for supportive therapy—was not significant. The remaining 110 patients (52 from interpretive therapy, 58 from supportive therapy) completed therapy, that is, attended eight or more sessions.

Each group was designated as homogeneous or heterogeneous on the basis of the percentage of high-QOR patients who completed the group, that is, patients who had attended 8 or more of the 12 sessions. We believed that completers represented the most relevant sample on which to conduct analyses because they had been a part of and experienced the same core composition of patients in the group for most of the 12 sessions. Most dropouts occurred early in the life of the group (65% by Session 4). Thus, unlike the completers, they did not fully experience the core composition of patients in the group. The percentage of high-QOR patients in the 18 groups ranged from 0% to 100%. The mean was 55%, and the standard deviation was 34%. The 18 therapy groups were separated into three distinct sets. Of these, 6 groups, with percentages ranging from 0% to 33%, were designated as homogeneous low-QOR groups. An additional 5 groups, with percentages ranging from 43% to 67%, were designated as heterogeneous mixed-QOR groups, and 7 groups, with percentages ranging from 71% to 100%, were designated homogeneous high-QOR groups. Also, 9 of the groups were interpretive, and 9 were supportive.

We hypothesized that patients in homogeneous groups would achieve better outcome than would patients in heterogeneous mixed-QOR groups treated with interpretive or supportive group therapy. However, support for this hypothesis was not found. Although the best outcomes were achieved by the homogeneous high-QOR patients who received interpretive group therapy, the poorest outcomes were achieved by the homogeneous low-QOR patients who received supportive therapy. The mixed groups had outcomes that fell in between. Even though our primary hypothesis did not receive support, we nevertheless found evidence for an important composition effect. We used a QOR cutoff score of 4.2, which we had also used in a previous study and which theoretically was descriptive of the midpoint of the 9-point scale. We designated each patient as high or low QOR and then calculated the proportion of high-QOR patients in each group. We discovered that the greater the proportion of high-QOR patients in the group, the better the outcome for all patients in that group. This was true regardless of the patient's own QOR score or the form of therapy (interpretive or supportive) that the patient had received. Thus, the high-QOR patients may beneficially provide peer support and serve as models in engaging in useful problem-solving behavior. In their absence, the more primitive behaviors of low-QOR patients may result in a group culture in which the provision of support and engagement in problem solving is regarded as intrusive and is met with suspicion and resistance.

Follow-Up

Once the efficacy of a form of therapy has been demonstrated, usually through randomized controlled trials, the question that follows naturally is, Will the effects last? To address the question concerning lasting effects, follow-up data are typically examined. However, for many disorders, follow-up data are either not available or they contain significant flaws. Typically, the nature of the follow-up sample is problematic. Inevitably, some patients do not return for their follow-up assessments. Thus, the sample will have decreased in size, which will compromise the statistical power of the analyses. The representativeness of the follow-up sample can also be questioned. Although missing data always create ambiguities, if the amount of missing data is relatively small and there is evidence that the sample of missing data is similar to the sample of nonmissing data, the findings are usually considered worthy of consideration. We believe that this is the case concerning the follow-up data from our composition trial.

Achieving lasting benefits from brief psychotherapies for certain disorders has proven to be difficult. Such has been the case for the treatment of depression. This is relevant to the treatment of patients with CG because of the overlap of symptoms with depression. Overall, the findings concerning the long-term benefits of brief therapies for depression have been disappointing. In the National Institute of Mental Health treatment of depression collaborative study (Elkin et al., 1989), patients received an average of 16 sessions of treatment. Only 33% of the patients who began therapy met recovery criteria, and nearly 40% of those relapsed within 18 months. The investigators concluded that "16 weeks of these specific forms of treatment are insufficient for most patients to achieve full recovery and lasting remission" (p. 782). Similar negative conclusions have been made regarding remission rates in the STAR*D clinical trial (Trivedi et al., 2006) by Fava and colleagues (2004) and in a recent meta-analytic review conducted by de Maat, Dekker, Schoevers, and de Jonghe (2006). In their review, the remission rate for cognitive therapy was 38%, and the relapse rate was 27%. Although these findings have been viewed as promising for advocates of psychosocial therapies, the relapse rates unfortunately have remained high at approximately 30%.

In the follow-up data from our composition trial, of the 110 completers in the study, 84 (77%) provided follow-up data. In addition, we compared patients who provided follow-up data with those who did not on 22 initial status variables. Only 1 of 22 variables was significant. Patients who did not provide follow-up data had higher Beck Depression scores ($M = 33$, $SD = 12$) than patients who provided follow-up data ($M = 25$, $SD = 12$), $t(106) = 2.99$, $p = .003$. However, given the number of analyses conducted, this could be due to error. Thus, there was little evidence of differences between patients who did and patients who did not provide follow-up data. Before examining the findings from our composition trial, several distinctions among types of follow-up and patient outcome need to be clear:

- *Maintenance* refers to recovery during treatment followed by maintenance of recovery during follow-up.
- *Relapse* refers to recovery during treatment followed by relapse during follow- up.
- *Delayed recovery* refers to nonrecovery during treatment followed by recovery during follow-up.
- *Nonrecovery* refers to nonrecovery during treatment followed by nonrecovery during follow-up.

These distinctions were used with the data from the 18 therapy groups of the composition trial. Outcome was represented by the achievement of clinical significance for two grief variables: intrusion and avoidance. Clinical significance was determined by the procedure of Jacobson and colleagues (Jacobson, Follette, & Revenstorf, 1984; Jacobson & Revenstorf, 1988). Recovery was defined as dropping below the clinical significance cutoff score and relapse as rising above the cutoff score. Next, we checked whether the overall proportion of patients who achieved clinical significance at posttherapy was different from the proportion of patients who achieved clinical significance at follow-up. Using the test for the difference between two dependent proportions, there was a significant increase from post therapy ($30/59 = .51$) to follow-up ($42/59 = .71$) in the proportion of patients who achieved clinical significance for intrusion, $z(N = 59) = 2.83$, $p = .004$. There was also a significant increase from posttherapy ($34/64 = .53$) to follow-up ($46/64 = .72$) for avoidance, $z(N = 64) = 2.88$, $p = .004$. Following this, we determined the percentages of patients for the four types of outcome described previously. For intrusion, there were 46% (27/59) maintenance patients, 5% (3/59) relapse patients, 25% (15/59) delayed-recovery patients, and 24% (14/59) nonrecovery patients. The results for avoidance were very similar with 48% (31/64) maintenance patients, 5% (3/64) relapse patients, 23% (15/64) delayed-recovery patients, and 23% (15/64) nonrecovery patients. Thus, a substantial percentage of the sample, nearly 75%, achieved clinically significant improvement on grief outcomes (intrusion, avoidance) by the end of follow-up, and a smaller proportion failed to maintain their recovered status or failed to recover at all.

Arbitrarily, we chose clinical significance for intrusion in our search for differences among the types of outcome. We were interested in learning more about the activities of the patients who experienced the four types of outcome. However, there were too few relapse patients to permit their inclusion in the statistical analyses. Therefore, we restricted our focus to the other three types of outcome (maintenance, delayed recovery, and nonrecovery). Because there was considerable similarity in the percentages of these three types of outcome in the cases of clinically significant change for intrusion and clinically significant change for avoidance, we did not need to conduct the analyses more than once.

We began our search by focusing on three events that took place during follow-up for patients. They represented potentially confounding factors or possible alternative explanations for the findings. For each of the two categorical variables, use of psychotropic medication and participation in psychosocial therapy, we conducted a two (yes vs. no) by three (types of change) chi-square analysis. For the continuous variable, social support, we conducted one-way analyses of variance in which types of outcome occupied the role of independent variable and social support the role of dependent variable. Of the patients, 73% reported that they had used a therapeutic dosage of psychotropic medication during follow-up. There were no significant differences in the use of medication for the three types of outcome, $\chi^2(4, N = 56) = 2.85$, $p = .58$. Also, 29% of the patients reported participating in psychosocial therapy. Once again, however, there were no significant differences for the three types of outcome, $\chi^2(4, N = 56) = 2.41, p = .66$.

In contrast to the analyses concerning psychosocial therapy, the one-way analysis of variance (ANOVA) for perceived level of social support at follow-up was significant, $F(2, 48) = 6.26, p = .004, \eta^2 = .21$. Tukey's honestly significant difference (HSD) test for multiple comparisons revealed that delayed-recovery patients perceived greater level of support ($M = 67.6, SD = 10.1$) at follow-up than maintenance patients ($M = 53.3, SD = 18.8$) and nonrecovery patients ($M = 44.4, SD = 18.4$). In addition, a similar one-way ANOVA, $F(2, 48) = 6.64, p = .003, \eta^2 = .22$, followed by Tukey's HSD test revealed that the three groups differed on perceived change in social support. The delayed-recovery patients perceived a significant increase (9.4), $t(12) = 2.55, p = .025$ in social support, whereas the maintenance patients perceived a significant decrease (−5.1), $t(24) = 2.29, p = .031$ in social support. The decrease (−2.8) in perceived social support for nonrecovery patients was not significant.

Social support generally refers to help that is available from or provided by one's friends and family that facilitates the individual's ability to cope with a stressful life event such as a death loss. Examples include expressing concern or care for the mourner, assisting with tasks of everyday living, providing information, or involving the mourner in social activities to provide diversion. The importance of social support to the successful resolution of grief symptoms has been illustrated in a number of studies (Engler & Lasker, 2000; Lund, Caserta, & Dimond, 1993; Reed, 1998). Greater social support has been associated with better bereavement outcome, as indicated by better physical health in the first year of bereavement (Stylianos & Vachon, 1993), less anxiety and depression (Gluhoski, Fishman, & Perry, 1997; Prigerson, Frank, Reynolds, George, & Kupfer, 1993) and lower use of psychotropic medication (Mor, McHorney, & Sherwood, 1986). From the measures used in the current study, we are unable to determine whether the higher levels of perceived social support for some of the patients came as a result of greater solicitation on the part of the patients or simply greater provision of support from concerned others who were pleased that the patients sought treatment for their grief symptoms.

Although social support at low to moderate levels may facilitate favorable outcome, there may be limits to the amount of support provided. Some research teams, including ours, have found a direct relationship between amount of family support and grief symptomatology (Arling, 1976; D. L. Morgan, 1989; Ogrodniczuk, Piper, Joyce, McCallum, & Rosie, 2002). They have suggested that too much support may lead to over dependency, which slows down the recovery process. Also, some reviewers (e.g., W. Stroebe, Zech, Stroebe, & Abakoumkin, 2005) have argued that the evidence supporting the value of social support is limited, although their study samples tended to be normal mourners rather than patients.

In addition, we checked the demographic, diagnostic, and initial disturbance variables that had been assessed prior to therapy for differences among the three types of outcome. To reduce the chances of Type I error, we made a Bonferroni adjustment to the p level for the seven demographic and diagnostic variables ($p = .05/7 = .007$) and the 13 outcome scores ($p = .05/13 = .004$). None of the demographic and diagnostic variables were significant. However, three of the 13 outcome variables were significant. These included the pathological grief items, $F(2, 53) = 11.13, p < .000, \eta^2 = .30$; intrusion, $F(2, 53) = 10.60, p < .000, \eta^2 = .29$; and Texas Revised Inventory of Grief feelings, $F(2, 53) = 6.31, p = .003, \eta^2 = .19$. Maintenance patients had lower levels of initial disturbance on the pathological grief items ($M = 10.1, SD = 4.6$) than delayed-recovery patients ($M = 16.0, SD = 4.5$) or nonrecovery patients ($M = 15.8, SD = 4.8$), lower levels of initial disturbance on intrusion ($M = 22.7, SD = 2.2$) than either delayed-recovery patients ($M = 28.1, SD = 5.5$) or nonrecovery patients ($M = 27.2$, $SD = 5.0$, $SD = 9.8$), and lower levels of initial disturbance on Texas Revised Inventory of Grief feelings ($M = 45.8$, $SD = 9.8$) than non-recovery patients ($M = 56.5$, $SD = 7.6$). In regard to the delayed-recovery patients, they had farther to go to traverse the cutoff criterion for CG. It should be noted, however, that this was not the case for general psychiatric symptoms. Their initial scores were not higher, yet delayed-recovery patients still took longer to achieve clinically significant improvement than maintenance patients.

Given the importance of discovering which forms of short-term therapies are associated with the most favorable outcomes during follow-up periods of time, the relatively small number of studies that have addressed this topic is surprising. As indicated in a review of the literature by Hollon, Stewart, and Strunk (2006), most studies have involved individually conducted cognitive–behavioral therapy for patients with depression or with anxiety disorders. They emphasized that other therapies, such as dynamic therapy or IPT, have not been adequately tested. There seemed to be some scattered successes of enduring effects with specific disorders, for example, family therapy with bipolar patients (Sandler et al.,2003), Internet-based cognitive–behavioral therapy with CG (Wagner & Maercker, 2007), and emotional expression for bereaved older adults (Segal, Chatman, Bogaards, & Becker (2001) but no substantial cumulative evidence. They also concluded that the nature of explanatory mechanisms remains to be determined. However, Blatt, Zuroff, and Hawley (2008) have argued that aspects of the patient's personality, denoted as psychological vulnerabilities, represent possible underlying mechanisms. In their opinion, it is the vulnerabilities rather than symptoms that require change to achieve lasting outcome effects.

The favorable outcome findings concerning pretherapy to posttherapy improvement, as originally reported by Piper et al. (2007), and the 6-month follow-up findings of the current report are inconsistent with the rather negative conclusions drawn by reviewers of studies concerning the efficacy of psychotherapy for CG (e.g., Jordan & Neimeyer, 2003). The authors who reached negative conclusions in their reviews usually provided a fairly long list of the shortcomings of the studies. These included insufficient intensity of treatment, insufficient duration of treatment, considerable time between the loss and the onset of treatment, lack of a theoretical base, methodological shortcomings, and undetected moderator variables that create high variation but only modest average outcome. In addition, many of the studies have involved nonpatient samples who may have manifested normal rather than complicated grief. Thus, there may have been less opportunity to change, that is, lower initial scores on the outcome variables. Each of these shortcomings is capable of preventing or interfering with a favorable outcome of therapy. If several were in effect, the probability of not achieving favorable outcome would be high. As we have indicated in previous sections, we believe that group therapy provides a number of unique and powerful therapeutic factors. Again, these include cohesion, universality, altruism, peer feedback, interpersonal learning, modeling, and group pressure to change (I. D. Yalom & Leszcz, 2005). To conclude that the efficacy of psychotherapy for CG has not been adequately tested would seem to be more appropriate than to conclude that it is not efficacious. The addition of delayed-recovery patients to those who were considered to have been successfully treated, that is, arriving at a total of approximately 75% (42/59) rather than 50% (27/59) of the patients, makes quite a difference in the overall impression of the usefulness of a treatment. Thus, researchers should not automatically conclude that treatment has failed if a patient has not achieved recovery by the end of short-term group therapy. Instead, they should carefully monitor patients over time, including follow-up periods. In this way, a more accurate impression of the total number of patients who benefited from treatment may be formed and the characteristics of the delayed-recovery patients and of delayed recovery itself can be studied.

There are a number of limitations associated with our follow-up study. Some involve the measure of social support. The measure did not differentiate between different types of social support (e.g., assisting the mourner with everyday tasks, involving the mourner in social activities). The measure did not assess whether the mourner's social needs were being met or whether the support was helpful. The identity of the "special person" was not disclosed. Other limitations involved the fact that only a small number of assessments were conducted over time. More frequent assessments permit more complex questions concerning change over time to be addressed. In addition, the findings may have been restricted to the particular patient sample (CG), the particular form of therapy (time-limited short-term group therapy), and the 6-month follow-up period of time that was studied.

One may also question whether the study design should have included a waiting-list control group of CG patients. We did not pursue that approach for two reasons. First, we had already demonstrated in our previous controlled trial (Piper et al., 1992) involving 16 therapy groups that patients who had been treated with short-term interpretive group therapy experienced considerably greater benefits than patients in a waiting-list control group. Subsequent to that study, we conducted our comparative trial, which also involved 16 short-term therapy groups (8 interpretive and 8 supportive), which revealed similar positive outcome findings for both interpretive and supportive forms of short-term group therapy (Piper, McCallum, et al., 2001). Second, a waiting-list control group in a follow-up study such as ours would mean a delay of treatment of 9 months for control patients. During this time there would be 3 months of treatment and 6 months of follow-up for immediate treatment patients. Such a delay in the treatment of control patients would be unethical.

It would also likely result in a considerable number of dropouts from the research project, which could threaten its internal validity.

It should be noted that although enduring favorable outcome effects from short-term therapies are desirable, there are other models of therapy that may also be desirable. For example, in the field of group therapy, there is Budman and Gurman's (1988) sequential model of therapy. They believe that it is quite appropriate and realistic to expect that a person might require a series of short-term therapies over his or her life span. They have pointed out that new stressors present themselves as people age, requiring serial brief therapy to help them face and resolve the problems. Similarly, in the field of behavior therapy, the practice of providing booster sessions is well accepted.

Finally, our findings concerning the number of patients in the four categories of follow-up outcome, in particular the delayed responders, merit future research attention. CG is a prevalent condition, especially among psychiatric outpatients. Continuing exploration of cost-effective and efficacious treatment remains an important objective.

CONCLUSION

Effect sizes for treatment of bereavement in general are very low, but with self-selected patients who may be or are experiencing CG, there is strong evidence that effect sizes are much higher. Likewise, when participants meet psychometric criteria for inclusion in a study of CG treatment, effect sizes in treatment conditions are much higher. People who are considered at risk of CG, for example, because of traumatic features of their loss, tend not to benefit from therapy as much as people who actually do meet criteria for CG or who seek out treatment for grief reactions (rather than being recruited by researchers).

Interventions for CG may have differential effects at different stages of bereavement—for example, improvements in mood may precede gains in adaptive resocialization. The evidence concerning optimal timing of interventions is mixed. The research literature does not presently provide clear guidance to clinicians about how much time should elapse following the death loss and before treatment should begin. In the absence of such guidance, severity of presenting complaints rather than a fixed policy regarding timing is a better indication for treatment.

Self-selection and timing are but two examples of factors that can mediate the effectiveness of treatments. Studies that do not account for these effects are methodologically weaker than those that do. In our trial studies of interpretive and supportive group therapies, mediating factors are controlled for, and effect sizes are significantly higher.

2

PREVALENCE OF COMPLICATED GRIEF

Death is omnipresent. This is a solemn fact that all people recognize and of which they are constantly reminded by various media, which tend to focus on the more traumatic and tragic deaths. Despite the ubiquitous nature of loss through death, people are often struck by the magnitude of how frequently it occurs. Although national mortality rates differ, we provide data from the U.S. Department of Health and Human Services (Minino, Heron, Murphy, & Kochanek, 2007); in the United States, there were approximately 2.4 million deaths in 2004. With increasing age, a person experiences the death loss of friends and family at a more rapid rate (see Table 2.1 for death rates across age groups). Widowhood, in particular, becomes increasingly frequent in late life. The number of people in the United States in 2004 who were widowed in the age groups 55–64, 65–74, and 75+ were 142,230, 215,471 and 430,343, respectively. In total, there were over 900,000 widowed people in the United States in 2004. For each death, not only is the spouse left behind but also children, siblings, friends, and parents.

Death losses are by no means restricted to older adults. For example, in 2004, there were nearly 28,000 infant (under 1 year of age) deaths in the United States. Although the death rate for children between ages 1 and 14 is

TABLE 2.1
Deaths by Age Group: United States 2004

Age	Number of deaths	Death rate per 100,000
All ages	2,397,615	816.5
Under 1 year	27,936	685.2
1–4 years	4,785	29.9
5–9 years	2,888	14.7
10–14 years	3,946	18.7
15–19 years	13,706	66.1
20–24 years	19,715	94.0
25–29 years	18,771	96.0
30–34 years	22,097	107.9
35–39 years	31,944	151.7
40–44 years	53,418	231.7
45–49 years	77,927	352.3
50–54 years	99,770	511.7
55–59 years	121,163	734.8
60–64 years	143,534	1,140.1
65–69 years	171,984	1,727.4
70–74 years	227,682	2,676.4
75–79 years	310,746	4,193.2
80–84 years	373,484	6,717.2
85 years and over	671,773	13,823.5

Note. Data from Minino, Heron, Murphy, and Kochanek (2007).

comparatively low, many deaths still occur. The rate increases substantially for the 15–19 age group. In total, there were 53,261 deaths of children under the age of 20 in 2004. These figures indicate that the loss of a child is not uncommon. Assuming that both parents of each child were alive at the time of the child's death, 106,522 young parents were bereaved in 2004. Of course, there are siblings, extended family, and friends, thus increasing the total number of bereaved people associated with each death of a child.

Even those in the youngest age groups do not escape the pain of experiencing death losses. The death of a parent has long been considered the most traumatic event that can occur in a child's life (Coddington, 1972; Yamamoto et al., 1996). Approximately 4% of children will experience the death of one of their parents by age 18 in Western countries (Harrison & Harrington, 2001; Haskey, 1998; U.S. Bureau of Census, 2001). In a representative sample of youths in an urban inner city in the United States, slightly more than half (51.9%) had experienced the sudden unexpected death of a close relative or friend by age 21, making it the most common serious negative life event (Breslau, Wilcox, Storr, Lucia, & Anthony, 2004).

It is clear from the figures that we have presented that death losses can affect anyone—from the very young to the very old. If one assumes that each death affects four people who were close to the person who died, then about 9.6 million Americans were bereaved in 2004 alone. Although most people who are confronted with the death of someone close to them recover without complications, some do not. These people may develop symptoms of complicated grief (CG), which, if left untreated, can lead to persistent impairments in psychological, social, and occupational functioning.

But how many people experience CG? Epidemiological studies examining the prevalence of CG are needed to address this question. Unfortunately, deriving accurate estimates of the prevalence of CG has been difficult. The most limiting factor is the lack of standardized criteria for CG. As we discussed in Chapter 1, various descriptions and definitions of the CG syndrome have been offered. Inconsistency in how the syndrome has been defined has led to variability in findings related to how many people satisfy criteria for the syndrome. Similarly, variability in assessment methods (e.g., self-report measure or clinical interview) and assessment times (e.g., 1 month or 1 year postloss) has contributed to differences in prevalence findings. Nevertheless, a review of the handful of studies that have directly assessed the prevalence of CG can provide a reasonable indication of how many people likely experience this debilitating syndrome.

To our knowledge, no study has attempted to estimate the prevalence of CG in the general population. Instead, studies have tended to focus on specific subgroups of the population, such as those that have high mortality rates (e.g., elderly people) or those that experience death losses that are particularly traumatic (e.g., survivors of suicide victims).

COMPLICATED GRIEF AMONG OLDER ADULTS

Most of the work on establishing the prevalence of CG has occurred within the context of studying older, often widowed, adults. Among such studies is that of Forstmeier and Maercker (2007). It may be the best with regard to producing generalizable prevalence figures because it used a random community sample of 570 elderly Swiss persons (not all of whom were bereaved). This study is also notable because it is the only one that we know of that has compared the two main diagnostic systems for CG (Horowitz et al., 1997; Prigerson et al., 1999). The criteria for these diagnostic systems are presented in Table 2.2. Results indicated that 18.9% of the sample had experienced a major bereavement an average of 15 years before participation in the study. Among those who had experienced a death loss, the percentage of people meeting criteria for CG was 22.2% using the Horowitz et al. (1997) system and 4.6% using the Prigerson et al. (1999) system. These figures translated into community prevalence rates of 4.2% and 0.9%, respectively. Agreement

TABLE 2.2
Comparison of Diagnostic Criteria for Complicated Grief

Criterion	Description
	Proposed by Prigerson et al. (1999)
Criterion A	1. The person has experienced the death of a significant other.
	2. The response involves intrusive, distressing preoccupation with the diseased person (e.g., yearning, longing, or searching).
Criterion B	In response to the death the following symptom(s) is/are marked and persistent:
	1. Frequent efforts to avoid reminders of the deceased (e.g., thoughts, feelings, activities, people, places).
	2. Purposelessness or feelings of futility about the future.
	3. Subjective sense of numbness, detachment, or absence of emotional responsiveness.
	4. Feeling stunned, dazed, or shocked.
	5. Difficulty acknowledging the death (e.g., disbelief).
	6. Feeling that life is empty or meaningless.
	7. Difficulty imagining a fulfilling life without the deceased.
	8. Feeling that part of oneself has died.
	9. Shattered worldview (e.g., lost sense of security, trust, or control).
	10. Assumes symptoms or harmful behaviors of, or related, to the deceased person.
	11. Excessive irritability, bitterness, or anger related to the death.
Criterion C	The duration of the disturbance (symptoms listed) is at least 2 months.
Criterion D	The disturbance causes clinically significant impairment in social, occupational, or other important areas of functioning.
	Proposed by Horowitz el al. (1997)
Event criterion/ prolong response criterion	Bereavement (loss of a spouse, other relative, or intimate partner) at least 14 months ago (12 months is avoided because of possible intense turbulence from an anniversary reaction).
Signs and symptoms criteria	In the last month, any three of the following seven symptoms with a severity that interferes with daily functioning: Intrusive symptoms:
	1. Unbidden memories or intrusive fantasies related to the lost relationship.
	2. Strong spells or pangs of severe emotion related to the lost relationship.
	3. Distressingly strong yearnings or wishes that the deceased were there.
	Signs of avoidance and failure to adapt:
	1. Feelings of being far too much alone or personally empty.
	2. Excessively staying away from people, places, or activities that remind the subject of the deceased.
	3. Unusual levels of sleep disturbances.
	Loss of interest in work, social, caretaking, or recreational activities to a maladaptive degree.

between the two systems was poor, with only two people satisfying criteria for CG on both systems. Forstmeier and Maercker concluded that the Horowitz et al. criteria set is more inclusive and less strict than the Prigerson et al. criteria set and thus leads to a higher prevalence. The two main reasons contributing to this difference are the disturbance criterion and the number of symptoms that have to be present to diagnose CG.

Only one other study used the Horowitz et al. (1997) criteria set in a volunteer sample of bereaved subjects. The sample consisted of persons between the ages of 21 and 55 years, 14 months after the death of their partners. The study found a prevalence of 41% of CG (Horowitz et al., 1997). This rate may be higher than the 22% rate in the Forstmeier and Maercker (2007) study because the Horowitz et al. sample was recruited through newspaper advertisements (not random community sampling) and had a shorter time since loss (14 months vs. an average of 15 years).

Holly Prigerson and her colleagues have conducted a series of studies on older widowed people, which has produced varying prevalence rates. In a community sample of older bereaved individuals, the prevalence decreased with increasing time since loss from 57% at 2 months postloss, 20% at 6 months, 6% at 13 months, to 7% at 25 months postloss (Prigerson et al., 1997). Similarly, Latham and Prigerson (2004) found a prevalence of 11% at 6 months and 7% at 11 months postloss in a community sample of older recently widowed people. In a sample of older people whose spouses died 2 to 34 months before, a prevalence of 18% was evidenced (Silverman et al., 2000). A subsequent study of recently widowed people by Silverman, Johnson, and Prigerson (2001) again found an 18% prevalence rate of CG. A study of 122 older widowed persons at 4 months and 9 months postloss evidenced prevalence rates of 10.7% and 8.2%, respectively. In summary, these studies, which used various versions of Prigerson et al.'s Inventory of Complicated Grief to diagnose CG, found prevalence rates ranging from a high of 57% to a low of 6%. Generally, prevalence rates were lower as the time since loss increased, yet even a 7% prevalence rate 2 years after a loss (e.g., Prigerson et al., 1997) suggests that a significant number of people experience the debilitating effects of CG.

Among older adults, baseline levels of health and adaptive capacity are lower and can be exacerbated by the stress associated with bereavement (Hansson & Stroebe, 2003). They may also have fewer economic and social resources to help them buffer the effects of loss. Among older adults, spousal bereavement is most common and is most frequently studied. The death of a spouse in old age may interact with or intensify the consequences of other stressors that tend to cluster in late life, such as chronic illness and disability, retirement, and involuntary change of residence (Hansson & Carpenter, 1994). Despite the fact that many older individuals may have had time to prepare for the death of their spouse, the loss of a lifelong relationship that may have continued for many decades may leave the survivor with a deep sense of loss and loneliness.

COMPLICATED GRIEF AMONG SURVIVORS
OF VICTIMS OF DISASTER EVENTS

In more recent years, investigators have started to examine the prevalence of CG in samples other than older widowed adults. One subgroup that has received attention lately consists of people who have experienced a death loss through a large-scale disaster event. For example, there has been much recent attention on survivors of those who lost their life in the September 11, 2001, terrorist attacks in the United States. One such study surveyed a sample of Project Liberty crisis counseling recipients approximately 1.5 years after the terrorist attacks to determine the proportion of respondents who screened positive for CG (Shear, Jackson, Essock, Donahue, & Felton, 2006). Of the 149 service recipients who were contacted, approximately half knew someone who had been killed in the attacks. Of those, 44% screened positive for CG.

In a similar study, a web-based survey of adults who experienced loss during the September 11, 2001, terrorist attacks examined the prevalence of CG 2.5 to 3.5 years after the attacks (Neria et al., 2007). Of the 704 bereaved adults who participated in the study, 43% screened positive for CG. Interestingly, a majority of the participants with CG reported receiving grief counseling and psychiatric medication after September 11, 2001.

Other studies have examined CG in the context of natural disasters. For example, Ghaffari-Nejad, Ahmadi-Mousavi, Gandomkar, and Reihani-Kermani (2007) examined the prevalence of CG among survivors of victims of the 2003 Bam earthquake in Iran, which killed 26,000 people. Using stratified multistage area sampling, the study included a sample of 400 survivors. The average age of the participants was 38 (range = 15–70). It was found that 76% of the participants satisfied criteria for CG. The authors concluded that the very strong familial bonds that are a part of Iranian culture may have contributed to the very high rate of CG—the assumption likely being that grief is more intense the closer one is to the person who died and thus more difficult to resolve.

All three studies referenced in the preceding paragraphs used Prigerson et al.'s (1999) system of diagnosing CG. The prevalence rates produced by these studies suggest that survivors of victims of large-scale disasters are at increased risk of the development of CG. Because research on CG in the context of catastrophic events is only in its infancy, data are not yet available to allow researchers to form conclusions about why the prevalence rate is so high. Is it the indiscriminate destruction, prolonged exposure to the aftermath, or some other factor(s) associated with such events that contribute to such widespread morbidity? More work is required to fully understand the phenomenology and underlying contributing factors of CG in this unique subpopulation.

COMPLICATED GRIEF AMONG SURVIVORS OF SUICIDE VICTIMS

Another specific subgroup of the population that has been the focus of recent attention by CG researchers consists of those who became bereaved through suicide. It has been suggested that deaths by suicide are among the most difficult with which mourners must contend (Rando, 1993). Survivors are left to agonize over the question, Why did he do this to me? The survivor has no way to answer this question and must contend with both the inevitability of never finding an answer and the strong affects, like anger, guilt, and shame, that this evokes. A study by Mitchell, Kim, Prigerson, and Mortimer-Stephens (2004) of 60 family members of suicide victims examined the prevalence of CG at 1 month postloss. They found that 43% of the sample satisfied criteria for CG. When they examined the relationship to the deceased and CG, they found that 80% of the children, 78% of the spouses, 67% of the parents, 57% of the siblings, and 28% of the in-laws met criteria for CG.

In another study, de Groot and colleagues (2007) examined CG among 122 relatives and spouses bereaved by suicide who participated in a grief counseling program to prevent CG. At 13 months postloss, the authors found that the prevalence of CG among participants who did not receive grief counseling was 32%. Among the participants who did receive grief counseling, 22% still developed CG. The difference was not significant.

Differences in the rates of CG reported in these studies could be due to differences in time since loss (1 month vs. 13 months postloss) and systems used to diagnose CG. Mitchell et al. (2004) used the Prigerson et al. (1999) system, whereas de Groot et al. (2007) used their own Inventory of Traumatic Grief. Despite the difference in rates that were reported, the findings indicate that CG is a syndrome that is experienced by no fewer than two out of every 10 people bereaved by the suicide of a family member.

COMPLICATED GRIEF AMONG PSYCHIATRIC OUTPATIENTS

A number of researchers have examined CG among psychiatric outpatients. It is believed that CG within this subgroup of the population may be particularly high. Authors have speculated that people with preexisting psychiatric difficulties are especially vulnerable to develop CG because of their already compromised mental health (Jones et al., 2003). Of course, it is also possible that CG can create vulnerability to other psychiatric illnesses. Because CG often is comorbid with major depression, posttraumatic stress disorder, and suicidal ideation, it is likely to be prevalent among those who access psychiatric care for these comorbid conditions.

Our research group conducted a large-scale study that investigated the prevalence of loss and CG among a large number of patients ($N = 729$) who sought services in two outpatient psychiatry departments—one in a suburban community hospital and the other in an urban university hospital (Piper, Ogrodniczuk, Azim, & Weideman, 2001). In contrast with many studies of loss through the death, our sample was not elderly: the patients' average age was 42. The most frequent losses involved parents, grandparents, and friends rather than partners or children. More than 55% of the sample had experienced one or more losses through death; the average was nearly three losses. Two levels of CG, moderate and severe, were defined on the basis of loss-specific symptoms, social dysfunction, and time since the loss. Patients who did not meet the criteria for CG were categorized as having minimal disturbance. We found that of all the patients who sought services at the two outpatient sites, 17% met the criteria for moderate CG, and 16% met the criteria for severe CG. Thus, 33% met or exceeded the criteria for moderate CG. In general, the three groups were well differentiated in terms of loss-specific variables, social dysfunction, and variables not specific to loss. The level of disturbance among those with severe CG was high.

Our findings agree with those of the two earlier surveys of Zisook and colleagues (Zisook & Lyons, 1989–1990; Zisook, Shuchter, & Schuckit, 1985). First, the age of the patients—adult but not elderly—and the most prevalent types of losses—those involving parents and grandparents—were similar. Second, the prevalence of loss was substantial in both of those studies (about 20%), and it was even higher in our study. Third, loss by itself was not necessarily related to higher levels of disturbance that are not specific to loss, such as depression. Finally, the average length of time since the loss, about 10 years, was considerable in both studies. Our study extended the results of these earlier surveys by using more comprehensive and standard measures of disturbance, assessing patients at two different sites, and distinguishing among various levels of CG.

Macias et al. (2004) conducted a study of people who had a diagnosis of a serious mental illness and who reported the death of a close friend or family member during a 5-year service evaluation project. In the sample of 148 individuals with serious mental illness, 12% reported the death of a close friend or family member as a significant life event that resulted in severe and prolonged grief. Unfortunately, standardized criteria were not used to define

CG. Nevertheless, the results suggested that a significant proportion of those with severe mental illness who regularly access community mental health care experience chronic difficulties associated with grief.

Prigerson et al. (2002) examined the prevalence of CG among attendees of a private psychiatric clinic in Karachi, Pakistan. The average age of the 151 recently bereaved patients who were assessed was 35 years. The most prevalent type of loss was siblings. Parents were also prevalent among the losses. Interestingly, among parental losses, 57% were classified as a violent death. Among the patients who were assessed, 34% met criteria for CG. A violent nature of death did not significantly increase the likelihood of CG. The rate of CG in this study was remarkably similar to the rate found in the Piper, Ogrodniczuk, Azim, et al. (2001) study.

Finally, Simon et al. (2005) examined the prevalence of CG within a specific subsample of psychiatric outpatients, those with bipolar disorder. In a survey of 120 patients with bipolar disorder, the authors found that 86% reported a significant loss. Similar to other studies of psychiatric outpatients, the loss of parents was prevalent. The loss of a grandparent was equally common. Among the patients with a significant loss, 24% met criteria for CG. The average time since loss among these patients was about 8 years.

These studies demonstrate that CG is highly prevalent among patients with psychiatric difficulties. Longitudinal studies that could help establish the nature of the association between CG and other mental illness (i.e., to determine the time course for illness development) are absent from the literature. Thus, we are unable to make conclusions about whether CG makes people more susceptible to other psychiatric disorders or vice versa. Nevertheless, the findings from available studies clearly suggest that by ignoring assessment and treatment of CG in psychiatric outpatients, therapists would be failing to provide satisfactory health care to a sizable segment of the population. The implication is that a significant proportion of people would experience chronic disability that would have negative effects on a personal, familial, and societal level.

COMPLICATED GRIEF IN OTHER GROUPS

Although grief has been studied in other subgroups of the population, very few have actually attempted to document the prevalence of CG in these groups. For example, grief researchers have been paying more attention to CG in children and adolescents who have lost a parent. Yet, none have provided estimates of how many likely experience the syndrome. That may change soon because a study that tested a modified version of the Inventory of Complicated Grief for children and adolescents was recently published (Melhem, Moritz, Walker, Shear, & Brent, 2007).

There are some exceptions of studies that did report prevalence figures for CG among subgroups of the population other than those reviewed previously. For example, Momartin, Silove, Manicavasagar, and Steel (2004) assessed the extent of CG among Bosnian refugees who relocated to Australia. Using the Core Bereavement Items scale (a rarely used measure) to assess symptoms of CG, the authors found that 31% of the 126 people who were assessed satisfied criteria for CG. The average time since loss was 5 years. The authors noted that a traumatic nature of the loss was associated with a greater likelihood of CG. Many participants reported particularly tragic and grotesque losses involving torture, public murder, or death by starvation. Momartin et al. concluded that refugees experience a wide array of stresses and traumas. Traumatic events that involved the violent deaths of close family members can lead to a complex pattern of reactions, including CG. Refugee services need to be mindful of the frequency with which CG is experienced by those who seek asylum in a new country and provide appropriate care.

Schulz, Boerner, Shear, Zhang, and Gitlin (2006) also reported prevalence figures for CG. They examined the extent of CG in caregivers of people with dementia. In a sample of 217 bereaved caregivers drawn from a larger group of 1,222 family caregivers of dementia patients, the authors found that 20% evidenced CG at an average of 18 weeks postloss. The authors concluded that the study shed new light on a bereavement experience that will become more commonplace as the population ages. Family caregiving is increasingly viewed as a major public health issue. To date, the spotlight has been on identifying caregivers at risk of negative health outcomes and ways in which they might be helped. The findings show that caregiving is closely intertwined with the bereavement experience that follows. Family members caring for relatives with advanced disease would not only benefit from traditional caregiving interventions designed to ease the burden of care but also from prebereavement treatments that better prepare them for the impending death of their loved one.

CONCLUSION

Despite the absence of any large-scale community-based epidemiological study of CG prevalence, the available literature suggests that a great number of people experience this debilitating syndrome. CG appears to occur at a rate that is equal to or greater than some of the more well-known psychiatric disorders, for example, obsessive–compulsive disorder or bulimia (Kaplan & Sadock, 1998). Within certain subgroups of the population, such as psychiatric outpatients or those who are bereaved by suicide, the prevalence rate of CG is very high.

Information about the prevalence of CG is important for service planning. The economic impact of CG has not been studied. However, Genevro, Marshall, and Miller (2004) reported that the Grief Recovery Institute Educational Foundation estimated that the hidden annual cost of grief in the United States related to the death of a loved one is $37.5 billion, on the basis of an assumption of one primary workplace griever for each death. The cost balloons to $44.5 billion when extended family members, colleagues, and friends are considered among the affected grievers. A number of studies have indicated that CG is associated with a wide variety of morbidities (Zhang, El-Jawahri, & Prigerson, 2006), a phenomenon that adds to the costs of CG. Given that CG is rarely diagnosed and/or treated appropriately and is typically a chronic illness, the year-over-year costs of the syndrome can quickly escalate. This implies that education of the public and health care providers needs to occur to raise awareness of CG. Ideally, increased awareness would lead to improved recognition and treatment of the illness.

Because assessment time is limited for most health providers and the amount and range of information they must collect during an interview are considerable, we suspect that questions concerning losses and reactions to losses often are not asked. If so, the presence of CG would be missed. What would be very useful is having a small number of screening questions that possess high sensitivity (i.e., identification of patients with CG) and high specificity (i.e., identification of patients without CG). Thus, we conducted a study (Piper, Ogrodniczuk, & Weideman, 2005) that attempted to identify just such a set of questions. We examined the responses of 235 outpatients to a set of items that have been used to define CG. We found that two items correctly identified nearly 90% of patients with and without CG. These items were transformed into questions that can be used in initial assessments. The questions were: During the past week did pictures about the loss pop into your mind? and During the past week did you try not to think about your loss? If a patient responds positively to one or both of these questions, the interviewer can acquire further information about the losses and/or refer the patient to someone who specializes in the assessment and treatment of patients with CG. We suspect that requesting assessors to ask two questions will succeed in identifying more patients with CG than requesting them to conduct a thorough assessment. In other words, less may provide more. Cost-efficient treatments such as short-term group therapy can effectively treat psychiatric outpatients with CG (Piper, McCallum, & Azim, 1992; Piper, McCallum, et al., 2001). Before it can be treated, however, CG needs to be identified. Although our study involved a large sample from two outpatient clinics, the findings would benefit from cross-validation. They may not apply to the general population. Different findings might emerge with different criteria for CG. Despite these limitations, we believe that the current study makes a reasonable case for the use of brief screening questions to identify psychiatric outpatients who are probably experiencing CG.

In addition, general education about CG may be especially important because some of the prevalence findings appear to contradict conventional wisdom. For example, studies of psychiatric outpatients, which typically focused on middle-aged individuals, found that parental losses were often associated with CG. Typically, these losses are regarded as "expected" and assumed to be easier to accept relative to some other types of losses (e.g., loss of a child). Also, a number of studies found that the time since the loss associated with CG was upward of 10 years, thus pointing to the chronicity of the syndrome. Although many people assume, and some studies have indicated (e.g., Prigerson et al., 1997), that the likelihood of fulfilling criteria for CG decreases with the passage of time, this is certainly not a universal phenomenon. Researchers will need to invest greater effort into identifying the factors that contribute to the chronicity of CG.

The field continues to move toward the point of consensus about the definition of CG. This includes defining standardized criteria and clarifying when (i.e., time postloss) it becomes appropriate to consider a diagnosis of CG. Method of assessment also needs to be standardized, as self-report and clinical interview methods are likely to produce different results. Once consensus is achieved, researchers will be able to engage in the types of large-scale studies that are required to accurately estimate the prevalence of CG in the general population. Still, at this time, there appears to be a reasonable foundation to conclude that CG is a commonly experienced syndrome. Thus, it becomes imperative to develop treatments that are specifically tailored to meet the unique needs of people experiencing CG. To do so, we must increase our understanding of the factors involved in the development of CG. In Chapter 3, we review risk factors for CG.

3

RISK FACTORS FOR
COMPLICATED GRIEF

Loss and grief are ubiquitous in the human experience—nearly everyone will at some point face the death of a significant other and enter into the bereavement process. Some find this encounter difficult but manageable, eventually adapting to the changes in their life and perhaps even demonstrating a transformation in perspective, attitudes, or relationship quality. Others experience their grief as overwhelming and disruptive to functioning at work and at home and fail to achieve any sense of resolution with the passage of time. "Grief affects everyone, but unequally. Some people are severely affected and die; others seemingly take it in stride, painfully acknowledging the loss but somehow managing to go on with their lives" (M. S. Stroebe, Stroebe, & Hansson, 1993, p. 267). What accounts for these individual differences in the quality of the grief process? What factors in an individual's life increase the probability that a complicated grief (CG) will emerge? It is commonly understood that the characteristics of the death, the individual's particular constellation of resources and frailties, and the provisions and demands of the individual's environment can all act to moderate the impact of the loss and the severity of the grief experience (M. S. Stroebe, Hansson, Stroebe, & Schut, 2001). Identifying and understanding the relationships between these variables and the quality of the grief process is the objective of this chapter.

In a number of respects, the study of risk factors in bereavement research is unique relative to other bodies of risk factor research. As noted, nearly everyone experiences grief over the loss of a significant other at some point during their life. Consequently, the focus of bereavement-related risk factors research is on the incidence of difficulties or dysfunction associated with a universal experience. This contrasts with studies of risk factors for particular health conditions of a medical (e.g., lung cancer) or psychiatric (e.g., schizophrenia) nature that affect only a relatively small proportion of the population. Further, research on bereavement is problematic because the condition of interest, CG, is not adequately represented by specific diagnostic criteria or a consensually accepted definition. Consequently, bereavement-related risk factor studies have examined the prediction of a number of outcomes of significant loss, including various forms of CG, depression, physical illness (morbidity), and even death (mortality). The outcome of interest is often defined differently from study to study. An important distinction between CG and the diagnosis of major depression (e.g., Ogrodniczuk, Piper, Joyce, Weideman, et al., 2003; Prigerson, Frank, et al., 1995) is not consistently addressed in risk factor studies.

The distinction between those risk factors that moderate the impact of the loss (impact factors) and those that influence the speed of resolution of the grief process (recovery factors) is often overlooked in bereavement research. Studies of the impact of bereavement have not always included a nonbereaved matched control group of the same age range to rule out nonbereavement-related explanations for changes in physical or mental health, a necessary step in the identification of putative impact factors associated with loss. With regard to recovery factors, bereavement-related risk factors research has not considered predictors of positive adaptation to bereavement, such as social reintegration or the undertaking of new social roles (Hansson & Stroebe, 2007). Moreover, research on risk factors for CG commonly considers predictors "that are different from risk factor profiles for other major psychiatric disorders" (Jacobs, 1999, p. 95), such as the quality of the pre-bereavement relationship or the coping style of the bereaved. Risk factors also rarely act in isolation; in most cases of bereavement, complex interactions of risk factors are possible and even likely. Finally, there remains considerable controversy about the specificity of identified risk factors to CG, although some factors appear to have an association with demarcated CG syndromes (e.g., delayed grief, chronic grief). The unique features of bereavement-related risk factor research underscore the complexity of the associated literature.

ORGANIZATIONAL SCHEME

In the following sections, we organize risk factors for complications of the grief process into four categories. The first to be considered is the nature of the bereavement stressor, reflecting the type (e.g., a sudden death, multiple deaths) and mode (e.g., accidental death, homicide) of the death loss. These factors tend to have a universal impact, that is, a sudden death or suicide will be problematic for any bereaved individual, over and above their personal strengths or environmental resources. The second category concerns those risk factors associated with the person of the bereaved; in addition to demographic and biographical characteristics, factors reflecting personality variables and coping style are also considered. These factors by definition represent individual differences and account for the greatest degree of variability in the quality of the grief process. They are also the factors most likely to be considered in the clinical situation. The third grouping of risk factors includes the individual's interpersonal context and the quality of the relationship with the deceased, the influence of kinship, and the availability of social support. The final category of risk factors is the circumstances surrounding the individual's loss experience, subdivided into antecedent and concurrent or consequent stressors.

Table 3.1 lists the risk factors considered in this chapter, the category of which each is a member, and a brief commentary summarizing the highlights of the review.

NATURE OF THE BEREAVEMENT

Bereavement takes many forms. It can be distinguished by the risk factors associated with the type of death.

Risk Factors Associated With the Type of Death

Two important risk factors for bereavement are the speed of death (sudden vs. nonsudden) and the cause of death (natural vs. nonnatural).

Sudden, Unexpected Death

Suddenness and an absence of anticipation are inherent in the experience of many deaths. This is by definition true for natural deaths from acute causes and accidental deaths (including disasters). It is also often the situation when the death is associated with war, suicide, and homicide, though not invariably. Because the incidence of accidental death tends to be greater for

TABLE 3.1
Risk Factors for Complicated Grief

Domain	Risk factor	Commentary
Nature of bereavement stressor	Sudden, unexpected death	These frequently involve deaths of children or adolescents. The shock of death can inhibit or prolong the grief process, elicit increased reactivity, or lead to *unexpected loss syndrome* (social avoidance, withdrawal). Interference with the grief process declines over time. Suddenness and untimeliness factors have less impact as age of deceased and bereaved increase.
	Traumatic death	Traumatic deaths (a) are sudden and unanticipated, (b) may involve violence, (c) are perceived as preventable or random, (d) may involve multiple losses, and (e) may involve the bereaved's personal encounter with death. Posttraumatic stress symptoms may be overlaid on the grief process.
	Multiple deaths	Multiple deaths can result in *bereavement overload* and lead to an inability or failure to mourn.
	Death following a chronic illness	The impact is associated with the demands and strains of caregiving. The impact can be magnified by degree of traumatic exposure associated with chronic illness. Mastery of these demands and facilitation of a "good death" can be associated with better grief resolution.
	Death of a child	Death contradicts the assumptions of "a natural order." The age of the child does not moderate the impact of a parental bereavement; mothers appear to be more affected. The impact can be exacerbated by the presence of other children and by the restriction of social support to the spouse. Such a death may also involve other risk factors such as suddenness and trauma.
	AIDS-related death	The bereaved may encounter social stigmatization as a barrier to the grief process. Other risk factors may be implicated (chronic illness, lack of social support, perceptions of preventability).
Mode of death	Natural versus unnatural death	Unnatural deaths demand a more profound psychological adjustment as a result of their violence, violation of the victim, and perceptions of the volition of the third-party perpetrator.

TABLE 3.1
Risk Factors for Complicated Grief   *(Continued)*

Domain	Risk factor	Commentary
	Accidental death	Such a death may reflect multiple risk factors (by definition sudden, unexpected, and seen as preventable; aspects of trauma). Factors associated with disaster (e.g., uncertainty regarding recovery of the body) or war (e.g., individual or societal attitudes) may also be implicated.
	Homicide	Deaths are by nature traumatic and represent "three Vs" (violence, violation, volition). Mourning is more affectively intense, with persistent anxiety. Social difficulties and secondary victimization are common.
	Suicide	Feelings of abandonment, humiliation, and personal diminishment are common and associated with a *conflicted mourning syndrome* and, frequently, secondary traumatization. However, no evidence that the bereavement differs in terms of pathology, complexity, or duration from other bereavements.
Personal risk factors: Sociodemographic and biographical	Age of bereaved	Younger bereaved suffer more health problems; associated deaths are more often unexpected and/or traumatic. Younger bereaved also report more frequent psychological problems, whereas older bereaved demonstrate greater increases in physical symptoms. Latter show more emotional problems over time because of chronic isolation and loneliness.
	Gender of bereaved	Widowers are more adversely affected than widows; this is attributed to differential availability or pursuit of social support by men versus women. Women may demonstrate more emotional difficulties; beyond gender differential for incidence of psychiatric conditions, this is attributed to nature of women's' attachment relationships and greater experience of environmental stressors (e.g., financial hardship) following the loss.

(continues)

TABLE 3.1
Risk Factors for Complicated Grief *(Continued)*

Domain	Risk factor	Commentary
	Family or personal history of emotional disorder	Prior mental illness appears to be a risk factor for various forms of problematic grief but evidence is inconsistent. Though studied less often, the presence of poor physical health prior to bereavement has been linked to a greater likelihood of complicated grief.
	Childhood loss	Loss of a parent in childhood—more accurately, the loss of early caretaker nurturance—is associated with a greater risk of depression following adult loss. Literature also suggests that early losses can facilitate good outcomes following adult bereavement. The type and timing of early loss experiences appears to be critical.
	Religiousness	Evidence is mixed regarding the association between religious beliefs and adjustment following bereavement. Evidence is more consistent about a positive relationship between religious practices (attending services, participating in a church community) and good bereavement outcomes. This is attributed to the social support accessed through participatory behavior.
Personal risk factors: Personality	Level of psychological adjustment	Evidence about the relationship between maladjustment and poor bereavement outcome is inconclusive. Problematic bereavement has been linked to *grief proneness* (clingy in relationships, tendency to pine), insecurity and anxiety in relationships, excessive anger and reproachfulness in relationships, or alexithymia. Greater neuroticism, poorer self-esteem, and less internal locus of control have been associated with poorer bereavement outcomes. Personality factors may affect the risk of acute complications of bereavement and influence the expression of grief over time.
	Attachment style	Individuals with an anxious-ambivalent style are more likely to demonstrate patterns of chronic grief. Individuals with an avoidant attachment style may be prone to *delayed grief.*

TABLE 3.1
Risk Factors for Complicated Grief   *(Continued)*

Domain	Risk factor	Commentary
	Coping style	Problem-focused coping may be effective in situations that are changeable (or restoration oriented), whereas emotion-focused coping may be effective in situations that are not (or loss oriented). Confrontation versus avoidance strategies may be effective at different points in grief process or with particular stressors associated with grieving. Rumination—focusing on negative aspects of the loss in a recurrent and passive manner—has been associated with a negative impact on recovery from bereavement. At certain times when resources are depleted or overextended, avoidance strategies may be appropriate and adaptive.
Risk factors associated with interpersonal relationships	Quality of relationship with the deceased	Greater intimacy and closeness in a spousal relationship has been associated with greater yearning and anxiety in the years after a loss. Greater ambivalence in a spousal relationship has been associated with poor bereavement outcomes, but more recent studies have suggested that the death may actually provide for resolution of conflictual feelings. Greater dependency on the relationship with the deceased has been consistently associated with more severe grief symptoms.
	Kinship relationships	Loss of a spouse or child has been shown to be more debilitating than the loss of a parent or sibling.
	Availability of social support	Availability of social support is positively associated with health in the bereaved. Social support has been directly linked to the success of restoration-oriented coping. Different social support provisions may be necessary for positive benefit at different times in the grief process. Family support may be critical for instrumental issues, whereas support from friends may be more critical for dealing with emotional issues.

(continues)

TABLE 3.1
Risk Factors for Complicated Grief   *(Continued)*

Domain	Risk factor	Commentary
Circumstances surrounding the loss	Antecedent life crises	Multiple antecedent crises, especially those reflecting disturbance in a marital relationship, have been associated with poorer bereavement outcomes.
	Concurrent or consequent life crises	Secondary effects of bereavement (concurrent problems) are more often shown by individuals with poor grief outcomes, but causal directions are unclear. Financial stressors are frequently mentioned in this context; this may reflect anxiety about making ends meet but also the limiting of social participation and support. Multiple death situations commonly give rise to secondary stressors (e.g., survivor guilt stimulated by social situations).

those under 40 years of age, sudden and unexpected deaths frequently involve children and adolescents. The death that is sudden and unexpected is generally held to contribute to poorer adjustment and a higher risk of mental and physical debilities during bereavement than when the loss has been anticipated. This is because the shock of the death overwhelms the individual's coping capacity, acts to inhibit or prolong the unfolding of the grief process, and elicits excessive physical and emotional reactivity (Lundin, 1984a, 1984b; Rando, 1983; Raphael, 1983; Sanders, 1989). The unexpected loss itself can represent a personal trauma for the bereaved, even in the absence of objectively traumatic circumstances. Additionally, the mourner is robbed of any opportunity to address unfinished business with the deceased and must contend with an abrupt loss of security and confidence in the world.

Evidence that sudden, unexpected deaths result in poorer adjustment among the bereaved originally emerged from the Harvard study of the widowed (Glick, Weiss, & Parkes, 1974; Parkes, 1975; Parkes & Weiss, 1983). Among the features of the death that emerged as major predictors of outcome in this study, those that correlated significantly with poor outcome on mental and physical health indices included a cause of death that was not cancer, a short duration of terminal illness, and the lack of opportunity to discuss death with the partner. From these findings, (Parkes, 1975; Parkes & Weiss, 1983) developed the profile of the "unexpected loss syndrome," characterized by social withdrawal, continued bewilderment, and protest. Rando concluded that the syndrome impaired functioning so severely that uncomplicated recovery could no longer be expected.

Although intellectually the mourner knows her loved one has died, she cannot accept this fact emotionally. The mourner's coping abilities are assaulted, and her adaptive capacities are completely overwhelmed. . . . The mourner perceives the world as a frightening place and fears that at any time she or someone else she loves may die. This causes profound insecurity and anxiety, to which the mourner may respond with avoidance and social withdrawal (Rando, 1993, p. 554).

Raphael (1983) has suggested that a sudden death, specifically when there is a target of blame, is a precipitant of a form of CG characterized by extreme and unremitting anger known as "distorted" grief. Raphael also noted that sudden death of all kinds is commonly associated with chronic grief, that is, a prolongation of acute grief symptoms with excessively delayed or no resolution. Lundin (1984a) reported that respondents who experienced a sudden death had significantly more somatic and psychiatric illnesses during the year following the loss when compared with persons who had experienced an anticipated death. At the end of 8 years, however, there were no differences between the groups in good versus poor outcome (Lundin, 1984b). These findings suggest that the suddenness of the loss may interfere with the initiation or early stages of the grief process but that this impact may tend to dissipate over time.

If a sudden and unexpected death has a profound negative impact on the grief process, it should be the case that with an expected death one would be prepared, and the death would tend to have a less severe effect. Ball (1976–1977) reported that widows who had engaged in a longer preparation for the death of their husbands reported grief reactions of diminished intensity. Carey (1977) also found that over the course of a 1-year follow-up, the "time to prepare" or forewarning appeared to have a buffering effect on the health of the surviving spouse. A retrospective study by Remondet, Hansson, Rule, and Winfrey (1987) looked at the impact of certain dimensions of *rehearsal* on adjustment to widowhood. These investigators found that whereas *behavioral* rehearsal (social comparison, planning and making changes) was associated with better adjustment, *cognitive* rehearsal (ruminating) appeared to be associated with increased emotional difficulty. Sanders (1983) divided a bereaved sample into three groups, depending on the type of death suffered by the loved one: sudden death, short-term chronic illness (less than 6 months), and long-term chronic illness. All three groups showed similar grief intensity at the first time point following bereavement. After 18 months, the short-term chronic illness group showed the most favorable adjustment, whereas the other two groups showed sustained grief intensity. Qualitatively, the sudden-death group exhibited more intrapunitive responses (anger directed inward and guilt) and physical difficulties, whereas the long-term chronic illness group reported greater feelings of isolation, alienation, and emotional upset. Thus, Sanders provided support for the view that deaths that have occurred unpredictably and with no anticipation lead to greater problems for survivors than those that are expected. However, the relationship is complex: If the terminal illness had been very protracted, the usefulness of preparation time tended to disappear, and survivors had difficulties, though of a different nature, equivalent to those surviving a sudden death. Factors contributing to these effects might include the loss of social supports over the course of the illness and the physical and emotional strain of caretaking (see the discussion that follows). It should be noted that the of length of preparation was confounded by type of relationship to the deceased in Sanders's (1983) study—the sudden-death group had the largest proportion of child deaths, whereas the short-term illness group had a larger proportion of parental over spousal deaths.

Nonsupportive findings regarding this relationship were reported by Bornstein, Clayton, Halikas, Maurice, and Robins (1973; see also Brecken-ridge, Gallagher, Thompson, & Peterson, 1986; Clayton, Halikas, Maurice, & Robins, 1973; Maddison & Walker, 1967), who reported no differences in depression between those who had experienced a sudden bereavement and those for whom the death of the partner had been expected. Subjects in this sample were generally elderly, however, leading Parkes (1975) to suggest that suddenness and untimeliness may both be required for a deleterious impact on bereavement outcome. The Bornstein et al. study also focused on depressive symptoms to the exclusion of other forms of emotional and physical difficulty subsequent to the loss. Sanders (1989) noted that survivors of sudden-death situations showed more anger and experienced more physical symptoms than those whose family member had died of a chronic illness. The unexpected deaths left survivors with feelings of loss of control and loss of trust in a world in which they had previously placed their faith. More recently, Barry, Kasl, and Prigerson (2002) found that feeling less prepared for the death was significantly associated with the diagnosis of CG at 4 months and 9 months postloss and with depression at 9 months.

The impact of a sudden death appears to be at least partly contingent on the relationship to the person who is lost and to the developmental life stage of the mourner. The same may be true regarding the beneficial effect of preparation time for the death. Thus, individuals experiencing the sudden death of a parent or a child (Sanders, 1983) will find this sudden impact more destabilizing than elderly adults abruptly losing a spouse to chronic ill health. The Changing Lives of Older Couples study (Carr, House, Wortman, Nesse, & Kessler, 2001; Carr, Nesse, & Wortman, 2005) examined the timing of a spouse's death on bereavement outcome. The sample was characterized by older age compared with previous studies; an unexpected death would thus be infrequent and less likely to be untimely or due to violent causes relative to younger samples. Forewarning or preparation time was found to have little effect on mental health at 6 or 18 months postloss. A sudden death was related in the short term to the incidence of intrusive thoughts. In contrast, a prolonged warning was associated with greater experience of anxiety at both 6 and 18 months postloss, presumably reflecting the accumulation of stressful experiences associated with the chronic illness (e.g., caregiving demands and illness exacerbations) and foreknowledge of the outcome.

Thus, the issue of the timing of the death may become less relevant in later life. At this juncture, issues associated with preparedness, the strains of caregiving and the hope for a "good death" become more pronounced. Carr (2003) examined the characteristics of a good death in old age and the effects on psychological distress among bereaved spouses. These characteristics include the deceased's acceptance and peace with death, a relative lack of pain, the timeliness of the death, the quality of relations with the spouse, dying at home with family rather than in a nursing home, being of little burden to caregivers, and having had the opportunity to lead a full life. Among the bereaved at 6 months postloss, four measures of bereavement-related distress were related to various indicators of the quality of the death. Continued yearning at 6 months was higher if the spouse had died in pain and if the marital relationship was positive in the last days. Continuing experience of intrusive thoughts was more likely if there had been high pain but lower if the mourner had been with the spouse at the time of the death. Anger was lower if the relationship had been positive before death and if the mourner was highly religious but was higher if the bereaved interpreted the death as being caused by substantial negligence of the medical staff. Loss-related anxiety was greater if the deceased spouse had been in great pain but lower if the spouse had been placed in a nursing home for some period prior to death.

Traumatic Death

Characteristics of traumatic experience are evident in many experiences of loss. As noted, sudden and unexpected deaths due to acute natural causes or accident can be personally traumatic for the mourner. Deaths by suicide, homicide, or due to war or disaster can be regarded as objectively traumatic and thus likely to have a consistently major impact on survivors. Rando (1993) has identified five factors associated with explicitly traumatic losses that may give rise to complications in the grief process. The factors that make a particular death traumatic include (a) suddenness and a lack of anticipation (see the preceding section); (b) violence, mutilation of the body, and destruction; (c) perceptions of the death's preventability or randomness; (d) multiple deaths (see the section that follows); and (e) the mourner's personal encounter with death, involving either a threat to personal survival or a confrontation with the death of others (e.g., surviving an automobile accident that proved fatal to a spouse). It is mainly the violence and destructiveness of traumatic deaths that distinguishes them from other deaths of a sudden nature; these dimensions are also the most significant in terms of complicating the grief process. Volkan (1981) and Horowitz (1986) have described how the violence associated with the death can stimulate extreme guilt in the mourner who is aware of prior aggressive feelings and fantasies regarding the deceased. Similarly, the violence that characterizes the death may also arouse hostility in the mourner, further fueling feelings of guilt and shame for aggressive thoughts and emotions. Not least, the mourner may also struggle with images of the suffering experienced by the victim of a violent, traumatic death and thus have to contend with profound anxiety and fear about the loved one's last moments and concerns regarding what the future might bring to other loved ones.

The experience of a traumatic death can thus give rise to an overlay of posttraumatic stress symptoms or a syndrome on the mourner's grief process. This can range from intensification of anxiety symptoms, feelings of helplessness and powerlessness, and survivor guilt to the stress response syndrome (Horowitz, 1986) and a full posttraumatic stress disorder (PTSD). A full PTSD is not uncommon following different forms of bereavement. On the basis of a sample of 350 widows and widowers assessed 2 months following the loss, Zisook, Chentsova-Dutton, and Shuchter (1998) identified PTSD in 10% of those whose spouses died after a chronic illness, 9% of those whose spouses died unexpectedly, and 36% of those whose spouses died from "unnatural" causes (i.e., suicide or accident). The development of posttraumatic problems is most likely if the mourner was involved in the same event that took the life of the deceased, feared for his or her own life, and experienced the event as beyond his or her individual control and if the event itself was unanticipated and shocking (Rando, 1993). A preexisting vulnerability associated with earlier traumatic experience can increase the likelihood of PTSD complications subsequent to a traumatic bereavement.

Multiple Deaths

The loss of two or more loved ones in the same event (e.g., a multiple fatality accident) or the occurrence of series of sequential losses over a short period of time (e.g., the AIDS-related deaths of a number of friends in a short period) meets the definition of multiple deaths. Kastenbaum (1969) referred to a serious consequence of multiple deaths with the concept of bereavement "overload." In effect, the mourner is faced with the untenable challenge of prioritizing which losses should be grieved first and which later. An unwillingness to enter into such a ranking can translate into an inability or failure to mourn (Lazare, 1979). Alternately, mourning for a selected loved one may be compromised by the avoided, neutralized, or delayed mourning for others lost at the same time (Rando, 1993). With multiple deaths, the mourner is essentially confronted with a concurrent crisis (see the section that follows) of additional losses when attending to the grief associated with a single loss.

Death Following a Chronic Illness

Chronic illness prior to death, especially in the elderly (Breckenridge et al., 1986; Heyman & Gianturco, 1973), frequently involves factors associated with the strains and potential benefits of caregiving. The chronic and progressive demands of caring for an older, ill person can result in caregiver strain and burnout (Hansson & Carpenter, 1994). At the same time, mastery of the tasks of caregiving, and the movement of the ill person toward a good death, may result in benefits to self-esteem and feelings of mastery, protective factors in the bereavement process. A number of studies are consistent with the view that a successful caregiving experience is associated with better coping during bereavement. Wells and Kendig (1997) found that widowed persons (in a sample of community-living people age 65 or older) who had been spousal caregivers were less likely to be diagnosed with depression compared with either spouses who were currently caregivers or widows who had not served as their spouse's caregiver.

Robinson-Whelen, Tata, MacCallum, McGuire, and Kiecolt-Glaser (2001) examined the consequences for a group of bereaved caregivers (mean age of 70 years) for 3 years after the death of their patient with comparisons across time to a matched group of continuing caregivers and a group of non-caregiving controls. At the prebereavement assessment, the caregiver groups were more depressed than controls but did not differ from one another, and this pattern continued for 3 years postbereavement. Bereaved caregivers also reported greater loneliness, but these feelings were found to decrease across the 3 years postbereavement while remaining stable for the controls. Also at the prebereavement assessment, perceived stress was highest in the caregiver-bereaved group; stress in this group decreased after the death to a level comparable to the continuing caregiver group. However, stress among caregivers never dropped to the level of controls. The consequences of caregiving in late life are thus substantial and can extend into the years after bereavement.

A number of studies have more directly focused on factors related to the burdens of caregiving. Schulz et al. (2001) classified recently widowed persons (mean age of 80 years) as having been strained or not-strained caregivers on the basis of the patient's health status and needed help and the caregiver's reported burden. Analyses compared caregivers' status during annual assessments immediately before and following the bereavement. Among the caregiver-strained group, depressive symptoms were significantly higher at prebereavement and remained unchanged at 1 year postbereavement. Among the not-strained caregiver group, prebereavement depression was low but increased at postbereavement to approach the experience of the caregiver-strained group. These data suggest that more strained caregivers are at greater risk but that for such persons the death actually eases the burden. Rossi Ferrario, Cardillo, Vicario, Balzarini, and Zotti (2004) also examined the implications of emotional burden among caregivers for older cancer patients. The caregivers, mostly wives and daughters (mean age of 56 years), experienced considerable emotional burden given the course of the disease. At 12 months postloss, emotional distress associated with bereavement remained elevated and was related to reported level of emotional stress with caregiving and from the nature of one's relationship to the deceased (i.e., spouses experienced more distress than adult child caregivers).

Prigerson et al. (2003) demonstrated that a caregiver's risk may sometimes extend beyond the consequences of caregiver burden to reflect traumatic exposure. The study monitored caregivers (all 65 years or older) of cancer patients over roughly 2 years. Caregivers indicated the extent to which they had witnessed their loved one in extreme distress (e.g., in pain, choking); witnessing such events was common and associated with feelings of helplessness. Caregivers who had more frequently witnessed these forms of traumatic patient distress were themselves more likely to meet criteria for major depression and for CG as well as showing diminished mental and physical health and social functioning. The effects on depression and quality of life were independent of the effects of caregiver burden.

Death of a Child

Parents who lose a child may be at risk for CG simply because of the overwhelming impact of this form of loss (Fish, 1986; Osterweis, Solomon, & Green, 1984; Rando, 1983; Sanders, 1980). As noted earlier, the death of a child violates "the natural order." The improbability of surviving their child means that parents are assumptively ill-equipped to deal with the reality of the event. The question of why the death occurred can become a persistent rumination. Because of their profound identification with the child, the parents often find that grief is doubly intense because a part of themselves also seems to have died. Most certainly, with the death the parents have also lost the hopes and dreams they held for that child. Consistently, then, the death of a child is identified as a profound high-risk factor in the development of CG. Those aspects of the relationship between parent and child that define its unique intimacy are the same factors that serve to intensify grief following the death (Rando, 1983).

Epidemiological surveys have indicated that the age of the child does not moderate the impact of a parental bereavement—the grief can be as profound when the child is a miscarried pregnancy, an infant, or an adult with family responsibilities of his or her own. Indeed, comparative studies of the kinship relationship have consistently shown that the loss of an adult child results in more intense or more persistent grief and depression than the loss of a spouse, parent, or sibling (Cleiren, 1991; Leahy, 1992–1993; Nolen-Hoeksema & Larson, 1999; Sanders, 1980). The child's age does, however, define some of the specific issues to be addressed in parental bereavement, in line with the developmental stage of the child and the parent–child relationship (Rando, 1993).

In a study focusing on mortality as an outcome, Rees and Lutkins (1967) found that the death of a spouse or a child was associated with significantly higher rates of death among the survivors compared with the death of a sibling or adult parents. This pattern of higher risk for spouses and parents holds true in studies that use psychological measures of the adjustment to bereavement. In a study comparing the grief of spouses, parents of children, and adult children of older parents, Sanders (1980) noted significantly greater intensities of grief in parental bereavement, with more somatic reactions, greater depression, and more anger and guilt with accompanying feelings of despair. Fish (1986) reported that bereaved mothers experienced greater levels of guilt and anger than did fathers, even 2 years after the loss. Mothers also experienced greater social isolation, feeling that they were the only persons still actively mourning. On the basis of her comparative kinship study, Sanders (1980) reported that the duration of parents' grief was prolonged and for the mothers actually intensified after the 1st year of bereavement. Cleiren (1991) reported a similar pattern of severe separation distress persisting beyond the first anniversary of the death of a child, and that was more problematic for bereaved mothers than for bereaved fathers. In a longer follow-up, Rando (1983) reported that parental grief actually escalated in the 3rd year of bereavement, making the period of mourning a long and draining ordeal.

Marital difficulties are not uncommon in couples dealing with the loss of a child, especially when the parents experience a differential intensity of grief. Rando (1991) has noted that mothers and fathers may be faced with different grief demands because of their respective roles in the family and the effects of sex role conditioning. When other children are present after the loss of a child, parents "must not only struggle with their own intense grief and mourning, they must fulfill the precise role with surviving children that they are struggling to relinquish with the deceased" (Rando, 1993, p. 622). Bereaved parents are also frequently the most stigmatized of mourners because their loss represents the worst fears of others. This rejection and social disenfranchisement of bereaved parents means that the availability of emotional support for the grief process may become restricted to the spouse, who can be in similar or greater need. Divorce and separation among bereaved parents is estimated to range anywhere from 50% to 90%, a proportion that is significantly higher than couples who have not lost a child (Rando, 1993).

The leading cause of death for children is accidents; for adolescents and young adults, accidents, suicide, and homicide are the leading causes of death (Rando, 1993). Thus, loss of a child often involves circumstances characterized by suddenness, trauma, and a sense that the death was preventable. Therefore, multiple risk factors converge to heighten the impact of the death of a child on the grief process. In this regard, the loss of a child has been regarded as the most severe form of bereavement. However, Rando (1993) has noted that existing models of mourning do not adequately fit the experience of the bereaved parent: "The simple fact is that what is considered abnormal or pathological in other losses is typical after the death of a child in the sense that it is experienced by the majority of bereaved parents" (p. 630).

AIDS-Related Death

The surviving family members or partners of someone who died of AIDS often face a bereavement experience characterized by social stigmatization (Doka, 1989). The fact that the majority of those infected with the disease are male homosexuals and intravenous drug users can compound the stigma associated with an AIDS-related death. Those experiencing an AIDS-related bereavement are at significant risk for CG because of risk factors associated with this type of death, specifically, a chronic illness, the mourner's perception of the death as preventable, and, in particular, the mourner's perceived lack of social support (Colburn & Malena, 1988; Martin, 1988; Rando, 1993; Worden, 1991b). Klein and Fletcher (1987) noted several problems typical of this grief situation, including societal disapproval, frequent exclusion from intensive care units and funeral plans, and even being shunned as likely carriers of the AIDS virus. Because AIDS is often not perceived in morally neutral terms, many of those facing an AIDS-related bereavement choose instead to keep their loss hidden. When these losses are revealed, the negative response of the wider environment (e.g., the extended family; Giacquinta, 1989) can bring additional distress to an already overburdened mourner.

The partners of those who die from AIDS-related causes typically experience intense and painful mourning, often accompanied by survivor guilt. In many respects, the bereavement is similar to that experienced by spouses of those who succumb to any other chronic illness. However, bereaved partners must also deal with the potential of their own infection with the HIV virus, social discrimination, and responses of others that invalidate the loss, the relationship, or the mourner (i.e., disenfranchisement; Doka, 1989). Frequently, the bereaved are also facing the experience of multiple losses from their same community, a form of bereavement overload (Kastenbaum, 1969). Martin (1988) found a direct association between the frequency of AIDS-related losses (i.e., deaths of lovers or close friends) and symptoms of traumatic stress response, feelings of demoralization, sleep problems, sedative or recreational drug use, and presentation for psychological services because of AIDS-related concerns.

It is unfortunately true that the issues faced by survivors of AIDS-related deaths, which constitute risk factors for grief complications, can also be borne by those bereaved by other causes that stimulate strong and polarized debate. These include losses associated with adoptions, abortions, or Alzheimer's disease (Rando, 1993). The difference is that the extent of the AIDS epidemic has encouraged more research on bereavements due to this cause than these others, rather than because of issues specific to an AIDS-related loss.

Mode of Death

The mode of death includes whether it is natural or unnatural.

Natural Versus Unnatural Death

In the case of a "death due to natural causes," exemplified by death due to old age, it is unlikely the mourner has to contend with feelings associated with the actions of third party, as in the case of homicide, suicide, many accidents, and disasters due to human error (Rando, 1993). The natural death is also unlikely to be perceived as preventable by the bereaved, though there may be problematic feelings associated with blame, including anger toward the deceased (e.g., a spouse who refused to quit smoking and died from lung cancer) or family members (e.g., for failing to get the deceased to a hospital in time), and guilt (e.g., for not being present during the deceased's final days). However, these are usually less intense than when the death is regarded as avoidable (e.g., as a result of a car accident). Aspects of the natural death that may pose difficulties for the bereavement process, that is, the unanticipated nature of the death from acute natural causes or the caregiver strain associated with the death following a chronic illness, have been mentioned.

In contrast, the unnatural death demands a more profound psychological adjustment on the part of the bereaved because the death is "characterized by horror, brutality, and calamity—abhorrent acts that are psychosocially dissonant and to some degree unacceptable" (Rynearson, 1986, p. 272). Rynearson described the unnatural death in terms of three critical characteristics: violence, violation, and volition. In other words, the unnatural death involves a degree of brutality, stands as an insult to the integrity of the victim, and is due to the willful intent of a third party. Each characteristic is related to a compensatory response on the part of the mourner. A violent death is associated with posttraumatic stress; perceptions of violation translate into issues associated with victimization; and the element of volition is associated with compulsive inquiry (Why?). Notably, Rynearson argued that these responses are the inevitable result of experiencing an unnatural death, "the psychological consequences of overwhelming affect and defensive collapse" (p. 274) and not necessarily indicative of pathology.

Accidental Death

Deaths due to accident are by definition sudden, unexpected, and perceived as preventable. They may also reflect aspects of violence and trauma. As a class, then, accidental deaths represent the action of multiple risk factors for CG. The bereaved's acute response to news of the accident is psychological and often physical shock. Depending on the influence of other risk factors such as the mourner's resiliency, the accidental death is most likely to give rise to the unexpected loss syndrome (Lehman, Wortman, & Williams, 1987; Lundin, 1984a, 1984b; Parkes, 1975). For example, Lehman et al. (1987) reported that a large proportion of mourners contending with an accidental death continued to struggle to find meaning in what had happened, even after 4 to 7 years had elapsed since the loss.

Accidental deaths occur disproportionately more often in younger age groups, meaning that the bereavement associated with an accidental death may frequently involve the parental loss of a child, discussed previously as a profound risk factor for CG. Accidental deaths are also very likely to reflect elements of violence, mutilation, and destruction and can thus lead to a traumatic impact on the mourner. The perceived preventability of an accidental death can be relative; those bereaved as a result of natural disaster may cope more adequately than those who lost loved ones in accidents following from avoidable human error (Bugen, 1979). This is not necessarily an absolute, however. The accidental death for which no third party can be identified and held accountable can be extremely difficult to grieve because the mourner's feelings of anger lack any outlet.

Disasters share all of the elements of accidental deaths but can be associated with additional risk factors because these events are frequently outside the range of usual experience. Raphael (1986) has noted that the uniqueness of a loss due to disaster leads to bereavements that are "rarely uncomplicated" (p. 100). Disasters often involve problems of locating and identifying the dead, for example, an airplane crash, a landslide. Consequently, the mourner can be left with uncertainty over the actuality of the death. In other circumstances, there is no doubt about the deaths and the mourner must contend with anxiety about what the loved one experienced at the end. Initiation of the mourning process can frequently be delayed or compromised by the intrusion of bureaucratic involvement (e.g., air traffic safety investigations, coroner's inquests) and problems returning the deceased's remains to the family.

By their nature, disasters often impact an entire community or involve multiple deaths, possibly affecting the availability of needed social support and constituting a form of bereavement overload.

Deaths due to war are regarded as a tragic cost of doing battle with an adversary. War deaths cannot strictly be considered to be accidental but, with deaths due to accident and disaster, they share the features of unexpectedness, violence, trauma, and perceived preventabililty (Rando, 1993). For the mourner, news of the war death may be unexpected but simultaneously may have been fearfully anticipated for an extended period of time. The impact of the death, then, may reflect the unique mixture of a lack of preparedness and a form of stress similar to that of a caregiver for a loved one with a long-standing chronic illness. Additionally, the mourner's grief over the war death of a loved one can be dramatically influenced by his or her attitudes and the larger society's attitudes toward the conflict itself. For example, the antiwar sentiment in the United States during the later stages of the Vietnam War would interact with the values of the surviving family and determine whether they felt supported or disenfranchised in their grief. Finally, the type of death event in the context of an armed conflict (e.g., during combat, as a prisoner of war, or in a noncombat accident) means that a range of additional risk factors may come into play. One study examined the impact of bereavement due to war relative to bereavement due to other causes (Shoham-Salomon, Vakstein, & Kruglanski, 1986, quoted in W. Stroebe & Stroebe, 1987). The authors found adjustment among war widows to be better and the depression lower than was the case among a matched sample of civilian widows. However, both samples showed poorer adjustment and greater depression than a nonbereaved matched control group. Differences were seen to be a function of economic support, patterns of interaction with family and friends, and the meaning of the loss for the widows in the two groups. W. Stroebe and Stroebe (1987, p. 213) suggest that two factors associated with war bereavements will determine the impact of the loss and the intensity of grief symptoms: first, the meaning ascribed to the loss (e.g., a noble and heroic death vs. a useless sacrifice) and, second, the support received after the loss, particularly from others with similar experiences and values (e.g., other war widows). Thus, a bereavement due to war is likely to be influenced by the mourner's personality and the availability of social support as additional risk factors for the emergence of complications.

Homicide

Homicide deaths incorporate many of the risk factors already discussed. First and foremost, a homicide death is horrifying and traumatic for the surviving family members. The traumatic impact can be compounded by the brutality of the murder, the availability of the remains for funeral rituals, and the presence of the mourner at the time of the homicide. Rynearson's (1986) "three Vs"—violence, violation, and volition—are intensely reflected in the homicide death, leaving mourners to contend with the possibility of developing posttraumatic symptoms, feelings of anger, resignation and anxiety regarding the safety and reliability of the world, and obsessive ruminations about the preventability of the death and the responsibilities of the perpetrator. Almost invariably, the mourner is unprepared for the sudden and unexpected loss brought about by the murder; the unanticipated mourning syndrome (Parkes, 1975) is common following a death by homicide. Vargas, Loya, and Hoddle-Vargas (1989) reported that those bereaved by homicide experienced more intense grief than those bereaved by accident, suicide, or natural deaths.

The consensus view of bereavement following homicide describes it as a form of PTSD, with symptomatic behaviors characteristic of PTSD present for up to 5 years following the loss (Masters, Friedman, & Getzel, 1988; Rando, 1993; Rinear, 1988; Rynearson, 1986; Rynearson & McCreery, 1993). The mourner's experience is thus a confluence of grief and traumatic response, potentially debilitating in its complexity. On the basis of extensive clinical involvement with the family survivors of homicide, Amick-McMullan, Kilpatrick, Veronen, and Smith (1989) argued that mourning in this circumstance differs from other bereavements in terms of affective intensity (i.e., the degree of horror, rage, and vengefulness), persistent anxiety symptoms (i.e., phobic avoidance), and social difficulties (i.e., problems adjusting because of involvement with the criminal justice system). Their research also highlighted the incidence of physiological symptomatology among the family survivors and the relationship between psychological adjustment and satisfaction with how the justice system dealt with the homicide. Masters et al. (1988) also noted that the psychological reactions of survivors of homicide deaths were equivalent across social class lines: Individuals of "widely differing ethnic, economic and social background share common emotions, defensive patterns, and processes of working through their pain" (p. 113).

A factor unfortunately often associated with losses due to homicide is secondary victimization brought about by the responses (or lack thereof) of those on whom the survivor depends for support (Ochberg, 1988). The horrifying elements of the murder, frequently sensationalized in the media, often provoke anxiety in others and the need to defend against fears of violence and chaos. Family and friends, the law enforcement and criminal justice personnel, the media, and health and social service workers can affect the experience of the mourner, not always constructively. The mourner's experience of secondary victimization emerges in terms of social isolation, blame and stigmatization, and feelings of injustice.

Suicide

Earlier clinical studies of survivors of suicide deaths (Cain, 1972; Rudestam, 1977) emphasized the mourner's problems in adjustment during bereavement due to feelings of guilt and bewilderment about the death. The deceased's action represents a rejection of loved ones in favor of death. Feelings of abandonment, humiliation, and "personal diminishment" (Rando, 1993) are common in survivors of suicide. Normal anger is intensified following suicide, approaching rage at the betrayal represented by the loved one's rejection, the emotional and social upheavals the bereaved must face, and the number of unresolved issues remaining in the relationship. Moreover, the natural target for these feelings and issues is now unavailable. Contending with feelings of sorrow and anger represents one of the most difficult tasks of grieving; for a survivor of suicide, this difficulty is compounded by the intensity and irresolvable nature of the anger toward the deceased. Feelings of guilt and shame are also common; frequently, the suicide represents the culmination of a conflicted relationship, and the mourner may also experience relief that the strain has now passed. The collision of these contrasting and intense feelings in the mourner's grief process can culminate in a conflicted mourning syndrome (Parkes & Weiss, 1983).

A death from suicide places more than psychological demands on the survivor. Family or societal responses to the suicide death, based on efforts to minimize the guilt and anguish stimulated by such a loss, can constitute a secondary trauma for the mourner. Rudestam and Imbroll (1983) observed that survivors of a suicide loss are viewed more negatively and with more blame than those bereaved by other forms of death. Mourners of a suicide death may engage in denial or a revision of events to protect against the further upset brought about by stigmatizing societal responses (Lazare, 1979), raising the likelihood of a delayed or protracted grief process. A comparison of individuals bereaved through suicide with groups bereaved through accident, homicide, or natural causes (Range & Calhoun, 1990) found that the former felt the expectation to explain the death to others and frequently lied about the cause of death. The bereaved as a result of suicide also reported less community support than the comparison groups.

Other risk factors are brought to bear by a suicide. The death is often unexpected, is frequently experienced as traumatic, and is often regarded by the survivors as preventable. Sheskin and Wallace (1976) compared samples of suicide survivors and widows of natural or accidental deaths from separate studies. Widows as a result of suicide were found to search for explanations much more intensely and to feel more blameworthy than nonsuicide survivors. Suicide survivors can face a number of unique social stressors during the bereavement (e.g., inquests, media portrayal, stigma, financial issues), often with little support from others. Wrobleski and McIntosh (1987) noted three problems unique to suicide survivors: separation from and isolation within and outside the family, rumination on the death scene, and difficulty in reconstructing events before the death.

Given these factors, the popular belief is that coping with bereavement following a suicide along with sudden accidental deaths and homicides may be among the most stressful of all types of bereavement. However, there is little empirical evidence to support this contention (Stroebe, Hansson, et al., 2001, p. 355). Studies that compared the psychological consequences of bereavement following suicide with bereavement following other modes of death have typically failed to find any marked differences in degree of pathology, complexity, or duration of the grief process (Cleiren, 1991; Farberow, Gallagher-Thompson, Gilewski, & Thompson, 1992; Shepherd & Barraclough, 1976; Sherkat & Reed, 1992; van der Wal, 1990). However, van der Wal (1990) did note that bereavement following suicide may be qualitatively different than the bereavement following other modes of death. Faberow et al. reported that although those bereaved by natural causes began to exhibit improvement in grief, depression, and symptoms of psychopathology after only 6 months, with another drop after 18 months, significant change among those bereaved by suicide appeared only in the final year of follow-up. More extensive longitudinal studies to track the reactions and course of the grief process in suicide survivors and other bereavement groups have been recommended, but problems associated with studying the experience of suicide survivors are also noted (Ness & Pfeffer, 1990).

PERSONAL RISK FACTORS

Personal risk factors include sociodemographic factors, age of the bereaved, gender of the bereaved, family and personal history of emotional disorder, childhood loss, and religiousness.

Sociodemographic Factors

Two sociodemographic variables that might be considered to have a bearing on the quality of grief process are social class and ethnicity. In general, however, the effect of these variables is difficult to tease apart from the influence of related, confounding factors, and the research addressing the risks associated with social class and ethnicity is inconclusive. Parkes (1975) argued that widows of lower socioeconomic status encountered more health-related difficulties than those of higher status. However, the health differential due to social class is the same for bereaved and nonbereaved groups alike (W. Stroebe

& Stroebe, 1987, p. 173), that is, lower socioeconomic status is a nonspecific risk factor for health problems. Research has not identified any specific effects of social class in the development of CG. It has proven difficult to study ethnic influences on bereavement outcome because of the frequent confounding of minority group status and other variables such as social class or religious practice. Using a covariate analysis approach, L. A. Morgan (1976) identified the importance of family interaction to the morale of widowed women of Mexican descent, relative to Black or White widowed women. Beyond similar descriptive findings, no clear conclusions can be drawn about the impact of bereavement on the health among members of different ethnic or racial groups. Racial or ethnic group comparisons reflect complex combinations of demographic, biological, social, and economic characteristics, so it is exceedingly difficult to tease out the influence of ethnicity on bereavement outcome.

Age of Bereaved

"It is the younger bereaved who appear to suffer more severe health deterioration" (W. Stroebe & Stroebe, 1987, p. 185). This pattern emerges most clearly from studies addressing mortality as an outcome of bereavement in which widowed-to-married ratios are more excessive in younger than older age groups in both cross-sectional (e.g., Kraus & Lilienfeld, 1959) and longitudinal studies (e.g., Helsing & Szklo, 1981). The same pattern has been reported for grief symptoms (Ball, 1976–1977) and other psychological and physical symptoms (Maddison & Walker, 1967) in studies of widows. This may be a function of the expectedness of the loss, that is, for younger people, the deaths are more frequently due to accident or suicide and thus sudden (Ball, 1976–1977; Clayton, 1974; Sheldon et al., 1981). The greater incidence of traumatic loss is no doubt responsible for the higher rates of clinical complications of bereavement among young adults; age differences are therefore potentially related as much to environmental factors as to personal factors (Jacobs, 1993, p. 144).

However, there is evidence that the relationship between age and more problematic bereavement is not a simple linear one. A longitudinal study by Sanders (1980–1981) found that soon after bereavement the younger widowed manifested greater grief intensities, whereas after 18 to 24 months it was the older bereaved who showed exacerbated grief reactions. Sanders attributed the later difficulties of the older widowed to a persisting situation of extreme isolation and loneliness. Parkes (1964, 1975) reported a similar pattern: The younger bereaved reported more frequent psychological problems, whereas the older bereaved experienced an increase in physical symptoms. In sum, age serves as an important predictor of bereavement outcome: The younger bereaved demonstrated increased mortality than the older and also appeared to experience a greater risk of emotional problems. The older bereaved may encounter more physical debility and, as time since the loss increases, the emergence of emotional problems associated with chronic isolation and loneliness.

Gender of Bereaved

It is well-known that there are gender effects on the incidence of certain psychiatric disorders, that is, a larger proportion of the female population presents with major depressive, anxiety, and somatization disorders. Thus, gender is a general risk factor for certain physical and mental health problems. However, the bereavement literature is inconsistent regarding the specific effects of gender on bereavement outcome.

Much of the literature concerning gender effects on bereavement outcome addresses the impact of spousal loss. Early studies noted no differences in bereavement outcome between men and women who lost their spouse to death (Clayton, 1974; Heyman & Gianturco, 1973), though some concluded that widows experienced more health consequences than did widowers (Carey, 1977; Lopata, 1973). On the other hand, several more recent studies have found that widowers sustain greater problems (Goldman, Korenman, & Weinstein, 1995; Helsing, Szklo, & Comstock, 1981; Martikainen & Valkonen, 1996; Rogers, 1995; M. S. Stroebe & Stroebe, 1983; Siegel & Kuykendall, 1990). When more rigorous, methodologically sound studies are considered, according to W. Stroebe and Stroebe (1987), "bereavement appears to have more extreme effects on the mental health of men than of women" (p. 182). "When widows and widowers are compared with same-sex, nonbereaved comparison persons (thus controlling for the main effects of sex on health) widowers are found to suffer greater detriments compared with married men than are widows compared with married women" (W. Stroebe & Stroebe, 1987, p. 178). These authors argued that the gender disparity might be related to a differential availability or pursuit of alternative (i.e., nonspousal) social support for men versus women. That is, in most Western societies, men are socialized to suppress emotional expression and rely primarily on their spouses as confidants. Siegel and Kuykendall (1990) supported the conclusion that widowers do less well than widows and reported that this gender difference was mediated by the nonaccessing of social support by most widowers. They also reported that widowed men who were active in their church or temple were less depressed than those without these social or religious connections. However, W. Stroebe, Stroebe, and Abakoumkin (1999) failed to find evidence for this mediating relationship; widows did receive more social support than widowers, but social support was unrelated to differential well-being.

Studies using mourner death as an outcome of bereavement show that widowers have more excessive mortality rates from all causes taken together than do widows compared with married men and women, respectively (M. S. Stroebe,

Stroebe, Gergen, & Gergen, 1981–1982). Widowers appear most at risk in the first 6 months of bereavement (Niemi, 1979; Parkes, Benjamin, & Fitzgerald, 1969), whereas for widows the peak in risk appears to occur during the 2nd year (McNeill, 1973, quoted in Stroebe & Stroebe, 1987). The longer time duration demonstrated for widows may suggest the competing influence of factors facilitative of resiliency (social support) versus factors detrimental to recovery (experiences of loneliness).

A recent review of the broader literature on risk factors is supportive of the conclusion that men fare worse following a death loss. W. Stroebe and Schut (2001) found considerable evidence that gender is a risk factor for health outcomes of bereavement. Bereaved men (compared with married men) generally demonstrated more depression in the short term and higher mortality rates. Findings from research on older bereaved adults are consistent with these conclusions (Lee, DeMaris, Bavin, & Sullivan, 2001; Lee, Willetts, & Seccombe, 1998; van Grootheest, Beekham, Broese van Groenou, & Deeg, 1999).

As noted, the studies discussed in this section were based on samples of bereaved spouses. If a broader sample base of research on bereavement outcome is considered, studies indicate that women are at greater risk for psychiatric complications. This is consistent with the higher risk for psychiatric disorder among women in general, that is, it is difficult to discriminate the general from the bereavement-specific risk effect of gender. However, it is possible that women's attachments differ from men's attachments, thereby predisposing women to a higher risk of bereavement complicated by emotional or mental health issues (Jacobs, 1993, p. 143). It was noted in an earlier discussion that mothers appear to grieve more deeply than do fathers after the loss of a child, and this could be attributed to the bonding of mothers to their infants early in life (Fish, 1986). Alternatively, women may be exposed to a greater risk of environmental stresses, such as economic hardship and role strain, when a spouse dies. Thus both personal and environmental explanations are possible for the gender differences in the psychological dimensions of grief and may operate in an additive fashion.

Family and Personal History of Emotional Disorder

It seems plausible that those with a history of poor mental or physical health should be more vulnerable to loss than those with a background of mental or physical fitness. Few studies actually compare nonbereaved persons in poor health with those who have been bereaved to examine relative adjustment. The evidence that is available does suggest a strong relationship between health prior to bereavement and subsequent outcome.

Positive personal and family histories of depression are not uncommon in bereaved spouses (Bruce, Kim, Leaf, & Jacobs, 1990; Gallagher, Breckenridge,

Thompson, & Peterson, 1983; Jacobs, Hansen, Berkman, Kasl, & Ostfeld, 1989). Some studies have not found this type of history to be a risk factor for depression following bereavement (Bruce et al., 1990; Jacobs et al., 1989), whereas others have found that a personal history of depression increases the risk of depression subsequent to bereavement roughly twofold (Richards & McCallum, 1979; Zisook & Shuchter, 1991). Bornstein et al. (1973) reported a history of mental illness (including major affective disorder, alcoholism, hysteria, and undiagnosed psychiatric illness) as a risk factor for depression during bereavement, yet the history of major affective illness itself did not emerge independently as a risk factor and was rare in their sample. Bunch (1972) examined the relationship of recent bereavement to suicide among spouses and adult children. Previous psychiatric admissions were more frequently found to have occurred among the bereaved who committed suicide than among those bereaved who did not. Parkes (1975; Parkes & Weiss, 1983) also confirmed the link between previous mental illness and poor bereavement outcome. Thus, it appears reasonable to conclude that prior mental illness is a high-risk factor for poor bereavement outcome.

With regard to physical health, the data are less compelling, but there is supportive evidence for a link between poorer health and problematic bereavement outcome. Perlin and Schmidt (1975) reported that the physically disabled and the physically ill were more vulnerable to poor bereavement outcome. There is also evidence that persons who used health services before the loss of a loved one were most susceptible to poor bereavement outcomes (Mor, McHorney, & Sherwood, 1986).

Childhood Loss

The preponderance of evidence on depression indicates that the childhood loss of a parent by death increases depressive risk by a factor of 2 to 3 (Lloyd, 1980). It has been argued that it is not the death of a parent in childhood itself that causes depression later in adulthood (Tennant, 1988) but rather that it is the failure to receive substitutive nurturance in the circumstances of such a loss that is associated with the later risk. Brown and Harris (1978) are renowned for linking early loss of mother to depression in adult life. Less evidence exists for the more specific question of whether persons who have experienced an early loss through death respond to a later bereavement much more poorly than those who had experienced no earlier loss. In fact, such evidence as does exist suggests the facilitation of good outcomes subsequent to earlier experiences with bereavement (Bornstein et al., 1973; Huston, 1971; Vachon, 1976). In this vein, Jacobs, Schaefer, Ostfeld, and Kasl (1987) found that death of or separation from parents in childhood was not related to scores on depression, anxiety, separation distress, or demoralization at a 1-year follow-up in a widowed sample. Antecedent loss, that is, early bereavement, is likely to have differing effects on the outcome of a current bereavement depending on (a) whether it occurred during childhood or adulthood and (b) the frequency and type of antecedent experiences of loss. The specific type and timing of these earlier loss experiences appears to be critical (Stroebe & Stroebe, 1987).

Religiousness

This risk factor refers to the strength of an individual's religious beliefs and practices. Early research suggested that religious beliefs helped bereaved persons overcome their loss and move on with life (e.g., Alexander & Adlerstein, 1959; Gorer, 1965). Later findings on the role of religious beliefs in coping with loss are more mixed. Some investigators claim positive associations (e.g., Bohannon, 1991; Clayton, Halikas, & Robins, 1973; Glick et al., 1974; Gray, 1987; Heyman & Gianturco, 1973; Levy, Martinowski, & Derby, 1994; Nolen-Hoeksema & Larson, 1999; Sherkat & Reed, 1992); others report no differences (e.g., Burks, Lund, Gregg, & Bluhm, 1988; Lund, Caserta, & Dimond, 1986) or even greater maladjustment among the more religious bereaved individuals (e.g., Amir & Sharon, 1982; Rosik, 1989). Many studies lack appropriate control groups, rendering the findings inconclusive. For example, religiousness was confounded with ethnicity and education in the Amir and Sharon study of widows in Israel. However, a study that attempted to avoid these problems by using a longitudinal design concluded that holding religious beliefs facilitated adjustment to loss. Levy et al. (1994) reported that religiousness discriminated between groups of bereaved individuals who had different trajectories in their depressive symptoms over time.

In terms of behavior, Bornstein et al. (1973) reported an association between religious practices, for example, attending church, and the prevention of depression following bereavement. Nolen-Hoeksema and Larson (1999) reported that participants who attended religious services at least occasionally had lower levels of depression at 13 and 18 but not at 6 months after bereavement relative to those who did not attend. As examples of the studies in this area, it is not clear whether these effects reflect the spiritual benefits or the opportunities for social contact afforded by religious involvement. Yamamoto, Okonogi, Iwasaki, and Yoshimura (1969) argued that in Japan it was the spiritual concepts that had a bearing on adaptation to loss, following a comparison of Japanese with British widows (Marris, 1958; Parkes, 1965). Sanders (1980) examined the impact of church attendance on outcome by dividing her sample into those who regularly attended church and those who did not. Attendance was associated with greater health on the Grief Experience Inventory and selected scales from the Minnesota Multiphasic Personality Inventory.

Other studies have failed to demonstrate the relationship between religious behavior and bereavement outcome (Parkes, 1971).

In sum, the evidence for the effect of religiousness on bereavement outcome is not consistent, nor is it clear whether the demonstrated associations with religiousness as measured are due to the spiritual benefit or to the availability of a supportive community (McIntosh, Silver, & Wortman, 1993; Stroebe & Stroebe, 1987). However, there is some empirical support for the mechanisms assumed to mediate the relationship between religious behavior, that is, attending church, and health. Nolen-Hoeksema and Larson (1999), who reported a relationship between church attendance and depression in the bereaved, also found a positive association between church attendance and levels of social support. Sherkat and Reed (1992) replicated the attendance–outcome relationship, but reported that this association became insignificant after adjusting for the influence of the individual's ratings of social support availability. McIntosh and colleagues found in a study of mothers who had lost a child to sudden infant death syndrome that social support mediated the association between church attendance and well-being. In the same study, the importance of religious involvement was positively related to effectiveness of cognitive processing and finding meaning in the death. Further, through these coping processes, religious beliefs were indirectly related to greater well-being and less distress among parents 18 months after their child's death.

Personality

Personality factors include level of psychological adjustment, attachment style, and coping style.

Level of Psychological Adjustment

An intractable problem in studies that include an assessment of personality as a predictor of bereavement outcome is the absence of baseline data on the personality traits—most often, the assessments take place after the loss has already occurred. The assumption that personality traits predate an acute or chronic disturbance such as CG should ideally be directly tested in longitudinal research. Until this can be done, there will always be reservations about claims that personality traits observed at the time a disturbance is evident are indeed preexisting moderating variables (Jacobs, 1993, p. 148).

It would nonetheless appear reasonable that individuals with stable and well-adjusted personalities would be better able to contend with the impact of a significant loss than those who are unstable and poorly adjusted. However, evidence from bereavement research has not been very conclusive on this relationship. Parkes and Weiss (1983) found "grief-prone" individuals who were intensely clinging and who pined for their deceased spouses to be at highest risk of poor outcome. Other personality profiles identified by Parkes and Weiss as characteristic of poor outcome were insecure, overanxious people with low self-esteem; excessively angry or reproachful persons; or those unable to express their feelings (*alexithymic*).

Lund et al. (1985–1986) attempted to avoid possible confounding between measures of personality and health by relating personality to bereavement-specific variables (e.g., shock, disbelief) as well as to somatic complaints and depression. In an elderly sample, low self-esteem in early bereavement was found to be predictive of poor coping at 2 years after bereavement. However, the self-esteem of the acutely bereaved was no different from that of matched nonbereaved controls. Self-esteem also remained stable over 2 years and did not vary as the process of grief evolved. Vachon et al. (1982) found that widowed women who were apprehensive, worrying, emotionally labile, and anxious were at risk for prolonged emotional distress after a loss. In contrast, women who were emotionally stable, mature, conscientious, traditional, and precise about social conventions had low levels of distress throughout the first 2 years of bereavement. The authors cautioned that the causal relationship is unclear: Were the high-distress individuals isolated because they were ordinarily unable to maintain relationships or because the grief situation had brought about their isolation?

Stroebe and Stroebe (1987) reported that a complicated bereavement was more frequently associated with higher neuroticism scores. In the same study, individuals with low internal control beliefs reacted with greater depression than those who believed that they had control over their environment when the loss was unexpected (W. Stroebe, Stroebe, & Domittner, 1988). Similarly, the differential impact of the expectedness of the loss was evident with bereaved of low, but not high, self-esteem (Stroebe et al., 1988). Jacobs (1993) observed that the widowed with high scores on neurotic defenses 2 months after the death of a spouse were more likely to have high scores on depression scales 13 months after the loss. Raphael and Middleton (1990) confirmed the observation of neuroticism and anxiety about relationships as risk factors for bereavement problems.

Sanders, Mauger, and Strong (1979) studied the relationships between personality and bereavement outcome longitudinally, that is, soon after the deaths and again 18 months to 2 years later when grief intensities had subsided. Four types of reaction to bereavement emerged: a disturbed group, a depressed high-grief group, a denial group, and a normal grief-contained group. Individuals in the disturbed group reported feelings of inadequacy, inferiority, and insecurity of a chronic nature. These individuals had few defenses and, following a significant loss, developed a long-lasting depression. The depressed high-grief group complained of lowered mood and tension as well as inordinate sensitivity. These bereaved almost always had a history of multiple losses. Because their anxiety was a trait issue with inordinate stress, the depressed group was also prone to intense emotionality. Although grief symptoms had abated 2 years after the loss, they still felt deeply saddened and remained withdrawn from others. The denial group demonstrated a contrasting pattern of behavior described as compulsive optimism. These bereaved used strong defense mechanisms to deal with crises, often developing physical symptoms as a means of resolving conflicts or avoiding responsibilities. They were unaware of using this form of defense. At follow-up, their emotional reactions were still suppressed, but they evidenced more psychosomatic symptoms than either of the other two problem groups. M. S. Stroebe and Stroebe (1991) reported a similar pattern: When bereaved spouses were followed through their first 2 years of bereavement, they found that widowers who sought distraction from grief work or who controlled their emotions closely did not make as good an adjustment as widowers who were less controlled.

In sum, the evidence is mixed for the assumption that personality traits can *intensify* the impact of bereavement, in contrast to the expectations expressed in theoretical writings. However, personality factors may affect the risk of acute complications of bereavement and influence the individual's expression of grief over time. The research can be faulted for not considering more than a narrow range of personality measures, for often failing to include nonbereaved control groups, and for an infrequent use of longitudinal designs. Despite the faults of this literature, the picture that emerges is one of an anxious, worrying, introverted, neurotic individual for whom an attachment relationship may serve critical supportive functions (see the section that follows) and who is sensitive to loss, particularly if perceived as a rejection (Parkes, 1985), that is, the "grief-prone personality." When a loss occurs to such an individual, he or she may be at a higher risk for poor adaptation and clinical complications (Jacobs, 1993, p. 150).

Attachment Style

A closely related construct is attachment style, the individual's characteristic behavior in relationships, that serves important emotion- and self-regulating functions. Attachment style is believed to arise out of prototypic experiences with early caregivers; the quality of those experiences is a determinant of the patterning of the individual's behavior in later significant relationships. The individual's attachment style would also be expected to influence the patterning of the grief response to a significant loss (Shaver & Tancredy, 2001; M. S. Stroebe, Stroebe, & Schut, 2005). Those individuals who have been treated in ways that allow them to feel secure find it easier to access attachment-related emotional memories. These individuals would thus be likely to resolve their grief and adjust to their loss. In contrast, individuals who do not have a secure orientation to attachment are likely to encounter problems in coping with a loss experience. For example, individuals with an anxious-ambivalent attachment style are highly emotional but unable to cope constructively with attachment-related feelings. These individuals have been found to show patterns of chronic grieving, characterized by an extension of the period of grieving that can be indefinite in extreme cases (Parkes & Weiss, 1983). The mourner in these instances was anxiously dependent on the deceased and required the deceased's presence, emotional support, or actual assistance to function (see Rando, 1993, p. 178ff.). Individuals with an avoidant style of insecure attachment are assumed to suppress or avoid attachment-related emotions. It is therefore plausible to relate this attachment style to *delayed grief*, a pathological style of grieving in which normal grief reactions occur only after an extensive delay, during which the expression of grief is inhibited. However, the prevalence of delayed grief may be quite low (Bonanno et al., 2002).

Clinical observers have noted ambivalent qualities in most relationships in the circumstances of a loss (see the section that follows). Parkes and Weiss (1983) had the widowed rate the degree of conflict in the marriage after the death of a spouse. They found that 38 bereaved spouses who reported high levels of marital conflict had significantly worse outcomes 2 and 4 years after the loss than counterparts who reported low conflict. It is unclear if other factors (illness in the family, socioeconomic issues) that could contribute to conflict were having an influence. Further, marital conflict is not necessarily equivalent to ambivalence. Rejection sensitivity, characteristic of insecure attachment, seems to be a prime risk factor for complications during bereavement but has not been operationalized in a systematic assessment (Jacobs, 1993, p. 150).

Coping Style

How an individual deals with loss and ensuing grief can reduce or amplify the effects of this stressful life event, not only during the initial acute grief but also as the months and years of bereavement unfold. Coping can influence levels of emotional distress, as well as the incidence and intensity of physical and mental disorders (Hansson & Stroebe, 2007, p. 26). *Adaptive* coping strategies would be those that actually lead to a *reduction* in the negative psychosocial and physical health consequences of bereavement or to a lowering of grief intensity. Certain strategies, but not others, would thus lead to a decrease in negative consequences of grief, short and long term. Relative to other factors such as the timing and nature of the death and personality, coping alone may have a relatively small influence on adjustment and recovery.

Nonetheless, coping is important because it is one of the few factors influencing bereavement outcome amenable to brief interventions (Folkman, 2001, p. 564).

Different strategies may be more effective at different times in the course of grief or for coping with different aspects of bereavement. A particular coping strategy may be useful in the short term but harmful in the long term, or it may positively affect physical health but increase emotional distress. In many instances, terms in the literature lack specificity. For example, it is difficult to distinguish yearning and pining, aspects of grieving that are associated with negative outcome (Nolen-Hoeksema, 2001) from grief work involving a constructive confrontation with the reality of loss that could lead to positive outcome (M. S. Stroebe, 1992–1993). Also, empirical studies have failed to confirm that confronting and working through a loss lead to better outcomes or that avoiding confrontation is necessarily detrimental to adaptation (Bonanno, 2001; M. S. Stroebe & Stroebe, 1991). Grief work may also apply more to Western than certain non-Western cultures in which the norm for grieving could call for suppression of emotions, a clearly different strategy that is not apparently associated with poor outcomes (Wikan, 1988). There is also now evidence that different bereaved individuals may follow quite different patterns or trajectories of grieving over a period of 4 or more years postloss (Hansson & Stroebe, 2007, p. 30). Grieving is a dynamic process of adjustment to an array of life changes that need to be worked through but that cannot all be attended to simultaneously.

Two general classes of coping strategies seem especially applicable to bereavement: problem- versus emotion-focused coping and confrontation versus avoidance. Problem-focused coping is directed at managing and changing the problem causing distress, for example, dealing with a drop in income after the death by taking employment. Emotion-focused coping is directed at managing the resulting emotion, for example, trying to suppress worries about the drop in income. Theorists argue that the former is appropriate in situations that are changeable, the latter in those that are unchangeable. Some aspects of bereavement may be best dealt with in an emotion-focused way because they are not changeable, others in a problem-focused manner because they can be altered. In a similar way, confrontation versus avoidance strategies can be differentially useful or effective given the multiple stressors associated with bereavement. Because of this array of stressors, some changeable and some not, one cannot simply confront or avoid as a general coping strategy.

Some authors have set out models of the grief process, highlighting what forms of coping may be pertinent and when. Rubin (1981, 1999) has put forward a two-track model of bereavement. The model specifies that a bereaved person will need to deal not only with the biopsychosocial reactions to bereavement but also with the implications of his or her attachment to the deceased, how this becomes transformed, and how a new relationship to the deceased is established. The two tracks are interlinked. Worden's (1991a) task model provides a more specific definition of the stressors that need active working through following bereavement. The four critical tasks include accepting the reality of loss, experiencing the pain of grief, adjusting to an environment without the deceased, and "relocating" the deceased emotionally to retain a form of connection while moving on. An integrative model has been offered by Bonanno and Kaltman (1999). Bereavement is considered in terms of four components. The first involves the context of the loss and refers to the risk factors such as type of death, age, gender, social support, and cultural setting. The second component involves the continuum of subjective meanings associated with loss, ranging from appraisals of everyday matters to existential concerns. The third component reflects changing representations of the lost relationship over time. The fourth component reflects the role of coping and emotion regulation processes. These authors argue that emotion regulation may at times involve deliberate or strategic processing, at other times more of a spontaneous or automatic regulatory processing not available to conscious awareness.

Recent reformulations of the coping model (Folkman, 2001) have also highlighted the importance of positive affect in the process of recovery from bereavement. "Positive affect is maintained by a class of meaning-based coping processes that is distinct from those that regulate distress, and it functions to sustain coping over the long term" (p. 573). Just as positive meaning has been linked to good outcome, so has ruminative coping—focusing on distressing aspects and meanings in a repetitive and passive manner (Nolen-Hoeksema, 2001)—been identified as a maladaptive strategy. Controlling for the amount of distress at the outset of evaluation, Nolen-Hoeksema and colleagues showed that disclosure of negative emotions actually had a harmful effect on later recovery from bereavement (Nolen-Hoeksema, Parker, & Larsen, 1994). Those with a more distractive style became less depressed over time. Similarly, investigators have provided evidence that avoidant strategies may be more functional than previously assumed.

Bonanno, Keltner, Holen, and Horowitz (1995) found a dissociation between physiologically measured arousal and indices of psychological upset. Bereaved men who showed high arousal but low psychological confrontation when talking to their deceased partner in a role play had good bereavement outcomes measured at a later point.

The dual-process model of Hansson and Stroebe specifies that the grieving process involves orientations to the loss experience and to the restoration of function (identifying and dealing with stressors other than those directly impacted by the loss) in the revised context, with oscillation between the tasks associated with each of these orientations over time. The oscillation also encompasses shifts between coping and not coping, that is, attention to and avoidance of different stressors associated with bereavement (Hansson & Stroebe, 2007, p. 48). It is not possible to attend to both the loss- and restoration-oriented stressors simultaneously, according to the model; oscillation is postulated to be essential for optimal adjustment over time. Generally, restoration-oriented issues become more dominant as time progresses. Martikainen and Valkonen (1996) reported patterns of excess mortality among the spousally bereaved in relation to durations of bereavement. Observed patterns of mortality indicated that stress and grief had short-term (loss-oriented) effects, whereas the effects of loss of social, material, and task support dominated at longer durations (restoration oriented) of bereavement (see also Richardson & Balaswamy, 2001). In a treatment study by Schut and colleagues (Schut, Stroebe, van den Bout, & de Keijser, 1997), differential effects were identified. Widowers, who tend to suppress feelings and address the restoration issues, benefited more from an emotion-focused intervention. In contrast, widows, typically more expressive of emotions (loss oriented), tended to benefit more from a problem-solving intervention.

Research on coping in bereavement has suggested that too much confrontation or too much avoidance is detrimental to adaptation. Both processes may be linked to negative health consequences if undertaken relentlessly, causing exhaustion. An adaptive process of bereavement likely involves, even necessitates, a balance between the tendency to confront with the tendency to avoid, deny, or suppress aspects of grieving. The mourner's environment should offer support for whatever form of coping is required at a given time. In this regard, Gass (1987) examined the potential influence of available coping resources on participants' appraisal of the difficulties they faced in their bereavement experience. Participants were widows (mean age of 71 years) in the 1st year of bereavement. Resources assessed included measures of social support, comforting religious beliefs and rituals, perceived control, good prior emotional health, the absence of concurrent losses, adequate finances, and so on. Those widows with greater resources (a) appraised their bereavement experience as less likely to involve additional losses, complications, or threats beyond the death itself and (b) exhibited significantly higher scores on measures of physical and psychological well-being.

RISK FACTORS ASSOCIATED WITH
INTERPERSONAL RELATIONSHIPS

Risk factors associated with interpersonal relationships include the quality of the relationship with the deceased, kinship relationships, and availability of social support.

Quality of the Relationship With the Deceased

Three aspects of relationship quality have been considered as risk factors for CG: intimacy and closeness, ambivalence, and dependence. The research to date addressing the quality of the relationship between the bereaved and deceased has invariably considered spousal bereavements. The *intimacy and closeness* of the marital relationship that is disrupted by the death of a spouse is important to the outcome of bereavement. The assumption is that the more intensely loved a partner was, the more that person will be grieved for after death. Carr and colleagues (2000) assessed important qualities of the marriage prior to the death as they related to bereavement adjustment. Results indicated that marriages that were emotionally close tended to result in greater yearning at 6 months postloss, whereas those characterized by more conflict were associated with less postloss yearning. Dependence on the deceased spouse for completion of instrumental tasks was also associated with increased post-loss yearning and anxiety. Prigerson, Maciejewski, and Rosenheck (2000) analyzed 3-year longitudinal data from older men and women with respect to the interaction of marital harmony and widowhood on health service use and estimated health costs postloss. Prior to the loss, high marital harmony was protective, being associated with lower total health costs. Among persons widowed between assessments, those widowed from a harmonious marriage experienced overall health costs 32% higher than those experienced by persons widowed from a nonharmonious marriage. These findings may reflect the increased disruption and trauma associated with losing a particularly close and valued partner and the mediating effects of the emerging CG symptoms. Additional studies providing evidence for the relationship between the strength of a positive, intimate relationship and the severity of grief symptoms include Piper, Ogrodniczuk, Joyce, et al. (2001), Scharlach (1991), and Van Doorn, Kasl, Beery, Jacobs, & Prigerson (1998).

A related but distinct assumption is that the existence of *ambivalence* in the marital relationship is associated with poor bereavement outcome. Ambivalence refers to the simultaneous presence of conflicting positive and negative feelings about the relationship. Ambivalent feelings are a common feature of most if not all relationships; considerations of ambivalence as a risk factor refers to a much greater intensity of opposing feelings. In his classic treatise on mourning and melancholia, Freud (1917/1957) emphasized that ambivalence toward the deceased can transform normal grief into melancholia (depression). Ambivalence also defines an insecure attachment, and the characteristic anger and anxiety may intensify when the attachment is severed through death. Parkes and Weiss (1983) and Lindemann (1944) wrote that the most severe grief reactions often occurred following an ambivalent relationship. It is important to note that in the Parkes and Weiss research, the survivors of ambivalent marriages showed better early adjustment to loss than those widowed after a happy marriage. It was only at the follow-up interviews 2 to 4 years after bereavement that survivors of ambivalent marriages demonstrated maladjustment and poor recovery. In the Parkes (1975) and Parkes and Weiss (1983) studies, ambivalence was inferred from scores on other variables such as anger and self-reproach.

Using more direct measures of ambivalence, Piper, Ogrodniczuk, Joyce, et al. (2001) reported an inverse relationship between ambivalence and the severity of grief symptoms. The finding was demonstrated with one large sample of psychiatric outpatients and cross-validated with a second sample. There are different ways to understand this finding. It suggests that the death actually offers a degree of resolution for the ambivalent individual. That is, following the death, the need to balance emotions in an ongoing relationship is no longer present. In the deceased's absence, the individual is able to focus on either the positive or negative feelings and consequently the intensity of the grief symptoms may be lessened. However, there is an alternative way to understand the meaning of an inverse relationship between ambivalence and severity of grief symptoms. The measure of ambivalence may actually be capturing a person's tolerance for ambivalence. That is, the patient reports a higher level of ambivalence because he is more in touch with (conscious of) experiencing both positive and negative feelings toward the lost person.

The third aspect of relationship quality, *dependency*, is strongly associated with other risk factors for CG such as early childhood losses and ambivalence in the relationship. Raphael (1983) identified dependency as one of three factors predisposing the bereaved to chronic mourning (the others being the sudden, unexpected death and the death of a child). Lopata (1973, 1979) found that widows who had been intensely involved in their husbands' lives and who were both socially and psychologically dependent on them had greater problems in adjustment during bereavement than those who were more autonomous. Parkes and Weiss (1983) described "clinging," dependent relationships as those leading to excessive yearning and chronic grief, consequently placing them in a high-risk category. These authors also suggest that those who have had significant losses in childhood will be more prone to dependency and subsequent severe grief than others who have had a more secure early life (Parkes, 1987; Sanders, 1980). Piper, Ogrodniczuk, Joyce, et al. (2001) provided evidence that a relationship in which the deceased was dependent on the bereaved (e.g., a caretaking relationship) was also associated with more severe grief symptoms.

In sum, the literature suggests that a close, intimate relationship can be particularly difficult to grieve, largely because of the trauma and life disruption brought about by the death of a "soul mate." The literature also identifies two negative characteristics of a marital relationship that raise the likelihood of poor bereavement outcome: ambivalence and dependency. Raphael (1983) argued that "These (ambivalence and dependency) may lead to greater risks of inhibited or disturbed grief, chronic grief, and depression, as well as other possible outcomes" (p. 221). Further research is needed to determine whether these risk factor effects are evident when the loss involves other types of significant nonmarital relationships.

Kinship Relationships

The attachment relationship differs according to whether it involves a parent, a spouse, a same-sex partner, a child, or a sibling. Relatively little has been done to examine the effect of this variable on the outcome of bereavement. As noted earlier, comparative studies of the kinship relationship have consistently shown that the loss of an adult child results in more intense or more persistent grief and depression than the loss of a spouse, parent, or sibling (Cleiren, 1991; Leahy, 1992–1993; Nolen-Hoeksema & Larson, 1999; Sanders, 1980). In a study that used mortality as an outcome, Rees and Lutkins (1967) found that the death of a spouse or a child was associated with significantly higher rates of death among the survivors compared with the death of a sibling or adult parents. Sanders (1980) found that bereaved parents experience more intense grief than do bereaved spouses or bereaved children who had an elderly parent die. In addition, the duration of the parents' grief was prolonged and, for the mothers, actually intensified after the 1st year of bereavement. McHorney and Mor (1988) found that the odds of an individual who lost a spouse being depressed about 4 months after a loss were significantly higher than for bereaved individuals who lost parents, siblings, or more distant relatives. Murrell and Himmelfarb (1989) reported that the death of a spouse, parent, or child—relative to the death of a sibling, grandchild, or good friend—was significantly associated with depression in the surviving family member within 1 year of the loss. Cleiren's study (1991) confirmed this pattern of depression, finding that bereaved spouses and parents were significantly more depressed than were bereaved siblings and children 4 months after a death.

Seltzer and Li (2000) found that older wives (mean age of 70 years) were more affected than daughters (mean age of 58 years) by entry into caregiving and also by the bereavement. Bernard and Guarnaccia (2002, 2003) compared bereavement reactions among older husbands (mean age of 64 years) and adult daughters (mean age of 41 years) after caring for breast cancer hospice patients. At 90 days postloss, intensity of grief did not differ between the two groups, although age was inversely related to grief adjustment for both. Among the husbands only, grief scores at 90 days postloss were significantly predicted by prebereavement symptoms of anxiety or depression, emotional strain, and physical health strain associated with caregiving.

On the whole, then, the death of a parent for adult children appears to be less distressing than the death of a child or spouse. The valence of the relationship has also been considered in studies, providing additional evidence for differential associations with bereavement outcome. For example, when the loss is a spouse, there is evidence of a direct association between a negative marital relationship and both grief and general distress but no association with depression (Bonanno, Notarius, Gunzerath, Keltner & Horowitz, 1998; BrintzenhofeSzoc, Smith & Zabora, 1999; Maercker, Bonanno, Znoj & Horowitz,1998; Zisook, Shuchter & Lyons, 1987). By way of contrast, when the loss involves a parent, a direct association emerges between a positive parental relationship and grief symptoms (Scharlach, 1991). A number of other studies of the kinship influence on bereavement outcome are available (see Jacobs, 1993, p. 148), but these are often uncontrolled. It should be noted that measures of depression and grief are often administered some time after the loss, so it is unclear whether the reported findings for kinship relationships indicate that the variable should be considered an impact factor or as a factor in recovery.

Availability of Social Support

In addition to the provision of instrumental and informational resources needed for survival, social support is viewed as fostering relational closeness, encouraging emotional expression, and facilitating feelings of mastery and self-sufficiency (Charles & Mavandadi, 2004). It is generally accepted that a lack of social support is a bereavement-specific as well as a general risk factor. Studies indicate that the availability of social support is positively associated with health in the bereaved; many, however, lack comparative samples, and thus it is not clear whether these findings may simply reflect the general positive association between social support and health. There is mixed evidence of a stress-buffering effect of support, that is, it is not consistently found to be protective or to foster recovery from symptoms specific to grief (W. Stroebe et al., 2005). "Support from other people cannot replace the deceased, alleviate the bereaved's loneliness, or lessen the need for loss-oriented coping. It may, however, help with restoration-oriented coping" (Hansson & Stroebe, 2007, p. 109). In other words, a positive effect on bereavement outcome is easier to identify for the instrumental aspects of social support, but evidence for an ameliorative effect of the emotional aspects of social support is more mixed. Another conceptual issue concerns whether the measurement of social support should address the objective component, that is, number of contacts in a network, or the subjective component, that is, the mourner's perceptions of the availability of or satisfaction with different forms of support from others.

The evidence for the beneficial effects of social support is frequently more implied than direct. Clayton and colleagues (Clayton, 1974; Clayton, Halikas, & Maurice, 1972; Bornstein et al., 1973) found that widowed individuals living with family had lower rates of depression than widowed living alone. Lopata (1973) reported that widowed with children living locally recovered from bereavement better than those who had no children living nearby. Bunch (1972) reported that bereaved persons who committed suicide had experienced more social disruption because of bereavement, were more likely to be living alone, and had been receiving less support from relatives (see also Bock & Webber, 1972; Wenz, 1977).

Different social support provisions may be necessary for positive benefit at different times in the grief process. Some studies have identified family support as critical to good outcome of bereavement (Bahr & Harvey, 1979, 1980; Maddison, 1968; L. A. Morgan, 1976), whereas other studies have emphasized the support received through interaction with friends (Arling, 1976; Pihlblad & Adams, 1972). In a study possibly offering a resolution of these mixed findings, Bankoff (1983) reported differential effects of support over time for young widows: Parents were most helpful early after bereavement, whereas later on single or other widowed friends were most beneficial in reducing distress. Psychological well-being in older bereaved persons generally has been found to be more closely associated with quality of friendships than with family relationships. In a study of widowers over age 60, psychological well-being (a balance of positive to negative affect) at 1 year postloss was significantly related to the degree of interaction with friends and neighbors but not to amount of contact and help available from children or siblings (Balaswamy & Richardson, 2001). For the older bereaved, family support may be more important in the more tangible areas of assistance and security, whereas support from friends may contribute more to psychological well-being. Individual characteristics, gender, family dynamics, and age may all influence access to and impact of social support.

Siegel and Kuykendall (1990) examined two forms of social ties with respect to the consequences of nonconjugal bereavement (loss of a parent, sibling, child, grandchild, or niece or nephew). Participants were seniors 65 years of age or older. The social ties of interest were marital status (married or widowed) and church or temple membership. Results demonstrated the importance of social resources but showed differential effects by gender. Among women, depressive symptoms were associated with conditions of poor health. Among men, however, depressed mood was associated with being older, being widowed, being in poor health, and having experienced a nonconjugal loss within the previous 6 months. Also among the men, the relationship between experiencing a nonconjugal loss and depression was higher if they were wid-owed or were not a member of a church or temple. The highest depression scores were found among men who had experienced a nonconjugal loss, were widowed, and also did not belong to a church or temple. These individuals were therefore dealing with the grief over a nonconjugal loss without the support available from a spouse or a peer group.

Norris and Murrell (1990) examined the role of social resources in coping with loss and comparing conjugal and nonconjugal bereavements. Assessments were conducted on three occasions at 6-month intervals. Each of the groups (widowed persons, married persons who had lost a parent or child between Assessments 1 and 3, and a matched sample of nonbereaved adults) involved adults with an average age of 65 years. Independent vari-ables included measures of *social embeddedness* in a helpful support network, global stress, and evidence of coping through pursuit of new life interests. The widowed group had the highest depression scores at Assessments 2 and 3 relative to the other groups. Widowed persons also had more health problems at Assessment 3 compared with those bereaved of a parent or child and reported greater global stress compared with the other groups. However, the widowed were the only group to demonstrate increases in social embedded-ness (between Assessments 1 and 2) and were the only group to develop new interests. The independent variables predicted depression and physical health more consistently among the widowed group. Widowed participants' depressive symptoms at Assessment 3 were associated with lower social embeddedness, fewer new interests, and greater global stress. In the other two groups, social embeddedness was unrelated to the outcome variables. Both bereavement groups had experienced an attachment loss. The death of a spouse, however, particularly later in life, also signals a major life transition and demands for (restoration-oriented) adaptations far beyond those associated with their grief (loss oriented). Thus, the provisions of social support tended to be more valued by the widowed and to figure more prominently in their ability to cope with bereavement.

More sophisticated research questions may be needed to disentangle the effects of specific forms of social support on specific aspects of grief experience. W. Stroebe, Stroebe, Abakoumkin, and Schut (1996) examined bereavement status and social support as moderators of two forms of loneliness, emotional loneliness (lack of a confidante) and social loneliness (lack of a network). They reported a main effect of bereavement (but not social support) on emotional loneliness, a main (inverse) effect of social support (but not bereavement) on social loneliness, and main effects of both social support and bereavement on measures of depression. The impact of bereavement on depression was found to be mediated by emotional loneliness, whereas the impact of social support on depression was found to be mediated by social loneliness. In sum, the research on social support generally suggests that (a) the presence of and interaction with others appears to ameliorate the negative effects of bereavement, (b) different persons may be most helpful at different times following a loss, and (c) different persons may be helpful to younger versus older bereaved (Stroebe & Stroebe, 1987). Again, the frequent absence of nonbereaved controls makes conclusions from many studies necessarily tentative. Contemporary studies of this variable have begun to partition support into subtypes (instrumental vs. emotional) and to examine effects on different aspects of the grief experience (e.g., emotional vs. social loneliness). More specific risk factor relationships involving the presence or absence of forms of social support may thus be identified in future research.

CIRCUMSTANCES SURROUNDING THE LOSS

It has to be noted that stressful life events include those that simply happen to the individual outside of his or her control (e.g., being mugged or hit by a vehicle) but also those that are attributable to the individual's own behavioral contributions. "(I)t is conceivable that depression or poor coping abilities of the bereaved person may have been responsible for the occurrence of 'multiple life crises' such as divorce or marital conflict" (W. Stroebe & Stroebe, 1987, p. 199–200) occurring before or after the death. Consequently, studies that examine the impact of additional stressors on bereavement outcome may fail to consider the potential for confounding with personality, coping style, or other variables.

Antecedent Life Crises

Multiple antecedent life crises, particularly those involving disturbance of the marital relationship (e.g., infidelity, pregnancy, possibility of divorce), was one factor Parkes (1975) reported as a predictor of poor outcome. (Two additional antecedent factors were low social class and lack of preparation for the loss.) Elizur and Kaffman (1983), in a longitudinal study of children of Israeli kibbutzim who lost their fathers through war, reported similar findings: Children of families with longstanding conflict and marital discord reacted to loss with intense and pervasive problems. These prebereavement factors were most influential in the early months of bereavement, whereas circumstances concurrent with and subsequent to the loss exacerbated bereavement reactions over the years of assessment. The suggestion is that the individual's capacities for coping and adaptation are overwhelmed by the loss if already strained to the limit, or, conversely, the individual has little reserve while engaged in the grief process if additional stressors arise.

More attention has been given to the impact of stressors subsequent to bereavement, whether these are consequences of the loss or independent events. Reporting on the Harvard study of the widowed, Parkes (1975) suggested that "secondary effects" of bereavement, such as problems with children, home, jobs, and financial difficulties, were all more likely to be mentioned by those whose outcome rating was poor. It could not be determined if these reports were a cause or effect of the poor outcomes. Parkes (1985) later ranked "social circumstances" according to their approximate order of importance for risk: (a) absence of family or perceptions of their unsupportiveness and lack of a confidant (see the preceding discussion), (b) detachment from traditional cultural and religious support systems (especially among immigrants), (c) unemployment, (d) presence of dependent children, (e) low socioeconomic status, and (f) other losses. Some investigators have suggested that poor adjustment to bereavement is attributable to the secondary economic effects of loss, such as sudden financial insecurity, and not to the change in status per se (Bahr & Harvey, 1980; Harvey & Bahr, 1974; L. A. Morgan, 1976). Sheldon et al. (1981) found that low socioeconomic status contributed to poor adjustment and negatively influenced health among widows. These observations were supported by Atchley (1975) in a working-class group of older widows in which inadequate income led to reduced social participation and, consequently, to reports of greater loneliness and anxiety. It does seem reasonable that concurrent financial stresses will exacerbate adjustment problems. This may be because of anxiety about "making ends meet," but it may also be associated with the limiting of social participation and the resulting isolation and lack of social support.

The debate over the impact of economic hardship following a bereavement has been continuous since the Harvard study. Glick et al. (1974) concluded that poor adjustment following bereavement is a direct consequence of an insecure economic position. In contrast, Sanders (1980) argued that low income did not contribute directly to poor bereavement outcome but, instead, was a preexisting factor that would contribute negatively to any stressful situation. L. A. Morgan (1976) statistically partialed out the effects of income and found that lowered morale was not attributable to bereavement in and of itself but was related primarily to the deprivation caused by lack of income. Thus, positive adjustment to bereavement is likely to be strongly associated with a firm financial situation in the case of a widowed person. Women appear most vulnerable to the economic consequences of conjugal loss (Lopata, 1993; Wortman, Silver, & Kessler, 1993); they are more likely to have been dependent on their spouse for current income, health insurance, the survivor's share of pensions, and so on. It is consistent that insufficient income in widowhood is associated with increased depressive symptoms (van Grootheest et al., 1999).

Concurrent or Consequent Life Crises

Concurrent stressors may include additional losses, including the multiple death situation, but also events such as loss of employment, divorce, loss of physical health, financial setbacks, and so on. Parkes (1964) and Raphael (1983) noted the serious implications of multiple death situations, particularly when several members of a family are lost in the same disaster, as a form of secondary stressor. Lifton (1964), in describing survivors of Hiroshima, described a "death guilt" as part of the survivor syndrome—survivors felt themselves saved at the cost of others' lives. This representation would frequently be triggered in social situations and reinforce feelings of shame and guilt; in this respect, a range of social situations became stressors secondary to the bereavement. Studies have shown that individuals involved in these multiple crises are at greater risk than others who are not so assailed (Parkes, 1975; Raphael & Middleton, 1990).

Murdock, Guarnaccia, Hayslip, and McKibbin (1998) compared the experience of recent widows with a married control group in terms of the impact of concurrent stressors on psychological health. The experience of small, disruptive life events during the last month accounted for significant variance in general psychological distress among the widows, even after the effects of poor health, education, lack of social support, and major life events—including the loss through death—had been statistically controlled. The findings from this study on older widowed women paralleled earlier findings from a similar study on both men and women (Zautra, Guarnaccia, Reich, & Dohrenwend, 1988). Again, the suggestion is that bereavement is a stressor that may dominate the individual's coping repertoire, such that relatively minor daily hassles are experienced with distress.

CONCLUSION

A predominant feature of the bereavement-related risk factors research literature is the apparent impossibility of considering the effects of any one factor in isolation. Findings regarding a particular factor invariably have to be qualified because of the influence of closely related factors or the presence of potential interactions involving other risk factors. This feature highlights the problems associated with research on risk factors for CG at the level of aggregated group-level data. At the same time, this feature also reflects the common clinical situation with the individual mourner—every bereaved person is unique because of his or her particular constellation of associated risk factors. With certain individuals, the unique combination of risk factors might suggest that complications of the grief process will be inevitable; another person with nearly the same presentation of risk factors may demonstrate progress toward recovery because of an apparently slight variation that has a decided impact, for example, the presence of a confidante or a capacity for flexibility in coping strategy.

Consequently, the body of risk factors research is unlikely to ever offer absolutes or algorithms regarding the impact of bereavement. It is true that certain risk factors are associated with profound impact for anyone (e.g., sudden or traumatic death, homicide, suicide), but there are always exceptional cases that behave in ways other than expected. Appreciating the form and intensity of a person's grief must by definition be idiographic in nature; research can outline potential nomothetic principles, but as noted, the complexity of the factors to be considered means these are more probabilistic than certain. The literature does however offer a general framework for understanding what must be considered when evaluating the status of the grieving person in terms of matching degree of dysfunction to level of intervention. Certainly, this represents the best use of a clinical science for a condition that ultimately confronts us all.

4

EFFECTS OF PATIENT
CHARACTERISTICS ON
THERAPEUTIC OUTCOME

The study of patient characteristics, and in particular patient personality variables, as predictors of important clinical events (e.g., dropping out, effective process, beneficial outcome) has a comparatively short history in the larger progression of psychotherapy research. A considerable number of studies and meta-analyses have demonstrated that different forms of psychotherapy "work" and are essentially equivalent in terms of effectiveness. However, it has often been noted in these reports that although the aggregate values for treatment groups have reflected clear benefit, the variation shown by individuals within those treatment groups has often been quite pronounced. That is, certain patients have not demonstrated clinically important gains, and indeed, others have demonstrated a worsening of symptoms or deterioration in some other respect. It is reasonable to suggest that differences in patient characteristics might be associated with these differences in response to the therapy.

Greater research attention was given to the impact of patient characteristics on the therapy process and outcome beginning in the 1980s. This consideration prompted an obvious but vexing question: Which of the multitude of patient variables should be selected for study? Said another way, Which of the long list of patient characteristics can be regarded as relevant to and capable of influencing the clinical phenomena of interest? Methodological recommendations, such as the use of aptitude–treatment interaction designs, were put forward as critical to reliably identifying potent patient variables. Even with these designs, however, the permutations and combinations of all treatment approaches and patient variables would require far greater investments of investigative time and research funding than would ever be available in the field (Beutler, Clarkin, & Bongar, 2000). It quickly became clear that the choice of which patient variables to examine had to be guided by the investigator's theory regarding the therapy approach and process. The patient variables themselves must therefore also have a clear theoretical relevance to the therapeutic model. In many instances, this can have the fortunate consequence of identifying variables with a definite clinical relevance as well.

As studies in this area have accumulated, certain patient characteristics have garnered evidence for having a definite influence on compliance with therapy, the quality of the process, and the ultimate benefit realized by the patient. Although often correlational in form, highlighting the difficulty of experimental studies in this area, a number of these relationships have gained additional support through the work of independent investigative teams. It is also the case that the bulk of this evidence has been obtained through studies of individual psychotherapy; there have been far fewer studies devoted to patient predictors in the group therapy context. Current opinion is that characteristics of the patient account for a greater proportion of the variation in therapy outcome than the effects of particular therapist interventions (Blatt, Quinlan, Pilkonis, & Shea, 1995; Zuroff et al., 2000; see also Clarkin & Levy, 2004). Reviewers (e.g., Lambert, 1992) have indeed concluded that personal characteristics and qualities of the patient account for the majority (approximately 40%) of the variation in treatment outcome. This perspective translates into an important clinical implication: "Identification of premorbid clinical and personality characteristics predictive of outcome might help clinicians guide treatment choices and revise treatment methods based on the needs of different types of clients" (Clarkin & Levy, 2004 p. 195). In short, knowledge of the individual patient's relevant characteristics can aid the clinician in formulating a tailored approach to the therapy.

This apparently positive state of affairs is, however, subject to some constraint. As Stiles, Honos-Webb, and Surko (1998) have argued, the influence of patient characteristics is not static over time. Instead, the responsiveness of the skilled therapist and the reciprocal impact of the therapy process on the patient can mitigate this influence such that nonsignificant relationships between patient variables and clinical events may be the rule rather than the exception. What this implies is that future research must endeavor to represent even more of the complexity of the clinical situation and include not only patient and treatment variables but also variables reflecting the skillfulness of the clinician and the facilitating quality of the therapy process to better understand how psychotherapy brings about change.

In this chapter, we offer a review of the patient characteristics considered as likely to have an impact on the course and outcome of short-term or time-limited group psychotherapy. The literature review spanned the years of 1985 to the present. In many instances, discussion of the patient variable is essentially speculative; evidence from studies of short-term or time-limited individual therapy was considered if there was a substantial likelihood that the relationships would translate across formats. Relationships with reasonably strong empirical support are highlighted. Patient-process and patient-outcome relations that have been studied and found to hold promise are also considered. The implications of the empirical evidence regarding each patient variable for the implementation of a short-term group treatment are addressed in each section.

We address patient variables in four domains: demographic characteristics, attitudinal and personality characteristics, interpersonal dimensions, and diagnostic variables. The domains addressing personality and interpersonal variables account for the bulk of this review. The structure of the review— providing a consideration of each patient characteristic on its own—represents something of a limitation. Patient variables are interdependent by definition and can act in concert with one another, with a given dimension acting to amplify or negate the effect of other characteristics. In the clinical setting, it is important to conduct a multidimensional evaluation of the patient and assess the range of patient variables that may be relevant to the therapy intervention being considered (Beutler et al. 2000). Table 4.1 summarizes the effects of patient characteristics that are discussed in this chapter.

PATIENT DEMOGRAPHIC CHARACTERISTICS

Demographic variables include two predictors (age and gender) that are static, that is, fixed and unchangeable, yet have broad impact on the therapy process and outcome. A third variable, social support, reflects an important quality of the patient's interpersonal environment, that is, the availability and helpfulness of others as a resource during episodes of distress. Social support also has broad effects, influencing the patient's presentation (i.e., an absence of sustaining support accentuates the patient's functional impairment; Beutler, Harwood, Alimohamed, & Malik, 2002) and response to therapy (i.e., the presence of support tends to reinforce gains in therapy). Further, social support can itself be impacted by changes brought about by therapy; for example, the patient acts in accord with an emerging intention to improve his or her social

TABLE 4.1

Patient Characteristics Likely to Influence Therapy Process and Outcomes

Characteristic	Type of variable	Examined as	Comment
Age	Static demographic characteristic	Direct predictor, moderator	Younger patients tend to be less compliant regarding attendance or engagement in therapy process. In group, age effects may be mediated by process variables (e.g., cohesion). Age may also interact with type of therapy approach.
Gender	Static demographic characteristic	Direct predictor, moderator	Therapy continuation and outcome are generally equivalent across the two genders. Some evidence supports the view that women fare better in therapy than men, with gender effects being mediated by process variables in group (e.g., commitment, compatibility).
Social support	Perceived quality of inter-personal environment	Direct predictor, moderator	Directly associated with therapy outcome. Effects may be restricted to specific sources of support (e.g., friends as opposed to family members).
Positive orientation to therapy	Attitudinal construct	Direct predictor	Assessed in a variety of ways, but generally highlighted as a predictor of benefit. *Autonomous motivation* most clearly defined. Can be facilitated through methods of preparing patients for therapy.
Treatment expectancies	Appraisal of likely patient and therapist behaviors, appraisal of likely benefits of therapy	Direct predictor, involved in mediation relationship	More realistic anticipation of therapy transaction associated with more positive process and outcome. Positive outcome expectancies associated with continuation and improvement. Direct effects may be mediated by the quality of the therapeutic alliance.
Stage of change	Motivational construct	Direct predictor, moderator	Lower stages (e.g., precontemplation) associated with therapy dropout and poorer outcome. Therapy strategies may have differential effects as a function of patient's stage of change.
Ego strength	Composite of personality traits	Direct predictor	Mixed evidence for a direct association with therapy outcome.
Resilience	Personality trait	Direct predictor	Directly related to speed of recovery.

Characteristic	Type	Role	Description
Psychological mindedness	Dynamic personality trait	Direct predictor, moderator	Predictive of continuation and positive process; predictive of therapy outcome, particularly in expressive (interpretive) approaches. May interact with other patient (e.g., type of personality disorder) and therapy approach (e.g., interpretive vs. supportive) variables.
Alexithymia	Composite of personality traits (deficits)	Direct predictor, moderator	Inversely associated with therapy outcome and directly associated with relapse or recurrence of depression following treatment. Negative impact on group outcome mediated by in-group behavior and corresponding therapist reaction.
Perfectionism	Personality trait	Direct predictor, moderator, involved in mediation relationship	Inversely associated with the outcomes of therapy. Impact is mediated by problems sustaining interpersonal relationships both within (alliance) and outside therapy (social support).
Reactance	Cognitive–affective disposition to resist or oppose directives	Moderator	Evidence for aptitude–treatment interactions with the directiveness of the therapy approach.
Coping style	Generalized response to stress or anxiety regulation	Direct predictor, moderator	Externalizing patients more likely to show poorer outcomes than internalizing patients. Evidence for aptitude–treatment interactions with externalizing patients faring better in skills training therapy and internalizing patients faring better in insight-oriented therapy.
Five-factor model	Higher order personality trait dimensions	Direct predictor, moderator	Neuroticism may be inversely associated with therapy outcome and may indicate preferential response to pharmacotherapy. Extraversion appears to be a predictor of improvement in therapy. Some evidence exists for a similar impact of agreeableness, but this may be particular to specific therapies. Evidence for openness and conscientiousness is inconsistent.
Quality of object relations (QOR)	Global interpersonal style	Direct predictor, moderator	Evidence for aptitude–treatment interaction involving the supportive versus expressive features of the therapy approach. Direct QOR–outcome relationship (interpretive groups) mediated by the balanced expression of affect during sessions. Inverse QOR–outcome relationship (supportive groups) mediated by dissatisfaction with the therapist. Evidence for a group-level composition effect (proportion of high-QOR members).

(continues)

TABLE 4.1
Patient Characteristics Likely to Influence Therapy Process and Outcomes   (Continued)

Characteristic	Type of variable	Examined as	Comment
Attachment style	Global interpersonal style	Direct predictor, moderator	Securely attached patients demonstrate more positive process and outcome in therapy. Dismissing attachment style has been associated with a problematic alliance but also the potential for substantial gains in therapy.
Symptom severity	Level of distress	Direct predictor	Greater severity associated with poorer outcomes of therapy or necessitating more treatment intensity (e.g., longer durations) to achieve similar outcomes. Subjective dimension, that is, distress, representative of motivation for treatment and directly associated with outcome.
Functional impairment	Negative impact of illness on level of functioning	Direct predictor	Greater degree of functional impairment is associated with a poorer prognosis and poorer therapy outcomes. Type of impairment may serve as an indicator for matching to treatment approach or the need to combine treatments.
Comorbidity	Presentation of multiple disorders (usually *DSM–IV–TR* Axis II)	Direct predictor, moderator	Presence of a comorbid *DSM–IV–TR* Axis II condition is associated with poorer outcomes in some forms of therapy.
Chronic pain	Presence of intractable physical pain in addition to mental health issues.	Direct predictor, moderator	Pain symptoms were inversely associated with outcomes of short-term group treatment for complicated grief, even after accounting for use of medication and alexithymia.

Note. *DSM–IV–TR* = *Diagnostic and Statistical Manual of Mental Disorders* (4th ed., text revision; American Psychiatric Association, 2000).

network, reflecting a more complicated reciprocal impact of treatment and this demographic characteristic.

Age

The patient's age appears to have a bearing on the likelihood of continuation or benefit in therapy, but the evidence for a clear relationship is inconsistent (Garfield, 1994; Piper, 1994). This may in part be due to the confounding of age with other developmental milestones (e.g., focus on school or a career, living with family or seeking an intimate partner) or because age is a proxy for aspects of maturity (e.g., a degree of verbal intelligence) that are required for engagement in the therapy process. Certain conditions targeted for treatment are also associated with particular age groupings, for example, anxiety disorders in school-age children, postpartum depression during a woman's child-bearing years. Further, patients of younger versus more advanced age may come to treatment with contrasting expectations for benefit.

A study of transference-focused individual psychotherapy for patients with borderline personality disorder identified younger age as a predictor of early treatment termination (Smith, Koenigsberg, Yeomans, Clarkin, & Selzer, 1995). A second important predictor of early termination was a high level of hostility at the outset of therapy. It is not difficult to imagine encountering more problems implementing therapy with the younger, angrier patients in this grouping. Studies of group therapy have reported that younger patients tend to attend fewer therapy sessions and are more likely to terminate prematurely (Chang & Saunders, 2002; Hadley, Reddon, & Reddick, 2000; Monras & Gual, 2000), but it should be noted that these investigations were in the forensic or substance rehabilitation context. However, in our comparative trial of two forms of short-term group therapy for complicated grief (CG), we also reported that age was directly associated with session attendance and completion of therapy (Ogrodniczuk, Piper, & Joyce, 2006). Moreover, the direct effect of age on attendance was mediated by the quality of the relationships among the group members (i.e., cohesion), that is, groups involving older patients tended to be more cohesive, and greater cohesion was predictive of greater benefit. These effects were largely confined to the supportive group approach. The general thrust of this collection of studies is that younger patients may be at more risk for poor treatment adherence.

In terms of therapy process, Taft, Murphy, Musser, and Remington (2004) reported that higher age was one of a set of eight predictors of a stronger therapeutic alliance among men participating in a cognitive–behavioral group treatment for domestic violence. Thus, older patients may be more likely to successfully engage in the therapy process. Pilkonis, Imber, Lewis, and Rubinsky (1984) conducted a comparative study of the outcomes of individual, group, and conjoint (couples) therapy. Evidence for differential effects of type of treatment was minimal, but there were indications of interactions between certain patient variables and therapy approach. With regard to age, older patients demonstrated more symptom improvement following group or conjoint therapy, whereas younger patients showed more gains following individual therapy. This study addressed a range of symptomatic outcomes. In contrast, there is some evidence that younger patients may respond better to therapy for major depression than older patients (Beutler, Blatt, Alimohamed, Levy, & Angtuaco, 2006; Piper, 1994). Generally, then, younger age may be associated with a higher risk of therapy dropout and poor treatment engagement. It may also serve as a contraindication for referral to certain forms of group therapy.

Gender

Patient gender is another variable that may "stand in" for related constructs (e.g., differences in socialization; Heatherington, Stets, & Mazzarella, 1986) or be implicated in specific interactions with treatment approach (e.g., problem-oriented vs. insight-oriented; Ogrodniczuk, Piper, Joyce, & McCallum, 2001a) or format (i.e., individual or group). Generally speaking, considerable research has indicated that therapy continuation and outcomes for the two genders are equivalent (Clarkin & Levy, 2004; Garfield, 1994; Thase et al., 1994). When significant differences have been found, these have consistently favored female over male patients (see Sue & Lam, 2002). For example, Talley, Butcher, Maguire, and Pinkerton (1992) reported that women fared better than males on an index of symptom reduction following brief individual therapy. Almost all of this research has involved the individual therapy format.

In the context of group psychotherapy, Holmes (2002) has suggested that women are at a disadvantage in mixed-gender psychotherapy groups because of a socially sanctioned tendency to defer to men. MacNab (1990) has argued the reverse, that because of their cultural heritage and biopsychosocial endowment, men are poorly equipped to participate in the intimate transactions that characterize psychotherapy groups. Empirical support for either of these positions is meager. On the basis of data from our comparative trial of interpretive and supportive short-term group therapies for CG (Piper, McCallum, et al., 2001), we examined the role of patient gender in the therapy process and treatment outcome (Ogrodniczuk, Piper, & Joyce, 2004b). The sample was restricted to those patients who also received a diagnosis of major depression and who provided complete outcome data ($N = 47$; 11 men, 36 women). Women were found to demonstrate better outcomes in both forms of group treatment compared with men. Additionally, men were found to be less committed to their therapy groups and were perceived by other members to be less compatible than women, factors that mediated the gender–outcome relationship. Although limited by the small number of men in the sample, these findings do suggest that male patients may find the experience of joining and working with a therapy group more challenging and difficult than women.

Social Support

It is a clinical aphorism that patients engaged in the therapy process can benefit from the availability and receipt of support from significant others in their life. Research has generally shown this to be true: Patients with higher levels of social support tend to demonstrate greater improvement in therapy for mood disorders (Beutler, Castonguay, & Follette, 2006) and for anxiety disorders (Newman, Crits-Christoph, Connolly-Gibbons, & Erickson, 2006). Social support can be measured objectively, for example, the number of family members or friends in an individual's network, or reflect the subjective sense that support is available. The evidence suggests that it is the individual's *perception* of the availability of resources that is associated with outcome and prevention of relapse. For example, in an analysis of data from the National Institute of Mental Health's Treatment of Depression Collaborative Research Program (NIMH TDCRP), patients reporting more satisfying close friendships demonstrated less depression on assessment at 6, 12, and 18 months after therapy termination (Zlotnick, Shea, Pilkonis, Elkin, & Ryan, 1996).

Social support is also widely believed to be among the most important moderators of grief resolution (Rando, 1993), and naturalistic studies of bereavement outcome tend to substantiate this assumption (Lund, Caserta, & Dimond, 1993; Prigerson, Frank, et al., 1995; Reed, 1998). However, there are reports suggesting no effect for social support on bereavement outcome (Murphy, 1988) or even a negative effect (Wortman & Silver, 1989). It has been suggested that these discrepant findings may be attributable to differential effects depending on the source—that is, family as opposed to friends—of the social support (Stylianos & Vachon, 1993). In a study examining the effect of perceived social support on the outcomes of short-term group therapy for CG, Ogrodniczuk, Piper, Joyce, McCallum, & Rosie (2002) reported that support available from friends was directly associated with treatment benefit, whereas support from family was inversely related to outcome for patients in both forms (interpretive, supportive) of group therapy. Further, perceived support from a special person was directly associated with improvement in grief symptoms for patients receiving the interpretive group treatment but unrelated to benefit for those in supportive group treatment. These findings suggest that there are disadvantages to the social support that individuals with CG may receive from family members (Lehman, Ellard, & Wortman, 1986), possibly because it may lead to reinforcement of the patient's dependency or represent a shared maladaptive grief reaction. Friendships tend to have broader boundaries than family relationships. The receipt of social support from friends may therefore not carry the same likelihood of infantilizing the patient or being colored by the individual's distress about the patient's loss. Consequently, social support from friends may be more constructive and helpful than the support received in the family. Knowledge of the patient's support network and resources should be obtained during the assessment for group treatment as a way of determining the level of support the patient may require during therapy.

PATIENT ATTITUDINAL AND PERSONALITY CHARACTERISTICS

The largest number of patient characteristics likely to influence the process and outcome of psychotherapy, in particular short-term group therapy for CG, fall into this category. Attitudinal variables that represent a positive stance on the part of the patient toward the demands of the therapy process, the gains likely from treatment, and a commitment to change appear to be critical to successful therapy. Personality variables cover a broad range of constructs, ranging from those with a long history in the literature (e.g., ego strength) to those of a more recent formulation (e.g., psychological mindedness, reactance, the five-factor model). Personality variables also range from specific traits (e.g., perfectionism) underpinning particular behaviors to more global dimensions (e.g., defensive or coping style) that serve to capture the individual's orientation to interpersonal transactions or dealing with stress. In broad terms, these variables represent the resources or deficits that the patient brings to the therapy enterprise; the patient's placement on a given dimension indicates whether this characteristic represents a strength that can be capitalized on in the therapy process or an obstacle requiring an accommodation or modification to the therapist's intervention strategy. In short, these variables often function as *moderators* of the response to therapy. Additionally, these constructs may also interact with characteristics of the treatment (e.g., quality of the therapy relationship, intervention technique) and highlight processes that serve as mechanisms of change, or *mediators*, associated with improvement.

Attitudinal Variables

Attitudinal variables include positive orientation for therapy, treatment expectancies, and the patient's stage of change.

Positive Orientation for Therapy

It represents clinical common sense to implement a therapy intervention on a foundation of the patient's endorsement of the approach and commitment to the process of change. Indeed, the conviction that the patient should understand and endorse the nature of the therapeutic work is the basis for various efforts at pretherapy patient preparation (Burlingame, Fuhriman, & Johnson, 2002). The evidence regarding this relationship is often stated in the negative. For example, a negative attitude toward the treatment was found to be associated with attrition from therapy for panic disorder (Grilo et al., 1998). A positive orientation for the therapy may be manifest in a number of ways, however. Better therapy outcomes have been associated with a positive orientation as represented by a more active perusal of therapy options and evaluation of the therapist's skill by a prospective patient (Seligman, 1995), a greater willingness to collaborate and cooperate with the therapist (Orlinsky, Rønnestad, & Willutzki, 2004), or greater openness to the demands of the therapeutic strategy (Orlinsky et al., 2004). Zuroff and colleagues (2007) identified a particular strong predictor of therapy outcomes in the patients' level of *autonomous motivation* for therapy. This is defined as the extent to which the patient sees the choice to enter therapy as having been freely and independently their own. Patients who scored high on autonomous motivation for therapy in the NIMH TDCRP were twice as likely to show a positive response relative to those with average scores and four times as likely to respond well relative to patients with low scores on the variable. Screening interviews conducted prior to the implementation of a short-term group can also be used to encourage a positive orientation toward the therapy and reinforce the patients' intrinsic motivation to engage in the change process.

Treatment Expectancies

Patients' expectancies regarding the treatment can be differentiated into two categories: *role* or *process expectancies* and *outcome expectancies*. Role expectancies refer to what patients expect will happen during therapy sessions, specifically in terms of their own behavior and the behavior of the therapist. Research on different methods of educating patients on the goals and process of therapy, using didactic materials, films or videos, or *role induction interviews*, has been a primary source of information regarding role expectancies (Fende Guajardo & Anderson, 2007). Generally, this research has suggested that patients who begin therapy with realistic expectations about what will happen tend to show greater benefit, even though the accumulated findings have been described as equivocal (Arnkoff, Glass, & Shapiro, 2002). An important element of patients' expectations is an anticipation that the therapy process will involve a degree of pain or embarrassment (Mohr, 1995). Patients with a more ambiguous initial understanding of the roles of the participants have demonstrated greater defensiveness, poorer process, and less satisfaction with treatment outcome (Tinsley, Bowman, & Barich, 1993). Again, pretherapy interviews with prospective group patients can be used to address patients' role expectancies to ensure that they are realistic and appropriate to the anticipated group process.

Outcome expectancies refer to the degree of confidence patients feel regarding the likelihood their therapy experience will lead to change or result in benefit. Arnkoff et al. (2002) emphasized that patients' expectations about the effectiveness of therapy are not the same as their motivation for treatment, that is, the desire for change or willingness to cooperate, and reflect more a degree of faith (Wampold, 2001) that psychotherapy can be helpful. Research regarding outcome expectancies has a firmer evidentiary base (Snyder, Michael, & Cheavens, 1999): Patients with a stronger faith in the effectiveness of the therapeutic process demonstrate greater improvement than patients with skepticism about the value of the experience (Glass, Arnkoff, & Shapiro, 2001; Kirsch, 1990). Summarizing this literature, Asay and Lambert (1999) postulated that approximately 15% of the variation in therapy outcomes can be accounted for by patients' expectancies about the effectiveness of their treatment. Clarkin and Levy (2004) concluded that outcome expectancies are also directly associated with continuation in treatment. Still, this research is primarily correlational in form, so it cannot be stated that patients' expectancies of therapeutic gain have direct or causal effects on outcome (Arnkoff et al., 2002). It is also true that initial (pretherapy) outcome expectancies undergo extensive modification as a function of the patient's actual experience in therapy, highlighting the critical importance of when outcome expectancies are assessed (Gunzberger, Henggeler, & Watson, 1985). Other aspects of therapy might need to be incorporated into conceptual models to clarify the expectancy–outcome relationship. For example, there is evidence that the impact of outcome expectancies is mediated by the development of a strong therapeutic alliance in both individual (Joyce, Ogrodniczuk, Piper, & McCallum, 2003; Meyer et al., 2002) and group psychotherapy (Abouguendia, Joyce, Piper, & Ogrodniczuk, 2004). Clearly, realistic and positive patient expectations about both the process and outcome of therapy are desirable because they likely serve as a foundation for a successful implementation of treatment. If the patient's expectancies about therapy are not naturally conducive to a positive group process and benefit, the therapist should capitalize on the opportunities afforded by pretherapy screening and preparatory interviews.

The Patient's Stage of Change

The guiding assumption of the transtheoretical model (Prochaska & DiClemente, 1983) is that behavioral change does not constitute a singular event but involves multiple processes demonstrating a trajectory through stages over time. The model was originally developed to reflect stages associated with cessation of smoking but is held to be representative of the behavioral change process regardless of domain (Prochaska & Norcross, 2002). The stages can be distinguished in terms of the individual's motivation and intention:

- *Precontemplation:* unaware of a need to change, no motivation or intention to change in the short term.
- *Contemplation:* ambivalent, but with an intention to change at some point in the future.
- *Preparation:* an intention to change in the near future, minor behavioral changes.
- *Action:* engagement in overt behavioral change, implementation of strategies.
- *Maintenance:* a focus on preventing relapse and consolidating change.
- *Termination:* no further likelihood of relapse and the experience of a sense of self-control.

The model suggests that therapeutic interventions should be accommodated to the specific stage of change occupied by the individual presenting for help, rather than assuming that the intervention can be applied in the same way across all patients. For example, studies have shown that using behavior-oriented interventions can be effective for patients in the preparation or action stages but may be ineffective or detrimental for patients in lower stages; the latter group tend to respond more positively to verbal interventions aimed at clarifying the problem (McConnaughy, DiClemente, Prochaska, & Velicer, 1989; Petrocelli, 2002; Prochaska, DiClemente, & Norcross, 1992; Satterfield, Buelow, Lyddon, & Johnson, 1995). Prochaska and Norcross (2002) discussed the various roles taken by the therapist working with patients in different stages of the change process. Further, although patients in successful therapies have been found to progress in a linear fashion through the stages over the treatment period, the model also allows for the possibility of stage regressions or the revisitation of certain stages later in the change process (Prochaska et al., 1992).

In studies of treatment for bulimia, patients who presented for therapy in either the action or maintenance stages had better outcomes than patients in the precontemplation or contemplation stages (Franko, 1997; Treasure et al., 1999; Wolk & Devlin, 2001). Similar predictive relationships have been demonstrated for patients with panic disorder (Beitman et al., 1994; Reid, Nair, Mistry, & Beitman, 1996) and men receiving treatment for domestic violence (Scott & Wolfe, 2003). Research has also demonstrated that patients in the precontemplation stage are the most likely to drop out of therapy prematurely, with those in the action phase least likely to do so (Brogan, Prochaska, & Prochaska, 1999; Rainer & Campbell, 2001; Smith, Subich, & Kalodner, 1995). To ensure that the patients considered for a group treatment can provide the appropriate commitment, it is important to establish that, at minimum, all patients have attained a contemplation stage of change.

Personality Variables

Personality variables include ego strength, resilience, psychological mindedness, alexithymia, perfectionism, reactance, and coping style.

Ego Strength

The construct of ego strength is a conglomerate of personality factors that, taken together, afford an individual with the capacity to tolerate the anxiety associated with conflicting environmental demands or internal concerns and to continually refine a flexible and differentiated coping style. As a composite variable, ego strength reflects the traits of frustration tolerance, impulse control, introspectiveness, good reality testing, creativity in problem solving, optimism, and self-confidence. This collection of traits and attitudes indicates that good ego strength is associated with healthy psychological adjustment and coping ability. In the Menninger Psychotherapy Project (Kernberg et al., 1972), a significant direct relationship between ego strength and outcome in psychoanalytic psychotherapy was demonstrated (see also Conte, Plutchik, Picard, & Karasu, 1991; Sexton, 1993). Ego strength was also directly associated with the outcome of group treatment for alcoholics (Lazic & Bamburac, 1991). However, other researchers (Luborsky et al., 1980; Weber, Bachrach, & Solomon, 1985) were not able to replicate this relationship in trials of similar therapies. Patients vary considerably in terms of ego strength, the more primitive or severely disordered patients showing less development of this capacity. Patients with good ego strength would be expected to engage readily in the therapeutic process; patients of poorer ego strength may require a greater proportion of supportive interventions and a period of time to develop a tolerance to the demands of therapy. Generally, patients of lower ego strength being considered for group treatment may require a greater investment in pretherapy, preparatory experiences, or time during early group sessions to acquire a facility with the process.

Resilience

Grief is an almost universal phenomenon, but the experience and expression of grief are variable. Bonanno and his colleagues (Bonanno, 2004; Bonanno, Moskowitz, Papa, & Folkman, 2005; Bonanno et al., 2002) have provided research and analysis that highlight individual differences in responses to losses, including the effect of resilience. In current parlance, some may prefer to represent ego strength by the concept of *resilience* (Bonanno, 2004;

Bonanno et al., 2002, 2005; Kumpfer, 1999; Stein, Fonagy, Ferguson, & Wisman, 2000;), which is defined as the capacity to recover quickly (Bonanno et al. 2002). These researchers point out that resilience is underestimated in much of the literature on grief treatment and unanticipated by the theoretical tradition that assumes both the invariable necessity for grief work in all survivors of loss and that people who do not show pronounced grief symptoms are experiencing *absent grief* or delayed grief, that is, a pathological variant that will disturb their lives in the future. Empirical evidence for delayed grief is minimal. Bonanno (2004) argued that features of the treatment literature could be better understood if there was recognition of various trajectories in postloss functioning, including resilience, recovery, and chronic grief. Chronic depression and distress are present in about 10% to 15% of all bereaved individuals. In a prospective study of 205 elderly people several years before the death of their spouse and 6 and 18 months postloss, Bonanno et al. (2002) identified five core bereavement patterns that captured most of the sample: common grief (which, despite its name, was only 10.7% of this sample), chronic grief (15.6%), chronic depression (7.8%), improvement during bereavement (10.2%), and resilience (45.9%, i.e., the most common pattern by far). The remaining 9.8% of the sample was made up of smaller patterns: delayed grief (3.9%), delayed improved (4.9%), and improved relapsed (1.0%). Delayed grief was thus present in the sample but it could not be described as prevalent. In the comparisons of chronic grief with chronic depression, the clearest predictor of chronic grief was excessive dependency, which included dependency on the spouse and dependency as a personality variable. Bonanno et al. (2005) reported on two studies. In one, they examined resilience in a group of middle-aged adults who had lost either a spouse or a child, which they matched with a group of middle-aged married adults. In the other, they examined resilience in a sample of bereaved gay men as they provided care for partners who were dying of AIDS and as they subsequently tried to recover from the loss. Some of these caregivers were also HIV-positive. Both of these studies provided a variety of types of evidence to support the existence of a prevalent resilience trajectory in the context of various death losses. Resilience was linked with normative rather than dysfunctional relationship patterns. Also, it was prevalent in a younger sample than had been previously studied and in a context of chronic stress and significant caregiver burden.

The literature on resilience serves to remind clinicians that CG affects a minority of bereaved people. However, this does not mean that CG is a rare condition, as was discussed in Chapter 2. Although figures of 10% to 15% for chronic depression and distress may seem small, given the universality of death they imply a huge population of people with disturbances of clinical severity (Allumbaugh & Hoyt, 1999). The clinician who encounters bereavement in a client's history should evaluate whether the client is experiencing CG (Ott, 2003: Prigerson & Jacobs, 2001). It is not useful or consistent with the research literature to assume that most bereavement requires treatment. Indeed, it has been strongly suggested that such an assumption may lead to harmful treatment (Bonanno, 2004; Neimeyer, 2000).

Psychological Mindedness

Psychological mindedness refers generally to an individual's ability to understand people and their problems in psychological terms. The psychologically minded individual will consider personal problems and those of others in terms of motives and the clash between desires and internal prohibitions, rather than in terms of external circumstances. More specifically, psychological mindedness is a dynamic personality trait reflecting both an interest in inner life and the capacity to be introspective, qualities that in turn are held to be related to an ability to acquire insight (see Conte & Ratto, 1997; McCallum & Piper, 1997b). As a way of thinking and perceiving, "psychological mindedness tends to be identified with a process reflecting a structure leading to an outcome" (McCallum & Piper, 1997a, p. 247). In the clinical context, the patient's psychological mindedness would be regarded as a favorable indication for psychotherapy (Appelbaum, 1973). Psychological mindedness has also been addressed by related terms, such as self-awareness (Marini & Case, 1994), private self-consciousness (Fenigstein, Scheier, & Buss, 1975), or personal intelligence (Park, Imboden, Park, Hulse, & Unger, 1992). The construct of alexithymia (Taylor, 1984), reflecting difficulties accessing and identifying inner content (i.e., feelings, thoughts, motives) or distinguishing these from bodily sensations, represents the conceptual obverse of psychological mindedness. These concepts have been operationalized by various investigators and measured using self-report questionnaires, clinical assessments (e.g., response to trial interpretations), or composite scores from measures of associated variables.

Our research group has administered the Psychological Mindedness Assessment Procedure (McCallum & Piper, 1990b, 1997a) to evaluate the construct among patients participating in clinical trials of various forms of time-limited dynamically oriented psychotherapy, including the short-term group interventions described in this volume. We operationally defined psychological mindedness (PM) as "the ability to identify dynamic (intrapsychic) components and to relate them to a person's difficulties." The Psychological Mindedness Assessment Procedure uses a scripted and simulated videotaped patient–therapist interaction as a standardized test stimulus. The person being assessed views an actress-patient describing a recent life event to her therapist. The vignette includes verbalizations reflecting dynamic components (e.g., conflicting wishes and fears, defensive maneuvers) and links between internal and external events. After viewing the videotape, the person being assessed responds to the question, "What seems to be troubling this person?" The narrative response is scored according to a 9-point scale. Higher scores reflect a greater appreciation of unconscious motivations and conflict, the importance of anxiety, and the purpose of defense mechanisms, that is, greater psychological mindedness.

The Psychological Mindedness Assessment Procedure has been shown to be reliably used by assessors. The PM score has also been shown to be independent of patient age or gender, level of education, intelligence, or other demographic variables, and indices of psychiatric symptomatology or distress. The PM variable's association with attrition, process, and outcome was investigated in a number of clinical trial studies of time-limited dynamically oriented psychotherapies in our setting. PM was predictive of remaining versus dropping out of short-term interpretive group therapy for CG (McCallum & Piper, 1990a; McCallum, Piper, & Joyce, 1992; see also Conte & Ratto, 1997). PM was consistently related to the patient's quality of work in group forms of dynamically oriented psychotherapy, for example, the short-term group approaches and intensive partial hospital treatment (McCallum & Piper, 1990a; McCallum, Piper, & O'Kelly, 1997; Piper, Joyce, Azim, & Rosie, 1994).

The evidence for the relationships between PM and therapy outcome is more complicated. In an early study using clinicians' ratings of patients' PM, PM was found to be directly associated with outcome for a short-term group therapy approach but unrelated to outcome for a long-term group approach or the corresponding forms (short-term, long-term) of individual therapy (Piper, Debbane, Bienvenu, & Garant, 1984). The variable was directly associated with benefit in day treatment (Piper et al., 1994) and in both interpretive and supportive forms of short-term time-limited group and individual therapy in earlier studies by our research team (Piper, Joyce, McCallum, & Azim, 1998; Piper, McCallum, et al., 2001). Later studies, which likely benefited from advancements in methodological rigor and reliability of the patient assessments, demonstrated differential findings as a function of patient diagnosis or type of treatment approach. McCallum and Piper (1999) found that PM interacted with the patient's category of personality disorder in predicting benefit from a partial hospital evening treatment program; PM was associated with outcome for patients with dependent personality disorder but unrelated to outcome for patients with paranoid or borderline personality disorder. Patients of higher PM demonstrated greater benefit in the interpretive therapy approach, and patients of lower PM demonstrated greater benefit in the supportive therapy approach in studies of short-term individual (Piper et al., 1998) and group psychotherapy (Piper, Ogrodnicuzuk, Joyce, Weideman, & Rosie, 2007).

The implications of these findings are relatively clear. PM appears to be a trait associated with the patient's ability to engage productively in psychodynamic forms of psychotherapy, particularly those emphasizing a more interpretive or expressive intervention strategy. We believe that PM reflects a general capacity of the patient to make effective use of therapeutic interventions and the therapy process to achieve insight and problem resolution; in this respect, PM represents a capacity for learning. Patients demonstrating a deficit in the aptitude to consider problems from this perspective seem to require treatments that place more emphasis on structure, guidance, and directed problem solving as well as the therapist's (and in group, the other members') provision of support and encouragement. Whether this pattern of relationships involving PM generalizes to other forms of psychotherapy has not yet been studied.

Alexithymia

As noted previously, the construct of alexithymia (Taylor, 1984) appears to represent the conceptual obverse of psychological mindedness, as it generally reflects a *deficit* in the cognitive processing and regulation of emotions (Taylor, 2000). Originally coined by Sifneos (1973), the term *alexithymia* refers to a marked difficulty describing subjective feelings, an impoverished fantasy life, and a cognitive style that is literal and externally oriented (i.e., focusing on concrete details of external events). Alexithymic individuals may have difficulty discriminating between emotions and physical sensations and often express emotional distress through somatic channels, for example, headaches. The construct is conceptualized as a deficit that can interfere with a patient's ability to benefit from the more expressive therapies that require reflection, introspection, and "working through" (McCallum, Piper, Ogrodniczuk, & Joyce, 2003).

The primary measure of this global personality trait is the 20-item Toronto Alexithymia Scale (Bagby, Parker, & Taylor, 1994). The factor structure of the Toronto Alexithymia Scale suggests that alexithymia encompasses problems in three domains: difficulty identifying feelings and distinguishing feelings from bodily sensations, difficulty communicating feelings to others, and externally oriented thinking. When relationships with outcome have been reported in previous research, alexithymia is often presented as a mediating variable, that is, improvement on alexithymia is regarded as mediating improvement on other outcome variables (e.g., Beresnevaite, 2000; de Groot, Rodin, & Olmsted, 1995). The construct has only recently been studied as a direct predictor or moderator of the outcomes of psychotherapy. McCallum et al. (2003) examined the relationship between alexithymia and treatment outcome in two clinical trials of short-term psychotherapy. Each trial had examined alternative forms of psychotherapy (interpretive, supportive) in a specific treatment format: One was our comparative trial for CG (Piper, McCallum, et al., 2001), and the other considered individual psychotherapy for a mixed diagnostic outpatient sample (Piper et al. 1998). Alexithymia was inversely associated with therapy outcome in both trials, and the therapy approach did not differentially affect the alexithymia–outcome relationship. Notably, alexithymia and PM were not found to be inversely correlated, as expected, but rather to represent independent constructs having unique, additive relationships with treatment outcome.

The alexithymia construct has been further examined in the context of these clinical trial studies. First, we reported that the first alexithymia factor—difficulty identifying feelings—was predictive of the persistence of residual symptoms in patients with depression who responded positively to short-term individual psychotherapy (Ogrodniczuk, Piper, & Joyce, 2004a). This relationship was identified after accounting for the patient's pretreatment levels of depression and anxiety, antidepressant medication use, and the form of therapy (interpretive, supportive) received. The presence of residual symptoms is a strong predictor of depression relapse (Judd et al., 1998), so these findings suggest that alexithymia may be a contributory factor to the relapse or recurrence of major depression, even after successful therapy.

Second, the inverse relationship between alexithymia and the outcome of short-term group therapy for CG was found to be mediated by negative therapist reactions to the alexithymic patient (Ogrodniczuk, Piper, & Joyce, 2005). That is, the higher the level of alexithymia (specifically, difficulty communicating feelings and externally oriented thinking), the less positive the therapist's reaction to a patient in the group and the poorer that patient's outcome. Third, a further analysis of the short-term group therapy comparative trial (Ogrodniczuk, Piper, & Joyce, 2008a) indicated that the higher the level of alexithymia (the same two dimensions), the less expression of positive affect by the patient in the group and the more negative the therapist's reaction to the patient. In essence, the impact of the patient's alexithymia on the therapist's reaction was itself mediated by less expression of positive affect on the part of the patient. Other researchers have identified that alexithymic patients may have problems developing an attachment to or relating collaboratively with their therapists (Mallinckrodt, King, & Coble, 1998; Rasting, Brosig, & Beutel, 2005). In sum, considerable evidence has accrued in a short period to indicate that the patient's alexithymia can represent an obstacle to the successful implementation and completion of psychotherapy interventions. Patients demonstrating pronounced alexithymia likely represent poor candidates for a referral to group treatment.

Perfectionism

Analyses of the NIMH TDCRP data by Blatt and colleagues provided strong support for the impact of a specific patient personality characteristic, perfectionism, on the treatment course and outcome (Blatt et al., 1995; Blatt,

Zuroff, Bondi, Sanislow, & Pilkonis, 1998; Zuroff et al., 2000). Patients involved in this controlled comparative trial of short-term treatments for major depression (i.e., cognitive–behavioral therapy, interpersonal therapy, imipramine plus clinical management, or placebo plus clinical management) completed the Dysfunctional Attitudes Scale (Weissman & Beck, 1978) at pre-treatment and at regular occasions during the course of and after treatment. The Dysfunctional Attitudes Scale assesses attitudes presumed to predispose an individual to depression. Factor analyses identified two principal dimensions to the Dysfunctional Attitudes Scale, labeled Need for Approval and Perfection-ism. The first factor taps into patients' dependence on others for self-esteem regulation; the second factor reflects a tendency to set inappropriately high expectations for self and to be self-punitive when these are not met. High pretreatment scores on the Need for Approval scale appeared to facilitate ben-efit from treatment, but these relationships did not attain statistical significance. In contrast, consistent effects involving Perfectionism were identified across all treatment conditions. Specifically, patients' pretreatment Perfectionism predicted poorer outcome at therapy termination (after 16 weeks of treatment) as well as at follow-up assessments 18 months after termination (Blatt et al., 1995; Blatt et al., 1998). Perfectionism was associated with a decrease in the rate of therapeutic progress in the latter stages of therapy, beginning between the 9th and the 12th therapy session (Blatt et al., 1998), suggesting that the perfectionistic patient's dissatisfaction becomes more of an obstacle later in the course of therapy. Zuroff et al. (2000) provided evidence that the impact of perfectionism on treatment benefit was mediated by the patient's contribution or lack thereof to the therapeutic alliance, again, especially in the latter half of the treatment. The more perfectionistic patients also reported greater impairment in their network of social supports outside of treatment; greater impairment in the social network was also found to mediate the relationship between perfectionism and treatment outcome (Shahar, Blatt, Zuroff, & Pilkonis, 2003). In short, perfectionistic patients demonstrate problems developing and maintaining sustaining interpersonal relationships both within and outside of the therapy process.

This research on the impact of perfectionism is notable because the mechanisms associated with the trait's inverse effect on treatment benefit have also been identified. A high level of perfectionism may be a contraindication to the offering of a therapy contract to the patient, and this risk might be further heightened if the treatment in question is group therapy (Zettle, Haflich, & Reynolds, 1992). The probability of the therapy being successful is increased if the therapist attends to the development of a strong therapeutic alliance with the perfectionistic patient and encourages understanding of "how their negative anticipation of self and others impairs their capacity to establish pro-ductive and satisfying interpersonal relationships" (Blatt, Shahar, & Zuroff,

2002, p. 328). In group therapy, feedback on this impact of perfectionism by fellow group members could represent an important pathway for change, but the evidence suggests that this might represent a high-risk treatment strategy for the perfectionistic patient. Studies regarding the impact of perfectionism as a patient characteristic in the context of group therapy interventions are clearly needed.

Reactance

The concept of *resistance* has had a long history in the literature on the clinical practice of psychotherapy. It has come to refer to transient episodes of patient defensiveness or avoidance in the course of therapy, often arising as a function of the emotional charge associated with certain issues being addressed. Confronting this situational or *state* manifestation of resistance—and dealing more directly with the avoided thoughts and feelings—is held to have value in the therapeutic process. This psychoanalytic meaning of resistance, however, is of no use in the planning of treatment, that is, when the clinician is considering tailoring the therapy approach to a particular patient.

Resistance can also refer to the behavioral style of a chronically defensive patient who seems incapable of working collaboratively and cooperatively with the therapist, for example, a perfectionistic patient may be regarded as highly resistant. In their review of therapy process research, Orlinsky et al. (2004) concluded that resistance to the processes of therapy, measured in a variety of ways, emerges as a strong predictor of poorer outcomes. In contrast, Orlinsky et al. (2004) identified *openness* in the sense of being nondefensive as a positive predictor of therapy benefit.

A related construct, originating from social psychology, is *psychological reactance* (Brehm & Brehm, 1981). Reactance refers to a cognitive–affective state prompted by the perception that there exists a threat to one's legitimate freedoms, "motivating the individual to restore the thwarted freedom" (Brehm & Brehm, 1981, p. 4). Once activated, reactance can be observed in the emergence of oppositional behavior, noncompliance, and rigidity. In terms of psychotherapy, reactance may be encountered when the therapist's suggestions or directives are perceived as threats to the patient's freedoms. Indeed, a firmly established aptitude–treatment interaction in psychotherapy research is that highly reactant patients tend to benefit more from therapies characterized as nondirective, whereas nonreactant patients tend to do better with more directive therapeutic procedures (Beutler, Moleiro, & Talebi, 2002). In other words, "the effectiveness of therapist directives and guidance are considered to be directly dependent on the patient's proneness to resist external control" (Beutler, Moleiro, & Talebi, 2002, p. 131). In turn, the degree of structure and directiveness implemented in the therapy approach should be accommodated to fit with the patient's level of reactance. It should be noted that there is also evidence that the reactant patient is more likely to respond in a positive direction to the therapist's use of *paradoxical interventions*, attempts to induce change by discouraging it (Beutler, Moleiro, & Talebi, 2002, p. 138), for example, the therapist "warns" the patient against engaging in rapid change (Shoham-Salomon, Avner, & Neeman, 1989). In the group therapy context, the therapist would need to be cognizant of the *reactance potential* of each of the members and adjust intervention strategies accordingly. It may be advantageous to consider composing groups to reflect a degree of homogeneity on the reactance dimension, that is, a nondirective approach, or paradoxical interventions, would be used with a group composed of more reactant patients and a more directive, structured group offered to members with equivalently low levels of reactance (see also Beutler, Machado, Engle, & Mohr, 1993; Horvath & Goheen, 1990).

Coping Style

Coping style is a broad term that refers to the characteristic habitual patterns of behavior an individual will demonstrate when confronting novel or problematic situations and needing to manage anxiety (Beutler, Harwood, et al., 2002). In response to stressful circumstances, then, a person will demonstrate the same cluster of related behaviors, a particular *style* of reacting to situational demands. Two contrasting coping styles are addressed in the research literature. The *internalizing* coping style reflects an orientation toward inhibition of behavior in response to stress and is characterized by withdrawal, suppression, interpersonal restraint, and a tendency toward self-blame and self-criticism. In contrast, the *externalizing* coping style reflects an orientation toward excitation and expression and is characterized by impulsivity, expressiveness, external attributions of cause, a tendency to blame others, and an action or task orientation. Although the majority of people can be assigned to one of these two coping styles, some may show different patterns of coping in response to different forms of stressor (e.g., interpersonal vs. impersonal). Studies examining patient coping styles as predictors of outcome have used standardized measures of personality like the Minnesota Multiphasic Personality Inventory or the California Personality Inventory, with the prototype coping styles being reflected by scores on distinct subscale combinations (e.g., Beutler et al., 1991).

Beutler et al. (2000) examined coping style as a prognostic indicator and reported that externalizing patients tend to show poorer outcomes than internalizing patients across a range of therapy interventions and presenting problems. The majority of studies addressing coping style have examined the variable as a potential moderator of treatment effects, that is, considering the patient's coping style as a *matching* dimension for different therapy approaches. The primary finding of this research is that therapies characterized by an orientation to insight and interpersonal dynamics are most effective for patients with an internalizing coping style, and therapies characterized by an orientation to skills training and a symptoms focus are most effective for patients with an externalizing coping style (e.g., Beutler et al., 1991; Beutler & Mitchell, 1981). Beutler et al. (1993) reported on follow-up findings of an earlier study matching patient coping style to form of therapy (group cognitive therapy, focused experiential therapy, supportive self-directed therapy; Beutler et al., 1991) and indicated that patients who were well matched to the treatment approach continued to demonstrate improvement, whereas patients who were mismatched demonstrated deterioration and, in some cases, problem relapse. In a study that drew on data collected in the NIMH TDCRP (Barber & Muenz, 1996), patients who relied on behavioral avoidance (an externalizing tactic) tended to show better improvement in cognitive therapy, whereas patients who relied on obsessive rumination (an internalizing strategy) tended to respond better to interpersonal therapy. Similar findings have been reported in the literature on treatments for alcoholism (Cooney, Kadden, Litt, & Getter, 1991; Kadden, Cooney, Getter, & Litt, 1989; Longabaugh et al., 1994). The coping style research has provided solid evidence for a reliable aptitude–treatment interaction.

In an interesting contribution to this literature, Tasca, Russell, and Busby (1994) allowed patients in a day treatment program to choose between a process-oriented psychodynamic group or a structured experiential activity-oriented group. These investigators used a self-report measure of defense mechanisms (Ihilevich & Gleser, 1986) to assess externalizing and internalizing styles. Patients tended to choose the group approach that was inconsistent with their defensive style: Patients with an externalizing style (turning anger against others and projection) selected the verbal, process-oriented therapy, whereas patients with an internalizing style (repression/denial and intellectualization) selected the structured activities-based therapy. In effect, this finding is in direct contrast to the aptitude–treatment interaction findings with coping style discussed previously. The authors argued that allowing patients to engage in their "typical resistances" early in therapy may allow for the development of a therapeutic alliance and, subsequently, more effective confrontation, leading to an eventual positive outcome. Outcomes were not evaluated in this study, however, so this alternative perspective has yet to be evaluated.

In terms of implementing a short-term group intervention, the findings regarding coping style suggest making an effort to compose groups homogenous for internalizing or externalizing patients. Patients who manifest patterns of emotional avoidance and self-criticism would benefit from a process-oriented group focused on interpersonal interaction and the development of insight. Patients manifesting an externalizing and task orientation would benefit from a group aimed at skills development, problem solving, and symptom resolution.

The Five-Factor Model of Personality

Identifying the requisite traits needed to comprehensively represent adult personality has occupied psychological researchers for many decades. A number of individual personality traits have been addressed in previous sections. In general, each of these individual traits reflects identifiable ways of thinking about problems or reacting to situational demands. An important development to emerge from the work of personality researchers has been the introduction of a higher order five-factor model of personality (Costa & McCrae, 1992a; Digman, 1990; John, 1990; McCrae & John, 1992). As the name suggests, the model posits that five dimensions (with each having a number of associated facets) are sufficient to capture all possible variations of personality. The Big Five dimensions include the following:

- *Neuroticism* represents the tendency to experience psychological distress and negative moods characterized by fear, sadness, or guilt.
- *Extraversion* reflects a capacity for sociability and assertiveness, excitement seeking, and a tendency to experience positive moods.
- *Openness* to experience refers to being imaginative, sensitive to art and aesthetics, intellectually curious and flexible, and having a rich and differentiated emotional life.
- *Agreeableness* reflects a tendency to be trusting, altruistic, and cooperative with others.
- *Conscientiousness* refers to a tendency to be well-organized, scrupulous, and disciplined.

The most popular measure of the five-factor model is the NEO Personality Inventory and its short-form version, the NEO Five-Factor Inventory (Costa & McCrae, 1992b). Research on the Big Five has demonstrated that the model is representative of constructs from a range of theoretical perspectives (e.g., McCrae & Costa, 1989), generalizes across different cultures (Paunonen, Jackson, Trzebinski, & Fosterling, 1992), is representative of genetically heritable traits (Bergeman et al., 1993), and is capable of predicting both physical (Russo et al., 1997) and mental health (Anderson & McClean, 1997; Scott, Williams, Brittlebank, & Ferrier, 1995). Studies have also demonstrated the temporal stability of these personality dimensions among adults (Costa & McCrae, 1994). Although derived using nonclinical populations, the five-factor model has also been replicated in psychiatric samples (Bagby et al., 1999; Reynolds & Clark, 2001).

There is speculation in the clinical literature about how different therapy approaches might be matched to patients based on their five-factor profile (e.g., Anderson, 1998; Miller, 1991). Bagby and Quilty (2006) summarized recommendations for interventions according to each of the five factors.

Despite these compelling speculations, there have been only a few studies examining the association between the five factors and treatment outcome; moreover, the focus in this research has often been on pharmacotherapy as the treatment intervention (Bagby, Joffe, Parker, Kalemba, & Harkness, 1995; Petersen, Bottonari, Alpert, Fava, & Nierenberg, 2001). Very few studies have examined the use of the model in predicting psychotherapy outcome (Bagby & Quilty, 2006). Associations between neuroticism and treatment outcome are inconsistent, with some studies suggesting that higher levels are predictive of a less favorable outcome (Miller, 1991; Ogrodniczuk, Piper, Joyce, McCallum, & Rosie, 2003) and others failing to demonstrate any relationship (Bagby et al., 1995). Bagby and Quilty (2006) described recent findings suggesting that higher neuroticism may be associated with a preferential response to antidepressant medication rather than psychotherapy for depressed patients. The evidence supports that higher levels of extraversion are associated with a more favorable outcome for treatment in general (Anderson, 1998; Ogrodniczuk, Piper, Joyce, McCallum, & Rosie, 2003). There is little evidence to indicate an association between openness and treatment outcome (but see Ogrodniczuk, Piper, Joyce, McCallum, & Rosie, 2003). Agreeableness has been associated with more favorable outcomes across a range of treatments (Miller, 1991); in our own work, this dimension was found to be differentially associated with treatment benefit for interpretive short-term group therapy but unrelated to the outcome of supportive short-term group therapy (Ogrodniczuk, Piper, Joyce, McCallum, & Rosie, 2003). The findings for conscientiousness have been mixed (Bagby & Quilty, 2006), with a few studies demonstrating a relationship to favorable outcomes (Anderson & McClean, 1997; Ogrodniczuk, Piper, Joyce, McCallum, & Rosie, 2003).

A recent study (Quilty et al., 2008) involved a sample of depressed patients randomly assigned to one of two antidepressant treatments and nonrandomly assigned to one of three forms of (individual) psychotherapy (supportive, cognitive–behavioral, or psychodynamic). Patients who responded to both medication and psychotherapy were characterized by lower neuroticism and higher extraversion and openness scores compared with nonresponders. Regression analyses, which controlled for influence shared by the five personality dimensions, identified neuroticism and conscientiousness as being significantly and specifically associated with response to treatment. Interestingly, these researchers also identified interactions among the five factors (e.g., Neuroticism × Extraversion or Extraversion × Conscientiousness) that accounted for larger proportions of outcome variation. Clearly, research has demonstrated that the five-factor model has the potential to inform patient–treatment matching decisions, but further studies may be required to clarify specific interactions between personality traits or facets and intervention strategies. In the context of a short-term group therapy for CG patients, low neuroticism and higher extraversion, conscientiousness, and openness would be expected to be predictive of positive process and benefit; indeed, this is what was found in our own use of the NEO Five-Factor Inventory (Ogrodniczuk, Piper, Joyce, McCallum, & Rosie, 2003).

INTERPERSONAL DIMENSIONS

In general terms, the patient's interpersonal characteristics reflect the likelihood of the patient making good use of the relationship opportunity afforded by the therapist or the opportunities afforded by the group. Patients with a more mature quality of object relations (QOR) or with a more secure attachment style tend to have fewer issues with the establishment of a collaborative relationship with the therapist and are thus more likely to engage readily in the kind of work required by the therapy approach being implemented. As with the attitudinal and personality characteristics discussed in the last section, the interpersonal dimensions of QOR and attachment have been found to function as direct predictors or moderators of therapy process or improvement or to interact with aspects of the therapy approach and point to mediators of change.

Quality of Object Relations

Establishing a sense of the patient's capacity for interpersonal relatedness (Clementel-Jones, Malan, & Trauer, 1990; Moras & Strupp, 1982) is regarded as a critical therapist task during the preparation of the patient for psychotherapy or during the early stage of treatment. To this end, the therapist can address the patient's interpersonal history (e.g., significant losses, involvements and separations), the patient's interpersonal functioning in current close relationships, or the patient's characteristic way of viewing relationships. The last perspective addresses the patient's perceptions of relationships, beliefs regarding relationship issues such as trust and reciprocity, and wishes and anxieties about the costs and provisions of relationships, all subsumed under the construct of QOR, Generally speaking, object relations refer to the conscious and unconscious mental representations of past interpersonal interactions developed through the processes of internalization over the course of the individual's interpersonal history. These representations of self and others include cognitive, affective, and experiential components and function to regulate and direct current interpersonal behavior (Blatt, Wiseman, Prince-Gibson, & Gatt, 1991).

A variety of measures and methods of assessment have been developed to evaluate patients' QOR in clinical research: the Object Relations Inventory of Blatt et al. (1991), the Reflective Functioning Scale of Fonagy and Target (1997), the Core Conflictual Relationship Theme of Luborsky and Crits-Cristoph (1997), and the Social Cognition and Object Relations Scale of Westen (1991). For a review of these measures, see Huprich and Greenberg (2003). Our research group developed the Quality of Object Relations Scale, and the construct has had a central role in all our treatment effectiveness studies.

We define QOR as a person's internal enduring tendency to establish certain types of relationships (Azim, Piper, Segal, Nixon, & Duncan, 1991). These relationship patterns range along a spectrum from primitive (character-ized by destructiveness and instability) to mature (characterized by reciprocity and mutuality). At the primitive level, the person reacts to perceived separation or loss of the object, or disapproval or rejection by the object, with intense anxiety and affect; there is inordinate dependence on the lost object, who provides a sense of identity for the person. In contrast, at the mature level, the person enjoys equitable relationships characterized by love, tenderness, and concern for objects of both sexes, and there is a capacity to mourn and tolerate unobtainable relationships. The QOR construct thus refers to the recurring pattern of relationships over the individual's life span, rather than to relationships during any one period (e.g., recent interpersonal functioning). Although for measurement purposes we focus on external relationships, we assume that these reflect the internal object representations and conflictual components of the patient's internal world. Again, what the QOR assessment attempts to capture is the patient's predominant pattern of relationships over the course of his or her life span.

The reliability and construct validity of the QOR variable is detailed in Piper and Duncan (1999). In general, QOR has been found to be independent of demographic and historic characteristics of the patient. The construct has also not been found to be related to *Diagnostic and Statistical Manual of Mental Disorders* (4th ed., text revision; *DSM–IV–TR*; American Psychiatric Associ-ation, 2000) Axis I diagnoses. As one would expect, patients with lower QOR scores (i.e., less than 4.5) tend to show more symptomatic disturbance and are more likely to have a *DSM–IV–TR* Axis II diagnosis than patients with higher QOR scores (i.e., equal to or greater than 4.5), although this over-lap is not considerable. The QOR variable has emerged as a strong direct pre-dictor and moderator of therapy process and outcome in time-limited forms of dynamically oriented psychotherapy.

In general, across a number of studies (Piper, Azim, McCallum, & Joyce, 1990; Piper, Azim, Joyce, McCallum, et al., 1991; Piper, de Carufel, & Szkrumelak, 1985; Piper et al., 1998); including our comparative trial, (Piper, McCallum, et al., 2001), high QOR has been shown to function as an important patient–treatment match for interpretive or expressive forms of psychotherapy in either the individual or group format. The high-QOR patient's history of meaningful give-and-take relationships appears to allow for the establishment of a strong collaboration with the therapist and greater readiness to make use of the interpretive approach. High-QOR patients also appear to have greater tolerance for the therapist's use of transference interpretations (Piper, Azim, Joyce, & McCallum, 1991). We engaged in a more detailed examination of the association of high QOR and benefit in the interpretive form of short-term group therapy for CG, to identify the mechanism through which this relationship might emerge (Piper, Ogrodniczuk, McCallum, Joyce, & Rosie, 2003). The focus in this analysis was the experience and expression of positive and negative affect during group sessions, as rated by the patient, the other members, and the therapist. High-QOR patients tended to demonstrate a greater balance of positive and negative affect expression, as reported by their peers in the group and the therapist, and a balanced expression of affect was associated with greater improvement on grief symptoms. The finding suggests that a favorable outcome in the therapy is facilitated by a greater tolerance and acceptance of the expression of conflicting feelings regarding the lost relationship. The high-QOR patient was more likely to demonstrate this in the therapy process. This finding corresponded well to the view expressed in the literature on grief that better adaptation following the loss of a significant other is associated with a greater tolerance of the ambivalent feelings involved in the grief process (Bonanno & Kaltman, 1999).

Though the evidence is less strong, there is reason to believe that low-QOR patients stand to gain more from a therapy approach oriented to the provision of support, problem solving, and advice regarding current circumstances. The treatment itself can provide the low-QOR patient with the experience of a clearly bounded and gratifying relationship, countering a lifelong experience of depriving or abusive relationships (see also Høglend, 1993a, 1993b; Horowitz, Marmar, Weiss, DeWitt, & Rosenbaum, 1984). Even within a supportive treatment, however, the low-QOR patient's relationship with the therapist can have a bearing on the success of the therapy. In the comparative trial of short-term group therapies for CG, we examined patients' feelings of dissatisfaction with their therapist. Patients in interpretive therapy provided higher ratings of dissatisfaction with their therapist than those in supportive therapy, in line with the more depriving and confrontative stance taken by the interpretive therapist. However, ratings of dissatisfaction were inversely predictive of outcome only for the supportive therapy approach, and the lower the patient's QOR, the stronger this relationship. The implication is that the low-QOR patient experienced negative feelings toward the therapist but suppressed these out of a concern about eliciting the therapist's rejection; at the time of the outcome assessment following the end of the group therapy, these feelings may have been expressed in terms of poorer outcomes (Ogrodniczuk, Joyce, & Piper, 2007). Low-QOR patients also apparently have less capacity to work with transference interpretations, indeed appearing to find this therapist technique at times injurious (Ogrodniczuk, Piper, Joyce, & McCallum, 1999; but see Høglend et al., 2006). Clearly, the evidence suggests that patients of low QOR may bring their maladaptive interpersonal style into the therapy process and, without sufficient efforts on the part of the therapist to address these patterns, be at increased risk of problematic outcomes.

Clinically, then, a formulation of the patient's internal object relations can reflect his or her capacity to form a collaborative working relationship with the therapist. A predisposition to establish a relatively trusting give-and-take relationship with an authority figure is an important indicator for a positive therapy process, an effective termination, and treatment benefit. The object relations formulation can provide an estimate of the patient's capacity to tolerate frustrations in the therapy relationship and facilitate predictions regarding the transference reactions that are likely to emerge (Joyce & McCallum, 2004). The more mature the patient's QOR, the more likely an expressive therapy approach can be undertaken. The more primitive the patient's QOR, the more problematic the patient's representations of interpersonal relatedness and capacity for self-regulation. With these patients, a supportive and open-ended therapy approach is more feasible, but the evidence suggests that the therapeutic collaboration can still be fraught with pitfalls given these patients' problematic representations of relationships. Whether engaging with the low-QOR patient in an interpretive or supportive approach, it is critical that the therapist monitor the patient's experience of the relationship and address negative feelings as they arise. The patient's QOR should thus be considered a primary determinant of the approach to therapy and the therapist's strategy within sessions.

Evidence from a recent study of short-term group therapy for CG indicates that the composition of the group may directly influence the benefit achieved by the members, including those of a low QOR. In our comparative trial, we previously reported aptitude–treatment interaction findings regarding QOR, that is, low-QOR patients showed greater benefit in the supportive short-term group treatment, whereas high-QOR patients demonstrated more improvement in the interpretive short-term group for general and grief symptoms (Piper, McCallum, et al., 2001). A study of groups composed to optimize this interaction, that is, homogenous high-QOR membership in an interpretive group, homogenous low-QOR membership in a supportive group, relative to the two approaches with a heterogenous membership, was recently published (Piper et al., 2007). The test of group homogeneity versus heterogeneity proved to be nonsignificant, but a composition effect was identified: The greater the proportion of more mature QOR patients in the group, the better the outcome for all patients in the group, regardless of the form of therapy or the individual patient's QOR score. This group-level effect suggests that the more mature patients engage in the therapeutic relationship opportunities offered by the group, "pulling" the less mature patients into a working group process and facilitating improvement for the group as a whole. Clinically, this finding suggests that the group clinician should seek to have a critical mass of high-QOR patients among the membership, either when establishing a new group or when replacing departing members. Such a group composition, particularly if an expressive or interpretive technical strategy is planned, can ensure that the low-QOR patients have a model of positive therapy process to follow, increasing the likelihood of treatment benefit for these patients.

Attachment Style

The individual's patterning of attachment behaviors, or attachment style, is similar to the QOR construct in being based on the development of mental representations of self and other catalyzed through early transactions with caregivers. Specifically, attachment style reflects the individual's disposition to seek proximity to significant others for security and protection in times of stress, initially established through the interaction between the developing child and the early caregiver, usually the mother. Through development, attachment reflects individuals' "comfort and confidence in close relationships, their fear of rejection and yearning for intimacy, and their preference for self-sufficiency or interpersonal distance" (Meyer & Pilkonis, 2002, p. 367). A secure attachment style develops from ongoing engagement with a caregiver who is attentive and responsive to the needs of the developing child. The secure individual develops with a representation of others as trustworthy and of self as worthy of others' responsiveness. Insecure attachment, or an anxious attachment style, is manifested in different behavioral patterns, for example, excessive dependence or defensive separation that develop in response to absent or inconsistent responsiveness on the part of the attachment figure. Following the seminal theoretical work by Bowlby (1969, 1980, 1988) and empirical studies of mother–infant attachments by Ainsworth (1964), the attachment model has been used as the underpinning for countless studies of adult behavior. In the area of psychotherapy research, a clear parallel has been drawn between the infant's attachment behaviors toward a caregiver during times of stress and the patient in distress seeking help in the therapeutic relationship.

According to Bowlby (1988), four attachment styles in infants or young children can be identified: secure, anxious-ambivalent, anxious-avoidant, and disorganized. Corresponding caregiver behaviors have also been identified, ranging from optimally responsive through inconsistent to rejecting or dismissing. Researchers of adult behavior, particularly in clinical settings, have identified variants of the attachment behavior observed in children, such as a *dismissing* form of anxious-avoidant attachment and a *preoccupied* form of anxious-ambivalent attachment.

Patient attachment styles have been associated with positive therapy process and beneficial outcome, but there have been inconsistent results across studies. These inconsistencies suggest that there may actually be interactions between the patient's attachment style and the particular treatment approach, but these have yet to be identified with certainty. Clearly, securely attached patients tend to engage in the therapy process more easily and to achieve greater benefit. Among a group of outpatients presenting with a diverse mix of *DSM–IV–TR* (American Psychiatric Association, 2000) Axis I disorders, those with a secure attachment style manifested less symptomatology at pretreatment and greater improvement after treatment (Meyer, Pilkonis, Proietti, Heape, & Egan, 2001). Securely attached patients have also been found to establish stronger alliances with the therapist (Satterfield & Lyddon, 1998) and to be able to do so in the earlier stages of therapy (Eames & Roth, 2000). In contrast, patients presenting with an anxious-avoidant attachment style tend to have the most problems establishing and maintaining a healthy alliance. Dozier (1990) reported that patients characterized by a dismissing attachment style are often resistant to treatment and have greater problems making use of the help offered by the therapist. Dismissing individuals often become disorganized when confronted with the emotional demands of the therapy process (Dozier, Lomax, & Tyrrell, 1996, cited in Clarkin & Levy, 2004). However, Eames and Roth (2000) reported that patients with dismissing or preoccupied attachment styles showed improvement in the quality of the therapeutic alliance as treatment progressed, suggesting that the therapy process was itself having a modifying impact on the patient's attachment behavior. Among nonpsychotic inpatients with severe personality disorder engaged in an intensive partial hospital treatment program, Fonagy and colleagues (1996) found that those classified as insecure-dismissive in their attachment behavior showed the best response to the intervention relative to other attachment subgroups. In terms of interpersonal functioning, then, these patients could be regarded as having the most to gain through the intensive treatment process.

Taken together, these findings generally suggest that patients who experience a high degree of anxiety about attachment relationships and who consequently have difficulty engaging in intimacy will also likely have problems establishing and making use of a healthy therapeutic alliance. These patients may require a higher degree of responsiveness on the part of the therapist. Research has indicated that variations in patient attachment style call for different responses from the therapist (Diamond et al., 1999). Hardy, Stiles,

Barkham, and Startup (1998) reported that therapists focused more on affect and relationship issues with patients characterized by a preoccupied attachment style but used a more cognitive strategy with those patients marked by a dismissive attachment style. At the same time, the evidence to date suggests that even problematic insecure attachment styles can be engaged in the therapy process over time to good results. As with the QOR construct, the more problematic the patient's attachment style, the more modifications will be required to the therapist's treatment approach to allow the patient to experience safety and trust in the relationship. In a long-term therapy, it may be possible as treatment goes on for the therapist to bring in certain types of interventions (e.g., comments regarding the transference) that earlier in the course of therapy would have proven too threatening to the patient. Knowledge of the patient's characteristic approach to attachment relationships can inform the therapist regarding the "best fit" treatment approach as well as sensitizing the clinician to changes in the patient's usual attachment style.

With regard to group treatment, and perhaps in contrast to the QOR variable, it is likely advisable to seek heterogeneity in the attachment styles of the membership. In our comparative trial of short-term group therapy for CG, the patients' level of attachment security was directly associated with treatment benefit after accounting for the initial level of grief symptoms and the type of group therapy received (Ogrodniczuk, Piper, McCallum, Joyce, & Rosie, 2002). Evidence for this relationship was also obtained from the independent sample obtained for the composition study (Joyce, Ogrodniczuk, Piper, & Sheptycki, 2010). The group interaction can demonstrate the differences in how the individual members approach the development of close interpersonal relationships, with feedback providing some balance to the more extreme positions assumed by members struggling with anxious attachment. A range of positions on the dimension of attachment security would ensure that the group interaction demonstrated diversity and energy, more so than would be the case if the membership reflected a primarily insecure form of attachment.

PATIENT DIAGNOSTIC CHARACTERISTICS

Diagnostic variables highlight the complexity of the problem presented by the patient coming for treatment. These dimensions may reflect the worrisome nature of the patient's symptoms or the severity of the patient's distress, the pervasiveness of the negative impact of the patient's illness, or the presence of additional disorders that also demand targeted treatment interventions. In effect, diagnostic considerations that go beyond the patient's presenting problem often indicate the need for a treatment plan of greater intensity (e.g., more frequent sessions or a longer treatment duration) or extensiveness (e.g., a "packaged" treatment involving a number of distinct and preferably complementary interventions).

Severity of Symptoms

Reviews of psychotherapy outcome research have consistently concluded that increasing severity of symptoms is associated with a poorer response to treatment (Garfield, 1994; Hoberman, Lewinsohn, & Tilson, 1988; Luborsky, Crits-Christoph, Mintz, & Auerbach, 1988). The most compelling evidence for this association came out of secondary analyses of the NIMH TDCRP dataset, that is, differential effects for the treatment condition variable only emerged for those patients presenting with depressive illnesses of greater severity. That is, among the less severely ill patients, the treatments were equivalent in effectiveness, but among the more severely ill patients, the medication with clinical management condition demonstrated greater effectiveness (Elkin et al., 1995). Similar findings from a study in the United Kingdom were reported by Shapiro and colleagues (Shapiro et al., 1994). Patients received either a cognitive–behavioral or psychodynamic interpersonal therapy of either 8- or 16-session durations. The two therapies were found to be equivalent in effectiveness across subgroups of varying severity of depression. Patients with more severe depression, however, demonstrated greater gains only in treatments of greater duration (16 session).

A related construct, though not to be considered as isomorphic to symptom severity, is the degree of subjective distress experienced by the patient. That is, certain patients may present with mild symptoms but a high level of subjective distress, whereas other patients presenting with profound symptoms may report little if any distress. As an internal state, the patient's level of distress is assumed to provide a degree of motivation for treatment; the greater the degree of felt distress, the greater the motivation to engage in treatment. This assumption is supported by evidence that psychotherapy has greater effectiveness with patients reporting moderate to high levels of subjective distress (Clarkin & Levy, 2004). Patients reporting the most severe subjective distress in the NIMH TDCRP demonstrated greater benefit in interpersonal therapy, whereas both interpersonal therapy and cognitive–behavioral therapy proved effective for those patients with mild to moderate distress (Elkin, Gibbons, Shea, & Shaw, 1996).

With regard to composing the membership for a short-term group therapy, the clinician would aim to select patients with moderate to high levels of subjective distress but levels of symptom severity that are commensurate with the bounded intensiveness of the treatment. That is, the patients should be strongly motivated to address their problem experience but not so ill that treatment benefit in the time available proves impossible.

Functional Impairment

A concept closely related to symptom severity or subjective distress is the degree of reduced or impaired functioning that is associated with development of the patient's illness. Commonly, severity and distress are assessed through patient self-report, whereas functional impairment is determined by ratings of external behavior, usually by a clinical assessor. Functional impairment can be observed in any of a number of domains, for example, work, home life, interpersonal relationships. More profound impairment usually implies dysfunction across multiple domains. Beutler, Harwood, and colleagues (2002) noted that a variety of patient characteristics can act in synergy to increase the level of the patient's functional impairment, for example, low QOR, previous psychiatric history, cognitive impairments. In general, the greater the degree of functional impairment, the worse the prognosis for the patient's illness and the greater the likelihood of poorer treatment outcomes. This relationship has been documented for a number of specific conditions (e.g., Beutler, Kim, Davison, Karno, & Fisher, 1996; Sotsky et al., 1991; see also Clarkin & Levy, 2004, p. 200; Beutler, Harwood, et al., 2002, pp. 150–159). Studies have indicated that patients of greater functional impairment may require more intensive treatments to demonstrate reasonable improvements. For example, Shapiro et al. (1994) reported that highly impaired patients, but not those with lower functional impairment, had a better response to 16 weeks of cognitive–behavioral or psychodynamic interpersonal therapy than to 8 weeks of either treatment.

There is also evidence that the specific domain of the patient's functional impairment can serve as an indicator for choosing the most appropriate therapy. Working with data gathered in the TDCRP, Sotsky and colleagues (1991) identified four specific indices of functional impairment that represented good treatment matches. Low functional impairment in social relationships was a predictor of greater benefit in interpersonal therapy. Less cognitive impairment predicted improvement in cognitive–behavioral therapy with antidepressant medication. Greater impairment at work predicted a good response to medication. Finally, higher severity of depression coupled with a more pervasive degree of functional impairment predicted the response to medication and to interpersonal therapy. In effect, the focus of the treatment is aligned with the patient's functional strength (e.g., low social dysfunction and interpersonal therapy) or weakness (e.g., impairment at work, or a more pervasive impairment and antidepressant treatment), and this alignment appears to promote effectiveness. Similarly, presentations of more profound illness involving a greater severity of symptoms and more pronounced functional impairment necessitate considerations of combined treatment (e.g., medications plus psychotherapy).

Comorbidity

Comorbidity refers to the presentation of multiple disorders, that is, usually involving two or more diagnoses. For example, the presentation of an anxiety disorder in the context of significant alcohol abuse would represent a comorbid presentation. The alcohol abuse disorder could be regarded as a form of functional impairment in the domain of self-care and would certainly require that the clinician develop a multidimensional strategy for the treatment plan. In outpatient or private practice settings where psychotherapy is offered, patients are more often comorbid in presentation than not. In the psychotherapy research literature, the construct of comorbidity commonly refers to the presence of a *DSM–IV–TR* (American Psychiatric Association, 2000) Axis II personality disorder in the context of the patient's presentation for treatment of a *DSM–IV–TR* Axis I clinical syndrome (e.g., an anxiety or mood disorder). Studies of the outcomes of therapy for patients with a major depressive disorder that have involved samples with and without comorbid personality disorder generally report poorer outcomes associated with the presence of any form of personality disorder (Burns & Nolen-Hoeksema, 1992; Diguer, Barber, & Luborsky, 1993; Hardy et al., 1995; Shea et al., 1990). Hardy and colleagues (1995) found that the presence of a Cluster C (anxious-fearful) personality disorder was inversely associated with outcome for the short-term psychodynamic interpersonal therapy condition in their trial but was unrelated to outcome for the cognitive–behavioral therapy. In addition to studies addressing the impact of having versus not having a personality disorder are those addressing the *loading* of personality pathology, that is, the number of personality disorders (Ogrodniczuk, Piper, Joyce, & McCallum, 2001b) or the severity of the personality disorder in association with the *DSM–IV–TR* (American Psychiatric Association, 2000) Axis I condition (e.g., a dependent personality disorder in the context of treatment for major depression; Beutler, Blatt, et al., 2006). Once again, these findings identify the negative impact of personality pathology on therapy outcome.

There are fewer studies addressing the impact of comorbid personality disorder in the treatment of anxiety or eating disorders, and those in the literature frequently involve small samples and anecdotal reportage (Clarkin & Levy, 2004). Nonetheless, the trend of the findings is the same: The presence of any personality disorder is associated with less benefit from therapy. The implication of this line of research is plain: It is critical that the therapist assess for the presence of clinical symptoms and personality disorder in the evaluation of the patient and plan treatment accordingly. As Clarkin and Levy suggested, "When an Axis II personality disorder is present, they should plan treatment for more modest gains, anticipate and address potential early patient dropout, and plan for disruptions in the treatment adherence and alliance" (p. 202). A longer treatment duration or the use of adjunctive treatments in addition to the planned psychotherapy is commonly considered when the patient's presentation includes the rigidities and maladaptive tendencies associated with comorbid personality disorder.

Chronic Pain

A relatively understudied construct associated with the diagnostic picture of the patient entering therapy is the severity of experience and interference with functioning determined by the patient's chronic pain symptoms. The presence of pain symptoms can intensify several aspects of a mood disorder; for example, greater pain has been associated with a greater number of depressive symptoms and more severe depression (von Korff & Simon, 1996). Further, as pain increases, patients struggling with depression confront greater functional limitation, a decreased quality of life, and poorer work functioning (Bair, Robinson, Katon, & Kroneke, 2003). It appears more than reasonable, then, to expect that pain symptoms may interfere with the therapeutic management of depressive illness and other psychiatric conditions. At present, however, few studies have been conducted to evaluate whether and how pain might reduce response to treatments for depression and other conditions. Bair and colleagues considered the impact of pain on the treatment of patients with major depression, dysthymia, and subsyndromal depression with antidepressant medication. Greater pain at baseline was associated with a poorer response to medication after 3 months of treatment. Karp and colleagues (2005) reported that higher pain at baseline was associated with a longer time to remission among patients with major depression who received a combined treatment (imipramine and interpersonal therapy).

Neither of these previous studies considered the impact of pain on the outcome of group psychotherapy, nor have these studies considered possible differential effects of pain on the outcomes of therapies with different intervention strategies. We considered the impact of pain symptoms on outcome for patients in our comparative trial of interpretive and supportive short-term group therapies for CG (Ogrodniczuk, Piper, & Joyce, 2008b). The patients in the sample were those who were comorbid for CG and major depression (44.9% of the 107 treatment completers). Roughly three quarters of these patients were also receiving antidepressant medication. More than half (58%) of the patients reported high levels of bodily pain. Greater pain at pretreatment was inversely associated with improvement on depression, general symptom distress, and social functioning, and these relationships were identified after accounting for type of group therapy received, use of antidepressants, and the patient's level of alexithymia (to account for the possible confounding of alexithymia with symptoms of both pain and depression). Pain accounted for up to 20% of the variation in outcomes, a substantial proportion for a single predictor in psychotherapy outcomes research. The findings were consistent with the previous studies in the literature (Bair et al., 2003; Karp et al., 2005) and could be considered even more robust given our accounting for differences in treatment regimen and alexithymia. These findings suggest that the presence of pain symptoms is a contributing factor to greater disability or functional impairment and therefore must be considered in the prognosis for treatment or in the treatment plan itself (i.e., more intensive or extensive therapy). Alternately, adjunctive pain treatment might need to be considered when evaluating a patient's appropriateness for psychotherapy. Consideration of patients' pain symptoms in the composing of a therapy group may also be critical. It is likely important that a patient dealing with chronic pain issues not be alone in dealing with same among the members of the group; the pain experience itself can be quite isolating, and these patients can benefit from the support of the group. Including a number of members with pain issues in the composition of the group (or composing a group to address chronic pain issues) may represent an appropriate strategy.

CONCLUSION

A clinician engaged in the assessment of a patient for psychotherapy, including forms of short-term group therapy, must evaluate a number of dimensions to determine that patient's appropriateness for the planned treatment. A substantial number of patient characteristics have been empirically studied, and evidence has been obtained that many function as direct predictors of therapy outcome and as moderators of the patient's response to certain intervention strategies and approaches or are even associated with certain change processes (mediators) that occur during the therapy experience. This is highly useful information for the clinician and should not be discounted when engaged in assessment of patients for psychotherapy.

Even so, the study of patient characteristics is still very much in its infancy. Simple relationships between certain patient variables and indices of therapy process and outcome may be modified when additional patient characteristics are addressed in a multivariate perspective; at present, the field offers very little information on how patient characteristics might function in an interdependent or even synergistic fashion (but see Beutler et al., 2000). Similarly, identification of important interactions between patient and treatment dimensions that illuminate the nature of change processes occurring during the therapy interaction has to date occurred only infrequently. Studies addressing these issues are still urgently needed and, indeed, are most likely to have an impact on clinical practice and psychologists' understanding of how psychotherapy brings about change in their patients.

In this chapter, the empirical literature regarding an admittedly selective set of patient characteristics was reviewed. Attitudinal and personality variables should be assessed to determine the patient's motivation for treatment and the "fit" between the patient's usual style of thinking or coping with problems and the therapy approach being considered. Measures of interpersonal relatedness also have a bearing on the consideration of a patient–treatment fit but more importantly reflect the degree to which the patient is likely to engage in the process and make good use of the opportunity provided by the therapist and therapy. Finally, diagnostic variables might reflect red flags about the limitations of a planned therapy approach for certain patients with problems of greater severity, negative functional impact, or complexity and augur the importance of greater intensity or extensiveness of the treatment plan.

5

EFFECTS OF PROCESS VARIABLES ON THERAPEUTIC OUTCOME

In Chapters 3 and 4 of this volume, we provide evidence that group therapy for complicated grief (CG) works and that for certain types of patients, we can expect better or worse outcomes. However, as important as these findings are, they tell us little of how group therapy for CG actually works. What actually goes on in these groups that facilitates improvement? Only by carefully examining the inner working of these groups (i.e., the group process) can we begin to answer this question. In general, group process refers to what happens in the group. As Corey and Corey (2002) described, group process

> pertains to dynamics such as the norms that govern the group, the level of cohesion among group members, how trust is generated, how resistance is manifested, how conflict emerges and is dealt with, the forces that bring about healing, intermember reactions, and the various stages in a group's development. (p. 7)

Group process can thus include dimensions that are observable (e.g., expressed affect, nonverbal behavior, or the quality of interpersonal interactions) as well as dimensions that must be inferred (e.g., members' experiences of therapist empathy or the level of group cohesion). These various group processes serve both adaptive, work-oriented ends, or defensive, work-avoidant, restrictive ends (Bernard et al., 2008). Group processes reflect the mechanisms through which therapeutic change occurs.

As Beck and Lewis (2000) described,

> Process research on group psychotherapy is the study of the group-as-a-whole system and changes in its development, the interactions within the patient and therapist subsystems, the patient and patient (dyadic or subgroup) subsystems, the therapist and therapist subsystem if there are coleaders, and the way each of the subsystems interacts with and is influenced by the group as a whole. The goal of process research is to identify the change processes in the interactions within and between these systems. (p. 8)

The complexity of group process is easily appreciated as one attempts to consider the dynamic flow of individual, dyadic, subgroup, and group-as-a-whole phenomena and how these synergistically affect members of the group. Because group process is so complex, the task of comprehensively understanding the variables that determine how therapeutic change occurs is difficult. Despite the challenges of this type of research, it is necessary to develop insight into how group therapy works. Although authors have been championing the need for group process research for decades, relatively few have attempted to engage in such research.

As noted by Burlingame, MacKenzie, and Strauss (2004) in their chapter on group therapy in the *Handbook of Psychotherapy and Behavioral Change*, our clinical research group is among the few that have systematically engaged in the study of group process. This has occurred in the context of trying to understand the mechanisms of change of group therapy for CG. Our studies have focused on a variety of group process variables, which can be generally categorized into (a) relationship factors and (b) working factors. In the remainder of this chapter, we provide a brief description of our work on these two types of group process factors.

RELATIONSHIP FACTORS

In his effort to understand the social climate and characteristics of growth-promoting environments, Moos (1984) identified relationship factors as among the most critical. A comprehensive understanding of relationships within a group therapy setting is made difficult by the presence of multiple types of relationships. Relationships in a group can be formed between members (member–member), between a member and the group leader (member–leader), and between a member and the group as a whole (member–group). As Johnson et al. (2006) described, the group environment is a representation of the outside environment for each of the individual members, all of whom have dyadic interpersonal relationships with various individuals in their lives, relationships with influential figures like bosses or parents, and relationships with certain groups such as their family or work group. However, the relationships within a group therapy setting are constructed to provide greater safety and support. The supportive relationships that are created and maintained by group therapy members working together toward similar goals can have substantial influence on their ability to resolve the problems that brought them to therapy. The relationship factors that our research has focused on are consistent with those that other authors have described as representing a core set of group therapeutic relationship constructs (Johnson, Burlingame, Olsen, Davies, & Gleave, 2005). These include cohesion and the therapeutic alliance.

The construct of cohesion has been highlighted as one of the most important therapeutic factors in group therapy (I. D. Yalom & Leszcz, 2005). Cohesion represents a complex construct that encompasses not only the patient's relationship (or bond) with the therapist but additionally the patient's relationships (or bonds) with the other patients and the patient's relationship (or bond) to the group as a whole (Burlingame, Fuhriman, & Johnson, 2002; Piper, Marrache, Lacroix, Richardsen, & Jones, 1983). According to I. D. Yalom and Leszcz (2005), cohesion is a necessary condition for meaningful work and change to occur in group therapy. Tschuschke and Dies (1994) reported that cohesion to the other patients in the group is directly associated with more meaningful self-disclosures, which in turn facilitate more frequent and intense feedback from fellow patients. Cohesion is of particular significance in short-term therapy groups as there is limited time for the creation of a safe working environment. Therefore, it is critical for the therapist in short-term groups to understand the concept of cohesion and how to rapidly facilitate its development within sessions (Budman, Simeone, Reilly, & Demby, 1994). An early development of cohesion may also lead to greater ability to tolerate the negative emotion and stress associated with the working stage of short-term group therapy (MacKenzie, 1994). In general, the suggestion is that cohesion, a network of affective bonds, serves as a base for therapeutic "work" in the group process.

The therapeutic alliance is a concept of central importance in the field of psychotherapy, particularly in individual therapy. It has frequently been the focus of clinical, theoretical, and research literature. In general, the alliance can be defined as the collaborative working relationship between the patient and the therapist. Alternatively, agreement between the patient and therapist on the patient's goals, his or her tasks, and a positive emotional bond between the patient and therapist represent generic components of the alliance. Over the years, several different terms have been used to refer to this relationship. These include *ego alliance* (Sterba, 1934), *therapeutic alliance* (Zetzel, 1956), *working alliance* (Greenson, 1965), and *helping alliance* (Luborsky, 1976). Authors have consistently regarded a strong alliance as a desirable condition of therapy.

Healing power has been attributed to the alliance itself and to its ability to facilitate therapeutic effects of therapist technique.

The definitions of *cohesion* and *alliance* may overlap in the group therapy context. Indeed, studies have provided evidence that the two constructs are significantly correlated, suggesting that they reflect similar phenomena (e.g., Budman et al., 1989; Gillaspy, Wright, Campbell, Stokes, & Adinoff, 2002). Analyses in the Gillaspy et al. (2002) study, however, suggested that the bonds between patients play a greater role in cohesion and the bond between the individual patient and therapist plays a greater role in the alliance.

It is an issue of theoretical and clinical interest whether the alliance, elements of cohesion, or both are associated with benefit in group therapy. Marziali, Munroe-Blum, and McCleary (1997) evaluated the impact of a short-term group treatment that adopted the techniques of interpersonal therapy (Klerman, Weissman, Rounsaville, & Chevron, 1984) for patients with borderline personality disorder (Marziali & Munroe-Blum, 1994). They reported that the alliance was related to the outcome of treatment and also that it was a stronger predictor of outcome than measures of cohesion. These findings were, however, weakened by a small sample and the high level of patient dropout in the trial. We were interested in whether Marziali et al.'s findings could be cross-validated in a similar brief group approach but involving a different clinical sample (i.e., outpatients presenting with CG).

For our study (Joyce, Piper, & Ogrodniczuk, 2007), which used data from our comparative trial of interpretive and supportive forms of group therapy for CG, we used measures that addressed cohesion and the alliance as distinct variables. The cohesion measures assessed important elements of the construct (i.e., the quality of the patient's relationship to the group as a whole [commitment] and the quality of the relationships with the therapist and the other members [compatibility]) from the perspectives of each group member and the therapist. The alliance measure assessed the degree of collaboration in the patient–therapist working relationship, again from the perspectives of each patient and the therapist. Few studies have systematically examined the relationships between cohesion and alliance and their relative contributions to group outcome. Our study is the only one to do so in group therapy for CG patients.

In terms of simple relations, the alliance variables were found to be more consistently associated with outcome than the cohesion indices. Moderate associations between the patient-rated alliance and each of the outcome factors were found, indicating that a stronger alliance was associated with greater improvement. Only a single cohesion variable evidenced a clear association with improvement. The therapist's perceptions of the patient's "fit" in the group had a significant simple relationship with improvement in general symptoms. Surprisingly, measures of cohesion based on the patient's own ratings (group commitment, compatibility with the other members and with the therapist) did not show significant simple associations with improvement. It is possible that our time-limited groups did not allow for the patient's experience of the group's emerging cohesiveness to develop sufficiently to function as a significant determinant of treatment benefit. The members of these groups were all dealing with the experience of CG. Commonly, a high level of sharing and a sense of universality surface very rapidly in these groups—the members can feel connected quite quickly. However, this intensity of connection may be quite distinct from the patient's impression of the collection of people having developed "groupness," or cohesion at the level of the group as a whole. In later sessions of a long-term group in which there has been greater opportunity for such development, these variables might indeed evidence stronger relationships with outcome.

We also examined the strength of the alliance and cohesion variables as joint predictors of group outcome. The patient-rated alliance proved to be significantly and directly associated with improvement on all three outcome factors over and above the effects of the therapist-rated alliance and cohesion variables as competing predictors. Two cohesion variables, the other members' and the therapist's ratings of the patient's compatibility, emerged as significant predictors of improvement in general or grief symptoms, respectively. The findings suggest that the patient's perceptions of the quality of his or her collaboration with the therapist and the view of others (other members, therapist) regarding the patient's compatibility or fit in the group are important elements independently associated with improvement.

In a separate study (McCallum, Piper, Ogrodniczuk, & Joyce, 2002), we found that the therapist's ratings of cohesion to the patient were also associated with dropping out of group therapy for CG. The therapist rated the dropouts as being less likable, less desirable as friends, and having less significance as group members. The therapist's ratings may reflect his or her early realization that the dropouts were subdued and detached, and subsequently the therapist may have rated them lower on the cohesion variables. Alternatively, perhaps the therapist (consciously or unconsciously) contributed to the departure of these "unlikable" patients from the group. This latter interpretation suggests the potency of the therapist's countertransferential feelings in patients' decisions to drop out of group. It is possible that the therapist was less likely to engage these patients in the therapeutic process, preferring to let them fade into the background and ultimately drift out of group. This finding may reflect the clinical analogy of Rosenthal and Jacobson's (1968) *Pgymalion in the Classroom*, in which the impact of the teacher's expectations on pupils' performance was revealed. Because the therapist did not view these patients as a good fit in the group, a self-fulfilling prophecy may have ensued such that these patients were "forced out." Our interpretation is consistent with one proposed by Stiwne

(1994) to explain his finding that during periods of group instability, therapists were prone to concentrate on those patients who became remainers.

WORKING FACTORS

The term *working factors* refers to aspects of the group process that reflect patients' efforts to engage in various activities of treatment. We have primarily focused on work with affects as one aspect of therapeutic activity. The patient's experience and expression of affects are regarded as important events by most psychotherapists. From one perspective, they may be viewed as therapy objectives, for example, experiencing and expressing positive rather than negative affect. Other common therapy objectives include increased awareness, tolerance, and regulation of affects. From another perspective, the experience and expression of affects may be viewed as components of therapeutic change processes. That is, changes in the experience and expression of affects may be required before certain therapy objectives can be achieved.

Many different conceptualizations of how the experience and expression of affects operate as therapeutic change events have been offered in the literature (Kennedy-Moore & Watson, 1999; Safran & Greenberg, 1991). Common to most of these conceptualizations is the linkage between affects and other types of constructs (e.g., cognitive, interpersonal, and behavioral constructs). Examples include cognitive–affective schemata (Foa & Kozak, 1991), interpersonal schemas (Safran & Segal, 1990), and action sequences (Perls, 1973). Affective change events are often viewed as interdependent with these other types of constructs and their associated change processes. Accordingly, affective change events are generally regarded as necessary but not sufficient to bring about favorable therapy outcome. For example, historically there has been considerable debate about the value of catharsis and whether, by itself, it is capable of bringing about favorable outcome. After conducting a review of the literature on catharsis, Kosmicki and Glickauf-Hughes (1997) suggested that when it is effective, catharsis should be viewed as an active process that occurs within a particular context (e.g., therapist empathy) and is well integrated with cognitive processing.

In the field of group therapy, catharsis has also been viewed as one of a number of different therapeutic factors (I. D. Yalom, 1995). It often has been cited by patients as important to therapeutic change. In group therapy, the public nature of the situation allows patients to be influenced by the affective expression of others as well as their own experience and expression. Rutan and Stone (2001) concluded that a major pathway to change in group therapy is the evocation of powerful feelings in the present followed by cognitive integration generally through interpretation.

For some types of problems, the expression of affect has been seen as particularly important to therapeutic change. One such problem is CG. The experience and expression of feelings associated with the loss and the lost person have been viewed by many experts as a necessary step in successful grief work (Rando, 1993; Worden, 1991a). However, there has been disagreement about what types of feelings should receive emphasis. Following Freud's original formulations about mourning and melancholia (Freud, 1917/1957), some investigators (Lazare, 1989; Osterweis, Solomon, & Green, 1984; Shuchter & Zisook, 1993) have emphasized the importance of experiencing and expressing negative feelings as a necessary part of successful grief work. They believe that such feelings tend to be defended against at considerable cost to the individual (e.g., guilt, self-reproach, and aggression toward the self).

In addition to focusing on affect exploration as a specific therapeutic activity, we have also focused on work as a more general construct. We have defined *work* as the degree to which the patient pursues the primary objectives of therapy. We believe that work represents a different type of construct that might act in combination with affect exploration to produce favorable outcome in group therapy for CG.

In our previous controlled study of time-limited short-term interpretive group therapy for patients with CG (Piper, McCallum, & Azim, 1992), we investigated the relationships between the experience and expression of both positive and negative affect and therapy outcome (McCallum, Piper, & Morin, 1993). The major finding revealed that the more the patient experienced or expressed positive affect during the group therapy sessions, the better the outcome. This finding was consistent with the social–functional formulations of Bonanno and Kaltman (1999). They believe that positive affect expression serves an adaptive function by increasing contact with and support from people in the patient's environment, in this case the other members of the therapy group. In addition to the affect variables, patient work was also measured. There was some evidence from the study that there was a direct relationship between work and favorable outcome and some, although minimal, evidence that the expression of negative affect was directly related to favorable outcome if accompanied by high levels of patient work.

More recently, we examined the effect of affect exploration and work in interpretive and supportive forms of short-term group therapy for CG patients (Piper, Ogrodniczuk, Joyce, McCallum, & Rosie, 2002). The study provided strong and consistent evidence of a direct relationship between the experience or expression of positive affect and favorable treatment outcome. In addition, there was some evidence, although less strong and consistent, for an inverse relationship between the experience or expression of negative affect and favorable outcome.

As with our previous study, these findings are consistent with the social–functional theory of Bonanno and Kaltman (1999). These investigators argued that during bereavement a continuing expression of negative affect tends to irritate, frustrate, and alienate sources of potential social support. In contrast, they believe that positive affect expression serves an adaptive function by increasing contact with and support from important people in the person's environment. From a more general perspective, Kennedy-Moore and Watson (1999) similarly concluded that the expression of positive affect can make the expression of distress more palatable to recipients. This tends to lead to greater cooperation and less avoidance.

In group therapy, obtaining support and assistance from other patients is a particularly important part of the therapeutic process. Because of their emphasis on loss, therapy groups for patients experiencing CG routinely focus on a variety of negative affects (e.g., sadness, fear, and guilt). In this context, the expression of positive affect may be salient. It may also convey optimism about the future and encourage other patients to join the patient in work activities. These may involve gaining insight into long-standing conflicts or formulating solutions to everyday problems, the two components of work highlighted in our study.

Direct relationships were also found between work and favorable outcome. The definitions of the two types of work that the therapists used for their ratings closely paralleled the primary objectives of the two forms of therapy (interpretive, supportive) that were provided, as discussed in Chapter 4 of this volume. Thus, it was not surprising that the more that patients pursued the objectives of the therapies, the more benefit they experienced.

The study also provided evidence that the combination (additive and interaction effects) of the experience or expression of affect with work had a stronger relationship to favorable outcome than either variable alone. The combination findings were stronger in the case of the positive affects. In addition to facilitating work among the patients in the immediate situation of the therapy group, the experience and expression of positive affect may encourage patients to apply what they have learned to different situations in their lives. From an insight-oriented perspective, this refers to the process of working through. From a behavioral problem-solving perspective, this refers to the process of generalization. Without affective involvement, the application of what patients have learned through working may remain limited. Similarly, the immediate benefits of experiencing and expressing positive affects in the group (e.g., cathartic relief and pleasurable interactions) may remain limited in the absence of work.

With regard to clinical implications, our findings suggest that therapists should consider encouraging patients to experience and express positive affects in therapy groups for CG in addition to engaging in work. This may require a concerted effort on the part of the therapist. The experience and expression of positive affects are not naturally occurring events in therapy groups for CG. In some cases (e.g., the experience of relief following the death of a significant other), the positive affect may be regarded as socially or personally inappropriate. In interpretive therapy, the therapist may need to interpret the meaning of resistance to expressing such positive affects. In supportive therapy, the therapist may need to directly encourage the expression of such affects.

The findings concerning negative affect, although less strong, also have clinical implications. Experiencing and expressing negative affects are natural processes in therapy groups for CG. However, too much attention to negative affect, particularly in the absence of positive affect, can be counterproductive. The findings suggest that therapists should be attentive to patients who primarily express negative affects. In group therapy, such patients may become isolated and may eventually become scapegoats.

We have examined not only the impact of affect exploration on the outcome of treatment but also its effect on dropping out of group therapy for CG (McCallum et al., 2002). Patients leave psychotherapy prematurely for a myriad of reasons. Not all departures represent therapeutic failures. However, when a patient makes a unilateral decision to stop therapy and this decision is contrary to the recommendation of the therapist, the therapy is usually considered a failure, and the patient is referred to as a dropout. When a dropout occurs, both patient and therapist may experience a sense of failure, wasted effort, and demoralization. In group therapy, the dropout may disrupt the treatment of the remaining members and precipitate additional dropouts. For group members, a preponderance of negative affect may be associated with dropping out, whereas a preponderance of positive affect may be associated with remaining. We examined this possibility in our comparative trial of interpretive and supportive forms of group therapy for CG.

We found that in the very first therapy session, dropouts reported experiencing significantly less positive affect (pleasure, warmth, acceptance, or optimism) than remainers. On the surface, this finding may appear as mere common sense: Patients who felt positive about the experience stayed; those who did not, left. This commonsense finding merits reporting, however, because "one reason for the gap between psychotherapy researchers and practitioners is the frequent failure of research to confirm the importance of variables that are self-evidently important to practitioners" (Stiles, Honos-Webb, & Surko, 1998, p. 439). However, the finding may be more relevant than merely confirming the obvious.

It is widely accepted that for patients to stay and benefit from therapy, they need to feel positive toward the experience. However, it has been our experience that clinicians tend to focus on negative feelings when assessing the value of a therapy session. Furthermore, whereas catharsis refers to the expression of both positive and negative affect, most theoretical writings have emphasized negative affect (Bohart, 1980; Greenberg & Safran, 1989; Nichols & Efran, 1985; Scheff & Bushnell, 1984). The emphasis on negative affect is particularly true of the loss literature, wherein the focus tends to be on the pain of grief.

Alternatively, it is possible that dropouts placed less importance on any type of emotional experience, perhaps reflecting their unsuitability for affect-focused therapy. We verified that dropouts did not differ from remainers in terms of negative affect. Dropouts and remainers reported experiencing comparable and moderate amounts of anxiety, sadness, anger, and pessimism (the negative feelings). Furthermore, whereas remainers experienced a comparable and moderate amount of both positive and negative affect, the dropouts experienced considerably less positive than negative affect.

A clinical implication of the findings is that when working with patients experiencing CG, perhaps the therapist should be as attentive to the encouragement of positive affect as he or she is to negative affect, group cohesion, group climate, and a positive therapeutic alliance. When working with such patients, the group therapist should be attentive to positive affect early in therapy. The therapist could directly invite reticent patients to participate in the group process. For example, before ending the first few group sessions, the therapist could invite members to identify anything positive they had experienced during the previous week, including that day's session. A second clinical implication of these findings is that the difference in positive feelings between dropouts and remainers may be manifested in other situations (e.g., socially or maritally). If it were evident prior to therapy, the clinician could address these difficulties before referral to group therapy. Finally, it is possible that patients who have difficulty experiencing positive feelings may be better suited to an alternative treatment. For example, having already established a positive investment in their loved ones, they may benefit from family or marital therapy.

GLOBAL FACTORS

Some authors have argued that many of the group process factors studied in group therapy research are highly interrelated and probably represent only a few underlying dimensions. One example of a more global process factor that has been described is group climate. Group climate refers to the general atmosphere within the group. MacKenzie (1983) has described the group climate as an environmental press, that is, a property or attribute of the group environment that facilitates or impedes the efforts of an individual to reach a particular goal. He has defined three key features of the group climate that are common to all therapy groups: (a) engagement (reflecting cohesion and work in the group), (b) avoidance (reflecting group members' reluctance to take responsibility for changing), and (c) conflict (reflecting interpersonal conflict and distrust).

MacKenzie (1983) and others (Kivlighan & Tarrant, 2001) have suggested that the group climate has an important influence on the outcome of treatment. Engagement, for example, reflects cohesion and self-disclosure among the members and also reflects group members' attempts to understand the meaning of their behavior. Challenge and tactful confrontation (also part of engagement) promote social learning. Positive change is more likely to occur with these behaviors. Avoidance perpetuates the members' dependence on the therapist or other group members for direction. Members are reluctant to address difficult issues (both personal issues that brought them to treatment and issues that develop within the group). Little change can be expected when group members avoid taking responsibility for addressing such difficulties. Finally, conflict does little to ease members' concerns about trust and heightens friction among the members. This is likely to lead to withdrawal or outbursts of anger, both of which can impede work within the group.

Using data from our comparative trial of interpretive and supportive forms of group therapy for CG, we examined the association between dimensions of the group climate and treatment outcome (Ogrodniczuk & Piper, 2003). We also examined the effect that early group climate had on treatment outcome as well as whether change in the group climate across the treatment period or the average level of group climate was associated with outcome.

We found evidence that the common factor of group climate was related to outcome of group psychotherapy. More specifically, our findings revealed that engagement was significantly related to favorable treatment outcome. The positive effect of engagement was evident as early as the beginning phase of therapy (i.e., after the fourth session). Engagement averaged across therapy was also found to be significantly associated with favorable outcome. These findings are consistent with the results of several previous studies (Braaten, 1989; Kivlighan & Lilly, 1997; Kivlighan & Tarrant, 2001). In contrast, change in engagement during treatment was not significantly related to outcome. In regard to other group climate dimensions, neither avoidance nor conflict (early ratings, averaged ratings, or change in ratings) was significantly related to outcome. The relationships between the group climate dimensions and outcome did not differ significantly between the two forms of therapy provided in the study.

MacKenzie (1983) argued that engagement captures many elements of cohesion. Thus, one possible explanation for the significant effect of engagement on treatment outcome is that group members who perceive that patients get along well with each other, particularly early in the life of the group, are better able to engage in the tasks of treatment and thus reap greater benefits from the group. Greater engagement, reflecting higher levels of cohesion, may provide patients with encouragement and reinforcement for their attempts to get better. This may facilitate optimism and expectation for improvement, which have been found to favorably influence treatment outcome (Joyce & Piper 1998). It may also encourage patients to take more risks in the group (e.g., being more open about uncomfortable emotions or trying new ways of interacting with others).

Furthermore, an engaged group climate reflects participants' efforts to understand their behavior, to self-disclose personal information or feelings, and to challenge and confront each other to sort out difficult issues. All of these behaviors represent different aspects of work in a psychotherapy group. Such work behaviors are believed to be necessary requirements for therapeutic change. Thus, perceptions of high engagement may have reflected the patients' greater involvement in work tasks, thus facilitating increased benefit from the group.

A significant interaction between engagement and conflict was also found after the first phase of therapy. When patients perceived conflict in the group, higher levels of engagement were related to less favorable grief symptoms outcome. However, when there was low perceived conflict, higher levels of engagement were related to more favorable grief symptoms outcome. When patients are working, they are engaged in activities such as self-disclosing personal information or feelings and challenging and confronting each other. There is a certain level of anxiety that is inherent in these work behaviors. Perceived conflict and friction in the group may exacerbate patients' symptoms, leading to little change or deterioration following group. Conversely, in the absence of perceived conflict among group members, work facilitates grief symptoms outcome, as we have described previously. This suggests that perceived conflict among group members interferes with work in the group.

Our findings concerning group climate have clinical relevance for group therapists. In attempting to maximize patient gains from group treatment, special attention should be paid to patients' perceptions of engagement in the beginning phase of therapy. Group leaders should look for ways to increase patients' sense of engagement in the group as a way to facilitate favorable outcome. Levine and Moreland (1990) suggested that this can be done by encouraging expressions of warmth and acceptance among group members or by serving as targets for the group members' projective identifications. Kivlighan and Tarrant (2001) have also found that the therapist may be able to facilitate engagement by decreasing attention to individual members in the group and by setting norms and goals for the group while maintaining a warm, supportive therapeutic stance.

The findings also suggest it is important for clinicians to be sensitive to all aspects of the group climate and how they interact to influence outcome. For example, we found that in some circumstances, high engagement was associated with good outcome, whereas in other circumstances, it was associated with poor outcome. This depended on the level of conflict in the group. The clinician will need to be attentive to the levels of these aspects of the group climate and intervene appropriately. For example, when engagement and conflict are both low, engagement should be increased. Strategies that may facilitate this include encouraging self-disclosure, providing interpretations and inviting patients' responses to interpretations, and creating a safe environment in which patients may challenge and confront each other. When engagement and conflict are both high, conflict should be minimized. Group-as-a-whole interpretations might be used to reduce or minimize conflict among group members by attributing responsibility for difficulties to all group members rather than any specific member. Kivlighan and Tarrant (2001) also suggested that maintaining group members' focus on the here and now will help decrease interpersonal conflict. Forming homogeneous groups may be another approach to minimizing conflict. It is important to reiterate that each aspect of the group climate should not be considered in isolation. Rather, clinicians should consider how the different aspects of the group climate interact to influence outcome. This will lead to a better understanding of the relation between group process and the outcome of therapy.

CONCLUSION

The study of the process of group psychotherapy will never be a readily controlled deterministic science. The interactions in groups are complex and sensitive to many different conditions. Yet, we believe there is order in the complexities of the psychotherapeutic process in therapy groups and have attempted to clarify aspects of the group process that are systematically related to improved outcome from short-term forms of group therapy for CG. By thoroughly studying the inner workings of these groups, we have been able to identify and describe various processes that appear to influence whether patients remain in therapy and how much benefit patients derive from treatment. Our findings can help clinicians develop a better understanding of how certain events that occur during therapy can impact the success of the group. We hope that improved clarity of the group process can enrich the conceptual framework that clinicians use in daily practice and improve their effectiveness by directing their attention to particular phenomena in the group that with increased attention from therapists can lead to greater patient improvement. Therapists may begin to influence the group process and success of treatment as early as the initial formation of the therapy group by composing homogeneous groups, that is, groups composed of similar patients. We discuss the role of group composition in Chapter 6.

6

EFFECTS OF GROUP COMPOSITION ON THERAPEUTIC OUTCOME

In preceding chapters (e.g., Chapter 4 on patient characteristics), we have provided evidence demonstrating that certain personal qualities of participants in our short-term therapy groups for complicated grief (CG) were significant determinants of the process and outcome of treatment. We discussed the consequences of these individual characteristics without regard to the characteristics of others in the group. The correlations between personal attributes and the process and outcome of therapy were considered under conditions of random or undetermined group composition in an attempt to establish general effects of these attributes. In a sense, these associations reflect consequences when other members in the group are average or typical with respect to the various personal characteristics—that is, the effects of these characteristics in the modal group. However, groups, by their very nature, are interactional, and as such, the individual cannot be seen in isolation from the group context. The success of group therapy is influenced to a large degree by the particular combination of members in the group, otherwise known as the group's composition. Thus, in this chapter, we shift our focus from the individual to the group system and consider group composition in the context of treating CG with short-term group therapy.

Composition is a group-level variable that represents the combination of individual characteristics. Different approaches to assembling a therapy group have been suggested, but by far the most commonly described approach refers to the homogeneity–heterogeneity approach (Dies, 1993; Kivlighan & Coleman, 1999; Lieberman, Wizlenberg, Golant, & Di Minno, 2005). Very simply, this refers to composing groups on the basis of similarity (homogeneity) or dissimilarity (heterogeneity) among group members. Although some authors have argued that heterogeneous groups offer members more variety of interactions and greater opportunity for interpersonal learning (Melnick & Woods, 1976), most appear to favor homogeneous groups (Lieberman et al., 2005; Perrone & Sedlacek, 2000; Siebert & Dorfman, 1995). The theoretical rationale underlying recommendations that groups be formed along homogeneous lines is cohesion theory (I. D. Yalom & Leszcz, 2005). Members who are more alike are expected to find more in common with each other, be more comfortable with each another, establish bonds more quickly, and establish a supportive atmosphere more quickly. Thus, participants will feel safe to explore their motives, fears, and ways of behaving. Through self-exploration, learning and change will occur. As MacKenzie (1997) described, when the group is set up so that the members have common or similar issues, it is easier for them to begin interacting because they can knowledgably share similar concerns and can become involved with one another on the basis of common experiences. In addition, if members have experienced similar stressful events or similar dysfunctional behaviors, they are in good position to recognize themselves in others. They are able to identify methods of resistance or label missed messages more easily. They cannot fall back on the rationale "you can't understand me because you haven't experienced what I have." Indeed, the opposite is often the case—issues can be understood only too well ("it takes one to know one" phenomenon). As a general rule, MacKenzie explained, the more constraints there are in terms of the group structure (e.g., duration, objectives), the more likely homogeneity is to be helpful. Thus, he strongly recommends that clinicians aim to achieve homogeneity in their groups if they are planning on offering short-term time-limited treatment (MacKenzie, 1990).

If one accepts the desirability of achieving homogeneity in short-term group therapy, the practical question that arises next is: Which patient characteristics should be given priority when composing a group? Brabender (2002) pointed out that the number of variables that could be considered in determining the optimal composition of the group "is as vast as the variation in the human condition itself" (p. 204). As the number of variables the clinician considers increases, the pool of candidates for the group decreases. Thus, to ensure that the group gets off the ground with a satisfactory number of patients, the clinician must discern which variables are most crucially related to the success of the group. We have previously described the usefulness of considering characteristics along a concrete–abstract dimension and the value of taking into account variables at more than one level of abstraction (McCallum & Piper, 1988). Examples of concrete variables are age, sex, presenting problem, and diagnosis. Examples of abstract variables include unconscious conflicts, relationship patterns, and personality styles. Most discussions of composition characteristics have focused on more concrete variables such as sex and age. However, several authors have described the immense value of considering more abstract variables as key composition ingredients (Budman, Bennett, & Wisneski, 1981; Goldberg, Schuyler, Bransfield, & Savino, 1983; Klein, 1993).

Ego strength has been discussed with some frequency as a critical variable that the clinician should consider when composing therapy groups. For example, V. J. Yalom and Vinogradov (1993) suggested that homogeneity of ego strength in a group allows the members to work together as a team, to communicate and interact fruitfully, to move forward at an even pace, and to attend to conflicts without impediment of a member who is weaker or more fragile than the others. The type of group implied by V. J. Yalom and Vinogradov is a relatively high-functioning group of patients with higher levels (i.e., more mature) of ego strength that is focused on exploratory, interpersonal work. Brabender (2002) further elaborated on the use of ego strength as a composition factor to consider the type of group necessary for patients with low ego strength. She argued that persons operating at a low level of ego functioning require support, warmth, and more individual attention to benefit from their group experience. The high level of anxiety these members bring to the group requires a high level of structure that has a containing role, enhancing members' sense of safety. Conversely, individuals operating at a higher level have a capacity to tolerate anxiety and to engage in exploratory work. This theme of composing groups consisting of high or low ego strength and matching the group structure and function to the capacities of the group has also been described by I. D. Yalom and Leszcz (2005) and MacKenzie (1997). I. D. Yalom and Leszcz, for example, have argued that patients who are less trusting, less altruistic, or less cooperative (each of which reflects low levels of ego functioning) will likely struggle with interpersonal exploration and feedback and may require more supportive groups.

Despite the fact that many clinicians believe in the importance of group composition and espouse certain strategies for composing therapy groups (e.g., creating homogeneous groups based on patients' levels of ego functioning), research on the topic is virtually nonexistent. Meta-analytic reviews of the literature (e.g., Ang & Hughes, 2002; Burlingame, Fuhriman, & Mosier, 2003) typically have compared the effect sizes of homogeneous groups from one set of studies with the effect sizes of heterogeneous groups from a different set of studies. A serious problem with this methodology is that no single study includes both homogeneous and heterogeneous groups. Thus, there are many uncontrolled variables that may be responsible for differences in their effect sizes. Conducting studies that involve the creation of both homogeneous and heterogeneous groups is challenging. Requirements include a large patient sample, efficient procedures for rapid assessment of patients, standard procedures for assigning patients to groups and conditions, a large number of groups, and a substantial number of trained therapists. As a substitute for group therapy studies in which composition is manipulated experimentally, I. D. Yalom and Leszcz (2005) attempted to discuss findings from the human growth and social psychology literatures in which composition was manipulated experimentally in nontherapy groups. However, extrapolating findings from these fields to the realm of group therapy requires a leap of faith that many group clinicians and researchers are not prepared to make. Given the absence of research evidence that could be used to guide composition decisions, we embarked on an ambitious study to examine the issue of whether homogeneous therapy groups were more advantageous than heterogeneous therapy groups for patients with CG (Piper, Ogrodniczuk, Joyce, Weidman, & Rosie, 2007).

In Chapter 1, we discussed findings from some of our previous studies that demonstrated that patients with higher levels of object relations had better outcome in interpretive group therapy and patients with lower levels of object relations had better outcomes in supportive group therapy. These findings suggest that the outcome of group therapy might be enhanced by referring high-quality-of-object-relations (QOR) patients to interpretive group therapy and low-QOR patients to supportive group therapy. However, our previous studies also found that the higher the percentage of high-QOR patients, the better the outcome for all patients in the group. This finding indicates that the QOR composition of the entire group was more important to the improvement of the individual patient than was the individual patient's own level of QOR or the form of group treatment received (interpretive or supportive). For example, a patient with a low-QOR score who is placed in a group composed of a relatively high percentage of high-QOR patients can be expected to do relatively well. Conversely, a patient with a high-QOR score who is placed in a group composed of a relatively low percentage of high-QOR patients cannot be expected to do well despite his or her high-QOR score. Another way of conceptualizing this group-level effect is that the more mature patients take advantage of therapeutic relationship opportunities offered by the group, "pulling" the less mature patients into relationships more conducive to work processes and, thus, facilitating improvement for the group as a whole.

Clinically, this finding suggests that the group clinician should seek to have a critical mass of high-QOR patients among the membership either when establishing a new group or when replacing departing members. Such a group composition, particularly if an expressive or interpretive technical strategy is planned, can ensure that the low-QOR patients have a model of positive therapy process to follow, increasing the likelihood of treatment benefit for these patients.

These possibilities are consistent with the reports of some investigators. For example, in their research involving the provision of interpersonal group therapy to outpatients who were homogeneous in terms of having been diagnosed with borderline personality disorder, Marziali and Munroe-Blum (1994) experienced very high dropout rates. Apparently, many patients could not tolerate a culture permeated by the primitive interpersonal processes of their peers. In contrast, therapy groups that are homogeneous in terms of high-QOR patients should not present a problem. The predominance of mature interpersonal processes should facilitate even greater benefit than that experienced in mixed-QOR groups. The validity of these possibilities is, of course, in need of verification by means of a direct process analysis of therapy-session behavior.

Many authors have expressed the view that the composition of therapy groups is important but unfortunately have been unable to cite convincing evidence. Investigating group composition has been an infrequent occurrence in the group therapy literature. Our discovery of a composition effect may have been facilitated by the specific nature of the composition variable (QOR), the nature of the patients' common problem (CG), and the type of treatment (short-term time-limited group therapy).

Patients with high-QOR scores have a lifelong tendency to engage others with a sense of respect and consideration. They demonstrate general interest in others, accompanied by altruistic concern. Although they make take risks to initiate or maintain relationships, in the end, the relationships tend to be rewarding to both parties. In short, they are accustomed to forming mutually productive give-and-take relationships. This is in contrast to patients with low-QOR scores, who have a tendency to engage others in patterns of intense, unstable, and destructive relationships. There is a marked interest in helping themselves rather than helping others. In the end, the relationships are often disappointing to both parties. In short, they are accustomed to forming nonproductive competitive relationships.

Having lost significant others, patients who are experiencing CG are in need of forming and maintaining mature relationships. Opportunities usually exist, both inside and outside of their therapy groups. In their groups, high-QOR patients can altruistically assist other patients in the work of the group, whether it consists of gaining insight into past conflicts and trauma (interpretive work) or solving everyday problems (supportive work). In the process of attempting to help others, they demonstrate to others how to form and maintain mutually rewarding relationships. In addition, altruistic behavior is also often rewarding to the provider.

Thus, it is possible that the presence of high-QOR patients facilitates relationships characterized by mature features, facilitates greater focus on others as opposed to a narcissistic focus on oneself, and facilitates work in line with the primary task associated with the particular form of therapy. Also, greater tolerance of the time pressures associated with time-limited short-term group therapy on the part of high-QOR patients may have a calming effect on the whole group.

Short-term time-limited group therapy provides a unique opportunity to examine issues related to loss in a situation in which new losses (therapist, other patients, the group) are reexperienced after a relatively short period of time. Such events as arriving late, missing sessions, and dropping out of therapy, which are viewed as problematic in most therapy groups, can usually be used productively in loss groups. In addition, the brief duration of the groups creates pressure to work without unnecessary delay.

The following vignettes help illustrate how the composition of a therapy group can affect how group members interact with each other.

LOW-QUALITY-OF-OBJECT-RELATIONS GROUP COMPOSITION VIGNETTE

The first vignette illustrates the interaction among members of a group composed of low-QOR patients (QOR scores ranged from 2.7 to 3.3). It is from the fourth session of a 12-session treatment. In the beginning of the segment, two of the patients discuss their anger and aggression toward their fathers, both of whom have passed away. This discussion incites anxiety in another patient, who, rather than empathizing or helping to explore the aggressive feelings being brought up in the group, mentions her own ambivalent feelings about her father. As a whole, the group is displaying high levels of unmodulated hostility toward people outside the group as well as anxiety about the discussion in the group. Rather than empathizing or working through their feelings with one another, the group members simply vent their own frustrations in response to one another's comments.

Anne: One of the things I found with my dad is there'd been so much bad stuff that happened between us since my mom had died, but even long before that, we just always fought. Um, I mean, I wanted to kill him so many times. Uh, but I didn't want him dead. I realized that when push comes to shove, I still wanted him around.

David: Uh, me too—my dad always pissed me off, made me furious. There were many times—I don't know how I contained myself, but I just felt like breaking his jaw. I don't know, but

I think some of my anger was misplaced, due to the fact that there were a lot of other issues. And I, I just didn't know what—why I was so angry, you know.

Anne: Did you ever figure out why you were angry?

David: No. I just knew I was angry.

Anne: That was good that you knew you were angry. I didn't even know that most of the time.

Alison: Did, did he abuse you at all?

David: No, no, he, he . . .

Therapist: Not overtly—at least?

David: Well, no, no, he, he, backed me up and everything—but, uh . . .

Anne: Was he emotionally there for you, or did he just sort of . . .

David: No, he wasn't emotionally there for me. Well, like, when I was 4, my brother died . . . but he never . . . it wasn't intentional. He, he never, he never laid a hand on me—actually, he did spank me once . . . I don't know, I just never felt like he loved . . . I don't even remember what the hell I was talking about.

Anne: Family.

Therapist: Well, also about people not being there in a way that you needed them. And also about feelings that, maybe, get displaced onto the wrong person or the right person. But not knowing what to do with those feelings.

Anne: It was always easy to blame Dad because, you know, he was the one I thought walked on water. Um, it was just easier, it was OK.

Therapist: So, who are you really angry with?

Anne: Me. I was a failure. And when I was a kid. I was failing all my life.

Therapist: So, where'd that nonsense come from?

Anne: Oh, well, that came from that, you know, Dad. You come home with 95% on a math test, and tell Dad, and he'd say what happened to the other five? And I got that from him all my life. It was that he wanted us to all be able to survive. He figured we needed to be tough because he was 17 when the Germans invaded Denmark—it wasn't a good place to be, and he needed to be tough to survive. He came to Canada, and he was accused a lot of being a DP, which was some-body that didn't immigrate but . . .

Alison: A deported person?

Anne: No, a displaced person.

Alison: That's what I feel like.

Anne: And people were mean to him when he came over—accusing him of stealing jobs from Canadians, and all of that. And so he figured we all needed to be tough, so he raised us to be tough. And it's been good in a lot of ways, but god damn it, the thing that sometimes is gonna kill me is the things I won't admit that I can't do, like feel pain, hurt . . .

Therapist: Sadness, fear . . .

Anne: Yeah.

Therapist: Regret, relief.

Anne: Yeah.

Therapist: All of those things I suspect.

Anne: Until I took the anger management course, I had no idea that that when I would take a strip off somebody, in my old way, verbally, that that was anger. I thought that was just normal, I thought that I was just being smart, intelligent about sticking up for myself. You know, I didn't realize that you could be angry and not wanna throw a chair around.

Carolynne: This noise is really making me crazy!

Therapist: It's what? Sorry?

Carolynne: It's upsetting me—that noise.

Therapist: Oh, those are the fans in the ceiling that circulate the air.

Carolynne: Ya know, we're talking about childhood issues, and I'm just remembering being in the basement hiding and my parents fighting, and you know, it's like, is this a safe place? I know in my head it is. But it's like, you know, cause when you guys were talking, I remember my childhood, and on Friday we went to a football game, my brothers and I. And we talked. My older brother was the one who made all the calls to the family about the interment. And, uh, I said, "Well, I invited Sandy," who is my dad's ex-wife, and Jason my brother said, "I wasn't sure whether or not to invite Dad." And, uh, my little brother said, "No way, 'cause he'll bring his new wife." You know, I was like, this . . . my parents were divorced. They had nothing to do with each other, you know, he (Dad) was there at the funeral, why'd he have to be there at the interment? And what it came down to was, uh, for me, was the realization that I realized, wouldn't it be nice to have a father who came here to support his kids, cause they lost their mom. Wouldn't that be nice?

Anne: I needed a father to be around when I needed him.

Carolynne: You know, I realize that his being there would not be for us. Rather, it would be like, she was my wife—it would be for him. It wouldn't be because he was our father and say he was there to support us. My stepdad has done that more than my own father. My father didn't come, and I'm kinda glad he didn't come. But, anyway, I was gonna spend time with my mom on Friday. I was gonna finish my business with my father, and not, like, say good-bye, but just say what I needed to say. I had this idea; well maybe he'll come into the city and we'll go have coffee. His girlfriend and Brian, my husband, can go have coffee somewhere and I could have an hour with him. But it's not gonna happen, you know, it's . . . and, uh, so, anyway, a while ago I called him, because it was his birthday, and we got him a lottery ticket, and I called and said, "I wanted to know if you received it, and how you're doing," and I just said, "I'm doing OK, I guess. It went OK, Mom's interment." I knew that he was aware of Mom's interment because his sister, my aunt, was there, so he must've known. I guess I was waiting for him to call back and say, "Why didn't you invite me?" or whatever. But he didn't. He finally called last night, when I wasn't home, and left a message, and said, "You know, I'm doing OK. I hope you're OK." Um, so it's just hard listening to you guys right now, so hard, but it's like realizing the past week that my dad . . . I know he's never been there. He's not able to be there. It's just like, wouldn't it be nice if he could just be a dad, you know, come and say it's going to be OK. You know, and I know I'm 32 years old, and I shouldn't need that, I want him to . . .

Alison: I'm 45.

Carolynne: I know.

Therapist: And, Alison, you're missing it too.

Alison: Oh, yeah.

Carolynne: You know, it's like he's so . . . he's right here living in the city. He's not dead, but he may as well be.

Therapist:	I think it illustrates very well David's point, and, Anne, your point, as well, you need to have your parents there for you, but . . .
Carolynne:	It's not gonna happen!
Therapist:	Well . . .
Carolynne:	Thirty-two friggin years without having a father to love you! If you look at the past it's like, I think, the one thing I now realize is that it's a fantasy—that one day my dad would come for me. And, you know, I said in the group, I said, "When will I give up that fantasy? Like, will he have to die? What will happen then, you know, to my fantasy?" And so my mom died, and it's like, now what?
Therapist:	So, I guess the other question would be, is there anything wrong with asking for what you need sometimes. I mean, you take a risk, because you don't know what the answer is going to be.
David:	Do we have to keep talking about this? All this discussion about how our dads screwed us over is really pissing me off! I wished he was there for me more, but now he's gone—nothing is gonna change now. I just get so angry when I think about him.
Carolynne:	I just get so sad . . . why are those damn fans so loud?

HIGH-QUALITY-OF-OBJECT-RELATIONS GROUP COMPOSITION VIGNETTE

The second vignette illustrates the interaction among members of a group composed of high-QOR patients (QOR scores ranged from 4.2 to 7.3). The segment begins with a discussion about the absence of a group member and moves into a discussion of the complications of needing to express oneself and be heard and empathized with. Group members display empathy, concern, and compassion for one another and engage in dynamic work. Affects are not simply expressed, they are discussed and interpreted.

Therapist:	I notice that nobody has mentioned the empty chair.
Annette:	I know, but I'm thinking about it. [sigh] He swore.
Lauren:	He gave his word.
Annette:	But if he can't, if he literally can't do it, you know. I've been in bed where I literally can't get those covers off.

Therapist:	Perhaps nobody has mentioned the empty chair because it's uncomfortable to talk about.
Gary:	It might also be that just, we're all like, maybe he has a good reason for not being here.
Claire:	I just think, well I don't know, I think the people who are here have needs, and let's get on with things.
Lauren:	I agree, you are making the effort to be here and it's very hard on you, and um, and so that person decided that it's not his time to do this.
Sharon:	I feel too that he can't make up his mind, you know, about whether he can make a commitment.
Annette:	I think that it was too soon after his trauma that he came here, compared to the rest of us, but I think he would have gotten something out of it just by sitting and listening.
Tamara:	I think he's not ready, to get help. You have to go further down, that's what's going to happen. He doesn't want to face his problems. He wants to still wallow.
Therapist:	Joseph is his name, but he is referred to as "he" and "him" in this discussion. Is that one way of not getting too close to Joseph and avoiding any feelings that we may have because of his absence?
Lauren:	I honestly didn't remember his name, now that's interesting.
Annette:	My fear with Joseph is that he is just too close to suicide; that's what my feeling is. That's why I really worry about him not being here. But I understand other people's, um, opinions that we should work on our own problems, but I feel this is a free, um, attempt to straighten ourselves around and that's great.
Claire:	But if we spend time talking about him, then we are avoiding our own stuff.
Annette:	Yeah, well, I know what you mean, but . . .
Lauren:	You can't stop.
Annette:	Actually you can have empathy for it.
Therapist:	What's the hard stuff that's being avoided?
Claire:	Are you asking me?
Therapist:	Mmmm.
Claire:	Well, I guess I feel really, really needy. Last week, when I left here . . . the talk at the end of last session about marriage

breakup and that, ah, brought up a lot of stuff for me. Um, my mom . . . she's unconscious and not taking any fluids or anything you know, or medication for her pain . . . it's just a matter of time. And I feel it's all related to being all alone, cause I'm all alone there with her all the time. My daughter who lives in town is in Atlanta right now but anyway . . . and then my dog, he had a biopsy done yesterday and he is 13 but he sleeps with me . . . he's, you know, he was the family dog when the kids were born, but I mean he's like, he's like my only companion, and he had a biopsy yesterday, and I find out this afternoon if he'll be okay. If I lose my dog . . . When you were talking I was thinking, oh, maybe he'll come to me in bed. Um, if there's anything wrong, I mean maybe it's just a fat lump, but it's also like it just churns up all my biopsies and all that sort of stuff.

Annette: Your dog's not with you though. She's in the hospital, so that makes you even more alone.

Claire: Well, um, she's just staring into space; her eyes are staring into space.

Therapist: Claire is describing feeling very needy, which raises the question, what need? The need for what?

Gary: Help.

Annette: Comforting.

Tamara   Compassion.

Lauren: Which one? All.

Claire: A friend who's been my friend since we were 3 and 4 . . . I had lunch with her yesterday. We talked about other people's weddings and stuff, but I didn't tell her one thing. I didn't tell her about the dog even though I'd just come from the vet. I didn't tell her. I just said my mom was getting weaker and worse but I didn't talk to her.

Annette: You are trying to protect other people from . . .

Claire: I don't know what I'm doing, I don't know.

Tamara: Maybe you feel that the person won't understand.

Claire: You know, you're right. With her, I can't talk, I can't go there with her and when I went there with my marriage stuff it was, "Claire, don't be stupid."

Annette: [very quickly] No empathy.

Claire: Just theoretical things about divorce and that you're supposed
             to get over it like this. [*snaps her fingers*] But you know it's just
             the fact that with her, I can't go there with my pain.

Lauren: Well let it out. You can let it out here.

Gary: Yeah.

Annette: And quite often, when you're asked here if you have any-
             thing to say you say "I forget" and let us move on to someone
             else. But really, you've got it all boiling in there, so we would
             like to hear from you.

Lauren: Yup, just let it out. Cause this is . . . when you say you are all
             alone . . . in a way I would hope that at least once a week you
             don't feel like you're alone when you come here.

Annette: I'm alone too, and next Wednesday my husband is getting
             remarried, and I have to wear a suit, and I can't use my right
             arm, even to get Kleenex, so I am hobbled up. When I come
             to these sessions . . . I've certainly been thinking about that
             too. I've been with him since I was 16, and I'm 58, so it's a
             long time.

Therapist: Claire mentioned a number of different stressors, and it looks
             as if the group is overwhelmed, a number of you look . . .

Gary: I guess it depends on what I am overwhelmed with. I can't
             take much more, I'm full.

Claire: And that's the way it's been, I mean since my breast cancer
             in '83, it's been like . . . and then another breast surgery, and
             then, you know it's just sort of like, give me a breather. My
             mother's been dying since '93. So, um, yeah, it's like, give me
             a break.

Gary: I don't know which piece to grab. Like, do I help talk to you
             about your dog or your mother or your job or . . . so, I'm getting
             a feeling of what you are going through.

Claire: I mean it sounds like, yeah, it sounds like if I told somebody
             these things they'd think I was crazy and making this up.
             Although I did, I do. I was talking to another friend last
             night who knows this stuff, and she keeps reminding me of
             this, helping me, so she is supportive. She knows that I'm not
             making it up, but if I had to tell somebody else this story, it
             sounds like it's ridiculous.

Therapist: You glanced at me when you said the words, "think that I'm
             crazy" and here we are in a psychiatric outpatient program.

	I wonder if your glance was your way of asking whether I think you are making it up.
Claire:	I don't, I don't think I'm, I know I'm not crazy. I know I'm not.
Therapist:	I think you are asking me if you are going to be judged as crazy, misjudged.
Claire:	No, I . . . no, I, I don't think . . .
Therapist:	If I would see you as psychotic?
Claire:	No, cause I know I'm not, and I really don't think that crosses my mind. It's just more like I'm concerned that people might think I'm making up stories. It's like I've been told before, "Ooh Claire, you're overreacting; you're making up the stories; you're making too much of things." But I don't really feel I'm over the deep end. I'm using crazy in the term of feeling . . .
Tamara:	That's how I felt.
Therapist:	It's safer to raise the specter of craziness so that it can be dismissed than to ask the sensitive question, am I overreacting?
Claire:	Yeah, I have certainly been told a lot I'm overreacting. People don't understand.
Annette:	I don't think you're overreacting. I think it's been like sticks piled on each other, and they're getting wobblier as they get higher, and then with the dog it's just . . . there'll be a lot of friends probably who would say, "Oh just put the dog down—that's one less worry," but that's not what you want. You want them to take the whole package or else don't make comments, you know, all the stories of what you had to go through, cause that's the reality.
Claire:	I mean . . . but I don't really talk to people, other than those two.
Lauren:	Well what are you going to do? Cause it sounds to me like you're going to burst or . . . what are you going to do?
Claire:	I'll carry on.
Annette:	Are you going to be more afraid? Are you going to be more afraid when you mom is gone? Of being alone, cause in some ways you know it's time for her to go on.
Claire:	Yeah, but it's not easy
Annette:	Oh I know.
Lauren:	I got some great drugs that can help you out. [laughter in the group]

CONCLUSION

At a general level, the clinical implications of our findings are clear, whereas at a specific level, they are in need of determination. In the case of short-term group therapy for CG, the findings suggest that if a therapist wishes to enhance the benefit of the group for all patients in the group, he or she should create a group composition that is characterized by a relatively high percentage of high-QOR patients. The question that remains, however, is how high should the percentage be? If it is set too high, patients who could benefit from therapy would be excluded. Also, waiting for a majority of high-QOR patients to become available could result in undesirable delays in starting groups. If the percentage is set too low, the entire group of patients may suffer. Thus, the determination of an optimal percentage is an important empirical question for future study.

In concluding this chapter, we would like to emphasize that homogeneity and heterogeneity in therapy groups are relative concepts. The reality is that all group members are similar in some ways and different in others. Groups can never be completely homogeneous or heterogeneous. Yet, they do have the potential to be relatively similar or dissimilar with respect to certain dimensions. Only to the extent that group interaction and member benefit can be shown to be influenced by the factors on which group members are similar or dissimilar will these specific dimensions have been demonstrated to be important. Our research has identified QOR as one such dimension. However, because of the minimal research specifically addressing composition of therapy groups, our recommended procedures in Chapter 7 for composing groups are only tentative. There is not likely to be an "ideal" group in terms of composition variables but rather particular group climates that are most facilitative of constructive change for particular kinds of group members.

II

THE MODELS: TREATING COMPLICATED GRIEF IN SHORT-TERM GROUP THERAPY

7

ASSESSMENT AND PREPARATION

In this chapter, we discuss how to assess patients, develop treatment plans, form groups, and prepare group members for treatment. These tasks are essential in creating a therapy group that has the potential of becoming an effective treatment for patients with complicated grief (CG; Bernard et al., 2008). One of the factors that facilitates these tasks is the quality of referrals. Suitable referrals are the life source of a group. In addition to being required for the beginning of a group, they are frequently required to replace dropouts (when appropriate). The better informed that referring sources and therapists are through education and preparation, the more likely the referrals will be appropriate and the more likely the group will operate smoothly. We have found it useful to provide sources of referral with a written list of suitability criteria and an invitation to discuss the criteria with us.

ASSESSING PATIENTS FOR COMPLICATED GRIEF

Identifying and referring patients for group therapy involves several clinical considerations. Primarily, the referring source must identify those patients experiencing CG. This identification is made difficult by the fact that patients rarely present for psychotherapy complaining of problems of CG. Rather, such patients tend to complain of interpersonal problems or psychiatric symptoms without identifying grief as a precipitant. Therefore, the clinician must consider the etiology of symptoms and complaints rather than focusing solely on their phenomenology. As we reported in Chapter 2 of this book, to facilitate the referring clinicians' task of identifying suitable patients for our therapy groups, our research team identified two screening questions to aide in the identification of people with CG (Piper, Ogrodniczuk, & Weideman, 2005). We found that if patients respond affirmatively to either of the following questions, nearly 90% of patients with CG are correctly identified: During the last week, did pictures about your loss pop into your mind? During the past week did you try not to think about your loss? Negative answers to these two questions identify nearly 90% of the patients who do not meet criteria. We believe that including these two questions in the therapist's inquiry about losses and their effects will be useful in making appropriate referrals. Along with these questions, the therapist can have patients complete the Loss Information Form (see Exhibit 7.1), which provides information about the nature of the losses.

ASSESSING WHETHER PATIENTS WOULD BENEFIT FROM SHORT-TERM GROUP THERAPY

It is important to keep in mind that therapists may encounter resistance from patients who are referred to group therapy. A number of aspects of the group therapy situation make it seem more intimidating. Compared with

EXHIBIT 7.1
Loss Information Form

Patient name: _____

Phone: _____ Cell: _____ Other: _____

DOB: _____ Age: _____ Sex: ☐ M or ☐ F

Intake assessor(s): _____

Name of lost person: _____

Relationship:	Father	Mother	Sister	Brother	Friend
(Circle one)	Husband	Wife	Daughter	Son	Other:

Year of the loss: _____ Time passed since the loss (in years or months): _____

Cause of death:	Illness	Accident	Suicide
(Circle one)	Homicide	Other	

Nature of death:	(Circle one)	Expected	Unexpected
	(Circle one)	Slow	Sudden

individual therapy, patients often experience a sense of less control in a group. Many people influence the flow of events. There can also be a diminished sense of individuality. The patient must accept that he or she is part of a group. There is also the potential for less complete understanding of events that transpire in a group session. There is less privacy in a group. Patients are continually exposed, and confidentiality is impossible to guarantee. There is also a diminished sense of safety for many patients in a group. Criticism can potentially come from many directions.

To counter such natural resistance to groups, therapists should attend carefully to selecting members for the group. This means carefully assessing whether patients possess characteristics that optimize their chances of working in, remaining in, and benefiting from brief therapy and group therapy. In regard to brief therapy, this means patients who have a focal problem and who can engage quickly in the therapeutic process. In regard to group therapy, this means patients who are capable of working in a group situation, that is, those who can tolerate social anxiety and work collaboratively, Rutan and Stone (2001) have identified other relevant factors to consider when selecting patients for group therapy. These include

- acknowledging the need for others (i.e., including some capacity to trust others),
- self-reflective capacity (i.e., ability to reflect on one's interactions with others),
- role flexibility (i.e., ability to lead and follow in a group context),
- ability to give and receive feedback,
- empathic capacity,
- frustration tolerance (i.e., can tolerate not always having one's needs met immediately), and
- preexisting relationships (i.e., a potential group member cannot have a preexisting relationships with any other potential group member that would inhibit the work of the group).

Other desirable characteristics for psychotherapy in general, such as realistic expectations and motivation to change, have been cited (Truant, 1998). It is also clear that some desirable characteristics are specific to the particular theoretical and technical orientation of the treatment. In our approach to group treatments for patients with CG, quality of object relations (QOR) is an important concept. Specifically, QOR refers to the lifelong pattern of relationships with others, which ranges from primitive to mature. We discuss QOR and its assessment in a separate section that follows.

In the process of considering selection factors, one must always be aware of situations and circumstances that make individuals inappropriate candidates for group therapy. Factors that we consider *exclusion* criteria include

- comorbid conditions that would interfere with effective participation in psychotherapy (e.g., organic brain disorder).
- problems that require immediate management (e.g., suicidal or homicidal tendencies),
- conditions that the patient and/or therapist decide should be treated first (e.g., phobic disorder),
- refusal to enter into a group,
- inability or unwillingness to abide by the ground rules of the group, and
- therapist discomfort with working with a particular individual.

It should be noted that strict adherence to these inclusion and exclusion criteria would likely render many patients ineligible for group therapy. Rather, these criteria represent ideals that the clinician will consider as he or she makes selection decisions.

ASSESSING QUALITY OF OBJECT RELATIONS

If it is determined that a patient would benefit from short-term group therapy, the clinician should assess QOR to determine what type of therapy would be most appropriate for the patient, interpretive therapy or supportive therapy.

As discussed in Chapter 4, we define *quality of object relations* as a person's internal enduring tendency to establish certain types of relationships (Azim, Piper, Segal, Nixon, & Duncan, 1991). These relationship patterns range along a spectrum from primitive (characterized by destructiveness and instability) to mature (characterized by reciprocity and mutuality). At the primitive level, the person reacts to perceived separation or loss of the object or disapproval or rejection by the object with intense anxiety and affect; there is inordinate dependence on the lost object, who provided a sense of identity for the person. In contrast, at the mature level, the person enjoys equitable relationships characterized by love, tenderness, and concern for objects of both sexes, and there is a capacity to mourn and tolerate unobtainable relationships. The QOR construct refers to the recurring pattern of relationships over the individual's life span, rather than to relationships during any one period (e.g., recent interpersonal functioning). Although for measurement purposes we focus on external relationships, we assume that these reflect the internal object representations and conflictual components of the patient's internal world.

The patient's QOR is evaluated by an experienced clinician during a 1-hour semistructured interview. The interviewer solicits information about four areas of functioning (behavioral manifestations, affect regulation, self-esteem regulation, and antecedent [etiological] factors) during three time periods of the patient's life (childhood, adolescence, and adulthood.) Tables 7.1 and 7.2 present the questions and corresponding criteria that are typically used.

To determine a specific score, the interviewer assigns greater weight to behavioral manifestations because they are observable, experience near, and often manifest during the interview itself. Following the interview, the assessor distributes 100 points across five levels of the QOR dimension (Primitive, Searching, Controlling, Triangular, and Mature). We recommend that the interviewer start by assigning points to the one or two levels that are most evident from conducting the interview. Once this is completed, the interviewer next considers the remaining points, which are assigned to levels that have fewer points.

An arithmetic formula is used to generate an overall score that ranges from 1 to 9—the higher the QOR score, the more mature the patient's object relations. This score is obtained in the following way. The number of points assigned to the Mature level is multiplied by .09; the number of points assigned to the Triangular level is multiplied by .07; the number of points assigned to the Controlling level is multiplied by .05; the number of points assigned to the Searching level is multiplied by .03; and the number of points assigned to the Primitive level is multiplied by .01. The product from each level is added to arrive at the overall score. A cutoff score of 4.2 or higher can be used to identify high-QOR patients, whereas low-QOR patients are those with scores of 4.1 or lower. Empirically, this cutoff was useful in our study, which showed a significant interaction between QOR and form of short-term group therapy (Piper, McCallum, Joyce, Rosie, & Ogrodniczuk, 2001), and in our study of group composition, which used QOR as the composition variable (Piper, Ogrodniczuk, Joyce, Weideman, & Rosie, 2007). Theoretically, the boundary between scale levels 4 and 5 marks the distinction between more primitive (searching) and more mature (controlling) types of relationships.

Veronica is an example of a low-QOR patient. Veronica was born into an unstable family with one older brother who emotionally, physically, and sexually abused her. She grew up frightened of him. She described her father as being a self-centered man who showed no love toward his children, often threatening and beating them. Her mother, on the other hand, was described as being warm but unable to be openly affectionate. From a young age, Veronica learned that she could not confide in either parent, and she withdrew into

TABLE 7.1
Key Interview Questions for Quality-of-Object-Relations Assessment

Period	Major criteria				
	Primitive	Searching	Controlling	Triangular	Mature
Childhood (family of origin)	Do you remember much abuse or disorder in your childhood?	Was there a major event that changed the course of your childhood?	How would you describe your parents in terms of your thoughts, feelings, or behavior?	Was there anything special or unique about your relationship with your (opposite-sex parent) that you did not share with your (same-sex parent)?	In what ways did members of your family express love and concern for each other?
Adolescence: period of transition (peers, parents)	Tell me about any incident you can recall in which you felt hurt or betrayed by peers at school or socially.	Were there any times as a teen or young adult at which you found yourself "falling in love"? How did those experiences turn out?	How did you engage in "rebellion" as a teen or young adult?	Can you tell me about any incident in which you and another were both vying for the attention of a third person? How did that work out?	Were there things about your high school friends that irritated you? How did it affect your relationships?
Adulthood (partners, children)	In what way would you say your intimate relationships have been stormy of hurtful?	Looking back over your relationships, have they been a bit like a roller coaster, lots of ups and downs?	Do you find yourself taking care of your partner, sort of looking out for him/her, trying to help him/her with his/her problems?	How would you say you've been competitive with people whom you are close to?	Do you have good male and female friends?

TABLE 7.2
Key Relationship Features for Quality-of-Object-Relations Assessment

Period	Major criteria				
	Primitive	Searching	Controlling	Triangular	Mature
Childhood (family of origin)	1. Persistent, destructive relationships 2. Inordinate attachment to objects 3. Loss, separation, rejection, disapproval, leads to extreme reaction	1. Repeated "falling in love" 2. Fear of loss and abandonment 3. Distancing behavior	1. Well-meaning attempts to control 2. Possessive behavior 3. Strong negative reaction, defiance or compliance to others' control	1. Repetitive, rivalrous relationships 2. Inordinate competition 3. Opposite sex viewed as a lover or parent	1. Capacity to express love for both sexes 2. At least one intimate dyadic relationship 3. Capacity for equitable (noncompetitive) relationships
Adolescence: period of transition (peers, parents)	4. Emotionally-laden relationships 5. Splitting 6. Impaired trust	4. Attempts to relive lost relationships 5. Initial optimism followed by loss and pessimism	4. Relationships tend to be formal	4. Triumphs followed by guilt	4. Capacity to take risks and be assertive 5. Object constancy despite disappointment 6. Tolerance of bad and appreciation of good in others 7. Capacity to mourn objects and relationships
Adulthood (partners, children)	7. Objects valued for utility				
Behavioral antecedents	1. Abuse 2. Rejection	1. Intensive attachment 2. Overindulgence	1. Over control 2. Discouragement of assertiveness	1. Oedipal competition 2. Oedipal triumph and guilt	1. Loving parenting 2. Identification with both parents

herself. Veronica remembered feeling sorry for her mother because of her father's controlling and abusive behavior. When Veronica was 8, her family moved out of a rural setting into a more urban environment. At 12, the family moved again to an even larger city. The transitions from her small rural birth town to the large city left Veronica feeling intimidated and fearful.

Throughout her teens and adult life, Veronica has been afraid of men and of authoritative women. She eventually married a man whom she considered safe but who was also very controlling. In her early 40s she slowly began to rebel against her husband's control, but out of a sense of guilt, she continued to go along with his demands. When Veronica was 45, her husband died. His death left Veronica feeling conflicted between a need to assert herself and a fear of the effects of her assertiveness on others. Now, at 58, she remains fearful of engaging in an intimate relationship with a man. This fear comes from having been controlled and stifled by her husband, as her mother had been.

The interviewer (rater) distributed the 100 points as follows: Primitive (50), Searching (20), Controlling (20), Triangular (10), and Mature (0). The elevation for the Primitive level was very high, which contributed considerably to her overall score of 2.8.

Bonnie is an example of a high-QOR patient. Bonnie describes a happy and secure childhood. She and her twin brother were the youngest of four children of which she was the only daughter. She remembers her relationships with her parents and brothers as being warm and caring. Her parents rarely fought, and there was no violence or abuse in the family. Of her two parents, Bonnie described feeling closer to her mother but also remembered a congenial relationship with her father, describing herself as "Daddy's little girl." Bonnie began many friendships in her childhood that have lasted through to her adult years. In her teens, she went through a state of mild rebellion, staying out later than her parents wished. Her parents, particularly her father, dealt with her rebellious behavior by having serious talks with her on the subject.

Bonnie's first and longest romantic and intimate relationship began at the age of 17 and lasted for 4 years. She described her relationship with this man as very supportive. However, when they began to think about getting married, she backed out. She convinced herself that she needed more experience with other men before committing herself to one person. When she was 21, Bonnie's mother died. Bonnie reacted to her mother's death by being excessively preoccupied by it for several months. She eventually developed panic attacks. Her difficulty dealing with the loss of her mother hindered her ability to take care of her father's needs before his death 2 years later. This resulted in considerable guilt. At age 26, Bonnie met her current boyfriend, whom she has been dating for a year. Her relationship with him has provided her with support in adapting to her parents' deaths.

The interviewer (rater) distributed the 100 points as follows: Primitive (0), Searching (20), Controlling (10), Triangular (30), and Mature (40). Elevations for the Mature and Triangular levels contributed to her overall score of 7.0.

The reliability and construct validity of the QOR variable is detailed in Piper and Duncan (1999). In general, QOR has been found to be independent of demographic and historic characteristics of the patient. The construct has also not been found to be related to *Diagnostic and Statistical Manual of Mental Disorders* (4th ed., text revision; *DSM–IV–TR*; American Psychiatric Association, 2000) Axis I diagnoses. As one would expect, patients with lower QOR scores (i.e., less than 4.2) tend to show more symptomatic disturbance and are more likely to have a *DSM–IV–TR* Axis II diagnosis than patients with higher QOR scores (i.e., equal to or greater than 4.2), although this overlap is not considerable. The QOR variable has emerged as a strong direct predictor and moderator of therapy process and outcome in time-limited forms of dynamically oriented psychotherapy.

In general, across a number of studies (Piper, Azim, Joyce, McCallum, et al., 1991; Piper, Azim, McCallum, & Joyce, 1990; Piper, de Carufel, & Szkrumelak, 1985; Piper et al., 1998), including our comparative trial (Piper, McCallum, et al., 2001), high QOR has been shown to function as an important patient–treatment match for interpretive or expressive forms of psychotherapy in either the individual or group format.

Though the evidence is less strong, there is reason to believe that low-QOR patients stand to gain more from a therapy approach oriented to the provision of support, problem solving, and advice regarding current circumstances than from interpretive therapy. The treatment itself can provide the low-QOR patient with the experience of a clearly bounded and gratifying relationship, countering a lifelong experience of depriving or abusive relationships (see also Høglend, 1993a, 1993b; Horowitz et al., 1984).

A predisposition to establish a relatively trusting give-and-take relationship with an authority figure is an important indicator for a positive therapy process, an effective termination, and treatment benefit. The object relations formulation can provide an estimate of the patient's capacity to tolerate frustrations in the therapy relationship and facilitate predictions regarding the transference reactions that are likely to emerge (Joyce & McCallum, 2004). The more mature the patient's QOR, the more likely an expressive therapy approach can be undertaken. The more primitive the patient's QOR, the more problematic the patient's representations of interpersonal relatedness and capacity for self-regulation. The patient's QOR should thus be considered a primary determinant of the approach to therapy and the therapist's strategy within sessions.

A complete manual for assessing QOR and a list of rating criteria are available online (http://pubs.apa.org/books/supp/short-term/).

ASSESSING OTHER FACTORS FOR SHORT-TERM
GROUP THERAPY

To maximize clinically effective outcomes, it is necessary for therapists to assess appropriate inclusion criteria, exclusion criteria, and risk factors. In busy clinical settings where it is desirable to form groups and get them started without undue delays, therapists need to strike a balance between including patients who will likely benefit from the treatment, both because of and despite their difficulties, and excluding patients who would likely not benefit and who could jeopardize the treatment of others. To include a probably unsuitable patient out of a wish to add enough members to make the group feasible is a mistake: Probable subsequent dropouts may include not only the unsuitable patient but also others who might have stayed in the group but for the misjudged inclusion.

Inclusion criteria are as follows: CG, an important loss at least 3 months prior to the intake assessment, a reasonable age match with other group members (of note, Rutan, Stone, & Shay, 2007, recommend a 20- to 25-year range of ages for adult psychodynamic groups), informed consent to treatment, and capability to work in a group. Exclusion criteria include comorbid conditions (e.g., organic brain disorder or primary substance abuse) that would interfere with group treatment, conditions that the patient chooses to attend to before CG (e.g., phobic disorder), or problems that require immediate management (e.g., acute suicidal risk; Piper et al., 2007).

Concurrent psychosocial therapy is a methodological complication for research studies. In regular clinical work in which research considerations are not a priority, concurrent treatment may nevertheless be excluded by institutional or insurance policies. Therapists need to judge whether treatment such as concurrent couples therapy or participation in Alcoholics Anonymous is likely to be helpful or an obstacle to progress in a loss group. Concurrent psychosocial treatment of CG features is more likely to be problematic.

Risk factors for CG were addressed in Chapter 3. These are not the same as risk factors for the treatment of CG, which are similar in general to risk factors associated with other treatments. If a patient were to become psychotic or suicidal during treatment or if another urgent clinical problem were to emerge, for example, a life-threatening physical illness, then the therapist would need to assess whether the CG treatment should be terminated or temporarily interrupted for that group member. Other unforeseen group complications, such as the revelation that two group members have formed an intimate relationship, would have to be addressed therapeutically, just as they would in any group therapy. Therapist limitations, such as discomfort with the intensity of affect that frequently occurs in a loss group, could be addressed by the standard recommendations of consultation and supervision, additional training, and/or personal therapy for the therapist. Administrative limitations, such as managerial discomfort with the selection of CG as an important treatment priority, should be addressed by building what Rutan et al. (2007) termed an *administrative alliance*.

DEVELOPING A TREATMENT PLAN

When CG is identified in a patient, the therapist should empathically educate him or her about the reality of CG, its probable contribution to psychological difficulties in his or her case, and its known responsiveness to treatment. That feedback itself can affect therapeutic outcome; thus, it must be undertaken with skill, compassion, and an adequate allocation of time. The therapist should inform the patient of available CG therapy and make an unambiguous recommendation for treatment. Advantages and disadvantages of treating other conditions should be openly discussed so that the best feasible treatment plan can be pursued. For example, it may be useful to pursue treatment for a phobic disorder before a CG group is scheduled to start. However, if the phobic disorder is not currently debilitating, it might be better to join an imminent CG group if there is not likely to be another one that the patient could access for another year.

CG is typically a chronic condition. Although the ideal is to provide targeted treatment without delay, this is often not realistically possible. Delayed treatment is better than no treatment. Logistical delays in the availability of therapy for CG are certainly not grounds for minimizing the reality of the condition. The patient should receive well-informed suggestions about what to do before the CG treatment is scheduled to start. Depending on their clinical condition, some patients could wait, that is, obtain treatment as usual, which may entail continuing with antidepressant medications, visits to primary health providers, and social support. Others, who may be more distressed or fragile or lacking in social support, could benefit from interim supportive individual or group therapy.

It would be consistent with the research literature on CG to instill an appropriate level of hope in the CG patient who is awaiting treatment. Experienced therapists know better than to overstate the benefits of recommended treatment. Nevertheless, it is appropriate for patients to look forward to addressing their unresolved and distressing grief in therapy that is specifically intended for that purpose.

FORMING A GROUP

The therapist who wishes to treat CG in groups may have to confront the same basic task that confronts many group therapists, that is, to disseminate and/or present the scientific literature on the outcome of group therapy. The CG therapist has to face an additional interesting challenge: Despite the prevalence of CG, many clinicians and administrators are not familiar with the condition or its treatment. Therefore, a basic task that may confront the clinician is to educate colleagues, for example, through inservices or workshops. Some aspects of such education, for example, training in QOR assessments, are useful as professional development opportunities even for therapists who will not go on to provide CG treatment.

In our experience, it is useful to set a target date for the start of a CG group and to be explicit with colleagues, referrers, and patients about that date. An explicit specific date can have the effect of redirecting collegial attention to the features of CG in the patients on their current case-loads. A specific date can also help to galvanize and organize the therapist's own behavior. Group rooms need to be reserved; measures need to be assembled; and consent forms need to be prepared in sufficient quantities, for example, if the group is to be observed and/or recorded.

The literature provides a number of potential guides for how a group should be formed. How these guides would best be implemented in a particular setting would depend on several factors, including suitable therapist availability, patient numbers, and administrative support. The following guidelines, derived mainly from our experience and research, are intended to be general. Their application to particular circumstances would inevitably require judgment. Consultation and collegial support are usually indispensable.

- Ensure that there are sufficient group therapists in the setting who could provide time-limited CG treatment in both of the two key approaches, that is, interpretive and supportive group therapy. It is reasonable to assume that a therapist who could provide treatment in both approaches would also be able to blend the approaches in response to the membership of a particular group. If there is only one such therapist in a setting, then the number of offered CG groups should obviously be compatible with his or her timetable.
- Ensure that intake screening procedures assess for the presence of CG.
- Set a target start date and aim to begin with a minimum of 10 patients, which would allow for up to four dropouts while still preserving an adequate number of group members.

- Assess the patients who are referred to the group for their level of object relations. Preferably, this assessment would involve a dedicated interview including the questions in Tables 7.1 and 7.2 and the calculation of a QOR score.
- Try to ensure that at least half of the group members are on the mature end of the QOR spectrum (i.e., mature, triangular, and not severely controlling). Preferably, no more than half the group members should have object relations that are predominantly on the immature end of the spectrum (i.e., primitive and searching). (This recommendation must be regarded as provisional.)
- If at least half the group is at the mature end of the QOR spectrum, be prepared to begin the group with an interpretive approach while paying attention to the responses of all group members, especially those at the less mature end of the spectrum. When clinically indicated, the therapist should be prepared to introduce supportive interventions (e.g., praise and encouragement) to preserve the therapeutic alliance and group cohesion and to avoid drop-outs.
- If the available referrals are predominantly at the less mature end of the QOR spectrum, be prepared to choose between two main choices: (a) Wait until some more mature QOR patients are available and then, if possible, assign those to the groups or (b) concede that only more damaged CG patients are available for treatment and provide the therapy with an emphasis on supportive techniques.

PREPARING GROUP MEMBERS FOR TREATMENT

Preparation refers to any pretherapy procedure that attempts to prepare patients for working in therapy. Immediate objectives include creating accurate expectations about desirable patient behavior, customary therapist behavior, typical therapy events, and realistic outcomes. Careful preparation can also reduce anxiety; establish positive bonds; and increase participation, self-disclosure, and interpersonal feedback. Many procedures for preparation have been described (Piper & Perrault, 1989). They involve different activities and stimuli. Some are provided to individual patients and some to groups of patients. Most procedures are relatively brief (an hour or less) and are integrated with routine clinical tasks such as conducting initial assessments and discussing treatment alternatives. Providing information and discussing issues in interviews are often supplemented with written material that the patient can take home. Sometimes audiovisual material is used to convey information and model (demonstrate) typical group processes. More elaborate procedures that involve the patient participating in experiential tasks that simulate therapy-like experiences have been described in the literature.

In our work in providing time-limited short-term group therapy to patients with CG, we have routinely used a one-page handout that covers "ground rules" for the following three areas: commitment, responsibilities in the group, and responsibilities outside the group (see Exhibit 7.2). We recommend that therapists use this handout or something similar.

The ground rules form a major part of the "contractual agreement" between the patient and therapist. Other aspects of this agreement are as follows:

- The patient agrees to work in a group with one therapist and approximately nine other patients for a fixed duration of 12 weeks.

EXHIBIT 7.2
Ground Rules for Group Therapy

Commitment: I understand that my commitment to the group is for all 12 sessions. The group will meet for 90 minutes each week. Group attendance must be a high priority, and unless there is a very good reason, such as severe illness, I will be there each week. In the event of such an absence, I will notify the therapist prior to the group, and at the next meeting I will share my reason with the rest of the group. I also recognize the importance of being on time because lateness interferes with the work of the group. If I am thinking about leaving the group, I will let others know. Should I decide to leave the group, I will come for one last session where people can say goodbye.

Responsibilities in the Group: I agree to work toward learning more about my own and others' problems. I will try to be open and self-examining. I will be as honest as possible in sharing what I am aware of in the group, that is, thoughts, feelings, and fantasies about myself, other group members (including the therapist), and other people in my life. I understand that I cannot come to group under the influence of alcohol or drugs. It is also not permissible to smoke, drink, or eat in the group. I also understand that physical violence will not be tolerated in the group.

Responsibilities Outside the Group: Confidentiality is essential so that each member can feel safe enough to share. I agree that I will not repeat anything that is said in the group outside of it, unless it concerns only me. I will not share information that might identify any member of the group. Extragroup socializing may prevent the work in the group. I understand that contact with another member (including the therapist) outside of the group may sabotage my own treatment, and I agree to discuss the details of any chance outside contacts in the group.

Signature:

[*Therapist's signature*]

Date:

Note. From *Adaptation to Loss: Short-Term Group Psychotherapy* (p. 61), by W. E. Piper, M. McCallum, and H. F. A. Azim, 1992, New York, NY: Guilford Press. Copyright 1992 by Guilford Press. Reprinted with permission.

- Group sessions of 90 minutes are held once weekly at regular prearranged times.
- Each session is ended by the therapist after the allotted time.
- The patients agree to talk freely about whatever occurs to them during each session.
- The therapist agrees to assist the patients in understanding and resolving problems that have brought them to therapy.

By attending to appropriate selection and careful preparation, we have been impressed with how quickly patients disclose personal material and become affectively involved in short-term group therapy for CG.

8

COMMON COMPONENTS
OF THE TWO MODELS

As we have discussed in the Introduction in this volume, the two short-term group therapy models for treating complicated grief (CG)—interpretive therapy and supportive therapy—have different objectives. Interpretive therapy seeks primarily to enhance the patient's insight about repetitive conflicts and trauma that serve to underlie and sustain the patient's presenting problems. In contrast, supportive therapy seeks primarily to improve the patient's immediate adaptation to his or her life situation. Yet, despite these different primary objectives, the two treatments share common components. Both treatments emphasize themes and roles; both rely on group-as-a-whole interventions; and both place significant emphasis on termination of the group. In this chapter, we explore these common components.

FOCUS ON THEMES AND ROLES

Given the limited time in short-term group therapies, therapists cannot be passive. Although patients often get off to a quick start, they can become bogged down as a result of the sensitive nature of the material that is discussed and the work that is required to bring about change. The therapist must keep the group on task. This is usually referred to as *maintaining a focus*. The focus is usually related to the commonalities that were used to compose the group. In addition, the focus can address content themes and patient roles that emerge in the group. Focus on themes and roles can alleviate resistance and provide a lively forum to enhance understanding and change. We regard a *group theme* as a psychological conflict that persists over the group sessions. Typical themes concern trust, survivor guilt, mortality, and termination. A *role*, in contrast, is a circumscribed set of patient behaviors that represents a particular relation to a theme.

There are various classifications of roles in the general literature on psychodynamic group therapy (Rutan, Stone, & Shay, 2007), Such classifications are interesting and instructive. However, therapists must be alert to the point that loss groups tend to give rise to particular roles that relate to loss themes or to loss-influenced expressions of roles that are familiar in group therapy in general.

Roles often express a wish regarding the therapist's behavior. Some examples follow:

- The *professor* role is played when a group member speaks informatively, even pedantically, about grief as a subject of knowledge and research, rather than about his or her own experience of grief. This role often expresses a wish that the therapist provide academic information about losses and how to cope with them. It serves as a defense against uncomfortable emotionality.
- The *professional nurturer* role is played when a group member is notably quick to respond to other group members by soothing them, reassuring, placating, and justifying whatever they say or do. This role expresses the wish that the therapist be more caring and gratifying.
- The *apparition* role is played when a group member has inconsistent attendance and a detached quality in the sessions that are attended. This role expresses the wish that the therapist be fully attentive to the ambivalence that group members experience about commitment to a brief therapeutic process that is designed to alleviate the distress arising from permanent loss. The apparition brings up themes such as trust and termination by acting in such a way as to preserve uncertainty about the very idea of group membership. Essentially, the apparition elicits the question, Is the patient in or is the patient out?
- The *monk* role is played when a group member appears to keep a "vow of silence" and deflects attention to others. This role expresses the wish to be recognized by the therapist and to be

singled out as deserving attention. The group may respond with gratitude for the monk's selflessness or with irritation about the monk's resigned endurance.

- The *scapegoat* role, which is well recognized in group therapy literature (Rutan et al., 2007), is played when a group member elicits disapproval or condemnation by saying what others only think or by goading the group in a seemingly self-destructive fashion into attacking him or her. The role expresses the wish that the therapist facilitate the expression of angry and aggressive feelings about losses. The therapist is often the only ally that the scapegoat could possibly find in the face of the general disapproval that has been elicited.

When subtle references to themes are made or roles appear to emerge, the therapist should not hesitate to interpret their meaning in terms of the associated conflicts. Skill as a therapist requires familiarity with common patient characteristics and group processes and willingness to work promptly with commonalities as they emerge.

GROUP-AS-A-WHOLE INTERVENTIONS

Themes and roles can be addressed effectively by means of group-as-a-whole interventions, which affect many if not all of the members of the group. Over the years, we have been struck with how effective a therapist can be in affectively involving most patients in the group with a sensitive group-as-a-whole intervention. Use of group-as-a-whole interventions that focus on commonalities serves to facilitate two therapeutic factors that have been heralded as important in group therapy (Piper & Ogrodniczuk, 2006). These are cohesion, which refers to bonds that unite members of a group, and universality, which refers to a sense of shared experience and acceptance in a group. Consistent sensitive focusing by the therapist is a demanding but necessary task in short-term group therapy for CG. When the therapist succeeds in enhancing cohesion and universality, it is likely that group members will respond by continuing to maintain and advance these factors.

Interpretive Group-as-a-Whole Interventions

In interpretive groups, group-as-a-whole interventions often focus on themes or roles. Although a role is played by an individual patient, it is usually assumed that the role expresses something for the entire group (e.g., a wish, a fear, or a defense). Because all patients are addressed in the group-as-a-whole intervention, individuals may feel personally responsible for whatever idea or conflict is being expressed. Thus, they may be more willing to respond and work with the intervention. A group-as-a-whole intervention is often useful as a way to delineate an emotion-laden theme that would evoke defensiveness if it were related to only one person.

The following excerpt illustrates the use of group as a whole. The therapist often uses the word *you* to refer to all of the patients. Some of these references are associated with dynamic components, such as underlying unexpressed feelings that have a dynamic impact.

Carol: I saw a counselor once, soon after leaving the hospital. I was out in less than 24 hours. They gave me tranquilizers to calm me down. I was totally devastated. I toyed with suicide but pushed on. I really didn't deal with the loss. I was angry with the doctors. I called the doctor who delivered my dead baby, but he said he wasn't allowed to talk to me in case there was a lawsuit. I was devastated by that. I found another doctor here at the university. They had done an autopsy but found nothing wrong. She was a girl. Since then I've had two boys by C-section because my body wouldn't release properly. I had gained 65 pounds. The doctor suggested that I not have any more babies because of the risk to the baby and me. So I had my tubes tied. Lately, I can't seem to let go of my baby's death. I still would like to know what happened.

Therapist: Carol has added another facet to peoples' decision to come to this group, can you trust doctors? Can you trust therapists? You have to depend on them sometimes, but it sounds as though they can be pretty insensitive. I wonder if that is an issue here today as you size up how I might treat you. Maybe I seemed a bit insensitive at the beginning today by asking Betty not to write.

Carol: I'm glad she is not writing.

Betty: I wasn't going to write anything bad. I just have trouble remembering names. I can't even remember yours.

Carol: Carol. No, I'm sure you weren't trying to offend anyone. But I thought that the therapists were going to announce you as an observer.

Betty: I didn't mean to freak anybody out. I just . . .

Therapist: I don't think that you were the only one worried about remembering names or whether you could understand things in this first session and take it with you. What I was really trying to touch upon was whether anyone was "freaked out"

> by my asking Betty not to write. Doctors and therapists are always telling people what to do, particularly about losses.

Betty: Can I offer an off the wall question? With you [Carol] losing a baby and teetering on suicide, isn't Compassionate Friends for parents who have lost a child? I wonder if that wouldn't be better than people telling their stories.

Therapist: Your question may not be such an off-the-wall one. I think that you might be responding to something. I was asking the group about how you think we'll interact with you, how much support is available here, whether there is enough to go around, and whether special problems can be coped with here.

Betty: Yah, uh, I was wondering whether Carol should be in a suicide prevention group or something specific to help her out.

Tom: I don't think anybody here is necessarily suicidal at the moment; maybe they were.

Carol: I'm not suicidal. I don't think that joining a "lost your child group" is what I need right now. A lot of things have piled up. My marriage is rocky; I got a DWI [driving while intoxicated] ticket last month; I can't go to different groups for all of these things.

Tom: Maybe there's a common thread here. Both Betty and Carol have a lot of anger toward somebody. As for me, I'm really angry at my ex-mother-in-law.

Therapist: So, as you sit here and size people up, you find that you have a lot in common. But getting beyond saying hello is problematic. In 12 weeks the group will end. You go through this process only to lose the group and the people who are members. It must have happened to you outside the group too.

In addition to the frequent use of *you,* in this last statement the therapist mentions *the group* three times. The excerpt is representative of the use of group-as-a-whole interventions in interpretive group therapy. All of the interventions focused on issues that involved the entire group of patients. Many addressed conflicts, sources of tension, concerns, worries, wishes, and unanswered questions present in the group. Most of the interventions were interpretations. Some were transference interpretations. The themes of trust, questionable health care professionals, and competing for scarce resources, which are common in loss groups, were addressed. The therapist made eye contact with the patients when making interventions and allowed himself to be facially expressive. Terminology such as "I wonder," "It seems as though," and "Maybe it seemed" conveyed a sense of tentativeness. Although the therapist was active, the group was not given directions about what to do, what to feel, or what to think. In that sense, the therapist withheld a certain level of potential support and promoted a tolerable level of anxiety, which in effect challenged the patients to work toward their own solutions. From the therapist's perspective, the result was an actively engaged group of patients. They worked well together over the course of the 12-session group and according to criteria used in our clinical trials, most patients clearly experienced a favorable outcome for one or more of their target objectives.

Supportive Group-as-a-Whole Interventions

The next excerpt is from a supportive group. The therapist uses such words as *the group* and *everyone* to address the entire group of patients in a supportive manner. The aim is to encourage and to reduce rather than promote anxiety. In comparison with support groups, there is a subtly increased emphasis not on shared dilemmas but on sharing and cohesiveness themselves.

Therapist:	Well, I think, that is sort of related to the question you asked last week, Colleen, in terms of family therapy, you know, is it OK? And, I guess, my answer to Colleen last week was, you know, everyone should get as much as they can. But I guess there can be a point where everyone becomes so immersed in grief that they don't have a chance to see life and, I guess, the real question is, like with any sort of helping profession including yours, is, um, you know, make sure we don't give it all away. Keep something for ourselves.
Katherine:	Yeah. I'm actually finding that listening to people's stories and stuff is, you know, talking about death, I feel like, talking about death all of the time, actually it's talking about life. You know, people are talking about their pride and joy, you know, people they love. So, anyway, doing that so I'm pretty tired.
Therapist:	It's completely understandable for everyone in the group to be tired. Everyone is dealing with their work and their life, which can include helping others. Plus at the same time, the group is dealing with grief, which is real work, extra work, which takes courage and determination. And everyone is doing it. No wonder everyone is tired. And so in the same way as I said to Colleen last week, "If there's anything you learn, bring it in here and share it with everyone." It's great how people exchange ideas here. There's a lot of creativity in this group, and we are making good use of it.

OBJECTIONS TO GROUP-AS-A-WHOLE INTERVENTIONS

During the 1960s and the 1970s, the advantages and disadvantages associated with the use of group-as-a-whole interventions in long-term group therapy were actively debated. For example, as Horwitz (1977) pointed out, proponents of group-as-a-whole interventions cited advantages such as decreased concern about unequal time for each patient, decreased therapist misunderstanding, and heightened sense of commonality. Opponents of group-as-a-whole interventions cited disadvantages such as restricted types of therapist interventions, ignored individual patient needs, and facilitated idealization of the therapist. For the most part, the debate concerning the use and frequency of group-as-a-whole interventions took place before the advent of short-term group therapy. It has been our experience that short-term group therapy has been and continues to be regarded with ambivalence by many patients and therapists. Both parties usually express a preference for individual psychotherapy. They are concerned about how much can be accomplished in a short period of time in a group situation. This is true despite the fact that reviews of the research literature have been quite favorable about the effectiveness of short-term group therapies (Burlingame, MacKenzie, & Strauss, 2004; Piper & Joyce, 1996).

A study by Malan, Balfour, Hood, and Shooter (1976) may have served to discourage many clinicians from using group-as-a-whole interventions. The study involved a long-term follow-up assessment of psychiatric outpatients who had been treated in therapy groups that emphasized group-as-a-whole interpretation at the Tavistock Clinic in London. Many patients were reported to have expressed frustration and disappointment with the therapists and their technique. The therapists were perceived to be cold, distant, passive, and noncaring. Patients found the therapists' interpretations difficult to understand and were considerably irritated when the therapists refused to explain what they meant. According to Malan et al., the therapists had rigidly used techniques that had been borrowed from long-term individual therapy. The Tavistock model represents an extreme form of using group-as-a-whole interpretations. Although it appears to have been useful to participants who wished to learn about group dynamics, the extreme form does not appear, on the evidence of that study, to be useful to psychiatric outpatients.

The negative impact on the patients may have been due to the style in which group-as-a-whole interpretations were delivered, rather than the content of the interpretations. Typically, the Tavistock group therapist avoids eye contact with group members, remains relatively expressionless, speaks in a definitive manner, and if requested, refuses to repeat interpretations or elaborate on them. This is in sharp contrast to a non-Tavistock-style group therapist who makes eye contact with patients when making group-as-a-whole interpretations, allows facial expressiveness, offers the group interpretation in a tentative manner, repeats the interpretation when asked, and is willing to elaborate on the interpretation to improve understanding. These stylistic differences may seem trivial or minor. However, it has been our experience that they can make a great deal of difference in how well interpretations are received and understood and how well they elicit work-oriented responses. We thus recommend using the non-Tavistock style to engage the patients in therapeutic processes, rather than distancing them, as seems all too likely if an austerely nongratifying approach were to be followed.

TERMINATION IN SHORT-TERM GROUP THERAPY FOR COMPLICATED GRIEF

It could be argued that the importance of termination in short-term group therapy is questionable. The loss groups consist of only 12 weekly sessions and usually include eight or nine patients. Given these structural features, one may question whether there is time to become very attached to the other patients in the group and to the therapist and whether there is much time to engage in the tasks of termination. In regard to the attachment issue, it has been our experience that the topic of losing others through death is an emotionally charged one that bonds members rather quickly and facilitates an affectively intense beginning to the groups. For a given patient, there are almost always one or two other patients with whom he or she can readily identify. Although individual therapy patients may find it easy to envision return visits to their therapist to resume therapy, this is not the case for group therapy. Groups that finish are never resumed, at least with the same membership. The termination of a group is final. Even a patient's voiced aspiration to meet with other patients after the end of the group is rarely realized. Thus, although we understand the skepticism of some authors regarding the importance of termination in short-term group therapy, our experience has been quite different (Joyce, Piper, Ogrodniczuk, & Klein, 2007). This may be because limited time is an especially sensitive topic for patients who are experiencing CG. In regard to the limited time to engage in the tasks of termination in short-term group therapy, our experience has been promising. The restricted time to engage in the tasks of termination tended to be used effectively, and the affective intensity of the group climate contributed to the process.

According to Rutan and Stone (2001), termination in group therapy is more public and more complicated because the patient is leaving many members, not just one therapist. They agree that there is less time, because of the presence of the other members, for detailed discussions about the associations and memories that are stirred up in the departing patient. They believe that patients experience less regression than patients in individual therapy. Although there is less opportunity and time in group therapy to engage in the processes of termination at the level of the individual patient, the topic of termination need not and should not be neglected. All of the patients can be addressed through accurate group interpretations. The therapists who lead groups in our program are trained to be particularly sensitive to termination issues and to keep the patients continually attuned to the inevitability of separation and loss as they experience it in the group itself.

CONCLUSION

The differences between the interpretive and supportive models are underscored in this book for expository purposes, but as we have emphasized, they should not be overstated. In this chapter, we have described some features of patients and some features of therapist interventions that cut across the differences between models and tend to blur the differences between their applications in practice. The needs of the patients and their common experiences as individuals dealing with CG are powerful determinants of well-judged therapeutic interventions. For example, there are times in a mainly interpretive loss group when a particular patient's distress is so poignant and despairing that supportive encouragement feels like the only appropriate intervention. Indeed, it is the intervention that will occur whether the therapist makes it or not: If the therapist does not, another patient will. On the other hand, there are times in a mainly supportive loss group when a tepid benign hopefulness prevails, and denial of any distress is in the air. The therapist in this situation feels that collusion with the one-dimensional tone of the interaction is a disservice to the group, so he or she poses the interpretive challenging question, What is being avoided in the discussion today?

A nontrivial benefit of a research study that contrasts the models is the sharpening for the participating therapists of awareness of the many points of differentiation between the two approaches. However, this sharpening does not require a research study to be achieved. It can also be achieved through training, observation, and supervision (which are aspects of careful research studies but which are, of course, routine professional activities in many settings, whether or not a research project is being conducted). It is one thing to be supportive or interpretive intuitively but another to be supportive or interpretive as a matter of choice. To be more fully aware of *what* one is doing as a therapist is an indispensable step on the way to knowing better *why* one is doing it.

Just as there are certain patient roles that may frequently occur in loss groups, as outlined previously, there are roles to which therapists may be drawn for reasons of their own, for example, their own training, professional development, and personalities. Apart from the roles that they may spontaneously assume, groups may pressure them in one direction or another. We believe that key differentiations between types of therapeutic activities, and hence therapist roles, lie in the multiple points of distinction between the supportive and interpretive models. A very general classification of therapist roles is thus bipartite: supportive and interpretive. This is not a crude or oversimplified classification. As we have emphasized, these two general labels encompass multiple potential choices in therapeutic interventions.

The great majority of therapists are supportive, well-intentioned, kind people. Supportive interventions come spontaneously to them. Unless therapists have had training in interpretive work, there is a real possibility that they will tend to avoid the anxiety that is intrinsically associated with the interpretive approach. The findings in our research studies indicate that such avoidance would be a disservice, at least in the sense of opportunities missed, in many situations. What situations? Specifically, situations in which there are sufficient group members who have sufficiently mature object relations to respond to the interpretations and the other challenges of the interpretive model.

The relation of research to practice is heuristic rather than narrowly prescriptive. However, the heuristic guidance that has already been assembled is instructive and clinically useful.

9

TIME-LIMITED SHORT-TERM INTERPRETIVE GROUP THERAPY

In this chapter, we describe techniques specific to time-limited short-term interpretive group therapy. We first review the theoretical approach, objectives, and implications for therapeutic techniques. Next, we describe the process of beginning the group and the primary techniques used throughout therapy. We then discuss what to do when common phenomena occur, such as a violation of ground rules. Finally, we describe the process of terminating the group.

THEORETICAL APPROACH AND OBJECTIVES

Use of the interpretive approach to short-term groups for complicated grief (CG) is based on the assumption that the impediments to the patients' mourning process can be overcome by understanding and resolving unconscious conflicts that underlie CG. Once the impediments are overcome, the resumption of the mourning process will naturally occur and continue until its completion.

The major differences between interpretive therapy and supportive therapy concern the overall objective, session objective, and therapist techniques:

- The primary overall objective of interpretive therapy is to enhance the patients' insight about repetitive conflicts (intrapsychic and interpersonal) and trauma, which underlie and sustain the patients' problems. There is an attempt to initiate a process of understanding and control that continues beyond the termination of therapy (working through). A secondary objective is to alleviate the immediate presenting problems that brought the patients into therapy.
- The session objective is to create a climate of tolerable tension and deprivation wherein conflicts can be examined through the use of immediate (here-and-now) experience. That involves an exploration of the relationship between the therapist and patients and the relationships among patients. The therapist's focus is on unconscious processes.
- The therapist's techniques are to (a) maintain pressure on the patients to talk, (b) encourage them to explore uncomfortable emotions, (c) make interpretations about conflicts, (d) direct attention to patients' subjective impressions of the therapist, (e) make links between the patients' relationships with the therapist or each other and the patients' relationships with others in their lives, (f) focus on the patients and therapist in the here-and-now treatment situation, and (g) direct attention to the patients' subjective impressions of others outside the treatment situation.

The interpretive group therapist actively minimizes use of therapist techniques characteristic of supportive therapy. Hence, he or she avoids (a) gratifying the patients; (b) providing noninterpretive interventions; (c) providing guidance; (d) engaging in problem-solving strategies; (e) externalizing responsibility for problems; (f) praising the patients; and (g) disclosing personal information, opinions, and values. Although the focus of therapist activity is on interpretive techniques, it is not expected that a "pure" form of interpretive therapy will be provided, that is, one that is consistently devoid of any and all supportive techniques. Rather, an emphasis on interpretive features is maintained.

IMPLICATIONS OF OBJECTIVES FOR THERAPIST TECHNIQUES

Regarding the primary objective, because the groups are homogeneously composed of patients experiencing CG, all patients are assumed to share similar conflicts that underlie CG. The therapist focuses on the limited and realizable goal of exploring the common themes or conflicts of the group. He or she will not pursue an idiosyncratic or unique problem of any one member but will tenaciously stay with only those conflicts common to all group members. These themes include wanting yet fearing a close relationship with another person; wanting to be autonomous and self-sufficient yet fearing isolation and loneliness; and experiencing ambivalent (conflictual) feelings toward the lost person, that is, anger and sadness, guilt and relief, attraction and repulsion.

The decision to maintain a focus on CG as the primary target of inter-pretive work is consistent with the short-term structure of the groups. It is assumed that relative to a superficial exploration of many conflict areas, a thorough exploration and understanding of this singular focal conflict area will be more beneficial to the patients. Given the potential range of conflict areas that could be explored for each patient, the therapist should remember that short-term group therapy is inevitably a partial treatment. Despite its partial nature it potentially can serve as an important model for understanding that can be applied to other areas of the patients' lives with or without the benefit of additional psychotherapy.

The time-limited aspect of therapy promotes the emergence of themes associated with all intrapsychic conflicts. The common wish of group members that the group continue past its predetermined termination date represents a wish for the unattainable. This wish is reminiscent of the conflictual, unattainable wishes that are denied gratification by society or its internal representation (conscience, superego). However, this common wish to avoid the "death" of the group is particularly significant for patients who may have wished to avoid the death that triggered their CG. For patients conflicted by loss, termination represents a unique opportunity to explore the related fears of isolation and abandonment. The interpretive therapist focuses on those aspects of conflicts that relate to issues of loss and CG.

The frustrating aspects of the group in terms of not being a "cure-all" is reminiscent of the anger and frustration that all patients feel with respect to the imperfection of themselves and the world. By exploring the limitations and frustrating aspects of therapy, patients can simultaneously explore other nongratifying situations outside the group. It is typically these other non-gratifying situations that are the focus of the patients' conscious concerns. Linking the unconscious intrapsychic conflicts with these more conscious interpersonal or intrapersonal problems is consistent with a secondary objec-tive of interpretive therapy. As previously mentioned, a secondary objective is to alleviate the immediate presenting problems that brought the patients into therapy. These presenting problems are often the consequence of or the maladaptive outcome of an intrapsychic conflict and are addressed as such.

This secondary objective of alleviating the patients' presenting prob-lems is also addressed in interpretive therapy by the homogeneity of group composition. Loneliness, isolation, and hopelessness are common presenting complaints of patients with CG. Homogeneity in the therapy group is assumed to promote cohesiveness among the patients as they recognize and identify with the similar complaints or concerns of each other. Consequently, in the group, the patients will not feel so alone, isolated, or hopeless. This similarity among group patients is elsewhere referred to as *universality*.

Regarding the session objective—to create a climate of tolerable tension and deprivation wherein conflicts can be examined through the use of immediate (here-and-now) experience—the therapist is active in rapidly focusing on the group defenses, transference reactions, termination issues, and unconscious themes by engaging in activities that characterize the interpretive approach to psychotherapy.

THE BEGINNING

The interpretive therapist begins the group by welcoming the patients in a direct, nondemonstrative manner. The therapist introduces him- or herself and invites the patients to introduce themselves:

> Good morning. This is the short-term group for loss. My name is [name], and I will be your therapist for the next 12 weeks. The group will always meet in this room. One of the things that I would like to emphasize is that this is your group. What we talk about, in particular how we begin each session, is largely determined by what you feel is important. Maybe you could begin today by introducing yourselves and saying whatever you wish about what brought you to the group.

The therapist is nondirective, active, and noneducative. A priority in this beginning session is to build a therapeutic alliance. Toward this end, the therapist facilitates cohesion among the group members by identifying similarities and common experiences. A second priority is to manage the anxiety in the group such that it does not become debilitating. Toward this end, the therapist intervenes to diminish anxiety that is seen as nonproductive but allows anxiety to mount if he or she believes that it is promoting work in the group. We have come to understand that the goal of therapy is not so much lessening the patient's level of anxiety as it is strengthening the patient's tolerance of anxiety as well as other painful aspects that are regularly associated with loss through death. In this book, we repeatedly empathize the ever presence (or inescapability) of death. If the patient can learn to function well in the face of death, he or she will have learned a very valuable skill.

With these priorities in mind, the group process is allowed to unfold in a typically open-ended manner. The therapist reflects back to the group the process that is emerging in the here and now. When he or she has enough evidence, the therapist attempts to link the group process with issues associated with loss. He or she may do this by identifying what is going on in the group and what is not going on in the group in terms of what is underneath the behavioral manifestations in the group, both verbal and nonverbal. It must be emphasized that the timing of interpretations is always contingent on the therapist's judgment that the group is receptive, which is based on his or her monitoring the therapeutic alliance and level of anxiety in the group.

> Now that you have all introduced yourself, you seem to be wondering what to do next. I imagine you all feel a little anxious about meeting each other and getting started. So maybe the silence is telling us that you are all feeling pretty alone in here today, despite all the feelings that you have in common.

Generally, the therapist does not respond directly to questions and requests for direction. Similarly, questions regarding medications are not dealt with on the manifest level. Rather the therapist invites the patients to explore the latent feelings and conflicts that underlie the manifest content of the group discussion. Toward this end, the therapist offers unambiguous interventions based on evidence provided by the manifest content. Links with unconscious latent conflicts are offered. Ultimately, the therapist attempts to associate here-and-now events with unconscious conflicts related to loss and the lost person(s). At the second session, the therapist waits for the patients to begin the group.

THERAPIST TECHNIQUES THROUGHOUT TREATMENT

This section expands on the techniques identified at the beginning of the chapter: (a) maintain pressure on the patients to talk, (b) encourage them to explore uncomfortable emotions, (c) make interpretations about conflicts, (d) direct attention to patients' subjective impressions of the therapist, (e) make links between the patients' relationships with the therapist or each other and the patients' relationships with others in their lives, (f) focus on the patients and therapist in the here-and-now treatment situation, and (g) direct attention to the patients' subjective impressions of others outside the treatment situation.

Maintain Pressure on the Patients to Talk

Given the short-term and time-limited modality, the therapist is active relative to longer term therapies. However, the nature of the therapist's activity is passive rather than directive and receptive rather than intrusive. This approach allows the therapist to listen, to empathize, to think, that is, to make associations, integrate material, formulate ideas, construct interpretations, and consider the appropriateness of his or her delivery. The patients do the majority of the talking. The process involves talkers and the listener who welcomes and encourages the provision of private material and who eventually offers clarifications and interpretations. The process should not resemble a conversation or a question and answer dialogue. Questions and other non-interpretive intervention should not be used to sustain the patients' speech. Pressuring the patients to accept ideas by means of therapist activity is antithetical to this approach. The passive-receptive approach creates a steady pressure on the patient to provide material. This pressure may serve to heighten anxiety and regressive reactions, which provide further material for interpretation.

Encourage the Patients to Explore Uncomfortable Emotions

Work in interpretive therapy is a collaborative activity. All participants (patients and therapist) must possess certain abilities and a willingness to pursue a particular kind of work, even when that is difficult. The patients must be willing to self-disclose, to experience unpleasant feelings, to think about interpretations that are partly experienced as puzzling and frightening, to learn even when it is painful and unflattering, to tolerate certain deprivations on the therapist's part, and to be patient. The therapist must be willing to tolerate tension and uncertainty, to withhold support and other immediately gratifying offerings (advice, instruction, compliments), to experience negative transference, to examine and contain personal countertransferential reactions, to continuously devote energy to understanding the patient and to providing useful interventions, and to be patient. Engaging in such work requires a trust in the intentions of the other participants and an optimism that in time the process will be useful. The presence of such trust, optimism, and willingness to engage in a particular kind of work is usually what is meant by a therapeutic alliance (helping alliance, working relationship).

Provide the Patients With Interpretations

Interpretations are defined as constructions that focus on the components of internal conflicts and the dynamic relationships among the components. This involves one or more wish-anxiety-defense-expression sequences. Elucidation of the people (objects) that are associated with the components is also regarded as important, in particular, ambivalent feelings toward the lost person. Topographically, interpretations are assumed to increase the patients' awareness of unconscious and preconscious material. Usually interpretations deal with only part of a conflict (or sequence). Integrative interpretations, that is, those that deal with multiple components of a conflict (or sequence), almost always follow interpretive work that is partial, repetitive, and applied to different objects and periods of time. In this context, linking similar patient relationships with different objects is viewed as important. The interpretive approach similarly tends to heighten anxiety and precipitate regressive reactions. It also serves to stimulate a progressive process of understanding and change.

Direct Attention to Patients' Subjective Impressions of the Therapist

The patients' transferential relationship with the therapist is viewed as an important axis for interpretive work. The immediacy and intensity of this relationship make it uniquely advantageous as a vehicle for exploring and understanding the patients' conflicts and difficulties. However, exclusive focus on therapist transferential reactions is not advocated. The importance of examining transferential reactions to other group members has been discussed previously. Examining transferential reactions to objects external to the group is also important, particularly when they can be related to transferential reactions involving the therapist and other group members. Because of tensions experienced by the patients and the therapist and the obvious importance of other relationships in the patients' lives, it is often easy for the therapist to neglect interpretive work involving the therapist as a transference object. Such neglect should be avoided.

Make Links Between the Patients' Relationships With Others

Interpretations that involve similar reactions to different objects are attempted. Initially, the therapist attempts to understand the nature of the patients' relationships with others in the group; with the therapist; with current relationships outside of therapy; and with past figures, especially parental figures and lost persons. Over time, and with the patients' assistance, the therapist attempts to explore similarities in the nature of the patients' conflicts as traced through their current relationships outside of therapy; their immediate relationship within therapy; and the patients' past relationships, especially with the lost person. The therapist may interpret, for example, that patients' ambivalence over dependency needs that were not satisfied by a parent is being displayed in their anger and disappointment with the therapist and patients' wishes to be taken care of by the lost person are being displayed in demands that the therapist give advice, be more active, answer their questions.

Focus on the Patients and Therapist in the Here-and-Now Treatment Situation

Given that therapy is provided in a group format, the therapist focuses on how the unconscious conflicts are emerging (manifested) in the here-and-now behavior in the group. For example, the therapist may interpret the way

- patients' fears of intimacy are being displayed in the lack of disclosure between the members or statements reflecting rationalizations such as, "Why get involved if it's only for 12 weeks?";
- patients' ambivalence over dependency needs is being displayed in their anger at other patients' neediness, despair of the "blind leading the blind," and disappointment with the therapist;
- patients' anger over the loss of the relationship is being displayed in their anger over the absenteeism and dropping out of other patients and of the inevitable termination of the group; and
- patients' guilt over the loss of the relationship is being displayed in the protective (defensive) maneuvers toward absent and dropping-out patients.

Direct Attention to the Patients' Subjective Impressions of Others

Interpretive therapy for patients experiencing CG offers the patients the opportunity to explore their relationship with the lost person as well as others. By emphasizing that the patients' impressions of their relationships with others are influenced by previous relationships and their memories of past relationships are influenced by subsequent relationships, the subjective nature of all relationships is emphasized. The ability to establish healthier, more realistic relationships becomes within the patients' domain. For example, patients may gain insight into how their conflicts with respect to the lost relationship continue to influence their reaction to any intimate relationship. Hence, patients may begin to understand the influence of their needs, fears, and defenses on their difficulties forming an intimate relationship with anyone.

THERAPIST TECHNIQUES WHEN COMMON PHENOMENA OCCUR

This includes the violation of ground rules, the empty chair, affect, acting out, silence, reaction to the therapist, patient roles, group-as-whole interventions, and time limit.

The Violation of Ground Rules

Although the interpretive therapist generally allows the group process to unfold unfettered, he or she ensures that the group is a safe place and facilitative for the work of therapy to occur. The therapist monitors the degree to which any violation of the "ground rules" (see Chapter 7, this volume) threatens the work or safety of the group as a whole or of any individual group member. Whereas minor infractions may be contained by examining them through interpretive work, whenever the therapist believes that a breach of the ground rules is significantly disruptive, he or she should directly intervene. This may involve confronting, containing, or in extreme instances even removing a group member.

Examples of breaches to the ground rules that have various disruptive potentials are included throughout this chapter.

The Empty Chair

This includes lateness, missed sessions, and dropouts.

Lateness

When a session begins with an empty chair but a dropout has not been confirmed, the therapist waits for the group to notice the empty chair. He or she does not inform the group of the reason for the absence. Rather, the therapist focuses on the group's response or lack thereof to the empty chair. This response may include exploring themes related to feeling abandoned, guilty, disappointed, or relieved. The response may include the group's identification with the absent member in terms of envying him or her for being elsewhere, that is, members' ambivalence with respect to the group as enacted by or projected onto the absent member. Ultimately, the therapist attempts to link the group's reaction to the absent member with patients' reactions to the lost persons.

> It seems that the group feels a mixture of feelings toward the empty chair. Some feel sort of put out, betrayed by Lynn, while others feel sort of responsible for driving her away. It's similar to the mixed feelings the group expressed toward those you've lost, a mixture of anger and guilt.

When a member arrives late the therapist does not inform him or her of what has transpired before his or her arrival. Rather, the therapist focuses on the group's reaction or lack thereof to the arrival. The meaning of the lateness for the late member may be explored, especially in later sessions; for example, the therapist may say, "Now that Lynn has arrived today, I'm struck by how you are reluctant to tell her directly how it felt not to have her here."

Missed Sessions

Missed sessions are discouraged and explored as reflecting multiple motivations. The absent member typically is not contacted after the first missed session unless the therapist believes that the patient's safety is at issue. Rather, the therapist waits for the member to return to the next session and explores in the group the motivations behind the absence and the group's reaction to the member's missed session. Even when the reason for an absence seems legitimate, the member's feelings with respect to the absence are nevertheless explored as is the group's reaction to the absence.

A member who misses two consecutive sessions is contacted. During a rather brief telephone contact, the reason for the absence is queried, and the member is reminded of his or her commitment to him- or herself and to the group. If the member expresses ambivalence regarding his or her return to the group, the therapist may reassure the patient that he or she is not the only member who feels ambivalent toward the group and encourages the member to return to the group to discuss these feelings or at the very least to say goodbye. The therapist may inform the patient that a third absence will be understood as his or her decision to terminate the group.

If the ambivalent member, or *apparition* (see Chapter 8, this volume), returns to the group, the therapist focuses on rhe role that the he or she may play for the group. Other members are invited to explore their identification with the patient by discussing their own ambivalence and disappointment with the group. They are also invited to explore their feelings regarding the patient. Ultimately, the therapist attempts to link the group's reaction to the ambivalent member with group members' reactions to the lost person.

> There seem to be lots of mixed feelings about Joe's absence last week and his difficulty being here today. In particular, we're hearing about how powerless you feel to make Joe stay in the group. I guess it's similar to the powerlessness you felt when you couldn't make your loved ones stay with you as they slipped into death.

If the therapist judges the ambivalent member's behavior to be disruptive to the group, the apparition may be discharged.

Dropouts

When the empty chair is because of a confirmed dropout, the chair is not removed from the circle but remains in place throughout the life of the group. The therapist may or may not confirm that the patient has dropped out. The professed reason for the departure is usually not provided to the group. Rather, the therapist encourages the group to fantasize about the reasons for the dropout's decision to leave the group and their reactions to the dropout. The therapist attempts to link the group's reactions to the dropout with patients' reactions to the lost persons.

> Well, some of you feel sad that Lynn has left the group, while others of you seem relieved that her comings and goings and the disruptions from that have finally stopped. It reminds me of the mixed feelings some of you felt when your loved ones succumbed to cancer. You felt sad but also somewhat relieved that they were no longer suffering and that your lives could get back to some sort of routine.

Affect

The interpretive therapist encourages the expression of all emotions, especially emotions that the patients are uncomfortable exploring. Similarly, the therapist labels nonverbalized affect that is present in the room. Cartharsis is seen as therapeutic but only if the affects are integrated with an exploration and understanding of the underlying conflicts associated with these affects. The guiding principle is that cartharsis is necessary but not sufficient for beneficial outcome. The therapist may empathize with affects being expressed in the group but pays particular attention to the exploration of affects that are not being expressed in the group. He or she also explores and interprets the conflictual aspects of all affects. Of particular importance is the exploration of patients' ambivalent feelings toward the lost persons and their difficulty tolerating this ambivalence. Ultimately, the therapist attempts to link the affect in the here-and-now group process with issues related to loss and the lost persons.

> We've heard about feeling many different feelings today: scared, sad, hurt, abandoned, and guilty. So I guess we're hearing that you have mixed feelings about the losses you've experienced. I imagine that leaves you feeling kind of confused.

Sometimes a group member may express affect that appears to serve a defensive function for the entire group. In such circumstances, the therapist does not focus on the "emotional conductor." Rather, he or she focuses on the role that the patient is enacting for the group. If the patient's cartharsis is seen as disruptive, the therapist may need to directly intervene to contain that patient.

> Diane, it seems that you're crying for everyone today. You certainly are in touch with the sadness in the group. My sense is that there are also other emotions that people are feeling in addition to the sadness. Somehow, it might be more frightening to get in touch with those other emotions, other emotions such as anger, resentment, for example.

If the therapist is aware that details associated with important losses are not being addressed, the therapist confronts this resistance but does not divulge the nature of the defended material. For example, if the therapist were aware that some of the women had had abortions but that they were not discussing them, the therapist would not divulge details about the abortions to the group. Rather, he or she might explore the themes of shame or relief around secrets.

Acting Out

If members begin to act out nonverbalized affects or unconscious conflicts, the therapist's response reflects his or her attempt to understand, explore, and interpret the behavior. Because the same acting-out behaviors may reflect various aspects of unconscious conflicts, the therapist weighs the evidence in deciding how to interpret any acting-out behavior. Typically, the maladaptive outcome of the conflict believed to be associated with the acting-out behavior is included in his or her intervention. The following examples demonstrate various responses to extragroup socializing by two group members or *pairing*.

> The wish seems to be that you could take the closeness you feel with Susie within the group and move it outside into the world so you could avoid taking risks all over again out there. What you may not realize, however, is how you end up alienating yourself from the rest of the group so that you feel alone inside as well as outside of group.

> The wish seems to be that you could express your feelings by doing things together rather than by having to rely on words. I suspect you are frustrated with me for expecting you only to use words and only during group. What you may not realize, however, is that by not using what the group can offer you, you deprive yourself of what the group could offer you.

> You seem to be wanting a more private, intimate, or exclusive relationship than the types of relationships offered here. I imagine you resent having to share Susie with the entire group. What you may not realize, however, is how excluded the rest of the group may feel.

> Perhaps the wish is that if you can transform the relationship from group members to friends, then you could avoid saying goodbye to one another. What you may not realize, however, is that by transforming the relationship, you threaten to destroy the group's trust in you.

If the interpretive therapeutic approach does not counteract and contain the behavior, the therapist makes a judgment concerning the behavior's destructive potential for the individual or the group in terms of work and safety. In cases in which the destructive potential is believed to be high, the therapist relies on group management techniques to confront and contain the behavior. In cases in which the destructive potential is believed to be low, the therapist persists with the interpretive approach.

Silence

When the group becomes silent, the therapist attempts to understand, explore, and interpret aspects of the unconscious conflict that underlie it. When a particular member continues to be silent in the group, the therapist addresses the group's reaction to the silent member, or *monk* (see Chapter 8, this volume), and the function this patient is fulfilling for the group. The patient is addressed primarily in terms of what he exemplifies for the group: "Perhaps Tom represents that part of all of you that would just as soon leave the Pandora's box tightly closed from fear of becoming overwhelmed by all the pain that is inside."

The monk and the apparition are patient roles that commonly emerge in short-term loss groups. Other familiar roles are discussed in Chapter 8.

Reaction to the Therapist

Using patient reactions to the therapist is an important part of the interpretive approach. The therapist attempts to understand, explore, and judiciously interpret transferential themes as they emerge in the here-and-now group situation. The therapist is cautioned against an overemphasis of transference interpretations, however, because that may only serve to strengthen resistance.

The therapist may represent various important objects for group members, for example, a parental figure, authority figure, caregiver, or medical expert. Of special utility is the exploration of ambivalence with respect to the lost persons through here-and-now exploration of ambivalence toward the therapist. In this respect, it is important to explore negative emotions such as anger, disappointment, and resentment with respect to the therapist and then link these emotions with respect to the lost persons. By grieving the fantasy of the idealized therapist, the patients may be able to more readily grieve the fantasy of the nurturing caregiver.

> I sense disappointment that I did not answer your questions. You seem to be feeling that I do not care about you, that I am deliberately withholding something helpful from you. I imagine it's like the disappointment you felt at home when your needs were not met, when you felt that you didn't count.

Patient Roles

When a patient seems to be occupying a particular role, the therapist understands it in terms of the patient responding to a need of the group. The therapist attempts to understand, explore, and interpret the function of the role for the entire group. Typically, patient roles serve a protective or defensive function for the group. The therapist directly addresses the dynamics of the role-taking member as these dynamics pertain to the group level conflict that is being enacted. It is believed that the function being served by the patient role is a function that the group wishes the therapist would fulfill. Consequently, the therapist often links the patient role to transferential wishes.

If the *professor* (see Chapter 8, this volume) emerges in the group, the therapist recognizes that the group is in need of anxiety reduction by using defenses such as rationalization and intellectualization. Hence, the therapist offers an interpretation to this effect:

> Well Rob, you seem to be trying to explain all these painful feelings. It is as if you believed that if you and the group could understand these feelings, if they somehow made sense, then maybe they wouldn't hurt so much. I think that Rob is not the only one who wishes this was so. I think Rob represents that part of all of you that is looking to make sense of all these confusing emotions.

If the *professional nurturer* (see Chapter 8, this volume) emerges in the group, the therapist recognizes that the group is in need of praise and encouragement and provides an interpretation to this effect:

> Diane, you seem to be trying to comfort various members of the group. I think in some ways the group would like to receive that support from me just as you wanted to receive affection and nurturance from the other people in your lives. I imagine you feel hurt and uncared for by myself and the others who disappointed you by not meeting these needs.

If a patient monopolizes the group, the therapist recognizes that the group is feeling vulnerable and in need of protection and provides an interpretation to this effect: "Richard, you're really letting the rest of the group avoid talking about their own issues, sort of letting them off the hook, and of course, they're letting you."

In extreme cases in which the group is being totally disrupted, the therapist may need to use group management techniques such as instructing the monopolizing member to be quiet or ultimately even to leave the session or group.

Group-as-a-Whole Interventions

The therapist conceptualizes the group as an entity whereby all members share common unconscious conflicts that emerge as group themes in the here-and-now group process. It is further believed that the emergence and/or persistence of any particular theme reflects the implicit permission of the group's members. In addressing these themes, the therapist conceptualizes the various aspects of unconscious conflicts as being enacted by individual members, dyads, or subgroups. He or she addresses these themes as such.

> We seem to be hearing a debate between the men and the women concerning the importance of having an intimate relationship. The women are saying they want a relationship, while the men are saying they don't. I think this debate reflects a debate that goes on in the mind of each one of you. You want a relationship, and you don't want a relationship. Or to be more precise, each of you wants intimacy and fears it at the same time. But of course, if the debate continues, in here and in your own mind, you can avoid looking for the intimacy that you both want and fear.

The Time Limit

Using the time limit is integral to the interpretive approach. The group's reaction to the limited time of the group is understood as reflecting its reaction to the limited time of life that is associated with the deaths of the lost persons. As a general rule, the interpretive group therapist does not repeatedly remind the group of the passage of time; the therapist is not a time manager or time-keeper. Rather, the therapist attempts to understand, explore, and interpret themes reflecting the time limit and then to link these to issues involving the lost person.

Common themes related to the time limit include feelings of deprivation, finality, futility, powerlessness, and competition for limited resources. Ambivalence with respect to involvement in the group given its time limit is also a common theme. This theme often reflects an underlying existential theme of ambivalence with respect to any involvement including life itself given the inherent limitations. Rather than emphasizing that the glass is half full or half empty, the interpretive therapist emphasizes that the glass is both. Hence, the limited available time is interpreted as an opportunity and as a deprivation.

> So with only a few sessions left, the feeling seems to be, Why get closer if it's all going to end in a few weeks anyway? That's sort of like asking

why get involved with anyone if it's not going to last forever. You want to enjoy the pleasure of someone's company yet fear losing them and missing them if you get too close. It's as if you regret ever knowing those people because they died and left you and you miss them.

THE TERMINATION

The principle guiding termination is for the group to experience and tolerate issues related to loss in the here-and-now group process and then to link these issues to lost persons. Of particular importance is an emphasis on recognizing and tolerating ambivalent feelings toward the loss of the group, the therapist, and lost persons. This ambivalence should include an exploration of defended feelings, especially anger and disappointment. This anger may be related to issues such as unfulfilled expectations, unresolved dependency needs, powerlessness to prevent or influence the timing of the loss, and others' participation in their own demise. The negative emotions associated with ambivalence are actively but not exclusively explored. The therapist emphasizes that termination is both an end and a beginning, a deprivation and an opportunity, anxiety-provoking and exciting.

> There is much sadness in the group today saying how much you appreciate each other and the time you spent together. I imagine that there are other feelings too. Perhaps feeling somewhat frustrated that just as you get comfortable with each other you have to say goodbye. And maybe there's also some relief that this ordeal is over. Sort of don't know whether it's a wake or a celebration.

The therapist does not rely on the last session to broach issues related to termination. These themes are addressed throughout the life of the group. The therapist persists with the interpretive technique throughout the last session. Pressure for the therapist to provide feedback, acknowledgement, or praise is explored and interpreted rather than being gratified:

> I'm struck by how much you wish I would provide you with some sort of report card. It is as if only my opinion counts. You seem reluctant to turn to each other for feedback or to appraise your own progress for that matter.

The therapist can express positive wishes when saying goodbye. For example, the therapist could say, "Good-bye, I wish you all the best." The therapist should also feel free to acknowledge the reality of a positive therapy outcome, if appropriate.

If members discuss their wish to continue meeting after the group ends, the therapist explores and interprets what this plan represents. Postgroup meetings can reflect members' wish to have an anxiety-free meeting, an attempt to avoid the finality of termination, a rebellion against the therapist's authority regarding termination, or a wish to retaliate and reject the therapist completely.

> So there seems to be a reluctance to say goodbye to each other. I guess the barbeque is really a way of avoiding the whole reality of what this last session represents—the death of this group. Saying goodbye is difficult, especially for this group.

In Chapter 10, we consider the theoretical approach, objectives, and technical approach taken by the supportive therapist. These features are in sharp contrast to those that we have just reviewed for the interpretive therapist. The difference in the therapist's behavior is particularly evident in the responses to the common phenomena, which often are forms of patient resistance.

10

TIME-LIMITED SHORT-TERM SUPPORTIVE GROUP THERAPY

In this chapter, we describe techniques specific to time-limited short-term supportive group therapy. We first review the theoretical approach, objectives, and implications for therapeutic techniques. Next, we describe the process of beginning the group and the primary techniques used throughout therapy. We then discuss what to do when common phenomena occur, such as a violation of ground rules. Finally, it describes the process of terminating the group.

THEORETICAL APPROACH AND OBJECTIVES

Use of the supportive approach to short-term groups for complicated grief (CG) is based on the assumption that improvements in symptomatology and life (role) functioning can be made through the provision of support. Once such improvements occur, the resumption of the mourning process will naturally occur and continue until its completion.

The major differences between supportive therapy and interpretive therapy concern the overall objective, session objective, and therapist techniques:

- The primary overall objective of supportive therapy is to improve the patients' immediate adaptation to their life situation. A secondary objective is to teach the patients problem-solving skills (build ego strength) that can be used in the future.
- The session objective is to create a climate of gratification wherein patients can share common experiences and feelings and receive praise (reinforcement) for their efforts at coping. The therapist's focus is on conscious processes.
- The therapist techniques are to (a) gratify the patients; (b) provide noninterpretive interventions; (c) provide guidance; (d) engage in problem-solving strategies; (e) externalize responsibility for problems; (f) praise the patients; and (g) disclose personal information, opinions, and values.

The supportive group therapist minimizes use of therapist techniques characteristic of interpretive therapy. Hence, he or she restricts (a) maintaining pressure on the patients to talk, (b) encouraging them to explore uncomfortable emotions, (c) making interpretations about conflicts, (d) directing the patients' attention to subjective impressions of the therapist, (e) making links between the patients' relationships with others and their relationship with the therapist, (f) focusing on the here-and-now situation, and (g) directing attention to patients' subjective impressions of others. Although the focus of therapist activity is on supportive techniques, it is not expected that a "pure" form of supportive therapy will be provided, that is, one that is consistently devoid of any and all interpretive techniques. Rather, an emphasis on supportive features is maintained.

IMPLICATIONS OF OBJECTIVES FOR THERAPIST TECHNIQUES

Regarding the primary objective, maladaptation is consistent with CG. The therapist highlights in his or her mind a constellation of psychodynamic conflicts conceptually related to CG. Attention is devoted to the manifestations (maladaptive outcomes) of the conflicts and practical methods of alleviating them. The underlying components of the conflicts, for example, wishes, fears, and defenses, which are often preconscious or unconscious, are not interpreted or explored. The supportive therapist encourages logical and rational thought processes. There is a *crisis intervention* orientation with an attempt to initiate restorative processes as soon as possible and strengthen them as therapy proceeds.

Regarding the secondary objective, the therapist seeks solutions to problems in the patients' current living situation by focusing on behavior and not the meaning of behavior. Generating solutions to problematic situations involves helping the patients map out more effective coping strategies or improving their adaptation. An important aspect of building ego strength is conveying to the patients that their feelings and predicaments are accurately understood.

Another important aspect of building ego strength involves a consideration of the patients' usual defense mechanisms. The therapist identifies adaptive defenses that should be supported, encouraged, and strengthened and maladaptive defenses that can safely be clarified, confronted, undermined, and actively discouraged without seriously compromising the patient's ability to function. Hence, defenses are evaluated according to their adaptational and homeostatic value. When defense mechanisms are reflected in the patient's resistance in the therapy situation, the therapist's response is consistent with the goal of strengthening adaptive defenses and weakening maladaptive defenses. Often, the patients' behaviors have ambiguous adaptational value, and the therapist must make a clinical judgment about strengthening, undermining, or ignoring the behaviors, resistances, or defenses.

Consistent with building ego strength, the patients' direct or indirect attempts to elicit praise and encouragement from the therapist are gratified. In response to the patients' effort to improve their adaptation, the therapist spontaneously offers praise and encouragement. He or she attempts to minimize anxiety and regression in the therapy sessions. Thus, the patients experience sessions as less frustrating. That experience is consistent with the session objectives of attempting to create a climate of gratification wherein patients can share common experiences and feelings and receive praise (reinforcement) for their efforts at coping.

Transference distortions involving the therapist are not encouraged. Rather, the therapist's "realness" is emphasized. The therapist promotes a feeling of security in the therapeutic relationship by communicating his or her interest in, liking for, or understanding of the patient. Negative transferences are dissipated immediately. The therapist's response to the patients' statements focus on the reality aspects of the communication. The emphasis is to explore interpersonal relationships outside the treatment situation. Hence, the patients are first confronted with the reality of the treatment relationship; second, the transferences are directed out of therapy as the therapist points out parallels in similar feelings toward significant others in the patients' lives.

Regarding the session objective, the aim in supportive therapy is to maintain a mildly positive transference that is not commented on. This is encouraged by the therapist being more real and somewhat gratifying of the patients. Distorted, excessively positive transference (e.g., idealizing or erotic) does not need to be responded to, though the therapist may indicate skepticism of the patients' idealization. The therapist's response will sometimes address specific defensive operations or distortions and at other times consist of guidance more appropriate to the family doctor role. Because the therapist's interventions include the latter, there is a danger that the therapist will attempt to overly influence the patients, that is, "Do as I do." The therapist should guard against such countertransference stringently.

THE BEGINNING

The therapist begins the group by welcoming the patients, introducing him- or herself, and inviting the patients to introduce themselves by name: "So, welcome to group. I am your therapist, and my name is [name]. Before we get started, let's go around the circle, and each of you tell us your name."

The therapist is directive, active, and educative. The therapist reminds the patients of the time frame of the group, the group process they can expect, and the ground rules and briefly highlights some of the therapeutic factors available from the group:

> The group will meet for 90 minutes, once a week, for 12 weeks. Each week you will have the opportunity to talk about the losses you have experienced, how the losses continue to affect your lives, and how you are coping with all that. You all received a copy of the group's ground rules that emphasize the importance of coming to group every week, of protecting the privacy of what is said here, and of not meeting with each other outside of group. The group is here to help you feel understood, to learn new coping skills from each other, and to think out some new solutions to your problems. We might begin by going around the circle again, but this time each of you could maybe say a little bit about what brings you to group.

The therapist responds directly to any questions and requests for direction. Similarly, questions regarding medications are clarified, and patients are encouraged to discuss their concerns with their prescribing physician. Ultimately, the therapist directs the discussion outside the group to people and situations in their lives. At the second session, the therapist welcomes the members back to the group and invites them to remind each other of their names.

THERAPIST TECHNIQUES THROUGHOUT TREATMENT

This section expands on the techniques identified at the beginning of the chapter: (a) gratify the patients; (b) provide noninterpretive interventions; (c) provide guidance; (d) engage in problem-solving strategies; (e) externalize responsibility for problems; (f) praise the patients; and (g) disclose personal information, opinions, and values.

Gratify the Patients

The supportive therapist accepts all patients' disclosures without interpretation. Active responses may include tracking (indicating that the therapist is following the patients), universalizing (clarifying that many people have similar feelings, wishes, or problems), or decatastrophizing (minimizing issues or problems the patients have exaggerated).

Provide Noninterpretive Interventions

The therapist can use clarifying interventions and confronting interventions.

Clarifying Interventions

The therapist clarifies by asking for more information, pointing out connections the patients have not made but could know, restating more directly what the patients have said, and reframing a more objective and less distorted view about the patients' life situation. Clarification has the goal of limited insight into conscious and preconscious material and connections.

Confronting Interventions

Confrontation refers to the therapist's forcefully directing the patients' attention to something in the treatment, particularly when behavioral incongruities indicate that conflict or defensive operations are marked.

Provide Guidance

The therapist can provide guidance in the form of suggestions and advice, environmental interventions, and management.

Suggestions and Advice

The therapist at times makes direct suggestions urging certain behaviors. The rationale for the advice is made explicit. Requests for advice are best handled by helping the patients consider alternatives.

Environmental Interventions

Interventions directly concerning the patients' functioning in their environment make it clear the therapist believes the patients can operate at a healthier level. Although important as a direct reality intervention, such comments also demonstrate the therapist's values and can influence the patients' ego and superego identifications.

Management

The therapist directly influences the patients' negative behaviors by making prohibitions and setting limits. Management interventions are again used sparingly and are based on understanding, trust, and positive transference.

Engage in Problem-Solving Strategies

Problem-solving strategies can include education, modeling, and competence.

Education

Educative comments help patients handle problems more effectively and also relieve anxiety by focusing attention on cognitive elements and away from unconscious conflict.

Modeling

The therapist's modeling of coping skills and values provides knowledge to be introjected and eventually identified with by the patients.

Competence

The therapist places emphasis on the patients' realistic strengths and talents and encourages sublimations congruent with the patients' character styles.

Externalize Responsibility for Problems

The therapist offers explanations that locate the responsibility for the patients' difficulties either outside themselves, in other people, or in body chemistry or physiology. These constructions diminish the patients' anxiety by relieving them of responsibility and by focusing attention away from the pathogenic unconscious conflict.

Praise the Patients

Praise can include providing morale and approval.

Morale

The giving of reassurance and hope must be based on an adequate understanding of the patients. Reassurance is effective when related to the patients' goals and past successes. Reassurance based on the therapist's expert knowledge can also be given.

Approval

Encouragement and praise are supportive of the patients' self-esteem but valuable only when given for what the patients hold as praiseworthy. A task of supportive therapy is to make the patients' assets sources of praise; however, praise is used moderately and ideally in the context of a good psychodynamic understanding of the patients, a basic level of trust, and a positive transference.

Disclose Personal Information, Opinions, and Values

The therapist encourages the working alliance by conveying that therapy is a joint effort. This task is aided by frequent use of the word *we*, by showing respect for the patients, by recognizing the patients' growing ability to use the basic tools of treatment, by referring to experiences that patients and therapist have been through together, and by engaging in a group effort for adaptation.

THERAPIST TECHNIQUES WHEN COMMON PHENOMENA OCCUR

Some common phenomena are the violation of ground rules, the empty chair, affect, acting out, silence, reaction to the therapist, patient roles, group-as-a-whole interventions, and the time limit.

The Violation of Ground Rules

Although the supportive therapist generally gratifies the patients, he or she is equally mindful of ensuring that the group is a safe place for the work of therapy to occur. The therapist monitors the degree to which any violation of the ground rules threatens the work or safety of the group as a whole or of any individual group member. Whenever the therapist believes that a breach of the ground rules is significantly disruptive, he or she should directly intervene. This may involve confronting, containing, or even removing a group member. Examples of breaches to the ground rules that have various disruptive potentials are included throughout this chapter.

The Empty Chair

The empty chair occurs when participants are late, miss sessions, and drop out.

Lateness

When a session begins with an empty chair, but a dropout has not been confirmed, the therapist may announce that the member is expected. If the therapist knows that the member will be late to or absent from the session, the therapist may inform the group. When a member arrives late to an early session, the therapist may inform him or her of what has transpired before his or her arrival. At later sessions of the group, the therapist may invite other group members to inform the late member of what he or she missed.

Missed Sessions

Whereas missed sessions are not encouraged, they are excused if rationalizations for practical reasons are offered. The absent member is contacted soon after the missed session; the reason for absence is queried and accepted; and the member is invited to return to the next session:

> We missed you in group today and wondered where you were . . . Ah, yes, it is annoying when babysitters don't show up when they're supposed to . . . So we'll expect you next week and look forward to seeing you then.

If the member expresses ambivalence regarding his or her return to the group, the therapist reassures the member that such feelings are normal and that coming to group usually gets easier. The therapist may inquire as to whether there is anything he or she can do to make it easier for the member in group. If the ambivalent member, or *apparition* (see Chap. 8, this volume), returns to the group, the therapist attempts to help the member feel comfortable by welcoming him or her back and by asking other group members to inform the apparition of what happened during the previous session(s). If the therapist judges the apparition's behavior to be disruptive to the group, the therapist reminds him or her of the ground rules, encouraging him or her to adhere to them. If the disruption continues and threatens the integrity of the group, the apparition may be discharged from the group.

Dropouts

When the empty chair is because of a confirmed dropout, the chair is removed from the circle before the members arrive for that day's session. The therapist announces that the member has dropped out and provides the professed reason for his or her departure. The therapist pauses to permit members the opportunity to spontaneously comment on the dropout if they wish, then redirects the discussion away from the dropout.

Affect

The supportive therapist encourages the expression of emotions that the patients are comfortable exploring and discourages the expression of emotions that they are uncomfortable exploring. The therapist empathizes with affect being expressed in the group and praises the members for its expression. Cartharsis is promoted as therapeutic. The guiding principles with respect to affect are to normalize and permit its expression and then to move on to strategies for coping with the affect. With respect to this latter principle, the therapist may need to contain negative affect by inviting other group members to offer advice or to problem solve strategies for coping with uncomfortable emotions: "Well, I think it is certainly very normal to feel hopeless at times. It's hard to talk about such feelings. Perhaps some other members can help by sharing how they've dealt with similar feelings."

The therapist does not explore or label the conflictual side of affect either with respect to the lost person or others in the here and now. Similarly, the therapist avoids labeling nonverbalized affect permeating the group. He or she may need to directly intervene to shut down any spontaneous discussions of this nature: "You said you feel sad and then relieved. Perhaps we can focus on one emotion at a time. Let's talk about how to deal with sadness."

Sometimes the group may express affect that appears to serve a defensive function, for example, idealization as a defense against anger, guilt as a defense against anger, or the displacement of anger toward the lost person to another object either inside or outside of the group. In such circumstances, the therapist's response follows the same general guidelines. He or she normalizes the emotion, reassures the group, contains intense emotional outbursts, and then moves on to problem-solving strategies regarding how to cope with the affect. The therapist avoids interpreting the defensive aspect of the affect but does not collude with its proliferation if it is seen as maladaptive. He or she may need to directly intervene to redirect the discussion: "OK, let's remember why we're here. The group is a place where you can get some support, not a place to attack each other."

If the therapist is aware that details and/or affect associated with important losses are not being addressed, the therapist does not confront this resistance.

Acting Out

If members begin to act out nonverbalized affects or unconscious conflicts, the therapist response reflects his or her judgment concerning the behavior's destructive potential for the individual or the group in terms of work and safety. For example, if a member brings candy for the group, the therapist may accept one and say thank you. Conversely, if a member expresses suicidal ideation, the therapist may gratify the patient's need for individualized attention without interpreting the anger, fear, or conflict underlying the behavior. Rather, in that case, the therapist demonstrates to the patient and the other group members that the therapist will provide the needed care.

If members begin to plan for extragroup socializing, the therapist may remind them of the ground rules. He or she provides educative interventions regarding the pitfalls of extragroup meetings. This contravention is especially crucial in cases of pairing and subgrouping: "I don't think you realize how much the rest of the group feels left out by your getting together between sessions."

Silence

When the group becomes silent, the therapist intervenes quickly and directly. Members of the group are invited specifically to discuss their week. The therapist should feel free to introduce topics for discussion.

When a particular member continues to be silent in the group, the therapist addresses the member directly: "Is it easier if you are invited to speak or just left to participate only when you feel comfortable? . . . Can you identify with anything that has been said in group today?"

The silent member, or *monk* (see Chapter 8, this volume), and the apparition are patient roles that commonly emerge in short-term loss groups. Other familiar roles are discussed in the section that follows.

Reaction to the Therapist

To preserve a strong therapeutic alliance, the supportive therapist encourages a mild positive transference that is typically not commented on. He or she dispels idealized transference and counteracts the emergence of hostile transferential material. This is accomplished by normalizing any emotions being expressed about the therapist, educating the members as to the role of the therapist, and deflecting the transferential focus onto the other group members or external persons.

> Yes, Jack, I do hear your frustration with me. The group will end next week as planned, and that is frustrating. The 12 weeks have gone by quickly, and another group is ready to meet after next week. Maybe some of the other members can help Jack plan what he can do to continue taking care of himself after next week.

Patient Roles

When a patient seems to be occupying a particular role, the therapist understands it in terms of the patient responding to a need of the group. Rather than interpreting the function of the role, the therapist usurps this role. The therapist addresses the role-taking member directly and highlights the positive aspect of his or her participation. Then, the therapist provides the group with what the role taker was attempting to provide. For example, if the *professor* (see Chap. 8, this volume) emerges in the group, the therapist recognizes that the group is in need of anxiety reduction by using defenses such as rationalization and intellectualization. Hence, the therapist offers an educative intervention: "Yes there are believed to be stages of grief, and everyone goes through those stages in their own way and according to their own schedule."

Similarly, if the *professional nurturer* emerges in the group, the therapist recognizes that the group is in need of praise and encouragement and provides this to the group: "I think you're all feeling closer to each other. You really ought to congratulate yourselves for persevering with the group."

If a patient monopolizes the group, the therapist may need to remind the patient that it is important that other members have an opportunity to participate. The therapist can then invite other members to participate, perhaps by providing feedback to the monopolizer on the same topic.

> It's good that you've been able to use this time today. You've brought up a very important topic that I'm sure has got many of the members thinking. Let's hear from the other members about their thoughts on this issue.

In extreme cases in which the group is being totally disrupted, the therapist may need to instruct the monopolizing member to be quiet or ultimately even to leave the session or group.

Group-as-a-Whole Interventions

The therapist encourages group cohesion by highlighting commonalities and by emphasizing that the group is a place where members share with each other, care about each other, feel understood by each other, and have many things in common. The therapist endeavors to keep the group alliance positive by emphasizing that every member is an important part of the team in helping each other in the group: "So you can really relate to what each of you is saying in here."

The Time Limit

As a general rule, the supportive group therapist does not remind the group of the passage of time. In the event that the therapist believes that the group is not working, the time pressure can be emphasized. In this case the therapist would remind the members to use the group's time to address their problems. The limited available time is presented as an opportunity to share rather than as a deprivation. The emphasis is on the "glass being half full rather than half empty." The therapist tries to ensure that each member has time to talk during every session. Toward this end the therapist may intervene by stating, "So how can you use the group time today? It's important that we hear from everyone today."

If a member does not use the opportunity to talk, the therapist may intervene by saying, "I think we can learn something from listening to each other; every member can teach us something helpful."

THE TERMINATION

The principle guiding termination is to praise the members for their accomplishments in the group. The therapist approaches the termination as a graduation, a celebration. He or she emphasizes that this is a new beginning, rather than an ending; it is exciting rather than anxiety provoking; it is an opportunity to say hello to the next chapter in their lives rather than a goodbye. The therapist may intervene by saying, "Let's sum up by reviewing all the changes you've all made."

The therapist reassures the group that the changes will continue. Toward this end, the therapist may help members problem solve how to replace the group's support in their everyday lives.

The therapist may express positive wishes by saying goodbye. He or she may say, "I wish you all the best; I've enjoyed working with you."

The therapist's goodbye should be global rather than individualistic. He or she can provide positive generalities, emphasizing their sense of achievement, their courage for persisting with the group, the difficulties they have overcome, the positive feelings they have felt for each other. The therapist can then reassure them that they can take these skills out into the world, thereby decatastrophizing the end of the group. The therapist avoids giving individual "report cards." Rather, he or she encourages the group members to give each other positive feedback.

If members plan to continue meeting after the group ends, the therapist can remind the group that the ground rules discourage them from meeting after the group. The rationale for this ground rule is that continuing contact with group members might interfere with forming new relationships that are more likely to last: "It could make it difficult for you to transfer into the real world the skills you have learned in the group."

AFTERWORD: FUTURE DIRECTIONS

The two forms of short-term group therapy that we have developed are powerful treatments that have brought about both significant and substantial benefits. This may be particularly the case if one attends to the apparent successful matches with interpretive therapy for high-quality-of-object-relations (QOR) patients and with supportive therapy for low-QOR patients. Our research also suggests that the group composition defined in terms of the proportion of high-QOR patients appears to make a difference in therapy outcome. It appears that a critical mass of high-QOR patients is important for both forms of therapy and especially for interpretive therapy.

Are there other reasons why our treatment outcome appeared to be significant and substantial although other attempts to discover effective treatments have not been particularly successful? First, in carrying out our trials, we were careful to avoid certain methodological shortcomings that have been present in other studies. Second, we believe that our sample of subjects definitely met criteria for complicated grief (CG). They came to the clinics not as volunteers for a study but as patients requiring assistance. In addition to reporting typical symptoms associated with CG, they reported difficulties in carrying out everyday role functions. Third, we believe that certain therapeutic factors that are only present in group therapies were actively present in our groups.

Future directions for practice can include training for therapists who wish to administer the models. We have provided short-term therapy groups for patients with CG and training for therapists in two separate clinical settings. Each was an outpatient psychiatry clinic located in a large university hospital. At each setting, there were approximately 8–10 full-time therapists who routinely conducted initial intake interviews and who provided psychotherapy when indicated. Group therapy was a commonly used method of treatment in the clinic. A subgroup of therapists who were interested in conducting loss groups met once weekly for 1 hour for purposes of training, supervision, or consultation, dependent on one's level of experience. During some sessions, tape-recorded excerpts from loss groups were discussed, and at other sessions, relevant papers (e.g., papers about themes and roles that emerge in loss groups) were discussed. Therapists typically observed or co-led a loss group before leading one by themselves. Thus, training was practice oriented and on-the-job. Since 1986, we have treated patients and trained therapists in more than 90 loss groups.

In addition to providing on-the-job training, we have often held training workshops at the annual meetings of organizations such as the American Group Psychotherapy Association and the Canadian Group Psychotherapy Association. Also, there is no reason why training in the assessment and group treatment of patients with CG cannot be a part of practicum, internship, or residency training.

However, essential to any of these types of training is a steady flow of suitable patients for the groups. As we have mentioned previously in this book, well-informed referral sources that make appropriate referrals are indispensible to the success of the treatment and training programs. The same may be said for the importance of administrative support for the programs. The administrator should be kept well informed about the progress of the program, and his or her expertise and advice should be solicited. Most administrators were previously clinicians and enjoy providing periodic consultation. Their support can be crucial, particularly in times of fiscal constraints, which have characterized many hospital and university budgets during the past decade.

With regard to future directions for research, several crucial areas deserve attention. There is a lack of information about the prevalence of CG in the general population. There is a lack of standard criteria for defining CG, although criteria have been proposed. There is a lack of baseline data on many variables prior to the loss. Finally, there is a lack of longitudinal data, which makes it difficult to understand certain causal relationships (e.g., the relationship between CG and comorbid conditions).

Although we think that we have identified some interesting and clinically useful findings concerning the matching of forms of therapy and patient personality characteristics, as well as the entire composition of the group, we know very little about the specific mechanisms that follow from these features to bring about favorable outcome. Consequently, we are currently embarking on an exploration of the therapy process of the 18 groups from the composition trial as revealed by means of audiotapes and written transcripts. We would like to discover what mediated the composition–outcome relationship. On theoretical grounds, we hypothesize that the greater the percentage of high-QOR patients in a group, (a) the greater the content of the group will reflect constructive, mutually productive, and hostility-free interactions; (b) the greater the focus will be on other patients rather than on oneself when a patient speaks; and (c) the more the group will engage in dynamic work. Identification of mediating mechanisms may suggest how they could be activated by means other than restrictive group composition (i.e., by excluding low-QOR patients). Instead, patient preparation or therapist technique could be used. That would facilitate including greater numbers of psychiatric patients with low QOR in short-term therapy groups for CG.

We believe that brief group therapy holds a great deal of promise as a therapy technique and when directed at problems such as CG can serve as an excellent model for exploring a variety of research topics. We hope that this book will inspire other clinicians and researchers to pursue some of the questions raised in this book that as yet do not have answers.

REFERENCES

Abouguendia, M., Joyce, A. S., Piper, W. E., & Ogrodniczuk, J. S. (2004). Alliance as a mediator of expectancy effects in short-term group psychotherapy. *Group Dynamics: Theory, Research, and Practice, 8*, 3–12.

Ainsworth, M. (1964). Patterns of attachment behavior shown by the infant in interaction with his mother. *Merrill-Palmer Quarterly, 10*, 51–58.

Alexander, I. E., & Adlerstein, A. M. (1959). Death and religion. In H. Feifel (Ed.), *The meaning of death* (pp. 271–283). New York, NY: McGraw-Hill.

Allumbaugh, D., & Hoyt, W. (1999). Effectiveness of grief counseling: A meta-analysis. *Journal of Counseling Psychology, 46*, 370–380.

American Psychiatric Association. (2000). *Diagnostic and statistical manual of mental disorders* (4th ed., text revision). Washington, DC: Author.

Amick-McMullan, A., Kilpatrick, D., Veronen, L., & Smith, S. (1989). Family survivors of homicide victims: Theoretical perspectives and an exploratory study. *Journal of Traumatic Stress, 2*, 21–35.

Amir, Y., & Sharon, I. (1982). Factors in the adjustment of war widows in Israel. In C. D. Spielberger, I. G. Sarason, & N. A. Milgram (Eds.), *Stress and anxiety* (Vol. 8, pp. 225–234). Washington, DC: Hemisphere Publication Services.

Anderson, K. W. (1998). Utility of the five-factor model of personality in psychotherapy aptitude-treatment interaction research. *Psychotherapy Research, 8*, 54–70.

Anderson, K. W., & McLean, P. D. (1997). Conscientiousness in depression: Tendencies, predictive utility, and longitudinal stability. *Cognitive Therapy and Research, 21*, 223–238.

Ang, R. P., & Hughes, J. N. (2002). Differential benefits of skills training with antisocial youth based on group composition: A meta-analytic investigation. *School Psychology Review, 31*, 164–185.

Appelbaum, S. A. (1973). Psychological mindedness: Work, concept, and essence. *International Journal of Psycho-Analysis, 54*, 35–46.

Arling, G. (1976). The elderly widow and her family, neighbors, and friends. *Journal of Marriage and the Family, 38*, 757–768.

Arnkoff, D. B., Glass, C. R., & Shapiro, S. J. (2002). Expectations and preferences. In J. C. Norcross (Ed.), *Psychotherapy relationships that work: Therapist contributions and responsiveness to patients* (pp. 335–356). New York, NY: Oxford University Press.

Asay, T. P., & Lambert, M. J. (1999). The empirical case for the common factors in therapy: Quantitative findings. In M. Hubble, B. L. Duncan, & S. D. Miller (Eds.), *The heart and soul of change: What works in therapy* (pp. 23–55). Washington, DC: American Psychological Association.

Atchley, R. C. (1975). Dimensions of widowhood in later life. *The Gerontologist, 15*, 176–178.

Azim, H. F. A., Piper, W. E., Segal, P. M., Nixon, G. W. H., & Duncan, S. (1991). The Quality of Object Relations Scale. *Bulletin of the Menninger Clinic, 55*, 323–343.

Bagby, R. M., Costa, P. T., McCrae, R. R., Livesley, W. J., Kennedy, S. H., Levitan, R. D., . . . Young, L. T. (1999). Replicating the five-factor model of personality in a psychiatric sample. *Personality and Individual Differences, 27*, 1135–1139.

Bagby, R. M., Joffe, R. T., Parker, J. D. A., Kalemba, V., & Harkness, K. L. (1995). Major depression and the five-factor model of personality. *Journal of Personality Disorders, 9*, 224–234.

Bagby, R. M., Parker, J. D. A., & Taylor, G. J. (1994). The twenty-item Toronto Alexithymia Scale I. Item selection and cross-validation of the factor structure. *Journal of Psychosomatic Research, 38*, 23–32.

Bagby, R. M., & Quilty, L. C. (2006). Personality traits can predict best treatment for depression. *Directions in Psychiatry, 26*, 199–208.

Bahr, H. M., & Harvey, C. D. (1979). Correlates of loneliness among widows bereaved in a mining disaster. *Psychological Reports, 44*, 367–385.

Bahr, H. M., & Harvey, C. D. (1980). Correlates of morale among the newly widowed. *Journal of Social Psychology, 110*, 219–233.

Bair, M. J., Robinson, R. L., Katon, W., & Kroneke, K. (2003). Depression and pain comorbidity: A literature review. *Archives of Internal Medicine, 163*, 2433–2445.

Balaswamy, S., & Richardson, V. E. (2001). The cumulative effects of life event, personal and social resources on subjective well-being of elderly widowers. *International Journal of Aging and Human Development, 53*, 311–327.

Ball, J. (1976–1977). Widow's grief: The impact of age and mode of death. *Omega: Journal of Death and Dying, 7*, 307–333.

Bankoff, E. (1983). Social support and adaptation to widowhood. *Journal of Marriage and the Family, 45*, 827–839.

Barber, J. P., & Meunz, L. R. (1996). The role of avoidance and obsessiveness in matching patients to cognitive and interpersonal psychotherapy: Empirical findings for the Treatment of Depression Collaborative Research Program. *Journal of Consulting and Clinical Psychology, 64*, 951–958.

Barry, L. C., Kasl, S. V., & Prigerson, H. G. (2002). Psychiatric disorders among bereaved persons: The role of perceived circumstances of death and preparedness for death. *American Journal of Geriatric Psychiatry, 10*, 447–457.

Beck, A. P., & Lewis, C. M (2000). *The process of group psychotherapy: Systems for analyzing change*. Washington, DC: American Psychological Association.

Bednar, R. L., & Kaul, T. J. (1994). Experiential group research: Can the canon fire? In A. R. Bergin & S. L. Garfield (Eds.), *Handbook of psychotherapy and behaviour change* (4th ed., pp. 631–663). Oxford, England: Wiley.

Beitman, B. D., Beck, N. C., Deuser, W. E., Carter, C. S., Davidson, J. R. T., & Maddock, R. J. (1994). Patient stage of change predicts outcome in panic disorder medication trial. *Anxiety, 1*, 64–69.

Beresnevaite, M. (2000). Exploring the benefits of group psychotherapy in reducing alexithymia in coronary heart disease patients: A preliminary study. *Psychotherapy and Psychosomatics, 69*, 117–122.

Bergeman, C. S., Chipuer, H. M., Plomin, R., Pedersen, N. L., McClearn, G. E., Nesselroade, J. R., . . . McCrae, R. R. (1993). Genetic and environmental effects on openness to experience, agreeableness, and conscientiousness: An adoption/twin study. *Journal of Personality, 61*, 159–179.

Bernard, H., Burlingame, G., Flores, P., Greene L., Joyce, A., Kobos, J. C., . . . Science to Service Task Force, American Group Psychotherapy Association. (2008). Clinical practice guidelines for group psychotherapy. *International Journal of Group Psychotherapy, 58*, 455–542.

Bernard, L. L., & Guarnaccia, C. A. (2002). Husband and adult-daughter caregivers' bereavement. *Omega: Journal of Death and Dying, 45*, 153–166.

Bernard, L. L., & Guarnaccia, C. A. (2003). Two models of caregiver strain and bereavement adjustment: A comparison of husband and daughter caregiver of breast cancer hospice patients. *The Gerontologist, 43*, 801–816.

Beutler, L. E., Blatt, S. J., Alimohamed, S., Levy, K. N., & Angtuaco, L. (2006). Participant factors in treating dysphoric disorders. In L. G. Castonguay & L. E. Beutler (Eds.), *Principles of therapeutic change that work* (pp. 13–63). New York, NY: Oxford University Press.

Beutler, L. E., Castonguay, L. G., & Follette, W. C. (2006). Integration of therapeutic factors in dysphoric disorders. In L. G. Castonguay & L. E. Beutler (Eds.), *Principles of therapeutic change that work* (pp. 111–117). New York, NY: Oxford University Press.

Beutler, L. E., Clarkin, J. F., & Bongar, B. (2000). *Guidelines for the systematic treatment of the depressed patient.* New York, NY: Oxford University Press.

Beutler, L. E., Engle, D., Mohr, D., Daldrup, R. J., Bergan, J., Meredith, K., & Merry, W. (1991). Predictors of differential and self-directed psychotherapeutic procedures. *Journal of Consulting and Clinical Psychology, 59*, 333–340.

Beutler, L. E., Harwood, T. M., Alimohamed, S., & Malik, M. M. (2002). Functional impairment and coping style. In J. C. Norcross (Ed.), *Psychotherapy relationships that work: Therapist contributions and responsiveness to patient needs* (pp. 145–170). New York, NY: Oxford University Press.

Beutler, L. E., Kim, E. J., Davison, E., Karno, M., & Fisher, D. (1996). Research contributions to improving managed care outcomes. *Psychotherapy, 33*, 197–206.

Beutler, L. E., Machado, P. P., Engle, D., & Mohr, D. (1993). Differential Patient × Treatment maintenance of treatment effects among cognitive, experiential, and self-directed psychotherapies. *Journal of Psychotherapy Integration, 3*, 15–31.

Beutler, L. E., & Mitchell, R. (1981). Differential psychotherapy outcome among depressed and impulsive patients as a function of analytic and experiential treatment procedures. *Psychiatry, 44*, 297–306.

Beutler, L. E., Moleiro, C. M., & Talebi, H. (2002). Resistance. In J. C. Norcross (Ed.), *Psychotherapy relationships that work: Therapist contributions to responsiveness to patients* (pp. 129–143). New York, NY: Oxford University Press.

Blatt, S. J., Quinlan, D. M., Pilkonis, P. A., & Shea, M. T. (1995). Impact of perfectionism and need for approval on the brief treatment of depression: The National Institute of Mental Health Treatment of Depression Collaborative Research Program revisited. *Journal of Consulting and Clinical Psychology, 63,* 125–132.

Blatt, S. J., Shahar, G., & Zuroff, D. C. (2002). Anaclitic/sociotropic and introjective/autonomous dimensions. In J. C. Norcross (Ed.), *Psychotherapy relationships that work: Therapist contributions to responsiveness to patients* (pp. 315–333). New York, NY: Oxford University Press.

Blatt, S. J., Wiseman, H., Prince-Gibson, E., & Gatt, C. (1991). Object representations and change in clinical functioning. *Psychotherapy, 28,* 273–283.

Blatt, S. J., Zuroff, D. C., Bondi, C. M., Sanislow, C. A., & Pilkonis, P. A. (1998). When and how perfectionism impedes the brief treatment of depression: Further analyses of the National Institute of Mental Health Treatment of Depression Collaborative Research Program. *Journal of Consulting and Clinical Psychology, 66,* 423–428.

Blatt, S. J., Zuroff, D. C., & Hawley, L. (2008). Factors contributing to sustained therapeutic gain in outpatient treatments of depression. In R. A. Levy & J. S. Ablon (Eds.), *Handbook of evidence-based psychodynamic psychotherapy: Bridging the gap between science and practice* (pp. 279–301). Towana, NJ: Humana Press.

Bock, E. W., & Webber, I. L. (1972). Suicide among the elderly: Isolating widowhood and mitigating alternatives. *Journal of Marriage and the Family, 34,* 24–31.

Boelen, P. A., de Keijser, J., van den Hout, M. A., & van den Bout, J. (2007). Treatment of complicated grief: A comparison between cognitive behavioral therapy and supportive counseling. *Journal of Consulting and Clinical Psychology, 75,* 277–284.

Bohannon, J. R. (1991). Religiosity related to grief levels of bereaved mothers and fathers. *Omega: Journal of Death and Dying, 23,* 153–159.

Bohart, A. C. (1980). Toward a cognitive theory of catharsis. *Psychotherapy: Theory, Research and Practice, 17,* 192–201.

Bonanno, G. A. (2001). Introduction: New directions in bereavement research and theory. *American Behavioral Scientist, 44,* 718–725

Bonanno, G. A. (2004). Loss, trauma, and human resilience: Have we underestimated the human capacity to thrive after extremely aversive events? *American Psychologist, 59,* 20–28.

Bonanno, G. A., & Kaltman, S. (1999). Toward and integrative perspective on bereavement. *Psychological Bulletin, 125,* 760–776.

Bonanno, G. A., Keltner, D., Holen, A., & Horowitz, M. J. (1995). When avoiding unpleasant emotions may not be such a bad thing: Verbal-automatic response dissociation and middle conjugal bereavement. *Journal of Personality and Social psychology, 69,* 975–989.

Bonanno, G. A., & Lilienfield, S. O. (2008). Let's be realistic: When grief counseling is effective and when it's not. *Professional Psychology: Research and Practice, 39*, 377–378.

Bonanno, G. A., Moskowitz, J. T., Papa, A., & Folkman, S. (2005). Resilience to loss in bereaved spouses, bereaved parents, and bereaved gay men. *Journal of Personality and Social Psychology, 88*, 827–843.

Bonanno, G. A., Notarius, C. L., Gunzerath, L., Keltner, D., & Horowitz, M. J. (1998). Interpersonal ambivalence, perceived relationship adjustment, and conjugal loss. *Journal of Counseling and Clinical Psychology, 66*, 1012–1022.

Bonanno, G. A., Wortman, C. B., Lehman, D. R., Tweed, R. G., Haring, M., Sonnega, J., . . . Nesse, R. M. (2002). Resilience to loss and chronic grief: a prospective study from preloss to 18-month postloss. *Journal of Personality and Social Psychology, 83*, 1150–1164.

Bornstein, P., Clayton, P., Halikas, J. Maurice, W., & Robins, E. (1973). The depression of widowhood after 13 months. *British Journal of psychiatry, 122*, 561–566.

Bowlby, J. (1969). Disruption of affectional bonds and its effects on behavior. *Canada's Mental Health Supplement, 59*, 12.

Bowlby, J. (1980). By ethology out of psycho-analysis: An experiment in interbreeding. *Animal Behaviour, 28*, 649–656.

Bowlby, J. (1988). *A secure base: Parent–child attachment and healthy human development.* New York, NY: Basic Books.

Braaten, L. J. (1989). Predicting positive goal attainment and symptom reduction from early group climate dimensions. *International Journal of Group Psychotherapy, 39*, 377–387.

Brabender, V. (2002). *Introduction to group therapy.* New York, NY: Wiley.

Breckenridge, J. N., Gallagher, D., Thompson, L., & Peterson, J. (1986). Characteristic depressive symptoms of bereaved elders. *Journal of Gerontology, 41*, 163–168.

Brehm, S. S., & Brehm, J. W. (1981). *Psychological reactance: A theory of freedom and control.* New York, NY: Academic Press.

Breslau, N., Wilcox, H. C., Storr, C. L., Lucia, V. C., & Anthony, J. C. (2004). Trauma exposure and posttraumatic stress disorder: A study of youths in urban America. *Journal of Urban Health, 81*, 530–544.

BrintzenhofeSzoc, K. M., Smith, E. D., & Zabora, J. R. (1999). Screening to predict complicated grief in spouses of cancer patients. *Cancer Practice, 7*, 233–239.

Brogan, M. M., Prochaska, J. O., & Prochaska, J. M. (1999). Predicting termination and continuation status in psychotherapy using the transtheoretical model. *Psychotherapy: Theory, Research, Practice, Training, 36*, 105–113.

Brown, G., & Harris, T. (1978). *The social origins of depression.* London, England: Tavistock.

Bruce, M., Kim, K., Leaf, P., & Jacobs, S. (1990). Depressive episodes and dysphoria resulting from conjugal psychotherapy. In S. H. Budman (Ed.), *Forms of brief therapy* (pp. 305–342). New York, NY: Guilford Press.

Budman, S. H., Bennett, M. J., & Wisneski, M. J. (1981). An adult developmental model of short-term group psychotherapy. In S. H. Budman (Ed.), *Forms of brief therapy* (pp. 305–342). New York, NY: Guilford Press.

Budman, S. H., & Gurman, A. S. (1988). *Theory and practice of brief therapy*. New York, NY: Guilford Press.

Budman, S. H., Simeone, P. G., Reilly, R., & Demby, R. A. (1994). Progress in short-term and time-limited group psychotherapy: Evidence and implications. In A. Fuhriman & G. M. Burlingame (Eds.), *Handbook of group psychotherapy: An empirical and clinical synthesis* (pp. 319–339). New York, NY: Wiley.

Budman, S. H., Soldz, S., Demby, A., Feldstein, M., Springer, T., & Davis, M. S. (1989). Cohesion, alliance and outcome in group psychotherapy. *Psychiatry, 52,* 339–350.

Bugen, L. (1979). Human grief: A model for prediction and intervention. In L. Bugen (Ed.), *Death and dying: Therapy, research, practice* (pp. 32–45). Dubuque, IA: William C. Brown Communications.

Bunch, J. (1972). Recent bereavement in relation to suicide. *Journal of Psychosomatic Research, 16,* 361–366.

Burks, V. K., Lund, D. A., Gregg, C. H., & Bluhm, H. P. (1988). Bereavement and marriage for older adults. *Death Studies, 12,* 51–60.

Burlingame, G. M., Fuhriman, A., & Johnson, J. (2002). Cohesion in group psychotherapy. In J. C. Norcross (Ed.), *Psychotherapy relationships that work: Therapist contributions and responsiveness to patients* (pp. 71–87). New York, NY: Oxford University Press.

Burlingame, G. M., Fuhriman, A., & Mosier, J. (2003). The differential effectiveness of group psychotherapy: A meta-analytic perspective. *Group Dynamics, 7,* 3–12.

Burlingame, G. M., MacKenzie, K. R. & Strauss, B. (2004). Small group treatment: Evidence for effectiveness and mechanisms of change. In A. E. Bergin & S. L. Garfield (Eds.), *Handbook of psychotherapy and behavioral change* (5th ed., pp. 647–696). New York, NY: Wiley.

Burns, D. D., & Nolen-Hoeksema, S. (1992). Therapeutic empathy and recovery from depression in cognitive–behavioral therapy: A structural equation model. *Journal of Consulting and Clinical Psychology, 60,* 441–449.

Cain, A. (1972). *Survivors of suicide.* Springfield, IL: Charles C Thomas.

Carey, R. (1977). The widowed: A year later. *Journal of Counseling psychology, 24,* 125–131.

Carr, D. (2003). A "global death" for whom? Quality of spouse's death and psychological distress among older widowed persons. *Journal of Health and Social Behavior, 44,* 215–232.

Carr, D., House, J. S., Kessler, R. C., Nesse, R. M., Sonnega, J., & Wortman, C. (2000). Marital quality and psychological adjustment to widowhood among older adults: A longitudinal analysis. *Journal of Gerontology: Social Sciences, 55B,* S197–S207.

Carr, D., House, J. S., Wortman, C. B., Nesse, R., & Kessler, R. C. (2001). Psychological adjustment to sudden and anticipated spousal death among the older widowed. *Journal of Gerontology: Social Sciences, 56B*, S237–S248.

Carr, D., Nesse, R, M., & Wortman, C. B. (2005). *Late life widowhood in the United States.* New York, NY: Springer.

Chang, H., & Saunders, D. G. (2002). Predictors of attrition in two types of group programs for men who batter. *Journal of Family Violence, 17,* 273–292.

Charles, S. T., & Mavandadi, S. (2004). Social support and physical health across the life span: Socioemotional influences. In F. R. Lang & K. L. Fingerman (Eds.), *Growing together: Personal relationships across the lifespan* (pp. 240–267). Cambridge, England: Cambridge University Press.

Clarkin, J. F., & Levy, K. N. (2004). The influence of client variables on psychotherapy. In M. J. Lambert (Ed.), *Bergin and Garfield's handbook of psychotherapy and behavior change* (5th ed., pp. 194–226). New York, NY: Wiley.

Clayton, P. (1974). Mortality and morbidity in the first years of widowhood. *Archives of General Psychiatry, 30,* 747–750.

Clayton, P., Halikas, J., & Maurice, W. (1972). The depression of widowhood. *British Journal of Psychiatry, 120,* 71–77.

Clayton, P., Halikas, J., Maurice, W., & Robins, E. (1973). Anticipatory grief and widowhood. *British Journal of Psychiatry, 122,* 47–51.

Clayton, P., Halikas, J. A., & Robins, E. (1973). Anticipatory grief and widowhood. *British Journal of Psychiatry, 122,* 47–51.

Cleiren, M. P. H. D. (1991). *Adaptation after bereavement.* Leiden, The Netherlands: DSWO Press.

Clementel-Jones, C., Malan, D., & Trauer, T. (1990). A retrospective follow-up of 84 clients treated with individual psychoanalytic psychotherapy: Outcome and predictive factors. *British Journal of Psychotherapy, 6,* 363–374.

Coddington, R. D. (1972). The significance of life events as etiological factors in the diseases of children: I. A survey of professional workers. *Journal of Psychosomatic Research, 16,* 7–18.

Colburn, K., & Malena, D. (1988). Bereavement issues for survivors of persons with AIDS: Coping with society's pressures. *The American Journal of Hospice Care, 5,* 20–25.

Conte, H. R., Plutchik, R., Picard, S., & Karasu, T. (1991). Can personality traits predict psychotherapy outcome? *Comprehensive Psychiatry, 32,* 66–72.

Conte, H. R., & Ratto, R. (1997). Self-report measures of psychological mindedness. In M. McCallum & W. E. Piper (Eds.), *Psychological mindedness: A contemporary understanding* (pp. 1–26). Mahwah, NJ: Erlbaum.

Cooney, N. L., Kadden, R. M., Litt, M. D., & Getter, H. (1991). Matching alcoholics to coping skills or interactional therapies: Two-year follow-up results. *Journal of Consulting and Clinical Psychology, 59,* 598–601.

Corey M. S., & Corey, G. (2002). *Groups: Process and practice* (6th ed.). Pacific Grove CA: Brooks/Cole.

Costa, P. T., & McCrae, R. R. (1992a). Normal personality assessment in clinical practice: The NEO personality inventory. *Psychological Assessment, 4*, 5–13.

Costa, P. T., & McCrae, R. R. (1992b). *Revised NEO Personality Inventory professional manual*. Odessa, FL: Psychological Assessment Resources.

Costa, P. T., & McCrae, R. R. (1994). Set like plaster? Evidence for the stability of adult personality. In T. F. Heatherton & J. L. Weinberger (Eds.), *Can personality change?* (pp. 21–40). Washington, DC: American Psychological Association.

Currier, J. M., Neimeyer, R. A., & Berman, J. S. (2008). The effectiveness of psychotherapeutic interventions for bereaved persons: A comprehensive quantitative review. *Psychological Bulletin, 134*, 648–661.

de Groot, M., de Keijser, J., Neeleman, J., Kerkhof, A., Nolen, W., & Burger, H. (2007, May 12). Cognitive behavior therapy to prevent complicated grief among relatives and spouses bereaved by suicide: Cluster randomised controlled trial. *BMJ, 334*, 994–999.

de Groot, J. M. de, Rodin, G., & Olmsted, M. P. (1995). Alexithymia, depression, and treatment outcome in bulimia nervosa. *Comprehensive Psychiatry, 36*, 53–60.

de Maat, S., Dekker, J., Schoevers, R., & de Jonghe, F. (2006). Relative efficacy of psychotherapy and pharmacotherapy in the treatment of depression: A meta-analysis. *Psychotherapy Research, 16*, 566–578.

Diamond, D., Clarkin, J., Levine, H., Levy, K., Foelsch, P., & Yeomans, F. (1999). Borderline conditions and attachment: A preliminary report. *Psychoanalytic Inquiry, 19*, 831–884.

Dies, R. R. (1993). Research of group psychotherapy: Overview and clinical applications. In A. Alonso & H. I. Swiller (Eds.), *Group therapy in clinical practice* (pp. 473–518). Washington, DC: American Psychiatric Publishing.

Digman, J. M. (1990). Personality structure: Emergence of the five-factor model. *Annual Review of Psychology, 41*, 417–440.

Diguer, L., Barber, J. P., & Luborsky, L. (1993). Three concomitants: Personality disorders, psychiatric severity and outcome of dynamic psychotherapy of major depression. *American Journal of Psychiatry, 150*, 1246–1248.

Doka, K. J. (1989). *Disenfranchised grief: Recognizing hidden sorrow*. Lexington, MA: Lexington Books.

Dozier, M. (1990). Attachment organization and treatment use for adults with serious psychopathological disorders. *Development and Psychopathology, 2*, 47–60.

Dozier, M., Lomax, L., & Tyrrell, C. (1996). *Psychotherapy's challenge for adults using deactivating attachment strategies*. Unpublished manuscript, Department of Psychology, University of Delaware, Newark.

Eames, V., & Roth, A. (2000). Patient attachment orientation and the early working alliance—A study of patient and therapist reports of alliance quality and ruptures. *Psychotherapy Research, 10*, 421–434.

Elizur, E., & Kaffman, M. (1983). Factors influencing the severity of childhood bereavement reactions. *American Journal of Orthopsychiatry, 53*, 668–676.

Elkin, I., Gibbons, R. D., Shea, M. T., & Shaw, B. F. (1996). Science is not a trial (but it can sometimes be a tribulation). *Journal of Consulting and Clinical Psychology, 64*, 92–103.

Elkin, I., Gibbons, R. D., Shea, M. T., Sotsky, S., Watkins, J., & Pilkonis, P. (1995). Initial severity and differential treatment outcome in the National Institute of Mental Health Treatment of Depression Collaborative Research Program. *Journal of Consulting and Clinical Psychology, 63*, 841–847.

Elkin, I., Shea, T, Watkins, J. T, Imber, S. D., Sotsky, S. M., Collins, J. E, . . . Parloff, M. B. (1989). National Institute of Mental Health Treatment of Depression Collaborative Research Program. *Archives of General Psychiatry, 46*, 971–982.

Engler, A. J., & Lasker, J. N. (2000). Predictors of maternal grief in the year after a newborn death. *Illness, Crisis, and Loss, 8*, 227–243.

Farberow, N. L., Gallagher-Thompson, D., Gilewski, M., & Thompson, L. (1992). Changes in grief and mental health of bereaved spouses of older suicides. *Journal of Gerontology, 47*, 357–366.

Fava, G. A., Ruini, C., Rafanelli, C., Finos, L., Conti, S., & Grandi, S. (2004). Six-year outcome of cognitive behaviour therapy for prevention of recurrent depression. *American Journal of Psychiatry, 161*, 1872–1876.

Fende Guajardo, J. M., & Anderson, T. (2007). An investigation of psychoeducational interventions about therapy. *Psychotherapy Research, 17*, 120–127.

Fenigstein, A., Scheier, M. F., & Buss, A. H. (1975). Public and private self-consciousness: Assessment and theory. *Journal of Consulting and Clinical Psychology, 43*, 522–527.

Fish, W. (1986). Differences of grief intensity in bereaved parents. In T. A., Rando (Ed.), *Parental loss of a child* (pp. 415–430). Champaign, IL: Research Press.

Foa, E. B., Hembree, E. A., & Rothbaum, B. O. (2007). *Prolonged exposure therapy for PTSD: Emotional processing of traumatic experiences: Therapist guide*. New York, NY: Oxford University Press.

Foa, E. B., & Kozak, M. J. (1991). Emotional processing: Theory, research, and clinical implications for anxiety disorders. In J. D. Safran, & L. S. Greenberg (Eds.), *Emotion, psychotherapy, and change* (pp. 21–49). New York, NY: Guilford Press.

Folkman, S. (2001). Revised coping theory and the process of bereavement. In M. S. Stroebe, R. O. Hanson, W. Stroebe, & H. Schut (Eds.), *Handbook of bereavement research: Consequences, coping, and care* (pp. 563–584). Washington, DC: American Psychological Association.

Fonagy, P., Leigh, T., Steele, M., Steele, H., Kennedy, R., Mattoon, G., . . . Gerber, A. (1996). The relation of attachment status, psychiatric classification, and response to psychotherapy. *Journal of Consulting and Clinical Psychology, 64*, 22–31.

Fonagy, P., & Target, M. (1997). Attachment and reflective function: Their role in self-organization. *Development and Psychopathology, 9*, 679–700.

Forstmeier, S., & Maercker, A. (2007). Comparison of two diagnostic systems for complicated grief. *Journal of Affective Disorders, 99*, 203–211.

Fortner, B. V. (1999). *The effectiveness of grief counseling and theory: A quantitative review.* Unpublished manuscript, University of Memphis, Memphis, TN.

Fortner, B. V. (2008). Stemming the TIDE: A correction of Fortner (1999) and a clarification of Larson and Hoyt (2007). *Professional Psychology: Research and Practice, 39*, 379–380.

Frank, E., Prigerson, H. G., Shear, M. K., & Reynolds, C. F. (1997). Phenomenology and treatment of bereavement-related distress in the elderly. *International Clinical Psychopharmacology, 12*, S25–S30.

Franko, D. L. (1997). Ready or not? Stages of change as predictors of brief group therapy outcome in bulimia nervosa. *Group, 21*, 39–45.

Freud, S. (1957). Mourning and melancholia. In J. Strachey (Ed. & Trans.), *The standard edition of the complete psychological works of Sigmund Freud* (Vol. 2, pp. 251–268). London, England: Hogarth. (Original work published 1917)

Fuhriman, A., & Burlingame, G. M. (2001). Group psychotherapy training and effectiveness. International Journal of Group Psychotherapy, 51, 399–416.

Gallagher, D. E., Beckenridge, J., Thompson, L., & Peterson, J. (1983). Effects of bereavement on indicators of mental health in elderly widows and widowers. *Journal of Gerontology, 38*, 565–571.

Garfield, S. L. (1994). Research on client variables in psychotherapy. In S. L. Garfield & A. E. Bergin (Eds.), *Handbook of psychotherapy and behavior change* (4th ed., pp. 190–228). New York, NY: Wiley.

Gass, K. A. (1987). The health of conjugal bereaved older widows: The role of appraisal, coping and resources. *Research in Nursing & Health, 10*, 39–47.

Genevro, J. L., Marshall, T., & Miller, T. (2004). Report on bereavement and grief research. *Death Studies, 28*, 491–575.

Ghaffari-Nejad, A., Ahmadi-Mousavi, M., Gandomkar, M., & Reihani-Kermani, H. (2007). The prevalence of complicated grief among Bam earthquake survivors in Iran. *Archives of Iranian Medicine, 10*, 525–528.

Giacquinta, B. (1989). Researching the effects of AIDS on families. *The American Journal of Hospice Care, 6*, 31–36.

Gillaspy, J. A., Jr., Wright, A. R., Campbell, C., Stokes, S., & Adinoff, B. (2002). Group alliance and cohesion as predictors of drug and alcohol abuse treatment outcomes. *Psychotherapy Research, 12*, 213–229.

Glass, C. R., Arnkoff, D. B., & Shapiro, S. J. (2001). Expectations and preferences. *Psychotherapy, 38*, 455–461.

Glick, I. O., Weis, R. S., & Parkes, C. M. (1974). *The first year of bereavement.* New York, NY: Wiley.

Gluhoski, V. L., Fishman, B., & Perry, S. W. (1997). Moderators of bereavement in a gay male sample. *Personality and Individual Differences, 23*, 761–767.

Goldberg, D. A., Schuyler, W. R., Bransfield, D., & Savino, P. (1983). Focal group psychotherapy: A dynamic approach. *International Journal of Group Psychotherapy*, *33*, 413–431.

Goldman, N., Korenman, S., & Weinstein, R. (1995). Marital status and health among the elderly. *Social Science and Medicine*, *40*, 1717–1730.

Gorer, G. (1965). *Death, grief, and mourning*. Garden City, NJ: Doubleday.

Gray, R. E. (1987). Adolescent response to the death of a parent. *Journal of Youth and Adolescence*, *16*, 511–525.

Greenberg, L. S., & Safran, J. D. (1989). Emotion in psychotherapy. *American Psychologist*, *44*, 19–29.

Greenson, R. R. (1965). The working alliance and the transference neuroses. *Psychoanalytic Quarterly*, *34*, 155–179.

Grilo, C. M., Money, R., Barlow, D. H., Goddard, A. W., Gorman, J. M, Hofmann, S. G., . . . Woods, S. W. (1998). Pretreatment client factors predicting attrition from a multicenter randomized controlled treatment study for panic disorder. *Comprehensive Psychiatry*, *39*, 323–332.

Gunzburger, D. W., Henggeler, S. W., & Watson, S. M. (1985). Factors related to premature termination of counseling relationships. *Journal of College Student Personnel*, *26*, 456–460.

Hadley, D. C., Reddon, J. R., & Reddick, R. D. (2000). Age, gender and treatment attendance among forensic psychiatric outpatients. *Journal of Offender Rehabilitation*, *32*, 55–66.

Hansson, R. O., & Carpenter, B. N. (1994). *Relationships in old age: Coping with the challenge of transition*. New York, NY: Guilford Press.

Hansson, R., & Stroebe, M. S. (2003). Grief, older adulthood. In T. P. Gullota & M. Bloom (Eds.), *Encyclopaedia of primary prevention and health promotion* (pp. 515–521). New York, NY: Plenum Press.

Hansson, R., & Stroebe, M. S. (2007). *Bereavement in late life: Coping, adaptation, and developmental influences*. Washington, DC: American Psychological Association.

Hardy, G. E., Barkham, M., Shapiro, D. A., Stiles, W. B., Rees, A., & Reynolds, S. (1995). Impact of Cluster C personality disorders on outcomes of contrasting brief psychotherapies for depression. *Journal of Consulting and Clinical Psychology*, *63*, 997–1004.

Hardy, G. E., Stiles, W. B., Barkham, M., & Startup, M. (1998). Therapist responsiveness to client interpersonal styles during time-limited treatments for depression. *Journal of Consulting and Clinical Psychology*, *66*, 304–312.

Harrison, L., & Harrington, R. (2001). Adolescent bereavement experiences: Prevalence, association with depressive symptoms, and use of service. *Journal of Adolescence*, *24*, 159–169.

Harvey, C. D., & Bahr, H. M. (1974). Widowhood, morale and affiliation. *Journal of Marriage and the Family*, *36*, 97–106.

Haskey, J. (1998). One-parent families and their dependent children in Great Britain. *Population Trends, 91*, 5–14.

Heatherington, L., Stets, J., & Mazzarella, S. (1986). Whither the bias: The female client's "edge" in psychotherapy? *Psychotherapy, 23*, 252–256.

Helsing, K. J., & Szklo, M. (1981). Mortality after bereavement. *American Journal of Epidemiology, 114*, 41–52.

Helsing, K. J., & Szklo, M., & Comstock, G. (1981). Factors associated with mortality after widowhood. *American Journal of Public Health, 71*, 802–809.

Heyman, D. K., & Gianturco, D. (1973). Long-term adaptation by the elderly to bereavement. *Journal of Gerontology, 28*, 359–362.

Hoberman, H. M., Lewinsohn, P. M., & Tilson, M. (1988). Group treatment of depression: Individual predictors of outcome. *Journal of Consulting and Clinical Psychology, 56*, 393–398.

Høglend, P. (1993a). Suitability for brief dynamic psychotherapy: Psychodynamic variables as predictors of outcome. *Acta Psychiatrica Scandinavica, 88*, 104–110.

Høglend, P. (1993b). Transference interpretations and long-term change after dynamic psychotherapy of brief to moderate length. *American Journal of Psychotherapy, 47*, 494–507.

Høglend, P., Amlo, S., Marble, A., Bøgwald, K-P., Sørbye, O., Sjaastad, M. C., & Hcyerdahl, O. (2006). Analysis of the patient–therapist relationship in dynamic psychotherapy: An experimental study of transference interpretations. *American Journal of Psychiatry, 163*, 1739–1746.

Hollon, S. D., Stewart, M. O., & Strunk, D. (2006). Enduring effects for cognitive therapy in the treatment of depression and anxiety. *Annual Review of Psychology, 57*, 285–315.

Holmes, L. (2002). Women in groups and women's groups. *International Journal of Group Psychotherapy, 52*, 171–188.

Horowitz, M. J. (1986). Stress-response syndromes: A review of posttraumatic and adjustment disorders. *Hospital and Community Psychiatry, 37*, 241–249.

Horowitz, M. J., Marmar, C. R., Weiss, D., DeWitt, K. N., & Rosenbaum, R. (1984). Brief psychotherapy of bereavement reactions: The relationship of process to outcome. *Archives of General Psychiatry, 41*, 438–448.

Horowitz, M. J., Siegel, B., Holen, A., Bonanno, G. A., Milbrath, C., & Stinson, C. H. (1997). Diagnostic criteria for complicated grief disorder. *American Journal of Psychiatry, 154*, 904–910.

Horvath, A. O., & Goheen, M. D. (1990). Factors mediating the success of defiance- and compliance-based interventions. *Journal of Counseling Psychology, 37*, 363–371.

Horwitz, L. (1977). A group-centered approach to group psychotherapy. *International Journal of Group Psychotherapy, 27*, 423–439.

Hoyt, W. T., & Larson, D. G. (2008). A realistic approach to drawing conclusions from scientific literature: Response to Bonanno and Lilienfeld (2008). *Professional Psychology: Research and Practice, 39*, 378–379.

Hughes, M. (1995). *Bereavement and support: Healing in a group environment.* Philadelphia, PA: Taylor & Francis.

Huprich, S. K., & Greenberg, R. (2003). Advances in the assessment of object relations in the 1990s. *Clinical Psychology Review, 23,* 665–698.

Huston, P. (1971). Neglected approach to cause and treatment of psychotic depression. *Archives of General Psychiatry, 35,* 429–431.

Ihilevich, D., & Gleser, G. C. (1986). *Defense mechanisms: Their classification, correlates and measurement with the Defense Mechanisms Inventory.* Owosso, MI: DMI Associates.

Jacobs, S. (1993). *Pathologic grief: Maladaptation to loss.* Washington DC: American Psychiatric Association.

Jacobs, S. (1999). *Traumatic grief: Diagnosis, treatment, and prevention.* Philadelphia, PA: Brunner/Mazel.

Jacobs, S., Hansen, F., Berkman, L., Kasl, S., & Ostfeld, A. (1989). Depressions of bereavement. *Comprehensive Psychiatry, 30,* 218–224.

Jacobs, S. C., Schaefer, C. A., Ostfeld, A. M., & Kasl, S. V. (1987). The first anniversary of bereavement. *The Israel Journal of Psychiatry and Related Sciences, 24,* 77–85.

Jacobson, N. S., Follette, W. C., & Revenstorf, D. (1984). Psychotherapy outcome research: Methods for reporting variability and evaluating clinical significance. *Behavior Therapy, 15,* 336–352.

Jacobson, N. S., & Revenstorf, D. (1988). Statistics for assessing the clinical significance of psychotherapy techniques: Issues, problems, and new developments. *Behavior Assessment, 10,* 133–145.

John, O. P. (1990). The "Big Five" factor taxonomy: Dimensions of personality in natural language and in questionnaires. In L. A. Pervin (Ed.), *Handbook of personality: Theory and research* (pp. 66–100). New York, NY: Guilford Press.

Johnson, J. E. (2008). Using research supported group treatments. *Journal of Clinical Psychology, 64,* 1206–1224.

Johnson, J. E., Burlingame, G. M., Olsen, J. A., Davies, D. R., & Gleave, R. L. (2005). Group climate, cohesion, alliance, and empathy in group psychotherapy: Multilevel structural equation models. *Journal of Counseling Psychology, 52,* 310–321.

Johnson, J. E., Pulsipher, D., Ferrin, S. L., Burlingame, G. M., Davies, D. R., & Gleave, R. (2006). Measuring group process: A comparison of the GCQ and CCI. *Group Dynamics, 10,* 136–145.

Jones, D., Harvey, J., Giza, D., Rodican, C., Barreira, P. J., & Macias, C. (2003). Parental death in the lived of people with serious mental illness. *Journal of Loss and Trauma, 8,* 307–322.

Jordan, J. R., & Neimeyer, R. (2003). Does grief counseling work? *Death Studies, 27,* 765–786.

Joyce, A. S., & McCallum, M. (2004). Assessing patient capacities for therapy: Psychological mindedness and quality of object relations. In D. Charman (Ed.),

Core processes in brief psychodynamic psychotherapy: Advancing effective practice (pp. 69–100). Mahwah, NJ: Erlbaum.

Joyce, A. S., Ogrodniczuk, J. S., Piper, W. E., & McCallum, M. (2003). The alliance as mediator of expectancy effects in short-term individual therapy. *Journal of Consulting and Clinical Psychology, 71*, 672–679.

Joyce, A. S., Ogrodniczuk, J. S., Piper, W. E., & Sheptycki, M. (2010). Interpersonal predictors of group therapy outcome for patients with complicated grief: A replication. *Clinical Psychology and Psychotherapy*. Advance online publication. doi:10.1002/cpp.686

Joyce, A. S., & Piper, W. E. (1998). Expectancy, the therapeutic alliance, and treatment outcome in short-term individual psychotherapy. *Journal of Psychotherapy Practice and Research, 7*, 237–248.

Joyce, A. S., Piper, W. E., & Ogrodniczuk, J. S. (2007). Therapeutic alliance and cohesion variables as predictors of outcome in short-term group psychotherapy. *International Journal of Group Psychotherapy, 57*, 269–296.

Joyce, A. S., Piper, W. E., Ogrodniczuk, J. S., & Klein, R. H. (2007). *The termination process in individual and group psychotherapy*. Washington, DC: American Psychological Association.

Judd, L. L., Akiskal, H. S., Maser, J. D., Zeller, P. J., Endicott, J., Coryell, W., . . . Keller, M. B. (1998). Major depressive disorder: A prospective study of residual subthreshold depressive symptoms as predictor of rapid relapse. *Journal of Affective Disorders, 50*, 97–108.

Kadden, R. M., Cooney, N. L., Getter, H., & Litt, M. D. (1989). Matching alcoholics to coping skills or interactional therapies: Posttreatment results. *Journal of Consulting and Clinical Psychology, 57*, 698–704.

Kaplan, H. I., & Sadock, B. J. (1998). *Synopsis of Psychiatry: Behavioral sciences/clinical psychiatry* (8th ed.). Baltimore, MD: Williams & Wilkins.

Karp, J. F., Scott, J., Houck, P., Reynolds, C. F., Kupfer, D. J., & Frank, E. (2005). Pain predicts longer time to remission during treatment of recurrent depression. *Journal of Clinical Psychiatry, 66*, 591–597.

Kastenbaum, R. (1969). Death and bereavement in later life. In A. H. Kutscher (Ed.), *Death and bereavement* (pp. 28–54). Springfield, IL: Charles C Thomas.

Kato, P. M., & Mann, T. (1999). A synthesis of psychological interventions for the bereaved, *Clinical Psychology Review, 19*, 275–296.

Kennedy-Moore, E., & Watson, J. C. (1999). *Expressing emotion: Myths, realities, and therapeutic strategies*. New York, NY: Guilford Press.

Kernberg, O. F., Burstein, E. D., Coyne, L., Appelbaum, A., Horowitz, L., & Voth, H. (1972). Psychotherapy and psychoanalysis: Final report of the Menninger Foundation's psychotherapy research project. *Bulletin of the Menninger Clinic, 36*, 1–275.

Kirsch, I. (1990). *Changing expectations: A key to effective psychotherapy*. Pacific Grove, CA: Brooks/Cole.

Kivlighan, D. M., & Coleman, M. N. (1999). Values, exchange relationships, group composition, and leader–member differences: A potpourri of reactions to Dose (1999). *Group Dynamics, 3*, 33–39.

Kivlighan, D. M., & Lilly, R. L. (1997). Developmental changes in group climate as they relate to therapeutic gain. *Group Dynamics: Theory, Research, and Practice, 1*, 208–221.

Kivlighan, D. M., & Tarrant, J. M. (2001). Does group climate mediate the group leadership–group member outcome relationship? A test of Yalom's hypotheses about leadership priorities. *Group Dynamics, 5*, 220–234.

Kleber, R. J., & Brom, D. (1987). Psychotherapy and pathological grief: Controlled outcome. *The Israel Journal of Psychiatry and Related Sciences, 24*, 99–109.

Kleber, R. J., & Brom, D. (1992). *Coping with trauma: Theory, prevention, and treatment.* Amsterdam, The Netherlands: Swets & Zeitlinger.

Klein, R. H. (1993). Short-term group psychotherapy. In H. I. Kaplan & B. J. Sadock (Eds.), *Comprehensive group psychotherapy* (3rd ed., pp. 256–270). Baltimore, MD: Williams & Wilkins.

Klein, S., & Fletcher, W. (1987). Gay grief: An examination of its uniqueness brought to light by the AIDS crisis. *Journal of Psychosocial Oncology, 4*, 15–25.

Klerman, G. L., Weissman, M. M., Rounsaville, B. J., & Chevron, S. E. (1984). *Interpersonal psychotherapy and depression.* New York, NY: Basic Books.

Kosmicki, F. X., & Glickauf-Hughes, C. (1997). Catharsis in psychotherapy. *Psychotherapy, 34*, 154–159.

Kraus, A. S., & Lilienfield, A. M. (1959). Some epidemiological aspects of the high mortality rate in the young widowed group. *Journal of Chronic Diseases, 10*, 207–217.

Kübler-Ross, E. (1993). *On death and dying.* New York, NY: Collier-Macmillan. (Original work published 1970)

Kumpfer, K. L. (1999). Factors and processes contributing to resilience: The resilience framework. In M. D. Glantz & J. L. Johnson (Eds.), *Resilience and development—Positive life adaptations: Longitudinal research in the social and behavioral sciences* (pp. 179–224). New York, NY: Kluwer Academic/Plenum Publishers.

Lambert, M. J. (1992). Psychotherapy outcome research: Implications for integrative and eclectic therapists. In J. C. Norcross & M. R. Goldfried (Eds.), *Handbook of psychotherapy integration* (pp. 94–129). New York, NY: Basic Books.

Larson, D. G., & Hoyt, W. T. (2007). What has become of grief therapy? An evaluation of the empirical foundations of the new pessimism. *Professional Psychology: Research and Practice, 38*, 347–355.

Latham, A. E., & Prigerson, H. G. (2004). Suicidality and bereavement: Complicated grief as psychiatric disorder presenting greatest risk for suicidality. *Suicide and Life-Threatening Behavior, 34*, 350–362.

Lazare, A. (1979). Unresolved grief. In A. Lazare (Ed.), *Outpatient psychiatry: Diagnosis and treatment* (pp. 498–512). Baltimore, MD: Williams & Wilkins.

Lazare, A. (1989). Unresolved grief. In A. Lazare (Ed.), *Outpatient psychiatry: Diagnosis and treatment* (2nd ed., pp. 381–397). Baltimore, MD: Williams & Wilkins.

Lazic, N., & Bamburac, J. (1991). The functioning of personality and the success of group psychotherapy of alcoholics. *Acta Medica Iugoslavica, 45*, 77–86.

Leahy, J. M. (1992–1993). A comparison of depression in women bereaved of a spouse, child, or a parent, *Omega: Journal of Death and Dying, 26*, 207–217.

Lee, G. R., DeMaris, A., Bavin, S., & Sullivan, R. (2001). Gender differences in the depressive effect of widowhood in later life. *Journal of Gerontology: Social Sciences, 56B*, S56–S61.

Lee, G. R., Willetts, M. C., & Seccombe, K. (1998). Widowhood and depression. *Research on Aging, 20*, 611–630.

Lehman, D. R., Ellard, J. H., & Wortman, C. B. (1986). Social support for the bereaved: Recipients' and providers' perspectives on what is helpful. *Journal of Consulting and Clinical Psychology, 54*, 438–446.

Lehman, D. R., Wortman, C., & Williams, A. (1987). Long-term effects of losing a spouse or child in a motor vehicle crash. *Journal of Personality and Social Psychology, 52*, 218–231.

Levine, J. M., & Moreland, R. L. (1990). Progress in small group research. *Annual Review of Psychology, 41*, 585–634.

Levy, L. H., Martinowski, K. S., & Deby, J. F. (1994). Differences in patterns of adaptation to conjugal bereavement: Their sources and potential significance, *Omega: Journal of Death and Dying, 28*, 71–87.

Lieberman, M. A., Wizlenberg, A., Golant, M., & Di Minno, M. (2005). The impact of group composition on Internet support groups: Homogeneous versus heterogeneous Parkinson's groups. *Group Dynamics, 9*, 239–250.

Lifton, R. J. (1964). On death and death symbolism: The Hiroshima disaster. *Psychiatry, 27*, 191–210.

Lindemann, E. (1944). Symptomatology and management of acute grief. *American Journal of Psychiatry, 101*, 141–148.

Lloyd, C. (1980). Life events and depressive disorders reviewed. *Archives of General Psychiatry, 37*, 529–539.

Longabaugh, R., Rubin, G. M., Malloy, P., Beattie, M., Clifford, P. R., & Noel, N. (1994). Drinking outcomes of alcohol abusers diagnosed as antisocial personality disorder. *Alcoholism: Clinical and Experimental Research, 18*, 778–785.

Lopata, H. Z. (1973). *Widowhood in an American city.* Cambridge, MA: Schenkman.

Lopata, H. Z. (1979). *Women as widows: Supportive systems.* New York, NY: Elsevier.

Lopata, H. Z. (1993). The support systems of American urban widows. In M. S. Stroebe, W. Stroebe, & R. O. Hansson (Eds.), *Handbook of bereavement: Theory, research, and intervention* (pp. 381–396). Cambridge, England: Cambridge University Press.

Luborsky, L. (1976). Helping alliances in psychotherapy. In J. Cleghorn (Ed.), *Successful psychotherapy* (pp. 92–116). New York, NY: Brunner/Mazel.

Luborsky, L., & Crits-Cristoph, P. (1997). *Understanding transference: The core conflictual relationship theme method* (2nd ed.). Washington DC: American Psychological Association.

Luborsky, L., Crits-Christoph, P., Mintz, J., & Auerbach, A. (1988). *Who will benefit from psychotherapy? Predicting therapeutic outcomes.* New York, NY: Basic Books.

Luborsky, L., Mintz, J., Auerbach, A., Christoph, P., Bachrach, H., Todd, T., . . . O'Brien, P. (1980). Predicting the outcome of psychotherapy: Findings of the Penn Psychotherapy Project. *Archives of General Psychiatry, 37,* 471–481.

Lund, D. A., Caserta, M. S., & Dimond, M. F. (1986). Gender differences through two years of bereavement among the elderly. *The Gerontologist, 26,* 314–320.

Lund, D. A., Caserta, M. S., & Dimond, M. F. (1993). The course of spousal bereavement in later life. In M. S. Stroebe, W. Stroebe, & R. O. Hansson (Eds.), *Handbook of bereavement: Theory, research, and intervention* (pp. 240–254). Cambridge, England: Cambridge University Press.

Lund, D. A., Dimond, M. F., Caserta, M. S., Johnsons, R., Poulton, J., & Connelly, J. (1985–1986). Identifying elderly with coping difficulties after two years of bereavement, *Omega: Journal of Death and Dying, 16,* 213–224.

Lundin, T. (1984a). Long-term outcome of bereavement. *British Journal of Psychiatry, 145,* 424–428.

Lundin, T. (1984b). Morbidity following sudden and unexpected bereavement. *British Journal of Psychiatry, 144,* 84–88.

Macias, C., Jones, D., Harvey, J., Barreira, P., Harding, C., & Rodican, C. (2004). Bereavement in the context of serious mental illness. *Psychiatric Service, 55,* 421–426.

MacKenzie, K. R. (1983). The clinical application of a group climate measure. In R. R. Dies & K. R. MacKenzie (Eds.), *Advances in group psychotherapy: Integrating research and practice* (pp. 159–170). Madison, CT: International Universities Press.

MacKenzie, K. R. (1990). *Introduction to time-limited group psychotherapy.* Washington, DC: American Psychiatric Publishing.

MacKenzie, K. R. (1994). Group development. In A. Fuhriman & G. M. Burlingame (Eds.), *Handbook of group psychotherapy: An empirical and clinical synthesis* (pp. 223–268). New York, NY: Wiley.

MacKenzie, K. R. (1997). *Time-managed group psychotherapy: Effective clinical applications.* Washington, DC: American Psychiatric Publishing.

MacNab, R. T. (1990). What do men want? Male rituals of initiation in group psychotherapy. *International Journal of Group Psychotherapy, 40,* 139–154.

Maddison, D. (1968). The relevance of conjugal bereavement for preventive psychiatry. *British Journal of Medical Psychology, 41,* 223–233.

Maddison, D., & Walter, W. L. (1967). Factors affecting the outcome of conjugal bereavement. *British Journal of Psychiatry, 113,* 1057–1067.

Maercker, A., Bonanno, G. A., Znoj, H., & Horowitz, M. J. (1998). Prediction of complicated grief by positive and negative themes in narratives. *Journal of Clinical Psychology, 54*, 1117–1136.

Malan, D. H., Balfour, F. H., Hood, V. G., & Shooter, A. M. (1976). Group psychotherapy: A long-term follow-up study. *Archives of General Psychiatry, 33*, 1303–1315.

Mallinckrodt, B., King, J. L., & Coble, H. M. (1998). Family dysfunction, alexithymia, and client attachment to therapist. *Journal of Counseling Psychology, 45*, 497–504.

Marini, Z., & Case, R. (1994). The development of abstract reasoning about the physical and social world. *Child Development, 65*, 147–159.

Marmar, C. R., Horowitz, M. J., Weiss, D. S., Wilner, N. R., & Kaltreider, N. B. (1988). A controlled trial of brief psychotherapy and mutual help group treatment of conjugal bereavement. *American Journal of Psychiatry, 145*, 203–209.

Marris, P. (1958). *Widows and their families*. London, England: Routledge & Kegan Paul.

Martikainen, P., & Valkonen, T. (1996). Mortality after death of a spouse in relation to duration of bereavement in Finland. *Journal of Epidemiology and Community Health, 50*, 264–268.

Martin, J. L. (1988). Psychological consequences of AIDS-related bereavement among gay men. *Journal of Consulting and Clinical Psychology, 56.* 856–862.

Marziali, E., & Munroe-Blum, H. (1994). *Interpersonal group psychotherapy for borderline personality disorder*. New York, NY: Basic Books.

Marziali, E., Munroe-Blum, H., & McCleary, L. (1997). The contribution of group cohesion and group alliance to the outcome of group psychotherapy. *International Journal of Group Psychotherapy, 47*, 475–497.

Masters, R., Friedman, L., & Getzel, G. (1988). Helping families of homicide victims: A multidimensional approach. *Journal of Traumatic Stress, 1*, 109–125.

Mawson, D., Marks, I. M., Ramm, L., & Stern, R. S. (1981). Guided mourning for morbid grief: a controlled study. *British Journal of Psychiatry, 138*, 185–193.

McCallum M., & Piper, W. E. (1988). Psychoanalytically oriented short-term groups for outpatients: Unsettled issues. *Group, 12*, 21–32.

McCallum, M., & Piper, W. E. (1990a). A controlled study of effectiveness and patient suitability for short-term group psychotherapy. *International Journal of Group Psychotherapy, 40*, 431–452.

McCallum, M., & Piper, W. E. (1990b). The psychological mindedness assessment procedure. *Psychological Assessment: A Journal of Consulting and Clinical Psychology, 2*, 412–418.

McCallum, M., & Piper, W. E. (1997a). Integration of psychological mindedness and related concepts. In M. McCallum & W. E. Piper (Eds.), *Psychological mindedness: A contemporary understanding* (pp. 237–258). Mahwah, NJ: Erlbaum.

McCallum, M., & Piper, W. E. (1997b). The psychological mindedness assessment procedure. In M. McCallum & W. E. Piper (Eds.), *Psychological mindedness: A contemporary understanding* (pp. 27–58). Mahwah, NJ: Erlbaum.

McCallum, M., & Piper, W. E. (1999). Personality disorders and response to group-oriented evening treatment. *Group Dynamics: Theory, Research, and Practice, 3,* 3–14.

McCallum, M., Piper, W. E., & Joyce, A. S. (1992). Dropping out from short-term group therapy. *Psychotherapy, 29,* 206–215.

McCallum, M., Piper, W. E., & Morin, H. (1993). Affect and outcome in short-term group psychotherapy for loss. *International Journal of Group Psychotherapy, 43,* 303–319.

McCallum, M., Piper, W. E., Ogrodniczuk, J. S., & Joyce, A. S. (2002). Early process and dropping out from short-term therapy for complicated grief. *Group Dynamics: Theory, Research, and Practice, 6,* 243–254.

McCallum, M., Piper, W. E., Ogrodniczuk, J. S., & Joyce, A. S. (2003). Relationships among psychological mindedness, alexithymia and outcome in four forms of short-term psychotherapy. *Psychology and Psychotherapy: Theory, Research and Practice, 76,* 133–144.

McCallum, M., Piper, W. E., & O'Kelly, J. (1997). Predicting patient benefit from a group-oriented, evening treatment program. *International Journal of Group Psychotherapy, 47,* 291–314.

McConnaughy, E. A., DiClemente, C. C., Prochaska, J. O., & Velicer, W. F. (1989). Stages of change in psychotherapy: A follow-up report. *Psychotherapy: Theory, Research, Practice, Training, 26,* 494–503.

McCrae, R. R., & Costa, P. T. (1989). Reinterpreting the Myers-Briggs Type Indicator from the perspective of the five-factor model of personality. *Journal of Personality, 57,* 17–40.

McCrae, R. R., & John, O. P. (1992). An introduction to the five-factor model and its applications. *Journal of Personality, 60,* 175–215.

McDermut, W., Miller, I. W., & Brown, R. A. (2001). The efficacy of group psychotherapy for depression: A meta-analysis and review of the empirical research. *Clinical Psychology: Science and Practice, 8,* 98–116.

McHorney, C. A., & Mor, V. (1988). Predictors of bereavement depression and its health services consequences. *Medical Care, 26,* 882–893.

McIntosh, D. N., Silver, R., & Wortman, C. B. (1993). Religion's role in adjustment to a negative life event: Coping with the loss of a child. *Journal of Personality and Social Psychology, 65,* 812–821.

McNeill, D. N. (1973). *Mortality among the widowed in Connecticut.* Unpublished master's dissertation, Yale University

McRoberts, C., Burlingame, G. M., & Hoag. M. J. (1998). Comparative efficacy of individual and group psychotherapy: A meta-analytic perspective. *Group Dynamics: Theory, Research, and Practice, 2,* 101–17.

Melhem, N. M., Moritz, G., Walker, M., Shear, M. K., & Brent, D. (2007). Phenomenology and correlates of complicated grief in children and adolescents. *Journal of the American Academy of Child and Adolescent Psychiatry, 46,* 493–499.

Melnick, J., & Woods, M. (1976). Analysis of group composition research and theory for psychotherapeutic and growth-oriented groups. *The Journal of Applied Behavioral Science, 12*, 493–512.

Meyer, B., & Pilkonis, P. A. (2002). Attachment style. In J. C. Norcross (Ed.), *Psychotherapy relationships that work: Therapist contributions and responsiveness to patients* (pp. 367–382). New York, NY: Oxford University Press.

Meyer, B., Pilkonis, P. A., Krupnick, J. L., Egan, M. K., Simmens, S. J., & Sotsky, S. M. (2002). Treatment expectancies, patient alliance, and outcome: Further analyses from the NIMH Treatment of Depression Collaborative Research Program. *Journal of Consulting and Clinical Psychology, 70*, 1051–1055.

Meyer, B., Pilkonis, P. A., Proietti, J. M., Heape, C. L., & Egan, M. (2001). Attachment styles, personality disorders, and response to treatment. *Journal of Personality Disorders, 15*, 371–389.

Miller, T. R. (1991). The psychotherapeutic utility of the five-factor model of personality: A clinician's experience. *Journal of Personality Assessment, 57*, 415–433.

Minino, A. M., Heron, M. P., Murphy, S. L., & Kochanek, K. D. (2007). Deaths: Final data from 2004. *National Vital Statistics Reports, 55*, 1–119.

Mitchell, A. M., Kim, Y., Prigerson, H. G., & Mortimer-Stephens, M. (2004). Complicated grief in survivors of suicide. *Crisis, 25*, 12–18.

Mohr, D. C. (1995). Negative outcome in psychotherapy: A critical review. *Clinical Psychology: Science and Practice, 2*, 1–27.

Momartin, S., Silove, D., Manicavasagar, V., & Steel, Z. (2004). Complicated grief in Bosnian refugees: Associated with posttraumatic stress disorder and depression. *Comprehensive Psychiatry, 45*, 475–482.

Monras, M., & Gual, A. (2000). Attrition in group therapy with alcoholics: A survival analysis. *Drug and Alcohol Review, 19*, 55–63.

Moos, R. H. (1984). Context and coping: Toward a unifying conceptual framework. *American Journal of Community Psychology, 12*, 5–25.

Mor, V., McHorney, C., & Sherwood, S. (1986). Secondary morbidity among the recently bereaved. *American Journal of Psychiatry, 143*, 158–163.

Moras, K., & Strupp, H. (1982). Pretherapy interpersonal relations, client's alliance, and outcome in brief therapy. *Archives of General Psychiatry, 39*, 405–409.

Morgan, D. L. (1989). Adjust to widowhood: Do social networks really make it easier? *Gerontologist, 29*, 101–107.

Morgan, L. A. (1976). A re-examination of widowhood and morale. *Journal of Gerontology, 31*, 687–695.

Murdock, M. E., Guarnaccia, C. A., Hayslip, B., Jr., & McKibbin, C. L. (1998). The contribution of small life events to the psychological distress of married and widowed older women. *Journal of Women & Aging, 10*, 3–22.

Murphy, S. A. (1988). Mental distress and recovery in a high-risk bereavement sample three years after untimely death. *Nursing Research, 37*, 30–35.

Murrell, S. A., & Himmelfarb, S. (1989). Effects of attachment bereavement and pre-event conditions on subsequent depressive symptoms in older adults. *Psychology and Aging, 4,* 166–172.

Neimeyer, R. A. (2000). Searching for the meaning: Grief therapy and the process of reconstruction. *Death Studies, 24,* 541–558.

Neria, Y., Gross, R., Litz, B., Maguem, S., Insel, B., Seirmarco, G., . . . Marshall, R. D. (2007). Prevalence and psychological correlates of complicated grief among bereaved adults 2.5–3.5 years after September 11th attacks. *Journal of Traumatic Stress, 20,* 251–262.

Ness, D. E., & Pfeffer, C. (1990). Sequelae of bereavement resulting from suicide. *American Journal of Psychiatry, 147,* 279–285.

Newman, M. G., Crits-Christoph, P., Connolly-Gibbons, M. B., & Erickson, T. M. (2006). Participant factors in treating anxiety disorders. In L. G. Castonguay & L. E. Beutler (Eds.), *Principles of therapeutic change that work* (pp. 121–153). New York, NY: Oxford University Press.

Nichols, M. P., & Efran, J. S. (1985). Catharsis in psychotherapy. *Psychotherapy: Theory, Research, Practice, Training, 22,* 46–58.

Niemi, T. (1979). The mortality of male old-age pensioners following a spouse's death. *Scandinavian Journal of Social Medicine, 7,* 115–117.

Nolen-Hoeksema, S. (2001). Ruminative coping and adjustment to bereavement. In M. S. Stroebe, R. O. Hansson, W. Stroebe, & H. Schut (Eds.), *Handbook of bereavement research: Consequences, coping and care* (pp. 545–562). Washington, DC: American Psychological Association.

Nolen-Hoeksema, S., & Larson, J. (1999). *Coping with loss.* Mahwah, NJ: Erlbaum.

Nolen-Hoeksema, S., Parker, L. E., & Larson, J. (1994). Ruminative coping with depressed mood following loss. *Journal of Personality and Social Psychology, 67,* 92–104.

Norris, F. H., & Murrell, S. A. (1990). Social support, life events, and stress as modifiers of adjustment to bereavement by older adults. *Psychology and Aging, 5,* 429–436.

Ochberg, F. (1988). *Post-traumatic therapy and victims of violence.* New York, NY: Brunner/Mazel.

Ogrodniczuk, J. S., Joyce, A. S., & Piper, W. E. (2007). Effect of patient dissatisfaction with the therapist on group therapy outcome. *Clinical Psychology and Psychotherapy, 14,* 126–134.

Ogrodniczuk, J. S., & Piper, W. E. (2003). The effect of group climate on outcome of two forms of short-term group therapy. *Group Dynamics: Theory, Research, and Practice, 7,* 64–76.

Ogrodniczuk, J. S., Piper, W. E., & Joyce, A. S. (2004a). Alexithymia as a predictor of residual symptoms in depressed patients who respond to short-term psychotherapy. *American Journal of Psychotherapy, 58,* 150–161.

Ogrodniczuk, J. S., Piper, W. E., & Joyce, A. S. (2004b). Differences in men's and women's responses to short-term group psychotherapy. *Psychotherapy Research, 14*, 231–243.

Ogrodniczuk, J. S., Piper, W. E., & Joyce, A. S. (2005). The negative effect of alexithymia on the outcome of group therapy for complicated grief: What role might the therapist play? *Comprehensive Psychiatry, 46*, 206–213.

Ogrodniczuk, J. S., Piper, W. E., & Joyce, A. S. (2006). Treatment compliance in different types of group psychotherapy: Exploring the effect of age. *Journal of Nervous and Mental Disease, 194*, 287–293.

Ogrodniczuk, J. S., Piper, W. E., & Joyce, A. S. (2008a). Alexithymia and therapist reactions to the patient: Expression of positive emotion as a mediator. *Psychiatry, 71*, 257–265.

Ogrodniczuk, J. S., Piper, W. E., & Joyce, A. S. (2008b). Impact of pain on the outcome of group psychotherapy. *International Journal of Clinical and Health Psychology, 8*, 399–409.

Ogrodniczuk, J. S., Piper, W. E., Joyce, A. S., & McCallum, M. (1999). Transference interpretations in short-term dynamic psychotherapy. *Journal of Nervous and Mental Disease, 187*, 571–578.

Ogrodniczuk, J. S., Piper, W. E., Joyce, A. S., & McCallum, M. (2001a). Effect of patient gender on outcome in two forms of short-term individual psychotherapy. *Journal of Psychotherapy Practice and Research, 10*, 69–78.

Ogrodniczuk, J. S., Piper, W. E., Joyce, A. S., & McCallum, M. (2001b). Using DSM Axis II information to predict outcome in short-term individual psychotherapy. *Journal of Personality Disorders, 15*, 110–122.

Ogrodniczuk, J. S., Piper, W. E., Joyce, A. S., McCallum, M., & Rosie, J. S. (2002). Social support as a predictor of response to group therapy for complicated grief. *Psychiatry, 65*, 346–357.

Ogrodniczuk, J. S., Piper, W. E., Joyce, A. S., McCallum, M., & Rosie, J. S. (2003). NEO-five factor personality traits as predictors of response to two forms of group psychotherapy. *International Journal of Group Psychotherapy, 53*, 417–442.

Ogrodniczuk, J. S., Piper, W. E., Joyce, Weideman, R., McCallum, M., Azim, H. F., & Rosie, J. S. (2003). Differentiating symptoms of complicated grief and depression among psychiatric outpatients. *Canadian Journal of Psychiatry, 48*, 87–93.

Ogrodniczuk, J. S., Piper, W. E., McCallum, M., Joyce, A. S., & Rosie, J. S. (2002). Interpersonal predictors of group therapy outcome for complicated grief. *International Journal of Group Psychotherapy, 52*, 511–535.

Orlinsky, D. E., Rønnestad, M. H., & Willutzki, U. (2004). Fifty years of psychotherapy process-outcome research: Continuity and change. In M. J. Lambert (Ed.), *Bergin and Garfield's handbook of psychotherapy and behavior change* (5th ed., pp. 307–389). New York, NY: Wiley.

Osterweis, M., Solomon, F., & Green, M. (1984). *Bereavement: Reactions, consequences, and care. A report of the Institute of Medicine, National Academy of Sciences.* Washington, DC: National Academy Press.

Ott, C. H. (2003). The impact of complicated grief on mental and physical health at various points in the bereavement process. *Death Studies, 27*, 249–272.

Park, L. C., Imboden, J. B., Park, T. J., Hulse, S. H., & Unger, H. T. (1992). Giftedness and psychological abuse in borderline personality disorder: Their relevance to genesis and treatment. *Journal of Personality Disorders, 6*, 226–240.

Parkes, C. M. (1964, August 1). Effects of bereavement on physical and mental health—A study of the medical records of widows. *British Medical Journal, 2*, 274–279.

Parkes, C. M. (1965). Bereavement and mental illness. *British Journal of Medical Psychology, 38*, 1–12.

Parkes, C. M. (1971). Determinants of outcome of bereavement. *Proceedings of the Royal Society of Medicine, 64*, 279.

Parkes, C. M. (1975). Determinants of outcome following bereavement. *Omega: Journal of Death and Dying,, 6*, 303–323.

Parkes, C. M. (1985). Bereavement. *British Journal of Psychiatry, 146*, 11–17.

Parkes, C. M. (1987). *Bereavement: Studies of grief in adult life* (2nd ed.). Madison, CT: International Universities Press.

Parkes, C. M., & Benjamin, B., & Fitzgerald, R. (1969, March 22). Broken heart: A statistical study of the increased mortality among widowers. *BMJ, 1*, 740–743.

Parkes, C. M., & Weiss, R. S. (1983). *Recovery from bereavement.* New York, NY: Basic Books.

Paunonen, S. V., Jackson, D. N., Trzebinski, J., & Forsterling, F. (1992). Personality structure across cultures: A multimethod estimation. *Journal of Personality and Social Psychology, 62*, 447–456.

Perlin, S., & Schmidt, A. (1975). Psychiatry. In S. Perlin (Ed.), *A handbook for the study of suicide* (pp.147–163). New York, NY: Oxford University Press.

Perls, F. (1973). *The Gestalt approach and eye witness therapy.* Palo Alto, CA: Science & Behavior Books.

Perrone, K. M., & Sedlacek, W. E. (2000). A comparison of group cohesiveness and client satisfaction in homogeneous and heterogeneous groups. *Journal for Specialists in Group Work, 25*, 243–251.

Petersen, T., Bottonari, K., Alpert, J. E., Fava, M., & Nierenberg, A. A. (2001). Use of the five-factor inventory in characterizing patients with major depressive disorder. *Comprehensive Psychiatry, 42*, 488–493.

Petrocelli, J. V. (2002). Processes and stages of change: Counseling with the trans-theoretical model of change. *Journal of Counseling and Development, 80*, 22–30.

Phares, E. J. (1992). *Clinical psychology: Concepts, methods, and profession* (4th ed.). Pacific Grove, CA: Brooks/Cole.

Pihlblad, C. T., & Adams, D. L. (1972). Widowhood, social participation, and life satisfaction. *Aging and Human Development, 3*, 323–330.

Pilkonis, P. A., Imber, S. D., Lewis, P., & Rubinsky, P. (1984). A comparative outcome study of individual, group, and conjoint psychotherapy. *Archives of General Psychiatry, 41*, 431–437.

Piper, W. E. (1994). Client variables. In A. Fuhriman & G. Burlingame (Eds.), *Handbook of group psychotherapy* (pp. 83–113). New York, NY: Wiley.

Piper, W. E., Azim, H. F. A., Joyce, A. S., & McCallum, M. (1991). Transference interpretations, therapeutic alliance and outcome in short-term individual psychotherapy. *Archives of General Psychiatry, 48,* 946–953.

Piper, W. E., Azim, H. F. A., Joyce, A. S., McCallum, M., Nixon, G. W. H., & Segal, P. S. (1991). Quality of object relations versus interpersonal functioning as predictors of therapeutic alliance and psychotherapy outcome. *Journal of Nervous and Mental Disease, 179,* 432–438.

Piper, W. E., Azim, H. F. A., McCallum, M., & Joyce, A. S. (1990). Patient suitability and outcome in short-term individual psychotherapy. *Journal of Consulting and Clinical Psychology, 58,* 475–481.

Piper, W. E., Debbane, E. G., Bienvenu, J. P., & Garant, J. (1984). A comparative study of four forms of psychotherapy. *Journal of Consulting and Clinical Psychology, 52,* 268–279.

Piper, W. E., de Carufel, F. L., & Szkrumelak, N. (1985). Patient predictors of process and outcome in short-term individual psychotherapy. *Journal of Nervous and Mental Disease, 173,* 726–733.

Piper, W. E., & Duncan, S. C. (1999). Object relations theory and short-term dynamic psychotherapy: Findings from the Quality of Object Relations scale. *Clinical Psychology Review, 19,* 669–685.

Piper, W. E., & Joyce, A. S. (1996). A consideration of factors influencing the utilization of time-limited, short-term group therapy. *International Journal of Group Psychotherapy, 46,* 311–328.

Piper, W. E., Joyce, A. S., Azim, H. F. A., & Rosie, J. S. (1994). Patient characteristics and success in day treatment. *Journal of Nervous and Mental Disease, 182,* 381–386.

Piper, W. E., Joyce, A. S., McCallum, M., & Azim, H. F. A. (1998). Interpretive and supportive forms of psychotherapy and patient personality variables. *Journal of Consulting and Clinical Psychology, 66,* 558–567.

Piper, W. E., Joyce, A. S., McCallum, M., Azim, H. F. A., & Ogrodniczuk, J. S. (2002). *Interpretive and supportive psychotherapies: Matching therapy and patient personality.* Washington, DC: American Psychological Association.

Piper, W. E., Marrache, M., Lacroix, R., Richardsen, A. M., & Jones, B. D. (1983). Cohesion as a basic bond in groups. *Human Relations, 36,* 93–108.

Piper, W. E., McCallum, M., & Azim, H. F. A. (1992). *Adaptation to loss through short-term group psychotherapy.* New York, NY: Guilford Press.

Piper, W. E., McCallum, M., Joyce, A. S., Rosie, J. S., & Ogrodniczuk, J. S. (2001). Patient personality and time-limited group psychotherapy for complicated grief. *International Journal of Group Psychotherapy, 51,* 525–552.

Piper, W. E., & Ogrodniczuk, J. S. (2006). Group-as-a-whole interpretations in short-term group psychotherapy. *Journal Contemporary Psychotherapy, 36,* 129–135.

Piper, W. E., Ogrodniczuk, J. S., Azim, H. F. A., & Weideman, R. (2001). Prevalence of loss and complicated grief among psychiatric outpatients. *Psychiatric Services, 52,* 1069–1074.

Piper, W. E., Ogrodniczuk, J. S., Joyce, A. S., McCallum, M., & Rosie, J. S. (2002). Relationships among affect, work, and outcome in group therapy for patients with complicated grief. *American Journal of Psychotherapy, 56,* 347–361.

Piper, W. E., Ogrodniczuk, J. S., Joyce, A. S., McCallum. M., Weideman, R., & Azim, H. F. A. (2001). Ambivalence and other relationship predictors of grief in psychiatric outpatients. *Journal of Nervous and Mental Disease, 189,* 781–787.

Piper, W. E., Ogrodniczuk, J. S., Joyce, A. S., Weideman, R., & Rosie, J. S. (2007). Group composition and group therapy for complicated grief. *Journal of Consulting and Clinical Psychology, 75,* 116–125.

Piper, W. E., Ogrodniczuk, J. S., McCallum, M., Joyce, A. S., & Rosie, J. S. (2003). Expression of affect as a mediator of the relationship between quality of object relations and group therapy outcome for patients with complicated grief. *Journal of Consulting and Clinical Psychology, 71,* 664–671.

Piper, W. E., Ogrodniczuk, J. S., & Weideman, R. (2005). Screening for complicated grief: When less may provide more. *Canadian Journal of Psychiatry, 50,* 680–683.

Piper, W. E., & Perrault, E. L. (1989). Pretherapy preparation for group members. *International Journal of Group Psychotherapy, 39,* 17–34.

Prigerson, H. G., Ahmed, I., Silverman, G. K., Saxena, A. K., Maciejewski, P. K., Jacobs, S. C., . . . Hamirani, M. (2002). Rates and risks of complicated grief among psychiatric clinic patients in Karachi, Pakistan. *Death Studies, 26,* 781–792.

Prigerson, H. G., Bierhals, A. J., Kasl, S. V., Reynolds, C. F., Shear, M. K., Day, N., . . . Jacobs, S. C. (1997). Traumatic grief as a risk for mental and physical morbidity. *American Journal of Psychiatry, 154,* 616–623.

Prigerson, H. G., Cherlin, E., Chen, J. H., Kasl, S. V., Hurzeler, R., & Bradley, E. H. (2003). The Stressful Caregiving Adult Reactions to Experiences of Dying (SCARED) Scale. *American Journal of Geriatric Psychiatry, 11,* 309–319.

Prigerson, H. G., Frank, E., Kasl, S. V., Reynolds, C. F., Anderson, B., Zubenko, G. S., . . . Kupfer, D. J. (1995). Complicated grief and bereavement-related depression as distinct disorders: Preliminary empirical validation in elderly bereaved spouses. *American Journal of Psychiatry, 152,* 22–30.

Prigerson, H. G., Frank, E., Reynolds, C. F., George, C. J., & Kupfer, D. J. (1993). Protective psychosocial factors in depression among spousally bereaved elders. *American Journal of Geriatric Psychiatry, 1,* 296–309.

Prigerson, H. G., & Jacobs, S. C. (2001). Caring for bereaved patients: "All the doctors just suddenly go". *Journal of the American Medical Association, 286,* 1369–1375.

Prigerson, H. G., Maciejewski, P. K., Reynolds, C. F., Beirhals, A. J., Newson, J. T., Fasiczka, A., . . . Miller, M. (1995). Inventory of Complicated Grief: A scale to measure maladaptive symptoms of loss. *Psychiatric Research, 59,* 65–79.

Prigerson, H. G., Maciejewski, P. K., & Rosenheck, R. A. (2000). Preliminary explorations of the harmful interactive effects of widowhood and marital harmony on health, health service use, and health care costs. *The Gerontologist, 40*, 349–357.

Prigerson, H. G., Shear, M. K., Jacobs, S. C., Reynolds, C. F., Maciejewski, P. K., Davidson, J. R., . . . Zisook, S. (1999). Consensus criteria for traumatic grief: a preliminary empirical test. *British Journal of Psychiatry, 174*, 67–73.

Prochaska, J. O., & DiClemente, C. C. (1983). Stages and processes of self-change of smoking: Toward an integrative model of change. *Journal of Consulting and Clinical Psychology, 51*, 390–395.

Prochaska, J. O., DiClemente, C. C., & Norcoss, J. C. (1992). In search of how people change: Applications to addiction behaviors. *American Psychologist, 47*, 1102–1114.

Prochaska, J. O., & Norcross, J. C. (2002). Stages of change. In J. C. Norcross (Ed.), *Psychotherapy relationships that work: Therapist contributions and responsiveness to patients* (pp. 303–313). New York, NY: Oxford University Press.

Quilty, L. C., De Fruyt, F., Rolland, J-P., Kennedy, S. H., Rouillon, P. F., & Bagby, R. M. (2008). Dimensional personality traits and treatment outcome in patients with major depressive disorder. *Journal of Affective Disorders, 108*, 241–250.

Rainer, J. P., & Campbell, L. F. (2001). Premature termination in psychotherapy: Identification and intervention. *Journal of Psychotherapy in Independent Practice, 2*, 19–41.

Rando, T. A. (1983). An investigation of grief and adaptation in parents whose children have died from cancer. *Journal of Paediatric Psychology, 8*, 3–20.

Rando, T. A. (1991). *Grieving: How to go on living when someone you love dies*. New York, NY: Bantam Books.

Rando, T. A. (1993). *Treatment of complicated mourning*. Champaign, IL: Research Press.

Range, L., & Calhoun, L. (1990). Responses following suicide and other types of death: The perspective of the bereaved. *Omega: Journal of Death and Dying, 21*, 311–320.

Raphael, B. (1983). *The anatomy of bereavement*. New York, NY: Basic Books.

Raphael, B. (1986). *When disaster strikes: How individuals and communities cope with catastrophe*. New York, NY: Basic Books.

Raphael, B., & Middleton, W. (1990). What is pathologic grief? *Psychiatric Annals, 20*, 304–307.

Raphael, B., Minkov, C., & Dobson, M. (2001). Psychotherapeutic and pharmacological intervention for bereaved persons. In M. S. Stroebe, R. O. Hansson, W. Stroebe, & H. Schut (Eds.), *Handbook of bereavement research: Consequences, coping, and care* (pp. 587–612). Washington, DC: American Psychological Association.

Rasting, M., Brosig, B., & Beutel, M. E. (2005). Alexithymic characteristics and patient–therapist interaction: A video analysis of facial affect display. *Psychopathology*, *38*, 105–111.

Reed, M. D. (1998). Predicting grief symptomatology among the suddenly bereaved. *Suicide and Life-Threatening Behavior*, *28*, 285–301.

Rees, W. D., & Lutkins, S. G. (1967, October 7). Mortality of bereavement. *BMJ*, 13–16.

Reid, J. C., Nair, S. S., Mistry, S. I., & Beitman, B. D. (1996). Effectiveness of stages of change and adinazolam SR in panic disorder: A neural network analysis. *Journal of Anxiety Disorders*, *10*, 331–345.

Remondet, J. H., Hansson, R. O., Rule, B., & Winfrey, G. (1987). Rehearsal for widowhood. *Journal of Social and Clinical Psychology*, *5*, 285–297.

Reynolds, S. K., & Clark, L. A. (2001). Predicting dimensions of personality disorder from domains and facets of the five-factor model. *Journal of Personality*, *69*, 199–222.

Richards, J. G., & McCallum, J. (1979). Bereavement in the elderly. *New Zealand Medical Journal*, *69*, 201–204.

Richardson, V. E., & Balaswamy, S. (2001). Coping with bereavement among elderly widowers. *Omega: Journal of Death and Dying*, *43*, 129–144.

Rinear, E. (1988). Psychological aspects of parental response patterns to the death of a child by homicide. *Journal of Traumatic Stress*, *1*, 305–322.

Robinson-Whelen, S., Tata, T., MacCallum, R. C., McGuire, L., & Kiecolt-Glaser, J. K. (2001). Long-term caregiving: What happens when it ends? *Journal of Abnormal Psychology*, *110*, 573–584.

Rockland, L. H. (1989). *Supportive, therapy: A psychodynamic approach*. New York, NY: Basic Books.

Rogers, R. G. (1995). Marriage, sex, and mortality. *Journal of Marriage and the Family*, *57*, 515–526.

Rosenthal, R., & Jacobson, L. (1968). *Pygmalion in the classroom*. New York, NY: Holt.

Rosik, C. H. (1989). The impact of religious orientation in conjugal bereavement among older adults. *International Journal of Aging and Human Development*, *28*, 251–260.

Rossi Ferrario, S., Cardillo, V., Vicario, F., Balzarini, E., & Zotti, A. M. (2004). Advanced cancer at home: Caregiving and bereavement. *Palliative Medicine*, *18*, 129–136.

Rubin, S. (1981). A two-track model of bereavement: Theory and application in research. *American Journal of Orthopsychiatry*, *51*, 101–109.

Rubin, S. (1999). The two-track model of bereavement: Overview, retrospect, and prospect. *Death Studies*, *23*, 681–714.

Rudestam, K. E. (1977). Physical and psychological responses to suicide in the family. *Journal of Consulting and Clinical Psychology*, *45*, 162–170.

Rudestam, K. E., & Imbroll, D. (1983). Societal reactions to a child's death by suicide. *Journal of Consulting and Clinical Psychology, 51*, 461–462.

Russo, J., Katon, W., Lin, E., Von Korff, M., Bush, T., Simon, G., & Walker, E. (1997). Neuroticism and extraversion as predictors of health outcomes in depressed primary care patients. *Psychosomatics, 38*, 339–348.

Rutan, J. S, & Stone, W. N. (2001a). *Psychodynamic group psychotherapy* (3rd ed.). New York, NY: Guilford Press.

Rutan, J. S., & Stone, W. N. (2001b). Termination in group psychotherapy. In J. S. Rutan, & W. N. Stone, *Psychodynamic group psychotherapy* (3rd ed., pp. 332–354). New York, NY: Guilford Press.

Rutan, J. S., Stone, W. N., & Shay, J. J. (2007). *Psychodynamic group psychotherapy* (4th ed.). New York, NY: Guilford Press.

Rynearson, E. K. (1986). Psychological effects of unnatural dying on bereavement. *Psychiatric Annals, 16*, 272–275.

Rynearson, E. K., & McCreery, J. (1993). Bereavement after homicide: A synergism of trauma and loss. *American Journal of Psychiatry, 150*, 258–261.

Safran, J. D., & Greenberg, L. S. (1991). *Emotion, psychotherapy, and change*. New York, NY: Guilford Press.

Safran, J. D., & Segel, Z. S. (1990). *Interpersonal process in cognitive therapy*. New York, NY: Basic Books.

Sanders, C. (1980). A comparison of adult bereavement in the death of a spouse, child, and a parent. *Omega: Journal of Death and Dying, 10*, 303–322.

Sanders, C. (1980–1981). Comparison of younger and older spouses in bereavement outcome. *Omega: Journal of Death and Dying, 11*, 217–231.

Sanders, C. (1983). Effects of sudden versus chronic illness death on bereavement outcome. *Omega: Journal of Death and Dying, 11*, 227–241.

Sanders, C. (1989). *Grief: The mourning after*. New York, NY: Wiley.

Sanders, C., Mauger, P. A., & Strong, P. N. (1979). *A manual for the Grief Experience Inventory*. Palo Alto, CA: Consulting Psychologists Press.

Sandler, I. N., Ayers, T. S., Wolchik, S. A., Tein, J., Kwok, O., Haine, R. A., . . . Griffin, W. A. (2003). The Family Bereavement Program: Efficacy evaluation of a theory-based prevention program for parentally bereaved children and adolescents. *Journal of Consulting and Clinical Psychology, 71*, 587–600.

Satterfield, W. A., Buelow, S. A., Lyddon, W. J., & Johnson, J. T. (1995). Client stages of change and expectations about counseling. *Journal of Counseling Psychology, 42*, 476–478.

Satterfield, W. A., & Lyddon, W. J. (1998). Client attachment and the working alliance. *Counselling Psychology Quarterly, 11*, 407–415.

Scharlach, A. E. (1991). Factors associated with filial grief following the death of an elderly parent. *American Journal of Orthopsychiatry, 61*, 307–313.

Scheff, T. J., & Bushnell, D. D. (1984). A theory of catharsis. *Journal of Research in Personality, 18*, 238–264.

Schulz, R., Beach, S. R., Lind, B., Martire, L. M., Zdaniuk, B., Hirsch, C., . . . Burton, L. (2001). Involvement in caregiving and adjustment to death of a spouse. *Journal of the American Medical Association, 285,* 3123–3129.

Schulz, R., Boerner, K., Shear, M. K., Zhang, S., & Gitlin, L. N. (2006). Predictors of complicated grief among dementia caregivers: A prospective study of bereavement. *American Journal of Geriatric Psychiatry, 14,* 650–658.

Schut, H., Stroebe, M. S., de Keijser, J., & van den Bout, J. (1997). Intervention for the bereaved: Gender differences in the efficacy of the two counseling programmes. *British Journal of Clinical Psychology, 36,* 63–72.

Schut, H., Stroebe, M. S., van den Bout, J., & de Keijser, J. (1997). Intervention for the bereaved: Gender differences in the efficacy of grief counselling. *British Journal of Clinical Psychology, 36,* 63–72.

Schut, H., Stroebe, M. S., van den Bout, J., & Terheggen, M. (2001). The efficacy of bereavement interventions: Determining who benefits. In M. S. Stroebe, R. O. Hansson, W. Stroebe, & H. Schut (Eds.), *Handbook of bereavement research: Consequences, coping, and care* (pp. 705–737). Washington, DC: American Psychological Association.

Scott, J., Williams, J. M. G., Brittlebank, A., & Ferrier, I. N. (1995). The relationship between premorbid neuroticism, cognitive dysfunction and persistence of depression: A 1-year follow-up. *Journal of Affective Disorders, 33,* 167–172.

Scott, K. L., & Wolfe, D. A. (2003). Readiness to change as a predictor of outcome in batterer treatment. *Journal of Consulting and Clinical Psychology, 71,* 879–889.

Segal, D. L., Chatman, C., Bogaards, J. A., & Becker, L. A. (2001). One-year follow-up of an emotional expression intervention for bereaved older adults. *Journal of Mental Health and Aging, 7,* 465–472.

Seltzer, M. M., & Li, L. W. (2000). The dynamics of caregiving: Transitions during a three-year prospective study. *The Gerontologist, 40,* 165–177.

Seligman, M. E. P. (1995). The effectiveness of psychotherapy: The Consumer Reports study. *American Psychologist, 50,* 965–974.

Sexton, H. (1993). Exploring a psychotherapeutic change sequence: Relating process to intersessional and posttreatment outcome. *Journal of Consulting and Clinical Psychology, 61,* 128–136.

Shahar, G., Blatt, S. J., Zuroff, D. C., & Pilkonis, P. A. (2003). Role of perfectionism and personality disorder features in response to brief treatment for depression. *Journal of Consulting and Clinical Psychology, 71,* 629–633.

Shapiro, D. A., Barkham, M., Rees, A., Hardy, G. E., Reynolds, S., & Startup, M. (1994). Effects of treatment duration and severity of depression on the effectiveness of cognitive–behavioral and psychodynamic–interpersonal psychotherapy. *Journal of Consulting and Clinical Psychology, 62,* 522–534.

Shaver, P. R., & Tancredy, C. M. (2001). Emotion, attachment, and bereavement: A conceptual commentary. In M. S. Stroebe, R. O. Hansson, W. Stroebe, & W. Schut (Eds.), *Handbook of bereavement research: Consequences, coping, and care* (pp. 63–88). Washington, DC: American Psychological Association.

Shea, M. T., Pilkonis, P. A., Beckham, E., Collins, J. F., Elkin, I., Sotsky, S. M., & Docherty, J. P. (1990). Personality disorders and treatment outcome in the NIMH Treatment of Depression Collaborative Research Program. *American Journal of Psychiatry, 147,* 711–718.

Shear, K., Frank, E., Foa, E., Cherry, C., Reynolds, C. F., Vander Bilt, J., & Masters, S. (2001). Traumatic grief treatment: A pilot study, *The American Journal of Psychiatry, 158,* 1506–1508.

Shear, K., Frank, E., Houck, P. R., & Reynolds, C. F. (2005). Treatment of complicated grief: A randomized controlled trial. *Journal of the American Medical Association, 293,* 2601–2608.

Shear, K., Jackson, C. T., Essock, S. M., Donahue, S. A., & Felton, C. J. (2006). Screening for complicated grief among Project Liberty service recipients 18 months after September 11, 2001. *Psychiatric Services, 57,* 1291–1297.

Sheldon, A. R., Cochrane, J., Vachon, M., Lyall, W., Rogers, J., & Freeman, S. (1981). A psychosocial analysis of risk of psychological impairment following bereavement. *Journal of Nervous and Mental Disease, 169,* 253–255.

Shepherd, D. M., & Barraclough, B. M. (1976). The aftermath of a parent suicide for children. *British Journal of Psychiatry, 129,* 267–276.

Sherkat, D. E., & Reed, M. D. (1992). The effects of religion and social support on self-esteem and depression among the suddenly bereaved. *Social Indicators Research, 26,* 259–275.

Sheskin, A., & Wallace, S. E. (1976). Differing bereavements: Suicide, natural and accidental deaths. *Omega: Journal of Death and Dying, 7,* 229–242.

Shoham-Salomon, V., Avner, R., & Neemen, R. (1989). You're changed if you do and changed if you don't: Mechanisms underlying paradoxical interventions. *Journal of Consulting and Clinical Psychology, 57,* 590–598.

Shoham-Salomon, V., Vakstein, H., & Kruglanski, A. (1986, July). *The differential pattern of bereavement of military and civilian widows in Israel.* Paper presented at the 21st International Congress of Applied Psychology, Jerusalem, Israel.

Shuchter, S. R., & Zisook, S. (1993). The course of normal grief. In M. S. Stroebe, W. Stroebe, & R. O. Hansson (Eds.), *Handbook of bereavement: Theory, research, and intervention* (pp. 23–43). Cambridge, England: Cambridge University Press.

Siebert, M. J., & Dorfman, W. I. (1995). Group composition and its impact on effective group treatment of HIV and AIDS patients. *Journal of Developmental and Physical Disabilities. 7,* 317–334.

Siegel, J. M., & Kuykendall, D. H. (1990). Loss, widowhood, and psychological distress among the elderly. *Journal of Consulting and Clinical Psychology, 58,* 519–524.

Sifneos, P. E., (1973). The prevalence of 'alexithymic' characteristics in psychosomatic patients. *Psychotherapy and Psychosomatics, 22,* 255–262.

Silverman, G. K., Jacobs, S. C., Kasl, S. V., Shear, M. K., Maciejewski, P. K., Noaghiul, F. S., & Prigerson, H. G. (2000). Quality of life impairments associated with diagnostic criteria for traumatic grief. *Psychological Medicine, 30,* 857–862.

Silverman, G. K., Johnson, J. G., & Prigerson, H. G. (2001). Preliminary explorations of the effects of prior trauma and loss on risk for psychiatric disorders in recently widowed people. *Israeli Journal of Psychiatry and Related Sciences, 38,* 202–215.

Simon, N. M., Pollack, M. H., Fischmann, D., Perlman, C. A., Murial, A. C., Morre, C. W., . . . Shear, M. K. (2005). Complicated grief and its correlates in patients with bipolar disorder. *Journal of Clinical Psychiatry, 66,* 1105–1110.

Sireling L., Cohen, D., & Marks, I. (1988). Guided mourning for morbid grief: A replication. *Behavior Therapy, 19,* 121–132.

Smith, K. J., Subich, L. M., & Kalodner, C. (1995). The transtheoretical model's stages and processes of change and their relation to premature termination. *Journal of Counseling Psychology, 42,* 34–39.

Smith, M., Glass, G., & Miller, T. (1980). *The benefits of psychotherapy.* Baltimore, MD: Johns Hopkins University Press.

Smith, M., Koenisgberg, H. W., Yeomans, F. E., Clarkin, J. F., & Selzer, M. A. (1995). Predictors of dropout in psychodynamic psychotherapy of borderline personality disorder. *Journal of Psychotherapy Practice and Research, 4,* 205–213.

Snyder, C. R., Michael, S. T., & Cheavens, J. S. (1999). Hope as a foundation of common factors, placebos, and expectancies. In M. Hubble, B. L. Duncan, & S. D. Miller (Eds.), *The heart and soul of change: What works in therapy* (pp. 179–200). Washington, DC: American Psychological Association.

Sotsky, S. M., Glass, D. R., Shea, T. M., Pilkonis, P. A., Collins, J. F., Elkin, I., . . . Moyer, J. (1991). Patient predictors of response to psychotherapy and pharmacotherapy: Findings in the NIMH Treatment of Depression Collaborative Research Program. *American Journal of Psychiatry, 148,* 997–1008.

Stein, H., Fonagy, P., Ferguson, K. S., & Wisman, M. (2000). Lives through time: An ideographic approach to the study of resilience. *Bulletin of the Menninger Clinic, 64,* 281–305.

Sterba, R. F. (1934). The fate of the ego in analytic therapy. *International Journal of Psychoanalysis, 15,* 117–126.

Stiles, W. B., Honos-Webb, L., & Surko, M. (1998). Responsiveness in psychotherapy. *Clinical Psychology: Science and Practice, 5,* 439–458.

Stiwne, D. (1994). Group psychotherapy with borderline patients: Contrasting remainers and dropouts. *Group, 18,* 37–45.

Stroebe, M. S. (1992–1993). Coping with bereavement: A review of the grief work hypothesis. *Omega: Journal of Death and Dying, 26,* 19–42

Stroebe, M. S., Hansson, R. O., Schut, H., & Stroebe, W. (2008). Bereavement research: 21st century prospects. In M. S. Stroebe, R. O. Hansson, H. Schut, & W. Stroebe (Eds.), *Handbook of bereavement research and practice: Advances in theory and intervention* (pp. 577–603). Washington, DC: American Psychological Association.

Stroebe, M. S., Hansson, R. O., Stroebe, W., & Schut, H. (2001). *Handbook of bereavement research: Consequences, coping, and care.* Washington, DC: American Psychological Association.

Stroebe, M. S., & Strobe, W. (1983). Who suffers more? Sex differences in health risks of the widowed. *Psychological Bulletin, 93*, 279–301.

Stroebe, M. S., & Stroebe, W. (1991). Does "grief work" work? *Journal of Consulting and Clinical Psychology, 59*, 479–482.

Stroebe, M. S., Stroebe, W., Gergen, K. J., & Gergen, M. (1981–1982). The broken heart: Real or myth? *Omega: Journal of Death and Dying, 12*, 87–106.

Stroebe, M. S., Stroebe, W., & Hansson, R. O. (1993). *Handbook of bereavement: Theory, research, and intervention.* Cambridge, England: Cambridge University Press.

Stroebe, M. S., Stroebe, W., & Schut, H. (2005). Attachment in coping with bereavement: A theoretical integration. *Review of General Psychology, 9*, 48–66.

Stroebe, M. S., von Son, M., Stroebe, W., Kleber, R., Schut, H., & van den Bout, J. (2000). On the classification and diagnosis of pathological grief. *Clinical Psychology Review, 20*, 57–75.

Stroebe, M. S., & Schut, H. (1999). The dual process model of coping with bereavement: Rationale and description. *Death Studies, 23*, 197–224.

Stroebe, W., & Schut, H. (2001). Risk factors in bereavement outcome: A methodological and empirical review. In M. S. Stroebe, R. O. Hansson, W. Stroebe, & H. Schut (Eds.), *Handbook of bereavement research: Consequences, coping, and care* (pp. 349–372). Washington, DC: American Psychological Association.

Stroebe, W., & Stroebe, M. S. (1987a). *Bereavement and health: The psychological and physical consequences of partner loss.* Cambridge, England: Cambridge University Press.

Stroebe, W., & Stroebe, M. S. (1987b). Risk factors in bereavement outcome. In W. Stroebe & M. S. Stroebe (Eds.), *Bereavement and health: The psychological and physical consequences of partner loss* (pp. 168–223). Cambridge, England; Cambridge University Press.

Stroebe, W., Stroebe, M. S., & Abakoumkin, G. (1999). Does differential social support cause sex differences in bereavement outcome? *Journal of Community & Applied Social Psychology, 9*, 1–12.

Stroebe, W., Stroebe, M. S., Abakoumkin, G., & Schut, H. (1996). Social and emotional loneliness: A comparison of attachment and stress theory explanations. *Journal of Personality and Social Psychology, 70*, 1241–1249.

Stroebe, W., Stroebe, M. S., & Domittner, G. (1988). Individual and situational differences in recovery from bereavement: A risk group identified. *Journal of Social Issues, 44*, 143–158.

Stroebe, W., Zech, E., Stroebe, M. S., & Abakoumkin, G. (2005). Does social support help in bereavement? *Journal of Social and Clinical Psychology, 24*, 1030–1050.

Stylianos, S. K., & Vachon, M. L. S. (1993). The role of social support in bereavement. In M. S. Stroebe, W. Stroebe, & R. O. Hansson (Eds.), *Handbook of bereavement:*

Theory, research, and intervention (pp. 397–410). Cambridge, England: Cambridge University Press.

Sue, S., & Lam, A. G. (2002). Cultural and demographic diversity. In J. C. Norcross (Ed.), *Psychotherapy relationships that work: Therapist contributions and responsiveness to patients* (pp. 401–421). New York, NY: Oxford University Press.

Taft, C. T., Murphy, C. M., Musser, P. H., & Remington, N. A. (2004). Personality, interpersonal, and motivational predictors of the working alliance in group cognitive–behavioral therapy for partner violent men. *Journal of Consulting and Clinical Psychology, 72,* 349–354.

Talley, J. E., Butcher, T., Maguire, M. A., & Pinkerton, R. S. (1992). The effects of very brief psychotherapy on symptoms of dysphoria. In J. E. Talley (Ed.), *The predictors of successful very brief psychotherapy: A study of differences by gender, age, and treatment variables* (pp. 12–45). Springfield, IL: Charles C Thomas.

Tasca, G. A., Russell, V., & Busby, K. (1994). Characteristics of patients who choose between two types of group psychotherapy. *International Journal of Group Psychotherapy, 44,* 499–508.

Taylor, G. J. (1984). Alexithymia: Concept, measurement, and implications for treatment. *American Journal of Psychiatry, 141,* 725–732.

Taylor, G. J. (2000). Recent developments in alexithymia theory and research. *Canadian Journal of Psychiatry, 45,* 134–142.

Tennant, C. (1988). Parental loss in childhood. *Archives of General Psychiatry, 45,* 1045–1050.

Thase, M. E., Reynolds, C. F., Frank, E., Simons, A. D., McGeary, J., Fasiczka, A. L., . . . Kupfer, D. J. (1994). Do depressed men and women respond similarly to cognitive behavior therapy? *American Journal of Psychiatry, 151,* 500–505.

Tinsley, H. E., Bowman, S. L., & Barich, A. W. (1993). Counseling psychologists' perception of the occurrence and effects of unrealistic expectations about counseling and psychotherapy among their clients. *Journal of Counseling Psychology, 40,* 46–52.

Treasure, J. L., Katzman, M., Schmidt, U., Troop, N., Todd, G., & DeSilva, P. (1999). Engagement and outcome in the treatment of bulimia nervosa: First phase of a sequential design comparing motivation enhancement therapy and cognitive behavioral therapy. *Behavior Research and Therapy, 37,* 405–418.

Trivedi, M. H., Rush, A. J., Wisniewski, S. R., Nierenberg, A. A., Warden, D., Ritz, L., . . . Fava, M. (2006). Evaluation of outcomes with citalopram for depression using measurement-based care in STAR*D: Implications for clinical practice. *American Journal of Psychiatry, 163,* 28–40.

Truant, G. S. (1998). Assessment of suitable for psychotherapy: I. Introduction and the assessment process. *American Journal of Psychotherapy, 52,* 397–411.

Tschuschke, V., & Dies, R. R. (1994). Intensive analysis of therapeutic factors and outcome in long-term impatient groups. *International Journal of Group Psychotherapy, 44,* 185–208.

U.S. Bureau of Census. (2001). *One-parent family groups with own children under 18, by marital status, and race and Hispanic origin of the reference person.* Washington, DC: Author.

U.S. Department of Health and Human Services. (1999). *Mental health: A report of the surgeon general.* Rockville, MD: U.S. Department of Health and Human Services, Substance Abuse and Mental Health Services Administration, Center for Mental Health Services.

Vachon, M. (1976). Grief and bereavement following the death of a spouse. *Canadian Psychiatric Association Journal, 21,* 35–44.

Vachon, M. L., Lyall, W. A., Rogers, J., Freedman-Letofsky, K., & Freeman, S. J. (1980). A controlled study of self-help interventions for widows. *American Journal of Psychiatry, 137,* 1380–1384.

Vachon, M. L., Sheldon, A., Lancee, W., Lyall, W., Rogers, J., & Freeman, S. (1982). Correlates of enduring distress patterns following bereavement: Social network, life situation, and personality. *Psychological Medicine, 12,* 783–788.

Van der Wal, J. (1990). The aftermath of suicide: A review of empirical evidence. *Omega: Journal of Death and Dying, 20,* 14–171.

Van Doorn, C., Kasl, S. V., Beery, L. C., Jacobs, S. C., & Prigerson, H. G. (1998). The influence of marital quality and attachment styles on traumatic grief and depressive symptoms. *Journal of Nervous and Mental disease, 186,* 566–573.

van Grootheest, D. S., Beekman, A. T. F., Broese van Groenou, M. I., & Deeg, D. J. H. (1999) Sex differences in depression after widowhood. Do men suffer more? *Social Psychiatry and Psychiatric Epidemiology, 34,* 391–398.

Vargas, L. A., Loya, F., & Hoddle-Vargas, J. (1989). Exploring the multidimensional aspects of grief reactions. *American Journal of Psychiatry, 146,* 1484–1488.

Volkan, V. (1981). *Linking object and linking phenomena: A study of the forms, symptoms, metapsychology, and therapy of complicated mourning.* New York, NY: International Universities Press.

von Korff, M., & Simon, G. (1996). The relationship between pain and depression. *British Journal of Psychiatry Supplement, 30,* 101–108.

Wagner, B., Knaevelsrud, C., & Maercker, A. (2005). Internet-based treatment for complicated grief: Concepts and case study. *Journal of Loss and Trauma, 10,* 409–432.

Wagner, B., Knaevelsrud, C., & Maercker, A. (2006). Internet-based cognitive–behavioral therapy for complicated grief: a randomized controlled trial. *Death Studies, 30,* 429–454.

Wagner, B., & Maercker, A. (2007). A 1.5-year follow-up of an Internet-based intervention for complicated grief. *Journal of Traumatic Stress, 20,* 625–629.

Wampold, B. E. (2001). *The great psychotherapy debate: Models, methods, and findings.* Mahwah, NJ: Erlbaum.

Weber, J. J., Bachrach, H. M., & Solomon, M. (1985). Factors associated with the outcome of psychoanalysis: Report of the Columbia Psychoanalytic Center Research Project: II. *International Review of Psycho-Analysis, 12,* 127–141.

Weissman, A. N., & Beck, A. T. (1978, August-September). *Development and validation of the Dysfunctional Attitudes Scale: A preliminary investigation.* Paper presented at the meeting of the American Psychological Association, Toronto, Ontario, Canada.

Wells, Y. D., & Kendig, H. L. (1997). Health and well-being of spouse caregivers and the widowed. *The Gerontologist, 37,* 666–674.

Wenz, F. (1977). Marital status, anomie, and forms of social isolation: A cause of high suicide rate among the widowed in an urban sub-area. *Diseases of the Nervous System, 38,* 891–895.

Werman, D. S. (1984). *The practice of supportive psychotherapy.* New York, NY: Brunner/Mazel.

Westen, D. (1991). Social cognition and object relations. *Psychological Bulletin, 109,* 429–455.

Wikan, U. (1988). Bereavement and loss in two Muslim communities: Egypt and Bali compared. *Social Science & Medicine, 27,* 451–460.

Winston, A., Pinsker, H., & McCullough, L. (1986). A review of supportive psychotherapy. *Hospital and Community Psychiatry, 37,* 1105–1114.

Wolk, S. L., & Devlin, M. J. (2001). Stage of change as a predictor of response to psychotherapy for bulimia nervosa. *International Journal of Eating Disorders, 30,* 96–100.

Worden, W. J. (1991a). *Grief counseling and grief therapy: A handbook for the mental health Practitioner* (2nd ed.). New York, NY: Springer.

Worden, W. J. (1991b). Grieving a loss from AIDS. *The Hospice Journal, 7,* 143–150.

Wortman, C. B., & Silver, R. C. (1989). The myths of coping with loss. *Journal of Consulting and Clinical Psychology, 57,* 349–357.

Wortman, C. B., Silver, R. C., & Kessler, R. C. (1993). The meaning of loss and adjustment to bereavement. In M. S. Stroebe, W. Stroebe, & R. O. Hansson (Eds.), *Handbook of bereavement: Theory, research, and intervention* (pp. 349–366). Cambridge, England: Cambridge University Press.

Wrobleski, A., & McIntosh, J. L. (1987). Problems of suicide survivors: A survey report. *Instrumental Journal of Psychiatry and Related Sciences, 24,* 137–142.

Yalom, I. D. (1995). *The theory and practice of group psychotherapy* (4th ed.). New York, NY: Basic Books.

Yalom, I. D., & Leszcz, M. (2005). *The theory and practice of group psychotherapy* (5th ed.). New York, NY: Basic Books.

Yalom, V. J., & Vinogradov, S. (1993). Interpersonal group psychotherapy. In H. I. Kaplan & B. J. Sadock (Eds.), *Comprehensive group psychotherapy* (3rd ed., pp.185–195). Baltimore, MD: Williams & Wilkins.

Yamamoto, J., Okonogi, K., Iwasaki, T., & Yoshimura, S. (1969). Mourning in Japan. *American Journal of Psychiatry, 125,* 1660–1665.

Yamamoto, K., Davis, O. L., Dylak, S., Whittaker, J., Marsh, C., & van der Westhuisen, P. C. (1996). Across six nations: stressful events in the lives of children. *Child Psychiatry and Human Development, 26,* 139–149.

Zautra, A. J., Guarnaccia, C. A., Reich, J. W., & Dohrenwend, B. P. (1988). The contribution of small life events to stress and distress. In L. H. Cohen (Ed.), *Life events and psychological functioning: Theoretical and methodological issues* (pp. 123–148). Newbury Park, CA: Sage.

Zettle, R. D., Haflich, J. L., & Reynolds, R. A. (1992). Responses to cognitive therapy as a function of treatment format and client personality dimensions. *Journal of Clinical Psychology, 48*, 787–797.

Zetzel, E. R. (1956). Current concepts of transference. *International Journal of Psycho-analysis, 37*, 369–376.

Zhang, B., El-Jawahri, A., & Prigerson, H. G. (2006). Update on bereavement research: Evidence-based guidelines for the diagnosis and treatment of complicated bereavement. *Journal of Palliative Medicine, 9*, 1188–1203.

Zisook, S., Chentsova-Dutton, Y., & Shuchter, S. R. (1998). PTSD following bereavement. *Annals of Clinical Psychiatry, 10*, 157–163.

Zisook, S., & Lyons, L. (1989–1990). Bereavement and unresolved grief in psychiatric outpatients. *Omega: Journal of Death and Dying, 20*, 307–322.

Zisook, S., & Shuchter, S. R. (1991). Depression through the first year after the death of a spouse. *American Journal of Psychiatry, 148*, 1346–1352.

Zisook, S., Shuchter, S. R., & Lyons, L. E. (1987). Predictors of psychological reaction during the early stages of widowhood. *Psychiatric Clinics of North America, 10*, 355–368.

Zisook, S., Shuchter, S. R., & Schuckit, M. (1985). Factors in the persistence of unresolved grief among psychiatric outpatients. *Psychosomatics, 26*, 497–503.

Zlotnick, C., Shea, M. T., Pilkonis, P. A., Elkin, I., & Ryan, C. (1996). Gender, type of treatment, dysfunctional attitudes, social support, life events, and depressive symptoms over naturalistic follow-up. *American Journal of Psychiatry, 153*, 1021–1027.

Zuroff, D. C., Blatt, S. J., Sotsky, S. M., Krupnick, J. L., Martin, D. J., Sanislow, C. A., & Simmons, S. (2000). Relation of therapeutic alliance and perfectionism to outcome in brief outpatient treatment of depression. *Journal of Consulting and Clinical Psychology, 68*, 114–124.

Zuroff, D. C., Koestner, R., Moskowitz, D. S., McBride, C., Marshall, M., & Bagby, R. M. (2007). Autonomous motivation for therapy: A new common factor in brief treatments for depression. *Psychotherapy Research, 17*, 137–148.

INDEX

Assessment(s), *continued*
  of psychological mindedness, 40,
    122–123
  of quality of object relations, 40,
    180–185
  for short-term group therapy, 178–180
Assistance, from patients, 152
Atchley, R. C., 104
Attachment style
  and ambivalence, 97
  as CG risk factor, 68, 92–93
  as patient characteristic, 112,
    136–138
  and termination of therapy, 200
Attendance
  church, 89, 90
  at therapy, 113. *See also* Empty chair
Attitudinal characteristics, 116–120
Autonomous motivation, 117
Avoidance
  as coping style/strategy, 69, 94–96,
    129
  in follow-up from composition
    analysis, 44–45
  in group climate, 155
Avoidant attachment style, 68, 93
Axis II diagnoses, 133
Azim, H., 35

Bagby, R. M., 131
Bair, M. J., 142
Balfour, F. H., 199
Ball, J., 71
Balzarini, E., 76
Bam earthquake, 56
Bankoff, E., 101
Barkham, M., 137–138
Barry, L. C., 72
BC Bereavement Helpline, 7
Beck, A. P., 146
Beck Depression Inventory, 43
Beginning session, 206–207, 224
Behavior
  altruism and altruistic, 5, 163
  destructive, 214–215
  in supportive group therapy, 223
Behavioral therapy, 30–32, 34
Bereavement interventions, 21–49
  comparative trials of, 40–41
  composition trials of, 41–43

controlled trials of, 35–40
follow-up data on, 43–49
individual treatment, 27–35
interpretive and supportive group
  therapies, 35–47
literature reviews of, 22–27
Bereavement overload, 66, 74, 78
Berman, J. S., 6, 7, 25–27
Bernard, L. L., 99
Beutler, L. E., 128, 129, 140
Biographical risk factors, 67–68, 84–90
Bipolar disorder, 59
Blame, 79, 83
Blatt, S. J., 47
Boelen, P. A., 34–35
Boerner, K., 60
Bonanno, G. A., 24, 95, 120, 121, 152
Bornstein, P., 72, 88, 89
Bosnian refugees, 60
Bowlby, J., 136
Brabender, V., 160, 161
Brief dynamic therapy, 28–29
Brom, D., 33, 34
Brown, G., 88
Budman, S. H., 49
Bunch, J., 88, 101
Busby, K., 129
Butcher, T., 114

Canadian Group Psychotherapy
  Association, 234
Canadian Institutes of Health Research,
  41
Cardillo, V., 76
Caregivers
  and attachment style, 136–137
  and death following chronic illness,
    75–76
  of dementia patients, 60
  resilience of, 121
  spouses and children as, 99–100
Caretaker nurturance, 68
Carey, R., 71
Carr, D., 73, 97
Catharsis, 150–151, 153–154, 229
CG. *See* Complicated grief
Change
  and catharsis/affect, 150–151
  and group climate, 155
  stages of, 110, 118–120

The Changing Lives of Older Couples study, 72
Childhood, in QOR assessment, 182, 183
Childhood loss, 68, 88–89, 98
Children. *See also* Death of a child; Death of a parent
 attachment styles of, 136
 bereaved parents and spouses vs., 99–100
 as caregivers, 99–100
 death rates of, 51–52
 prevalence of CG in, 59
 social support from, 101
Chronic depression, 121
Chronic grief, 121
Chronic illness, 66, 75–76
Chronic mourning, 98
Chronic pain, 112, 142–143
Church attendance, 89, 90
Church membership, 101–102
Clarifying interventions, 225
Clarkin, J. F., 107, 118, 141
Clayton, P., 72
Cleiren, M. P. H. D., 77, 99
Climate, group, 154–157
Closeness, 97
Cognitive–behavioral therapy, 30–34, 47
Cognitive impairment, 140
Cognitive restructuring (CR), 34–35
Cognitive therapy, 43–44
Cohen, D., 30
Cohesion
 and age of patients, 113
 and engagement, 155–156
 and group-as-a-whole interventions, 195
 and homogeneity of groups, 160
 in interpretive group therapy, 206
 as relationship variable, 147–150
 in supportive group interventions, 198
Cohesive social microcosm, 4
Collaboration, 134, 135, 208, 209
Commitment, 148, 190
Common grief, 121
Comorbidity, 112, 141–142, 186
Comparative trials (of interpretive and supportive group therapies), 40–41
Compassionate Friends, 7

Compatibility, 148, 149
Competence, in supportive group therapy, 226
Complicated grief (CG), 3–17. *See also related topics, e.g.:* Prevalence of complicated grief
 assessments of, 177–178
 and common support groups, 6–7
 diagnosing, 3–4, 53–55
 future research, directions for, 234–235
 group therapy for, 4–5
 interpretive group therapy for, 5, 8–10, 12–16
 short-term group therapy for, 16–17
 supportive group therapy for, 5, 8–12
 treatment outcomes for, 233
Composition of therapy groups. *See* Group composition
Composition trials (of interpretive and supportive group therapies), 41–49, 235
Concrete patient characteristics, 161
Concurrent life crises, 105
Confidentiality, 190
Conflict(s)
 and group climate, 155
 as group theme, 194
 in interpretive group therapy, 38, 203, 205, 207, 210, 214, 217
 marital, 93, 103
 minimizing, 157
 perceived, 156
 repetitive, 9
 in supportive group therapy, 222, 229–230
Conflicted mourning syndrome, 67, 83
Confrontation (coping strategy), 69, 94–96
Confronting interventions, 225
Conjugal bereavement, 102. *See also* Death of a spouse
Conscientiousness, 130, 131
Consequent life crises, 105
Constructive confrontation, 94
Contemplation stage of change, 119
"Contractual agreement," of patient and therapist, 190–191
Control, 91, 103
Control groups, waiting-list, 48

Controlled trials (of interpretive group therapy), 35–40
Controlling level of QOR, 182, 183
Coping counseling, 34
Coping style (coping strategies)
 as CG risk factor, 69, 93–96
 as patient characteristic, 111, 128–129
 and social support, 100
Core Bereavement Items scale, 60
Corey, G., 145
Corey, M. S., 145
Costs, of treating CG, 61
Countertransferential feelings, 149
Couples therapy, 114
CR (cognitive restructuring), 34–35
Crisis intervention, 8, 222
Culture, 56, 94
Currier, J. M., 6

Death(s)
 accidental, 67, 80–81
 AIDS-related, 66, 78–79
 following chronic illness, 66, 75–76
 "good," 66, 73
 mode of, 66–67, 79–84
 multiple, 66, 74–75, 105
 natural, 66, 79, 84
 and prevalence of CG, 51–53
 sudden, unexpected, 65, 66, 70–73, 78
 traumatic, 66, 73–74
 type of, 65–66, 70–79
 unnatural, 66, 79–80
Death guilt, 105
Death of a child, 32
 as CG risk factor, 69, 76–78
 conventional wisdom on, 62
 and other kinship relationships, 69, 99–100
 and social support, 90
Death of a parent
 and antecedent life crisis, 103
 as childhood loss, 68, 88–89, 98
 conventional wisdom on, 62
 and other kinship relationships, 69, 99–100
 prevalence of, 52
Death of a spouse. *See also* Spouses
 and gender of bereaved, 86
 and other kinship losses, 99–100
 and quality of relationship, 97–99

Death rates, 51–52, 99
Defense mechanisms, of patients, 223
Defensive aspects of affect, 213–214, 229
de Groot, M., 57
de Jonghe, F., 43
de Keijser, J., 34, 96
Dekker, J., 43
Delayed grief, 68, 93, 120
Delayed mourning, 74
Delayed recovery, 44–48
Delays, in treatment of CG, 187
de Maat, S., 43
Dementia patients, caregivers of, 60
Demographic characteristics, 109, 113–116
Denial, 92
Dependency, 98
Depression
 and accidental death, 81
 and alexithymia, 125
 and caregiving, 75, 76
 and childhood loss, 68, 88
 chronic, 121
 and economic position, 104
 and five-factor personality model, 131
 and functional impairment, 140
 and kinship relationship, 99
 and pain, 142
 and psychological adjustment, 91–92
 and religiousness, 89
 remission rates for, 43–44
 and risk factors for CG, 64, 87–88
 and social support, 101–103, 115
 and timing of death, 72
Destructive behavior, 214–215
Deterioration effect, treatment-induced, 24
DeWitt, K. N., 28–29
Diagnosis, of CG, 3–4, 53–55
Diagnostic and Statistical Manual of Mental Disorders (4th ed., text revision; DSM–IV–TR), 3, 133, 141, 185
Diagnostic characteristics, 138–143
Dies, R. R., 147
Disappointment, 199
Disaster victims
 accidental deaths of, 67, 80–81
 CG in survivors of, 56–57
Dismissive attachment style, 137, 138

Harwood, T. M., 140
Hawley, L., 47
Hayslip, B., Jr., 105
Health
    as CG risk factor, 88
    and concurrent stressors, 105
    and social class, 84–85
    and social support, 100
Helping alliance, 147. *See also*
        Therapeutic alliance
Here-and-now experience, 157, 206,
        210, 215
Heterogeneous groups, 160, 173
High-QOR patients, 134, 233
    assessment of, 181, 184–185
    in composition trial, 41–43
    and group composition, 16, 162–163,
        168–172
    interpretive therapy for, 185
Himmelfarb, S., 99
Hiroshima, 105
Hoddle-Vargas, J., 82
Holen, A., 95
Hollon, S. D., 47
Holmes, L., 114
Homicide, 67, 81–82
Homogeneity–heterogeneity approach
        (group composition), 160
Homogeneous groups, 157, 161–162,
        173, 206
Honos-Webb, L., 107
Hood, V. G., 199
Hope, 187
Horowitz, M. J., 28–29, 53–55, 74, 95
Horwitz, L., 199
Hostility, 113
Hoyt, W., 22–24
Hughes, M., 4
Hypnotherapy, 33, 34

ICG. *See* Inventory of Complicated
        Grief
Illness, chronic, 66, 75–76
Imber, S. D., 113–114
Imbroll, D., 83
Immediate experience, 206, 210
Impairment, functional, 112, 140
Impressions, of patients, 209, 210
Inclusion criteria, 179, 180, 186
Income, 104

Indicated interventions, 26
Individuality, 179
Individual therapy
    effect size for, 22–24, 26–27
    gender of patients in, 114
    group therapy vs., 4, 114, 123, 199,
        200–201
    patient characteristics in, 107
    and quality of object relations, 40–41
    therapeutic alliance, 147
    time-limited short-term, 39–40
Individual treatment, 27–35
Inferred group processes, 145
Initial disturbance, follow-up and, 46–47
Insecure attachment style, 136
Insight, 9
Integrative interpretations, 209
Integrative model of bereavement, 95
Internal conflicts, 38
Internal control beliefs, 91
Internalizing coping style, 128, 129
Internet, 7, 32–33
Internet-based cognitive–behavioral
        therapy, 47
Interpersonal characteristics, 16, 132–138
Interpersonal exploration, 160, 161
Interpersonal learning, 5, 160
Interpersonal relatedness, 16. *See also*
        Quality of object relations (QOR)
Interpersonal relationships
    and perfectionism, 126
    and risk factors for CG, 69, 96–103
Interpersonal therapy (IPT), 31, 140
Interpretations, 208–209
Interpretive group therapy, 203–219
    affect exploration and work in,
        151–152
    approach and objectives of, 9,
        203–206
    beginning session of, 206–207
    for CG, 5
    comparative trials of supportive and,
        40–41
    controlled trials of, 35–40
    disruptive phenomena in, 210–218
    focus of, 193–195
    follow-up data on, 43–49
    and group-as-a-whole interventions,
        195–198
    group composition trials of, 41–49

Preoccupied form of attachment, 137, 138
Preparation, of patients, 189–191
Preparation stage of change, 119
Prevalence of complicated grief, 51–62
    and assessment of CG, 61–62
    in children, refugees, and caregivers, 59–60
    and death losses, 51–53
    in older adults, 53–56
    in psychiatric outpatients, 57–59
    and resilience, 121–122
    in survivors of disaster victims, 56–57
    in survivors of suicide victims, 57
Prigerson, H. G., 30, 53–55, 57, 59, 72, 97
Primary interventions, 25
Primitive level of QOR, 180, 182, 183, 185
Private self-consciousness, 122
Problem-focused coping, 69, 94, 96
Problem-focused counseling, 34
Problem-solving skills, 8, 226
Process-oriented psychodynamic groups, 129
Prochaska, J. O., 119
Professional nurturer role, 194, 216, 231
Professor role, 194, 216, 231
Project Liberty, 56
Psychiatric outpatients, 57–59, 98, 199, 234
Psychoanalytic psychotherapy, 120
Psychodynamic theory, 9
Psychodynamic therapy
    as group therapy, 39
    as individual therapy, 28–29, 33, 34
    and psychological mindedness, 123–124
    roles in, 194–195
Psychological adjustment, 68, 82, 90–92
Psychological health, 105
Psychological mindedness (PM), 40, 111, 122–124
Psychological Mindedness Assessment Procedure, 122–123
Psychological reactance, 111, 119, 127–128
Psychological well-being, 101
Psychosocial treatment, 39, 45, 186

Psychotherapy
    and degree of subjective distress, 139
    efficacy of, 48
    and interpretive group therapy, 39
    and patient characteristics, 107
    and psychological mindedness, 122
    reactance in, 127–128
Psychotropic medication, 45, 46
PTSD. *See* Posttraumatic stress disorder
Pygmalion in the Classroom (R. Rosenthal & L. Jacobson), 149

Quality of object relations (QOR)
    assessments of, 180–185
    defined, 40
    and group composition, 162–164
    and group formation, 189
    high-QOR patients, 168–172
    and interpretive/supportive group therapies, 40–43, 233
    low-QOR patients, 164–168
    and patient characteristics, 111, 132–136
    as patient selection factor, 179–185
    and treatment approach, 16
Quality of Object Relations Scale, 133
Quality of relationship with the deceased, 69, 72, 73, 97–99
Quilty, L. C., 131

Rainbows, 7
Ramm, L., 30
Rando, T. A., 71, 73, 77, 78
Raphael, B., 71, 80, 91–92, 98, 99, 105
Reactance, 111, 119, 127–128
Reactions, of patients to therapists, 215, 230–231
Recovery
    delayed, 44–48
    nonrecovery, 44–46
    spontaneous, 23
Reed, M. D., 90
Rees, W. D., 99
Referrals, 21, 177–178, 189, 234
Refugees, 60
Reihani-Kermani, H., 56
Rejection sensitivity, 93
Relapse, 44
Relationship factors, 146–150

and five-factor personality model, 131–132
and group-as-a-whole interventions, 199
group composition for, 173
improving outcome of, 157
limitations of, 16–17
new losses in, 164
and psychological mindedness, 123
and quality of object relations, 134–136
termination in, 200–201
Shuchter, S. R., 58
Siblings, loss of, 99–100
SIDS (sudden infant death syndrome), 90
Siegel, J. M., 101
Silence, 194–195, 215, 230
Silove, D., 60
Silverman, G. K., 55
Simon, N. M., 59
Sireling, L., 30
Smith, S., 82
Social class, 84–85
Social embeddedness, 102
Social–functional theory, 151
Social loneliness, 102–103
Social support, 48
    as CG risk factor, 69, 100–103
    and church attendance, 89, 90
    and gender of bereaved, 67, 86–87
    and intrusion, 45–46
    as patient characteristic, 109, 110, 113, 115–116
    and perfectionism, 126
Sociodemographic risk factors, 67–68, 84
Socioeconomic status, 84–85, 104
Sotsky, S. M., 140
Specialized support groups, 6–7
Spontaneous recovery, 23
Spousal relationship, 69. *See also* Marital relationship
Spouses, 97–99. *See also related topics, e.g.:* Death of a spouse
    bereaved parents and children vs., 99–100
    as caregivers, 99–100
    denial by, 92
    depression of, 87–88, 99
    emotional support from, 77
    mortality of, 95

quality of relationship for, 97–99
sudden, unexpected deaths of, 72–73
Stages of change, 110, 118–120
STAR*D clinical trial, 43
Startup, M., 137–138
Steel, Z., 60
Stern, R. S., 30
Stewart, M. O., 47
Stigmatization, 66, 77, 78, 83
Stiles, W. B., 107, 137–138
Stiwne, D., 149–150
Stone, W. N., 150, 179, 200–201
Stress and stressors, 69, 75, 103–105
Stress-response model, 32
Stroebe, M. S., 25, 34, 63, 81, 86, 91, 92, 95, 96, 102
Stroebe, W., 81, 86, 91, 92, 100, 102
Strunk, D., 47
Subjective distress, degree of, 139
Subjective impressions, of patients, 209, 210
Sudden, unexpected death, 65, 66, 70–73, 78
Sudden infant death syndrome (SIDS), 90
Suggestions, 225
Suicide
    as CG risk factor, 67, 83–84
    and history of emotional disorder, 88
    and prevalence of CG, 57
    and social support, 101
Support, from patients, 152. *See also* Social support
Support groups, 6–7
Supportive group therapy, 221–235
    and affect exploration, 151–152
    approach and objectives of, 8–9, 221–224
    beginning session of, 224
    for CG, 5
    comparative trials of interpretive and, 40–41
    disruptive phenomena in, 227–232
    focus of, 193–195
    follow-up data on, 43–49
    and group-as-a-whole interventions, 198–200
    group composition trials of, 41–49
    overview of, 8–10
    and pain, 142–143

Toronto Alexithymia Scale, 124
Training, of therapists, 23, 29, 234
Transference
    and group therapy, 5
    in interpretive group therapy, 209,
        215
    and quality of object relations, 134
    in supportive group therapy,
        223–224, 230
    unconscious, 9, 10
Transtheoretical model, 118–119
Trauma desensitization, 33
Traumatic death, 66, 73–74
Traumatic grief, 30–31
Traumatic nature of loss, 60, 85
Treatment expectancies, 110, 117–118
Treatment-induced deterioration
        effect, 24
Treatment of Depression Collaborative
        Research Program. See National
        Institute of Mental Health
        Treatment of Depression
        Collaborative Research Program
Treatment outcome, 157, 233. See also
        specific treatments
Treatment plans, 187
Triangular level of QOR, 182, 183
Trust, 208
Tschuschke, V., 147
Two-track model of bereavement,
        94–95
Type of death, 65–66, 70–79

Unanticipated mourning syndrome,
        82
Uncomfortable emotions, 208
Unconscious conflict
    in interpretive group therapy, 203,
        207, 210, 214, 217
    in supportive group therapy,
        229–230
Unconscious transference, 9, 10
Unexpected loss syndrome, 66, 70, 80
Universal interventions, 26
Universality, 5, 149, 195, 206
University of Alberta Hospital, 35
"Unlikable" patients, 149
Unnatural death, 66, 79–80
U.S. Department of Health and Human
        Services, 51

Vachon, M. L., 27–28, 91
Valkonen, T., 95
Values, 227
van den Bout, J., 25, 34, 96
van der Wal, J., 84
Vargas, L. A., 82
Veronen, L., 82
Vicario, F., 76
Victimization, secondary, 82
Vietnam War, 81
Vinogradov, S., 161
Violation, 67, 79, 82
Violence, 67, 73–74, 79, 82
Volition, 67, 79–80, 82
Volkan, V., 74

Wagner, B., 32
Waiting-list control groups, 48
Wallace, S. E., 83
War, 67, 81, 103
Watson, J. C., 152
Weideman, R., 61–62
Weiss, D., 28–29
Weiss, R. S., 90–91, 93, 97–98
Wells, Y. D., 75
Western culture, 94
Widowed people. See also Widowers;
        Widows
    gender effects on bereavement for,
        86
    older adults as, 55–56
    prevalence of CG in, 53–56
    PTSD of, 74
    quality of relationship for, 93
    social support of, 101, 102
    as spousal caregivers, 75–76
    and unexpected death, 70
Widowers, 67, 86–87, 101. See also
        Men
Widows. See also Women
    and age as CG risk factor, 85
    brief dynamic individual therapy
        for, 29
    coping resources of, 96
    dependency of, 98
    economic position of, 104
    ethnicity and family interactions
        of, 85
    personality of, 91
    social class of, 84–85

Widows, *continued*
    social support for, 101
    and sudden, unexpected deaths, 71
    as survivors of suicide victims, 83–84
    of war victims, 81
    widowers vs., 67, 86–87
Widow-to-widow counseling, 27–28
Wilner, N. R., 29
Winfrey, G., 71
Wish-anxiety-defense-expression
        sequences, 208–209
Women. *See also* Gender
    financial stressors for, 104
    group therapy for, 114, 115
    social support of, 67
Worden, W. J., 95

Working alliance, 147, 227. *See also*
        Therapeutic alliance
Working factors, 150–154
Working through process, 152
Wrobleski, A., 84

Yalom, I. D., 147, 161, 162
Yalom, V. J., 161
Yamamoto, J., 89
Yearning, 73, 94, 97, 98
Yoshimura, S., 89

Zhang, S., 60
Zisook, S., 58
Zotti, A. M., 76
Zuroff, D. C., 47, 117, 126

ABOUT THE AUTHORS

William E. Piper, PhD, is a professor and director of the psychotherapy program in the Department of Psychiatry, University of British Columbia, Vancouver, Canada. His primary research interests include process and outcome research for both individual and group forms of psychotherapy. He has received many research grants and published more than 180 journal articles and book chapters.

He has also published five other books: *Adaptation to Loss Through Short-Term Psychotherapy*; *Time-Limited Day Treatment for Personality Disorders*; *Psychological Mindedness: A Contemporary Understanding*; *Interpretative and Supportive Psychotherapies: Matching Therapy and Patient Personality*; and *Termination in Psychotherapy: A Psychodynamic Model of Progresses and Outcomes*. He is past president of the Society for Psychotherapy Research and past editor of the *International Journal of Group Psychotherapy*.

John S. Ogrodniczuk, PhD, is an associate professor and associate director of the psychotherapy program in the Department of Psychiatry, University of British Columbia, Vancouver, Canada. His psychotherapy research program examines relationships among pretherapy characteristics of patients, therapy process patterns believed to mediate change, and multivariate outcomes. His research has involved a variety of psychotherapies and patient populations, but he has a particular interest in studying psychodynamic psychotherapy, personality disorder, and men's mental health. Dr. Ogrodniczuk has held several grants to support his research and has published extensively, with nearly 100 publications to date. He is a recipient of the Outstanding Early Career Achievement Award presented by the Society for Psychotherapy Research.

In addition to his research, Dr. Ogrodniczuk is involved with teaching medical students and psychiatry residents, serves as an associate editor for *Psychotherapy Research*, serves on the editorial board for *Group Dynamics* and *Journal of Personality Disorders*, provides regular reviews for more than a dozen scientific and clinical journals, and consults with mental health clinics about service provision and evaluation. To learn more about Dr. Ogrodniczuk's work, please visit http://www.psychotherapyprogram.ca.

Anthony S. Joyce, PhD, is a professor and coordinator of the Psychotherapy Research and Evaluation Unit in the Department of Psychiatry at the University of Alberta, Edmonton, Alberta, Canada. A strong believer in the scientist–practitioner model for psychologists, he is also active as an individual and group psychotherapist in the department's outpatient service. In the larger departmental context, he serves as the director of the graduate program, which offers postgraduate degrees in many areas of psychiatric research, and as a supervisor for psychiatric residents learning the practice of psychotherapy.

His research interests include the relationships between patient characteristics and therapy process variables and how these relationships function as mediators, moderators, or direct predictors of positive therapy outcome. He is also interested in the development of effective treatments for patients with personality disorders. These interests encompass short- and long-term forms of individual and group psychotherapy and intensive partial hospitalization group programs. Among ongoing contributions to the psychotherapy research literature are three coauthored books, including *Termination in Psychotherapy* for which he served as lead author. He is a long-standing member of the Society for Psychotherapy Research and the Canadian and American Group Psychotherapy Associations.

Rene Weideman, PhD, is director of the Clinical Psychology Centre in the Department of Psychology, Simon Fraser University, Burnaby, British Columbia, Canada, and associate director of faculty affairs in the psychotherapy program in the Department of Psychiatry, University of British Columbia, Vancouver, Canada. He conducts a part-time private practice in Vancouver. He previously worked for many years in the outpatient psychiatry program at Vancouver General Hospital. He has strong interests in psychotherapy training and supervision, and he has been a coauthor with Dr. Piper and colleagues of five research articles related to complicated grief.